Ward Newcomb: *The Handbook* has been like the answer to a prayer! It is an immense help and especially so when one is planning a PCT hike from 3,000 miles away.

Chris Oswald and **Andris Olins**: Ray and Jenny's more extensive experience convinced us to give their *PCT Hiker's Handbook's* ideas a try. And we're glad we did!

Thomas Winnett, (President, Wilderness Press): All trekkers and would-be trekkers are in Jardine's debt for his excellent and extensive advice for long-distance walking.

Scott Conover (PCT 94): *The Handbook* is a very worthwhile source of information for anyone contemplating much hiking. It prompted me to make some major changes in my thinking.

Chris Townsend (PCT, CDT, etc.): Jardine has carefully considered all aspects of backpacking and has come to some startling conclusions. His *PCT Hiker's Handbook* challenges many standard views and is a refreshing and important addition to the literature. I recommend it highly.

Scott Smouse: *The Handbook* touched on several important subjects that have never been mentioned by other writers. It was a real eye opener for me, and I learned some important lessons. Jardine's stealth camping, for example, is an idea whose time has come.

Erma Marak & Judy Gianandrea (PCT 93 "Mother/Daughter Team"): *The Handbook* helped us tremendously to prepare for the PCT, and steered us clear of several major mistakes.

Libby Sendek: *The Handbook* is very well read. Along the trail Jardine's name is mentioned by nearly every hiker out for longer than the weekend. He's made people rethink this whole thing - and that's good!

Ruth Pfeifer: (AT 86, LT 87): I find *The Handbook* extremely informative and inspiring.

Charles Porter (PCT 94): A contribution to the hiking community and the planet.

David Paulson (AT 87): Essential reading in preparing for any long hike.

Garrett and Leisha Holmes: An incredible inspiration and technical juggernaut!

Matt Antonelli (PCT 94): I'm really glad that I got a hold of the *Handbook* - I doubt that I could have organized my hike in the last month-and-a-half without it. The itineraries made it easy.

Scott Blanton: *The PCT Handbook* is informative and a pleasure to read. It's an invaluable source of advice.

Karl Ullman (PCT in sections; Founder, Pacific Crest Leadership School): *The PCT Hiker's Handbook* helped pave the way for the most incredible journey of my life. As much as a PCT through-hike is a wilderness experience, it is also a physical and logistical task, and one's preparation must reflect this. The trick is to minimize any problems associated with the hike so that you can enjoy yourself. Several hikers I met along the way did not plan well (mostly out of arrogance) and they have been humbled. So, step number one is to read this book thoroughly. It really accelerates the learning curve.

Greg Walter (AT 91 and 93, LT 94): I've read *The PCT Hiker's Handbook* several times and find it extremely valuable.

Robert Prestegaard: *The Handbook* is on to something that will make the wilderness experience even more pleasurable!

Danica Ankele: A wonderful source of practical inspiration.

Steve Roper: (Originator of The Sierra High Route and author of its guide book): Never have I seen such a detailed treatment of long-distance hiking. And I especially enjoyed browsing through the philosophical sections.

Alan Julliard (PCT 75): I was climbing in Yosemite Valley when Jardine was there, and have used the "Friends" protection devices since the beginning. So I have been familiar with his name for quite awhile. I was therefore surprised and glad to see *The PCT Hiker's Handbook*. Jardine seems to have successfully put the same inventiveness and attention to detail that he used to create "Friends" into his hiking book, in a straightforward and well organized format. In an insecure person, such a considerable background might have come through in the book as a sermon or a chance to brag. Instead, it is honest, practical and warm. He has done a fantastic job.

THE AMERICAN HIKER: Ray Jardine is best known among mountaineers for inventing the "Friend," an invaluable tool for technical rock climbing. But among hikers, he and his wife, Jenny, may be better known for their lightweight approach to hiking. Their typical packweights are remarkable, and their *PCT Hiker's Handbook* is a superb first stop for those in the dreaming stage. Even if you're not planning to hike the PCT, Jardine's philosophy of traveling lightly through the landscape is a good one, and is well presented. Virtually all hikers, no matter how experienced, will pick up invaluable tips for the trail. This book would be a welcome addition to any backpacker's library.

C. Huddleston, USMC: Just received and finished reading *The PCT Hiker's Handbook*. Enjoyed it. However, I now find I need more. Please send me the PCT guide books.

Accolades for The PCT Hiker's Handbook

Frederick D. Coleman: A roaring round of applause for *The PCT Hiker's Handbook!* This one small volume may, indeed, be changing a whole generation's thinking on how to approach, not only long distance trails, but backpacking in general.

Tom Culton: *The PCT Hiker's Handbook* is the most unique hiking book on the market – there are no others that even come close.

Jonathan Blees: *The PCT Hiker's Handbook* is one of the best books I have ever read. It has an extraordinary combination of detailed practical advice coupled with spiritual and emotional insight. Jardine's joy in hiking, his love of Nature and of God, and his commitment to serving others shine through his words.

Michael Anderson (two time PCT section hiker): If there was ever a book perfectly suited to the hiker's needs, the *Handbook* is it. It is filled with fresh, new and vital information. Believe me when I say that *The PCT Hiker's Handbook* will become a classic!

George Metcalf: (PCT 93): *The Handbook* is the only "how to" book in my experience that goes way out on a limb with radical ideas and makes no concession to conventional wisdom. It revolutionized my thinking and was a major ingredient in my success.

Rob Reish: I have read *The PCT Hiker's Handbook* several times and am constantly referring back to it. Its ideas, experience and practical knowledge have been invaluable in planning my hike. It has made an astronomical contribution to me and to all thru-hikers.

Abe Allen: Based on 35 years of backpacking experience I can honestly say that *The PCT Hiker's Handbook* rates among the top books on the subject.

Bill Valentine: I couldn't sit still after reading it!

J.H. Horak, MD (AT, LT, etc): I really enjoyed *The PCT Hiker's Handbook*. I frequently found myself saying "Yes! Right on! That's what I think too!" or "Yes! I thought I was the only one who had thought of that!"

Bill Wesp: I view the *Handbook* as some sort of personal watershed in my mountain traveling style.

Denny Fixmer (PCT 94): My copy looks more like rainbows of colors with many parts underlined and highlighted.

Jason Ontjes (AT 91): *The Handbook* impressed me for its content and style. I've sold my friends on many of its ideas, citing it with authority. They are all quite impressed with the logic of these snippets. Jardine's gospel, it seems, is getting out.

Dennis Hill (PCT and 5-time AT thru-hiker): *The Handbook* is a MUST READ for all hikers. I bought three more copies for my friends.

David Brace (PCT 94): *The Handbook* opened my eyes and changed my way of thinking towards hiking principles I had always considered standard practice. Great information!

Ray Hogan (PCT 94): I wouldn't have tried the PCT without the *Handbook*. Thanks to its advice and information my hike was a great success.

Dan Dotson: When I first read *The PCT Hiker's Handbook* several years ago it was like receiving a breath of fresh air.

Dustin LaRose & Julia Bauer (PCT 94): *The PCT Hiker's Handbook* had a great impact on us both.

Scott Murdock: An outstanding job on the book! It's great!!!

Carl Sanders: An incredible source of sensible backpacker's know-how.

Paul Grubb: I almost have the *PCT Hiker's Handbook* memorized.

Richard Strehlau: I can't say enough about *The PCT Hiker's Handbook* and the well of experience from which it flows. It is utterly absorbing.

Andrew Helliwell (PCT 95): I read the *Handbook* for the third time and still found gems of useful information.

Steve Budelier (PCT 94): *The Handbook* has been unbelievably helpful in my adventure planning.

Jack Brady: I enjoy Ray's ideas and enthusiasm immensely and also his willingness to share it! My eyes have certainly been opened.

Steve Leigh: The book is much more than practical. Ray puts the experience of grandeur into fanciful words of achievement. Words that inspire dreams.

Phil Hough (PCT 94): Useful as well as provocative. New, fresh approaches to age old challenges.

Dennis, Valerie, Cody, Rulon, & Colin Clark and hiking partner **David Rose**: Our first long-distance PCT hike was delightfully successful because we relied on the ideas in *The PCT Hiker's Handbook*. Ray Jardine is an innovative thinker and his personality smiles out of every page, making his advice a pleasure to absorb.

Jerry Meyers: How do you thank someone for inspiration and dream building? *The PCT Hiker's Handbook* has been a constant source of motivation for me.

Tod Bloxham (PCT 93): *The Handbook* is a great asset to the hiking community. I recommend it frequently.

Anders Åhnberg: My congratulations for an excellent book. The "Ray Way" is starting in Sweden too.

The Pacific Crest Trail
Hiker's Handbook

Innovative Techniques
and Trail Tested Instruction
For the Long Distance Hiker

Ray Jardine

First Printing 1992; Second Printing 1993; Third Printing 1994.
Second Edition, 1996

Published by
AdventureLore Press
Box 804, LaPine OR 97739

Library of Congress Catalogue Card Number: 95-83681
Ray Jardine, *The Pacific Crest Trail Hiker's Handbook*, Second Edition, AdventureLore Press, LaPine Oregon.

ISBN 0-9632359-2-3

Printed on 100% recycled paper.

Front Cover: Jenny Jardine on the PCT in the Goat Rocks Wilderness; Mt. Rainier in the background.

To Jenny:

Companion in 15 years of exploring,
and constant assistant in the preparation of this book.

And to our readers:

"fellow-adventurers on a bright journey to understand
the things that are." – Richard Bach

May you cast your visions far;
load your backpacks lightly and leave your cars at home;
and may you cherish and protect the lands you explore.

For ye shall go out with joy, and be led forth with peace;
the mountains and the hills shall break forth before you into singing,
and all the trees of the field shall clap their hands.

– Isaiah 55:12

Contents

Caution

The PCT is not meant to be an all season, all weather route

As the Pacific Crest Trail winds more than two and a half thousand miles along the length of western United States, it leads the hiker through extremes in elevation and climate. As such, it is not an all season, all weather route. Normally, the trail through the higher regions is passable only from late spring to early fall. And these higher regions extend, intermittently, from Mt. Laguna, 40 miles from the Mexican border, all the way to the Canadian border.

Spring arrives in the high country, not according to the calendar, but to the latitude, the elevation, and the depth of the previous winter's snowpack. This depth can vary dramatically, winter to winter. In years of *extreme low* deposition, hikers may encounter very little snow if they begin at the Mexican border in late April. In years of *exceptionally heavy* snowpack they would begin not until a month or so later, and even then they could find the trail buried in the higher regions. In most years, though, northbound PCT thru-hikers will encounter snow only here and there, as long as they follow one of the itineraries in this book.

In any year, summer can end abruptly in the high country, and early winter can hit hard with bitter temperatures and surprisingly heavy snowfall. The higher the elevation, the earlier and the harder hitting. Normally, the hiking season in the High Sierra ends in late August, and in the North Cascades in early October. But again, these dates will vary from year to year. Often, a few storms will bring an early winter to the region, and although the weather will remain cold, the sunshine may return. This autumnal snowpack is usually powdery and not difficult to walk through, although if deep enough it can obliterate all traces of the trail and make route-finding very difficult.

And of course, Mother Nature is well known for bringing snow and blizzards to the mountains even in mid summer.

The PCT is a fair weather trail, not built to accommodate these variable conditions. And with good reason. It was designed to allow the greatest number of hikers to enjoy the greatest expanse of high country, in good-to-fair weather, which, in the average year, persists through most of July and August. For every early-season PCT thru-hiker who finds him or herself wallowing in pervasive snowpack while searching for the route on the Fuller Ridge, for example, there will be 5,000 hikers ambling the dusty trail later in the summer. The PCT trail planners were concerned with the masses, and we thru-hikers are the exceptions. Our potential for adventure is vastly greater, but the burden is on us to remain alert to the conditions, and use our own judgment to assess the dangers.

For example, the construction crew may have routed a section of trail in late summer, rock-hopping across a creek. Thru-hikers who arrive there in springtime may find it a roaring torrent of snowmelt run-off. Don't be lured by the trail emerging from the opposite bank. Head upstream and look for a safe crossing, or turn around and find another way, even though it may require a detour of several hours, or even days.

Where the trail builders blasted the track out of a cliff in summertime, thru-hikers can find it buried in snow – steep, slippery, and hanging over a precipice. Do not attempt to cross unless you are absolutely certain of your abilities. Otherwise, turn around and select a safer route.

The trail crew probably built the path along the high, exposed crestline during fine weather. Thru-hikers might arrive to find approaching black clouds spitting lightning. If so, they should descend to safer ground well before the storm arrives.

The vast majority of PCT hikers have safe journeys. But each season there are a few accidents, sometimes very serious ones. So remember: There is nothing sacred about the Pacific Crest Trail. And there is nothing about your adventure worth staking your life on. Danger may be an inescapable fact of life, but lack of vigilance is not. If you encounter a dangerous situation, turn around and find another way, or wait until the conditions improve.

Preface

> A true friend is somebody
> who can make us do what we can.
>
> – *Emerson*

Prior to the advent of *The PCT Hiker's Handbook in* 1992, the drop-out rate among aspiring PCT thru-hikers was almost 95%. In fact, of the 150 or so who started each spring, less than 20% managed to hike even the first 100 miles.

Imagine the planning and preparing that had gone on for months; the packaging of resupply boxes with a summer's food and provisions, the studying of equipment catalogs and the purchase of hundreds of dollars worth of specialized clothing and gear. Imagine these people quitting their jobs, saying good-bye to friends and family, and setting out on one of life's grandest adventures – only to have the whole plan come crashing into a heap of despair within the first week's travel. Trail life, these discouraged hikers discovered, was not at all what they had imagined. The heavy pack, the interminable fatigue, the blisters, the heat or the cold. The disappointment was no doubt abysmal, and it was practically an epidemic.

If this mass defeat was regrettable it was also greatly ironic. Those who lost their will to continue did so, generally, for the same reasons every year. The fact is, everyone had read the same books and the same magazine articles and advertisements that promoted the same ideas. So they all had the same opinions, and they all talked with the same hikers who only reinforced those opinions. The problem was, Nature had different ideas, and when these "well informed" hikers confronted Nature they discovered that their methods, which had looked great in the magazines, were not very workable in the mountains.

Our first PCT hike

In 1987 Jenny and I decided to thru-hike from Mexico to Canada generally along the PCT. In those 4½ months we made many of the same mistakes as the others, along with a host of our own invention. We did, however, manage to fall in with the fortunate 5% and go the distance. Yet in many ways, despite our years of backpacking experience, the rigors of that trek had us feeling like beginners. The hike, the trail, and practically everything about the journey were not what we had expected.

At the Canadian border we found an anonymously penned note which echoed these same sentiments: *"I began this journey with many hopes and many fears. Glittering expectations blinded me as I crossed my trailheads. What I wanted to find and what I found never matched, yet the experience has granted me profound illumination."*

Our journey had greatly enriched our lives also, and the more I pondered its meaning, the more I began to identify some of our mistakes, and those of some of the other hikers we had met.

Our second PCT hike

Three years later we returned to thru-hike the PCT, this time with the intent of sticking to the trail, at least where safe and practicable. But now our attitudes had been tempered by our previous struggles with trail reality. Humbled and ultimately molded by the rigors of our first hike, our intent was now to throw open the doors of our minds to Nature's profusion of teachings. Manning Park – the goal, we decided, could take care of itself.

As such, nearly every day of this second trek proved one of enlightenment. And indeed, the more we yielded to the lessons encountered, and the more we experimented with ways of changing ourselves to accommodate them, the more the truths of Nature began weaving themselves into a tapestry of a heightened wilderness consciousness. We found ourselves moving more in harmony with Nature's cadence. And as a bonus, the miles began reeling past as never before.

After reaching Canada we returned home and I wrote the first edition of this *Handbook*. Then we spent the summer thru-hiking the Continental Divide Trail, and the next summer the Appalachian Trail. Meanwhile, we were pleased to see that the success rate among PCT hikers had risen dramatically.

Our third PCT hike

The summer after the AT we decided to hike the PCT from the Canadian border to Elk Lake in central Oregon, near our home. This plan changed along the way, for we found that we were enjoying the summer so much that we decided to continue to the Mexican border. Reaching Elk Lake, we detoured home and worked for 2½ days on business and one more day preparing for the additional 2,000 miles of hiking.

The remaining trek to Mexico went extremely well, and I must say that the overall journey was by far our easiest and most enjoyable PCT trek to date. It was also our fastest, at three months and four days, border to border, total elapsed time, walk every inch of the way, no vehicle support, no flip-flopping, and stick with the trail 99% of the way. However, this is not to suggest that we were trying to set any records. Such would be out of character with the wilderness experience, which is the very basis for our backcountry enjoyment. The PCT is not a race track; but it certainly is a great place to practice hiking ultra-long distances with greater efficiency.

Quest for knowledge

The person using the Standard Backpacking Method is essentially a product of today's commercialism. I broke away from the system in the mid 1970's and started making my own clothing and gear, and hiking according to my own plan. Since then I have continually analyzed my methods and equipment with an eye toward refinement. While preparing for each of our mega-hikes, I looked for ways to improve our gear and techniques. As such, each hike became something of a multi-month field test. This break away from the standard methods produced excellent results, but I imagine we were only rediscovering some of the concepts and skills that our primal ancestors used for millennia.

My quest for knowledge has not focused entirely on what works best, most of the time, for Jenny and myself. I am also concerned with what seems to work best, most of the time, for other hikers, primarily those of lesser experience. As a result of writing the first edition of this *Handbook* I received about 2,500 letters. Most were valuable sources of feedback. During our southbound journey we met scores of people traveling the other way, and saw that most were using ideas from the *Handbook*. We always tried to stop and talk awhile, and even if we didn't discuss gear and techniques, I could see which of the book's techniques were working for the hiker and which were not.

The result has been a system of knowledge, tried, tested, modified, and tested again. And yes, many of my concepts fly in the face of conventional "wisdom." But as my more recent journeys demonstrated, and as those of several other hikers have verified, these methods work. I will be the first to admit that there is no right or wrong way to hike the PCT. Virtually every idea in this book is subjective. Like selecting vegetables at the supermarket, then, you are welcome to adopt a few ideas here and a few there. By all means think for yourself. But remember a fair amount of experience is needed to grasp the import of many of these concepts. And in many cases it would be easier to grasp them in the planning stages rather than in the struggling stages.

At any rate, I hope this Second Edition will make your wilderness adventures safer and more enjoyable. If it does, then we both will have succeeded.

The Pacific Crest

The Land, the Trail, and its Hikers

The Pacific Crest is a geologic uplift similar to the great Continental Divide of the mountain states, but at a distance of 40 to 180 miles from the Pacific Ocean. As it wends along the edge of the continent, it traverses the United States through California, Oregon and Washington.

Much of this uplift is clad in coniferous forests, mainly in the higher regions, and these are overseen by the National Forest Service and in a few cases by the National Park Service. These forests have had some protection from encroaching civilization which tends to "improve" the landscape with an unbroken patina of buildings and asphalt. The lower crest regions are generally warmer and more arid, and in most cases these are the domain of the Bureau of Land Management, which again has done much to protect them from development.

Thus, we have a vast corridor which has not felt the crush of man at the controls of his bulldozer. Granted, the forests have been logged almost to the tree, but in most places they have recovered sufficiently to instill at least the illusion of vitality, which is the best we dare hope for and a great deal better than nothing. So perhaps we should just say that to the casual eye these lofty mountain ranges, expansive forests, and high desert reaches are in a condition which resembles what the early Native Americans, explorers, and pioneers must have known well.

The trail

The Pacific Crest Trail leads along this marvelous crest from Mexico to Canada. Some 30 years in the making at a cost of millions of dollars and incalculable hours of volunteer labor, it is a walkway of unprecedented diversity and genuine awe. As such, Congress has granted it the status of National Scenic Trail.

In my mind, the construction of the PCT was an investment in the American future, on par with the purchase of Alaska or the funding of the space program. Decades ago, people with vision acted on their dreams, and left us with a national treasure. And rightly so, for of the thousands of hiking trails in this country and abroad, the PCT is unique in many ways.

It is one of the longest continuous trails on earth. And with its length comes unparalleled diversity. Diversity of elevation, from 140 feet at the Columbia River to 13,200 feet at Forester Pass; of temperatures from below freezing in the High Sierra and North Cascades to over 100 degrees Fahrenheit in the deserts; of weather patterns from continuous weeks of fine weather to periods of heavy rain, perhaps laced with strong winds, lightning and even snowfall. And of course it displays a strong diversity of flora and fauna, from the desert chaparral to the exposed lichens above timberline. For the hiker making way along this trail, these elements can change frequently and often with surprising abruptness. The trail through southern California, for example, traverses mountain ranges one after the next, each interspersed with a section of low desert. One day the hiker will be at 8,500 feet trudging through snow, and a few days later at 2,500 feet sweltering in the heat.

At last count, this National Scenic Trail leads through two dozen National Forests and 33 congressionally designated Wilderness Areas. It wanders through seven National Parks and six State and Provincial Parks. Blend in a National Monument, a National Recreation Area, four BLM Management areas, and several parcels of private land, large and small, and we have a recipe for an unparalleled hiking adventure.

And yet, we celebrate not the trail, but the wild places it passes through. The trail is merely a means of enjoying the end. It is also a long, winding invitation to shed the ennui; a beckoner of souls who would travel its higher regions, if only for a few glorious weeks or months.

The PCT offers an exemplary, extended, yet convenient wilderness experience. It rarely leads us within sight, sound, or smell of civilization. And it often affords exceptional views. We can stand on a high vantage and scan unlimited miles in every direction. What do we see? Prominent landmarks on the horizon behind us which a week earlier had stood on the horizon ahead. And forests and lowlands everywhere empty of cities, highways, and the rising dust of progress. The air will be clear and silent, accented only with the chortle of a raven or whisper of breeze in the pines.

Ironically, this massive tract of unsullied land is easily accessible. We need not travel to the far corners of the earth in order to find the "tonic of the wilderness," as Thoreau put it. Nor do we have to use air drops for food resupplies. Post offices and backcountry resorts suffice. These "resupply stations" are spaced several days apart, and as we reach one, we can load our backpacks with provisions mailed to ourselves earlier, and set off again into another vast stretch of backcountry. And we can repeat the process for a few weeks at a time, or for several months. Exemplary, extended, yet convenient.

Unlike its eastern counterpart, the Appalachian Trail, the PCT could not have followed every ridgeline and climbed every mountain along the way. The Crest is often so rugged and lofty that such a trail would have been nearly impossible to build, and even then it would have eliminated all but the most exceptional athletes and exposed them to great risk. So the PCT planners compromised. They wound the trail in and among the highlands in the most pleasing and safe manner. They made it sufficiently challenging to hold our interest, without sacrificing the pure wistful pleasures of the experience. They routed the trail up and down the mountainsides in gentle switchbacks designed to free our minds from the bodies' exertions and allow them to alight on the beauties of the surroundings.

In the same vein, the PCT planners showed great wisdom when they routed the trail away from towns. Distance is a great barrier to those who do not respect the land and who would come into its pristine regions to paint its rocks and leave its forests littered with spent cartridges and empty beer cans. It is also a great barrier to those who would menace the hikers.

And who are these hikers? Just about anyone it seems; for the PCT makes no distinction between the young and old, rich and poor, fit and flabby, Type-A and carefree. It knows nothing of race, gender, or creed. Nor does it care whether hikers pass through in groups, pairs, or singles; equipped with high-tech or Army surplus. And it has been known to grant passage to the handi-capped person of particular grit. The only traits it insists on, and this at times emphatically, are perseverance and a willingness to shed whatever miscon-ceptions do not align with reality.

The Meaning

What is the meaning of the PCT experience? Naturally, this varies with the individual. But in my mind a multi-month journey along this national treasure can be a perfect example of the long-distance hiker's dream. First and fore-most it is an escape from structured, citified living; a temporary withdrawal from our fellow metronauts. It is a return to Nature, and possibly a journey in search of what parts of ourselves might lie within its deserts, forests, and far-flung mountains. Trail life can be a time of rising early, of traipsing wet footed through meadow grass, and later of feeling the luxurious warmth of the morning sun. It can be a time of ambling through quiet, hallowed forests, and perhaps in the same day, of laboring to gain a high vantage, and finally in conquest to feel the supremacy of the mountaineer.

A rejuvenation of self

Trail life is also a time of gaining better control of ourselves, and of expand-ing our capacities for personal growth. It is a time of shedding lethargy; of losing weight perhaps, and of growing stronger and healthier. It can be a time of meeting kindred spirits; of relating to other distance-hikers whose aspira-tions and experiences generally parallel our own. It is also a chance to discover innumerable out of the way places, inaccessible to mechanized travelers and in fact unknown to most people.

Distance-hikers rely almost entirely on their own resources. Turning their back on the demoralizing world of politics and crime, they alone decide the course of the day's events. In toil and privation, and in joys inexpressible they will be awakening their senses and gaining better understandings of their strengths and weaknesses, and of their natural surroundings – the biosphere that sustains all life. And in surmounting the many problems along the way they will be forging self confidence. Thus equipped, they no longer need compare themselves with their contemporaries back at home in order to interpret their own self images.

The trail lures these restless buccaneers ever onward. Granted, the way is garnished with toil and fatigue, but they are the right kinds of toil and fatigue. And of course the wilderness features the usual adversities of snowpack, mosquitoes and so forth. But adversities only strengthen those who learn to accept and adjust to them, who are open to personal growth. So indeed, the journey is a test of abilities: not only of physical strength and stamina, but of adaptability as well. It is truly, a test of selves.

The Handbook

This *Pacific Crest Trail Hiker's Handbook* is a collection of trail tested information and instruction addressing all the aspects of planning, preparing, and actually hiking the PCT. It is also a manual in the art and skills of ultra-long-distance hiking relevant to just about any trail. It's main focus is on the thru-hike: the long and distinguished journey afoot, border to border in a single season. For after all, the full benefits of long distance hiking come only when we have fully attuned, usually after a month or two on the trail. However, most people cannot afford that much time away from work and family. So they hike the PCT in segments, spending a weekend or a week on the trail, and returning year after year. These folks, too, should find a great deal of useful information in these pages. For after all, the techniques are designed to increase hiking efficiency, safety, and enjoyment. And what works for the long distance hiker should work as well for the weekend hiker.

Part 1
Planning and Preparations

Preparedness is the key to victory.

— *General Douglas MacArthur*

Goals

The way you activate the seeds of your creation is by making choices about the results you want to create. When you make a choice, you mobilize vast human energies and resources which otherwise go untapped. All too often people fail to focus their choices upon results, and therefore their choices are ineffective. If you limit your choices only to what seems possible or reasonable, you disconnect yourself from what you truly want, and all that is left is a compromise.

– Robert Fritz

As we press into the 21st Century, our lives encompass the new and the old: the new technology – launching us into the future, and our old foundation as Homo sapiens - with traits and instincts designed to insure our survival. The new measures change in days; the old, in millennia. The new strives to create and live in a sophisticated society where progress is measured in how far Nature is bulldozed away. But the old was designed to function in that natural world, where physical exertion and exposure to the elements were a part of life. Technology has freed us from those pressures of raw survival, but its freedom is not without price. The industrialization and luxuries which shelter us from discomfort also keep us from exploring new realms.

I believe if we address those primitive, survival instincts every now and then, our lives can become more sharply focused. About the only way we can do it in this day and age is to invent goals for ourselves – goals which involve sweat-induced labor and a measure of discomfort, and which reintroduce us to uncertainty and risk. For it is only by confronting these challenges that we can even begin to experience our full capabilities as human beings.

In his book *Personal Best*, George Sheehan draws a compelling likeness of recovering alcoholics and runners, (or distance hikers) in that people in each group are summoned into battle against the forces that would consume their lives. The ruinous agent the recovering alcoholic battles is of course liquor, and that which the athlete or adventurer dreads is languor. As A. Conan Doyle wrote in one of his dialogues, "My life is spent in one long effort to escape from the commonplaces of existence."

Yes, the goals are to be contrived. Of themselves, they do not exist. What may exist are our dreams. But dreams are like electricity without wires: ineffective despite tremendous potential. All of us have dreams, but not all of us forge them into goals. Instead, most people simply await the right opportunities. But even if the right opportunities were to happen along they might only ensnare us to the wills of the people who created them. Self-wrought goals, on the other hand, beckon us ahead of our own volition.

Dispersed campfire coals extinguish themselves. But scooped together they can ignite the kindling to produce a heartening blaze. And so it is with dreams. Scoop them carefully and purposefully together, fan some life into them, and they can engender a blaze of resolve and purpose. And scoop together the disparate but glowing fragments of our lives: the innate talents, abilities and courage within us all, and we become far more capable.

Society views physical labor as a personal indignity – something to be avoided. But for the distance hiker, the labor, the moving along the high and rugged trail, is an expression of life itself. And when this expression is directed toward a goal the journey becomes a pilgrimage and the long distance hiker becomes a pioneer, exploring the realities of human existence and the glories of Nature, which sustains all life.

The Avalanche of Adversity

We cannot direct the wind, but we can adjust the sails.

– Unknown

One of the more powerful forces of Nature is the climax avalanche. In its terrible maws even the largest and strongest trees are snapped like match sticks, hurled into the air, and driven far into the valleys where they are piled in tangled heaps. Yet imagine the irony. The avalanche does not strip the slopes bare. It takes the stalwart but leaves the willow and young aspen. These simply bend to its incredible pressures and spring back upright when it has passed.

In much the same way, Nature can rebuff the rigid minded hiker. And she will usually begin testing and prodding from day one of any wilderness outing. Those who proceed ahead with unrealistic ideals are likely to meet with obstacles every step of the way. And as likely as not those hikers will retreat, if not sooner then later. But those who recognize the need to bend and flex to Nature's ways are far more capable of living and traveling safely and enjoyably.

The Avalanche of Adversity comes in many forms. Wet brush on the trail. Dry brush on the trail. Incessant rain or driving thirst. Trails too steep or too gradual. Deep snow or tormenting heat. Bridgeless fords or dry creek beds, mosquitoes, bears, resupply stations too far from the trail or towns too close to it. And other hikers complaining about the same.

The fact is, we are usually stressed far more by our views of these adversities. This is because our minds tend to treat imagined possibilities as real, and our central nervous systems have no way of distinguishing the differences. It took me thousands of miles of trudging to learn to project my consciousness through these realities of Nature.

For best results in our wilderness quests, then, we need to cast aside some of our citified thinking. As an example, when city people go into a restaurant they expect the service to be punctual and polite. They expect the food to be fresh and hot. If they are non-smokers then they expect smoke not to come wafting into their faces. If each of these conditions is not met, they might complain to the management or at least they will not return. Granted, the customer is paying for these services, and for the most part these expectations are justified. But it is this attitude of demanding that all situations meet our expectations which lies at the root of our unhappiness in the wilderness.

More examples of rigid thinking are found in war and sports. The Army teaches its recruits to do-or-die-trying. The football coach hammers his team into delivering absolute maximum performance. This approach might stand up to the powers of other people, but in all my experience I have yet to find it effective in confronting the vastly superior powers of Nature.

Jenny and I once met a fellow on the PCT wearing camouflage and clasping the requisite cigar stub in one corner of the mouth. Nearby was his backpack, a gargantuan affair loaded with all manner of what appeared to be Army surplus gear. It wasn't surplus we soon learned. One hundred and twenty five pound's worth, the fellow said, and he could carry it only 15 minutes between rests. I asked why he didn't lighten his load by sending a few things home. "I started with it," he replied, "and by God I'm gonna finish with it. I come from the military and that's how we operate."

One of the great benefits of hiking is that each of us is free to pursue our goals however we like. We all have idiosyncrasies, our own ambitions, hiking parameters and philosophies. But when it comes to dealing with the natural obstacles along the way, known or unknown, physical or mental, I believe our best approach is to remain flexible.

Brush on the trail? Think of yourself as skiing in deep powder. Ignore the brush and simply plow through it. Rarely will it physically stop you, or even slow you down. Struggles and frustrations with brush on the trail are actually struggles with our own unrealistic demands. Wet brush on the trail? Forge ahead wearing nylon pants and running shoes. They will dry soon enough. Incessant rain? Anticipate it by carrying an umbrella. Driving thirst? Carry more water. Trails too steep or too gradual? Accept these as part of the reality of the moment. Deep snow? You probably started your hike too early in the season. Haul out for a few weeks' layover and allow the snow to melt and consolidate. Tormenting heat? Wear the minimum of clothing and make it lightweight and loose-fitting; carry plenty of water and hike beneath a mylar covered umbrella. Bridgeless fords? Head upstream in search of a fallen tree bridging the creek. Dry creek beds? Again, carry more water. Mosquitoes? Wear mosquito-proof clothing. Bears? Practice stealth camping away from their nightly haunts. Resupply stations too far from the trail? Choose your resupply stations carefully ahead of time. Towns too close to the trail? Not usually. Other hikers complaining about all the above? Point out the positive aspects of the moment, and if your pleasant mood doesn't rub off on them, then look for other companions and leave the complainers to interpret their journeys in their own ways.

If we confront the Avalanche of Adversity with rigid expectations it will weaken us and rob us of the moment's happiness. Yet it is mostly imagined. For best results we must find ways of operating within the parameters of Nature, and then of projecting our consciousness through the inevitable obstacles. We do this by remaining flexible, like the willows.

*Obstacles are those frightful things you see
when you take your mind off your goals.*

– Author not known

The Pyramid of Hiking Style

"Come to the edge," he said.
They said, "We are afraid."
"Come to the edge," he said.
They came.
He pushed them...
And they flew.

– Guillaume Apollinaire

Imagine a hypothetical pyramid, with steps leading up its flanks representing the levels of hiking style. The broad base represents the ultimate in incompetence; the lofty apex, the ultimate in proficiency. Each hiker chooses his or her position somewhere on the pyramid's flanks. But this position is not entirely fixed. The hiker can take a few steps up or down by adjusting attitude or equipment. The lower on the pyramid, the more arduous the journey. The higher, the easier.

A descent

Let's start midway on the pyramid's flanks and begin an unfavorable descent. Such descents are unintentional, but they happen with great regularity. In the following scenario we are planning to thru-hike the PCT, but because we have six months of free time, we are in no great hurry. This hike is going to be a vacation.

At one point in the journey we are planning for an 8 day trek between resupply stations. Intent on taking our time and enjoying life, we add more food, a thick paperback, and perhaps a harmonica. But because the extra gear won't fit into our already overloaded backpack, we might as well buy a bigger (and consequently heavier) one.

While carrying this new and heavier pack loaded with the extra belongings, the hiking will be more strenuous. But we will compensate by allowing ourselves longer rests, and by sleeping in whenever we feel like it. After all, we are in no hurry. So we might as well plan for an extra day's travel to the distant waypoint.

In order to accommodate the additional day we will need to pack more food and stove fuel. Granted, these will increase our load once again, but not to worry: the new backpack has plenty of space. And after all, it was advertised to carry heavy loads in comfort. So because we will be carrying more food we can plan for more variety. Let's include a frying pan.

Ostensibly, we are catering to our sense of enjoyment. But in actual fact the heavier pack lessens our enjoyment by increasing the work load and extending it. The heavier load also lessens our daily mileage, while lessening our agility, making us more prone to stumbling and sustaining injuries of impact. And of course it increases our chances of feet and leg problems.

Originally the plan was to take life easy; this hike is supposed to be enjoyable. So let's divide the segment by hiking out to a distant resupply station midway along its length. This will allow us to lighten our load somewhat. The resupply is a nine mile hike, each way, then a long hitchhike from the trailhead. So we will add two more days; one for going to and from our main route, and one for relaxing and enjoying town life.

Adding those two days to the nine, the eight day journey lengthens to eleven. But during each of the two segments we need carry only 5½ days of food and fuel. So we still have plenty of room for accouterments. Might as well bring along a backpacker's chair and a couple of extra lenses for the SLR.

As we descend the Pyramid of Style our journey lengthens in time and distance, our overall load increases, we become more susceptible to injury, and contrary to our intentions our hiking enjoyment diminishes. We have attempted to reduce our packweight by dividing the section, resupplying at an intervening and trail-distant station. In theory we are lightening our packs somewhat, but in truth we are only carrying more weight over a longer distance. We are, in short, descending the Pyramid of Hiking Style.

As a general rule, less efficient travelers are less capable ones. Bandaging self esteem, these people are fond of criticizing those who travel with greater efficiency and enthusiasm. "I just don't understand the 25-mile-a-day endurance hikers who plow along and don't see anything," they might say. "I prefer hiking five or ten miles a day and taking a greater interest in my surroundings." The fact is, daily mileage is a function of energy and vitality, and has nothing to do with one's enjoyment of the wilderness environment. How many 5-mile-a-day types do we find spending their entire summers in the wilds? Few, if any; but we regularly encounter 25-mile-a-day folks spending, not just one summer in the wilds, but several. So which is seeing more wilderness? And which is motivated by a greater sense of enjoyment? In reality, more efficient hiking is a lot more fun.

An ascent

Let's return to the starting point, midway on the pyramid's flanks, and begin an ascent.

Again we are planning to hike the original distance in 8 days, and we intend to do so while enjoying the traveling. Staying tuned to the goal of hiking the entire two and a half thousand miles in one season, we will exercise a little more discipline.

Hiking 17 miles a day at 2.75 miles an hour will require us to hike 6.2 hours each day, not including the rest stops. Surely we can hike more than 6.2 hours a day! Let's get going an hour earlier. Disciplining ourselves into hiking 7.2 hours each day, and allowing 8 hours of sleep each night, still we have 8.8 hours for resting and relaxing every day. So let's hike another half hour in the afternoon. Assuming we travel at the same 2.75 mph, our daily mileage will expand to over 21 miles. That extra 1½ hours on the trail makes a huge difference.

At 21 miles a day we would travel the total distance, not in 8 days but in less than 6½. Subtracting that 1½ days from our itinerary, we can remove the same amount of food and fuel from our pack.

Now, because our load is less ponderous, we will hike – not faster – but with less fatigue. The lessened packweight will virtually offset the extra time spent hiking. Covering the 21 miles per day while carrying a lighter pack, we will arrive in camp no more fatigued than had we hiked 17 miles a day carrying the heavier one. The magic in this system is that we gain extra mileage with little, if any, extra effort.

Distance hikers who grasp this principle are well on their way up the pyramid. Let's look at a few more techniques:

Let's send home a few items we haven't used in weeks. If sometime we need them, then too bad. We'll make do without them. Meanwhile, we won't be lugging them unprofitably every hour and every step of the way.

We'll send back the spare fleece sweater, the rain pants, two pairs of the most worn (and dirtiest) socks, the down booties, four pads of the moleskin, the cotton T-shirt emblazoned with the nifty art and worn only in camp, two tent stakes, the carabiner dangling affectatiously off the pack, the salt and pepper shaker (keeping a spoonful of salt in a small plastic bag), the candle lantern (keeping a few pieces of one of the candles for emergency fire-starting), and the electronic pedometer.

That makes a surprisingly large pile of non-essentials. Ridding ourselves of it lessens the pack's mass and increases its maneuverability. Greater maneuverability means easier and safer hiking, snow tromping and creek crossings. And because we will be carrying less weight, we will move ahead with less strain, meaning that we will be less prone to stress injuries. And because we will be traveling with less discomfort, we will be traveling with more enjoyment.

As we ponder the pile of things we're sending home, we have to admit that it wasn't increasing our enjoyment after all. It was lessening it. The pile weighs close to 5 pounds. Subtracting the 5 pounds from the original 50, we have lessened our burden by 10%. Transposing that ahead, we should be able to hike an additional 2 miles each day, while exerting no additional effort. Accordingly we would cover the distance to the next resupply station in less time.

Once again, we are not compromising enjoyment. On the contrary: the aesthetics of the journey will increase as we travel less encumbered. But here is another very important concept with the Pyramid of Hiking Style: we are not striving to increase our hiking speed. **Speed is not the issue.** Trying to hike fast only reduces long-term mileage and increases the chances of an injury.

Having readjusted our itinerary, we can now remove, say, a breakfast and a lunch from the pack. That lightens the pack and reduces its size yet again, lessening hiking time further. We're climbing higher on the Pyramid of Style, and are now looking far down at those hikers more heavily burdened. Now let's take a GIANT step upward.

We've been on the trail a few weeks, and have met hikers wearing running shoes, passing by and continuing on ahead of us. Oddly, they did not appear to be straining more than we. Let's send home our boots in favor of running shoes.

Removing weight from our feet is far more effective than removing it from our pack. Switching from boots to running shoes will increase our daily range dramatically – with no additional effort. This works because we will use far less energy, so we can hike, not faster, but more hours each day. But of course lightweight shoes work best for those who have trained in them, and strengthened the ankles properly.

We've gone from hiking 17 miles a day to hiking marathon distances without increasing the effort required. So once again, out comes more food and fuel. And that, again, helps our mileage.

Dizzy from the heights? Let's take another step upward. We have improved our hiking style so dramatically that we might now be in a position to skip the resupply at station B, which is at a considerable distance from the trail. Instead, we might hike another 2.5 days, in this example, to station C. Our packs will be quite light by the time we bypass station B, so those final 2.5 days should be quick and easy. This tactic will save us perhaps a full day, hiking out to station B and spending time sorting the resupply, etc. The disadvantage is that we are adding back the weight of 2.5 days' supplies to our packs. But because station B is at a considerable distance from the trail, skipping it will more than compensate for the weight gain.

Let's summarize the two scenarios. Those hikers on the pyramid's lower flanks trudge to resupply station B in 11 days. The marathoners on the upper slopes of the pyramid bypass station B and hike to station C in just over 7 days. The net result: the higher-style hikers very quickly out-distance the others, with no extra effort.

※

Climbing the Pyramid of Hiking Style is not easy because it requires us to more sharply define our wants from our needs, something we are not normally accustomed to doing in society. But I have found that when we humble ourselves and open our eyes to the realities of the natural world all around us, we also open ourselves to personal growth. And that is what climbing this pyramid is all about.

Training

Making Light of Toil

> Success to the strongest,
> who are always, at last,
> the wisest and best.
>
> — *Emerson*

Imagine someone starting out on a marathon run, out of shape but with the notion of conditioning themselves during the event. I don't know anyone foolish enough to try something like that. Yet every year, poorly-conditioned PCT hikers start from the Mexican border and try to hike, not just 26.2 miles, but a hundred times that. One hundred marathons with little prior conditioning. It sounds absurd, but people try it all the time.

Novice hikers imagine that they will condition themselves to the rigors of the journey during its initial stages. This might work if they hiked only a few hours a day while carrying very light packs, and if they took a day's rest every other day. But with the Canadian border in mind, thru-hikers have little time for such dallying. The season is comparatively short and the distances are vast. So these ill-prepared travelers hike eight or ten hours a day, carrying all the necessary gear, food, and sometimes a big load of water. And they try to keep this up day after day. This strategy places tremendous strains on their bodies, and is quite likely to cause a stress injury, if not sooner then later. Either way, much of the fun goes out of their journeys. Miles of beautiful, stimulating country pass by, and all they can think about is how much they hurt. They are not adjusting to the rigors of trail life. They are surviving.

Some hikers start their journeys out of shape, imagining that once they begin the trek, the trail's magical qualities will somehow buoy them along. The fact is, walking two and a half thousand miles while climbing and descending hundreds of thousands of feet in elevation, in all types of weather – all in a few short months – is an intense physical challenge. Don't underestimate the demands and difficulties, and don't over-estimate your abilities to handle them.

Another mistake is to confuse experience with strength, and vice-versa. If you have hiked one long trail, don't assume that you are still in shape. And if you are accustomed to carrying a heavy pack during the occasional week-long trip, don't imagine that you have the strength and stamina required to carry it day after day, all summer long.

PCT hiking is supposed to be enjoyable. And for the fully trained hiker it can be tremendously so. And so can the pre-hike training, when properly done.

The benefits of training

One of the most important features of the pre-hike training program is the rest day it affords between each training day. Then at the end of the five month training period the well-conditioned hiker may no longer need many rest days, as long as he or she carries a lighter load and eats well. It works exactly the opposite for the out-of-shape hiker using the actual journey as the conditioning. He or she will desperately need many rest days, but will not be able to take them.

Let me illustrate this with a typical comparison: Setting off from the Mexican Border, the un-trained hiker might manage ten miles the first day, while the well-trained hiker might cover twice that. Both feel they have exerted themselves equally. However, training's main benefit comes not at the end of the first day but at the beginning of the second. The out-of-shape hiker will struggle out of the sleeping bag stiff, muscle sore, and feeling inclined to take a layover day. The well-conditioned hiker is apt to arise feeling in excellent condition despite the previous day's exertions, and anxious to resume the trek. And of course, he or she will enjoy far greater chances of vitality and success in the ensuing weeks and months.

Over the years I have met several hundred long distance hikers plying the PCT and AT. One of the more obvious distinctions I have noticed is that almost without exception, those who had trained for their hikes were making far better progress and enjoying themselves much more than those who had not.

Training time reduces trekking time

Every hour you spend conditioning can lessen the duration of your distance hike Spend 5 months training beforehand, hiking maybe 450 miles in the process, and rid your packweight of every needless ounce, and your chances of hiking the trail in 4½ months are excellent. I am not inferring that the faster thru-hike is the superior one. But the more enjoyable hike certainly is, and enjoyment stems from energy and enthusiasm. The higher daily mileages are merely a spin-off.

The thru-hikers training technique

Start your training five months prior to your actual hike. Every other day walk a short distance over gentle but irregular terrain, initially while carrying no backpack. By "short distance" I mean whatever mileage you feel comfortable with. If you don't normally walk everyday for exercise, start by going out for 15 minutes, then turning around and walking back. Add mileage a week at a time until you are up to five miles.

Walking exerts the muscles of the legs and lower back: muscle groups used to some degree in everyday living. But carrying a backpack also exercises the groups supporting the shoulder girdle. So training with a gradually heavier pack is essential. When you have increased your every-other-day walks to five miles, it's time to start carrying a backpack – empty at first, then containing gradually more weight with the passing of weeks. Water makes excellent ballast because you can pour some of it out if you find, midway on your training hike, that you are tiring. I also recommend carrying the "ten essentials"[1], along with a few items of creature comfort. If the weather is cold you might carry an insulating pad to sit on, a thermos of hot soup or hot chocolate, and a warm jacket and hat to put on at the rest stops.

When you have worked up to five miles while carrying a 35 pound load, without stressing yourself, you can start increasing your distances once again. My target load is 35 pounds, and Jenny and I normally hike a 12 mile loop.

Keep a log of your training mileage. 450 miles prior to the summer's thru-hike would be about right. This may seem like a lot, but those training miles add up quickly when regularly done.

The more we train, the easier

A common misconception is that the training becomes progressively tougher. Not so. With the passing of weeks you should find that you can walk a little farther without tiring. And here you will discover the main benefits of training. As you build strength and stamina you become more capable. So although the differences between the first training jaunt and the last one can be astronomical, you would not feel the differences.

The key is to train with utmost gentleness. Don't make the routine so difficult that it ceases to be fun. Motivation is fueled by positive feedback; frustration by negative. If you find yourself tiring, then you are either going at it too vigorously or you are in need of food. Snacking during the training hike can lift your energy level and your spirits dramatically. And if you find that

---

[1] The Ten Essentials: Map, compass, knife, matches, fire starter, flashlight, first aid kit, extra food, extra clothing, sun protection.

your training hikes give you headaches or backaches, it is probably because the exertion is dehydrating you. Drink more water; a lot more water.

Additionally, the further you progress with your training program the more you will need to increase your nutritional intake. I recommend eating a certain amount of corn pasta during the training period, but more importantly that you concentrate mainly on fresh foods. These will help build your reserves. You might also boost your calcium intake to help strengthen the bones of your feet and legs. And don't forget to stretch out those calves every day.

Wherever you can walk, you can train for the PCT

If you can find a hill to climb during your regular forays, so much the better. If not, it doesn't matter. What does matter while training for the PCT is mileage and packweight. The PCT is gradually inclined, and it takes great, long switchbacks to climb and descend the mountains. So wherever you can walk, you can train for the PCT. I should note, though, that walking on flat surfaces does not properly strengthen the lateral muscles, tendons, and ligaments of the ankles and feet. Therefore, your training is best done on uneven ground. The idea here is to gently work those ankles.

Supplementary exercises

What about training on a stair climbing machine? In my opinion these exercises are so machine-specific that they do very little to condition the hiker for the trail.

I do, however, recommend two exercises for strengthening the legs. These can help the heavily burdened hiker climb out of snowpack post holes and moats, surmount steep terrain, and climb over wind-felled timber blocking the way.

- When performed correctly the barbell squat is generally considered a safe and effective thigh strengthening exercise. The technique is to stand erect, hold a barbell across your shoulders and behind your head, and squat down. A barbell? As a beginner, use a broom handle with no added weight. Or simply hold a few bottles of water. As you squat, keep your chin up and your spine as erect as possible. And avoid squatting below the comfort level. Any knee pain indicates that you are squatting too low.

- And speaking of knee pain, one way to help prevent it is to practice the foot lift, an exercise done while seated. Place the leg to be exercised over the chair's arm rest and let the foot hang free. Loop a small weight, suspended by a short length of rope or webbing, over the foot. Then slowly straighten the leg as far as it will go, then bend it again. Exercise gently, and use very little weight to begin with. If your knee makes grating noises, reduce the weight and hold it stationary rather than trying to straighten it.

Developing a sense of balance

During the training program you might practice balancing on one leg while looking ahead and upward. Performed every day for a month, this simple exercise can improve your balance a hundred fold. A well developed sense of balance will hold you in good stead not only when standing one-legged while dumping gravel out of a shoe, but also when balancing across a log spanning a swift-flowing creek.

"Weston the Pedestrian"

In 1909, Edward Weston walked 4,500 miles across the US in 105 days. The following year, at the age of 72, he repeated the journey in the opposite direction, in 76 days – for a remarkable average of 59 miles a day. One of the most accomplished walkers of our era, Weston believed that walking was as healthful and natural as sleeping, and throughout most of his life he walked 12 to 15 miles every day of the week except Sunday. He disdained the notion of "training," and considered his daily walking merely a part of his lifestyle.

So if you disdain the notion of training as well, just make your pre-hike walks a regular part of your lifestyle too.

I wish to preach, not the doctrine of ignoble ease
but the doctrine of the strenuous life.

– Theodore Roosevelt

Ice Axe Self-Arrest

The ice axe is the PCT hiker's parachute. Inconvenient to carry, fairly heavy, and rarely needed – but life saving when it is needed. When the hiker slips on a steep snow slope, he or she digs the pick of the axe into the snow to prevent sliding down into the rocks and trees. The technique is called the "self-arrest," and like riding a bicycle it is not difficult to learn with a little help from an instructor, yet once learned the skill will stay with you for life.

Snow travel on a PCT thru-hike is practically inevitable. Make sure you are prepared for it by carrying an ice axe and knowing how to use it.

PCT thru-hikers must start fairly early in the hiking season, when at least some, or perhaps much, of the trail is snowbound. The trail designers realized that the thousands of visitors do not go into the high country until the snow has melted. So the planner's intentions were to lead the hikers from the sultry lowlands to those cool, pleasant heights, and show them some of the country's most spectacular scenery along the way. And by "heights" I am referring to eleven and twelve thousand feet. From early September through to the end of June that is normally snow country.

Often, novice thru-hikers will assume that if the trail is mostly snow free then it will be safe enough to hike without an axe. The fact is, whether the previous winter's snowfall was massive or minuscule the dangers are about the same. The main hazards are not with the expansive, deep snowfields, but the steep little ribbons of sometimes rock-hard snow covering just a few yards of trail. They are too long to circumvent by climbing or descending around, and they can be quite dangerous to cross without an ice axe.

Granted, a great many hikers from all parts of the country have hiked the PCT without ice axes or even the rudiments of self-arrest skills. Chalk it up to good luck. Those prospective PCT hikers who are absolutely certain that their luck is good might choose to follow suit. To increase the odds a thousand-fold they should avoid setting off from Campo ahead of the *Handbook's* itineraries, regardless of how little snow might have fallen the previous winter. And they should try not to slip.

The fact is, many PCT hikers have slipped on steep snow slopes. We rarely hear about such slips by the ones carrying ice axes because they stopped themselves immediately, and carried on unharmed. And we rarely hear about the slips of the ones not carrying ice axes, because the rescue agencies involved have not wanted the publicity. But I have heard about plenty of them, in several cases first hand. And I can assure you that a number of ice axe-less PCT hikers have injured themselves from plummeting down steep slopes.

Schooling in the proper techniques

Once you learn to self-arrest, your confidence in negotiating steeper sections of snow will soar, and this will allow you to hike the high and wild places with far greater safety and peace of mind.

The safest and best way to learn the ice axe self-arrest is under the watchful eye of a qualified instructor, on a gentle practice slope with a safe run-out. If at all possible, enroll in an accredited class during the pre-hike winter months. Consider the costs of the lessons a form of insurance: Pay the one-time premium, and you're covered for life.

To locate various schools, check with your nearby universities, backpacking or mountaineering supply shops, or with your research librarian. If these prove fruitless, call some of the major equipment outlets – in other states if necessary.

The pointed end of the shaft is called the spike. The other end is called the head, and consists of the spoon-shaped, step-chopping and daily cat-hole digging blade called the adze (pronounced "adds"). Opposite that is the long and narrow blade called the pick, used for self-arrest. The adze needn't be razor sharp, and I don't imagine that using it to dig daily cat holes would dull the edge appreciably, if done with a little care.

The self-arrest described

The accompanying picture shows Jenny in the self-arrest position. She demonstrates on a concrete slab so that the pick of the axe is not buried in the snow, obscuring the important nuances of the position.

Note that the body does not lie on the surface, but is held up off of it. This exerts maximum plowing pressure on the axe and the feet. These are the three points of contact, and they form a triangle, with the legs spread apart somewhat for lateral stability.

Note also that the head of the axe is held closely to the body for a secure grip, but safely away from the face. THE greatest danger when learning to self-arrest without an instructor is in dropping down onto the slope in the self-arrest position and allowing the axe to gouge you in the face. So before dropping down onto the slope, hold your axe firmly in the self-arrest position, and with only one thought in mind: holding the adze *away* from your face.

Practice the self-arrest position in your backyard. Not dropping down onto the ground like you would on snow, but just lying there thinking about bracing your body off the ground, about spreading your feet, and about holding the adze away from your face. Once you get the position right, memorize it. Then go over it in your mind on occasion.

Actual practice

Lying in your backyard, face down in the self-arrest position, you will learn much amount about the proper technique. But you must also practice on a snow slope in order to coordinate the aggressive movements of jamming the pick of your axe into the snow. Here you must be very careful to choose a gentle practice slope which has a safe run-out. The slope must be forgiving of any mistakes you might make. Remember to keep a tight grip on the axe, and to keep the adze away from your face. With every practice fall, concentrate mainly on that adze.

Always hold the head of the axe with your strongest arm. If you are right-handed, grasp the head in your right hand. Visa versa if you are left handed. Should you suddenly slip, you will not have time to think about which hand goes where. It must be a reflex action, and the best way for beginners to develop this is to do it the same way every time. Resist the temptation to switch hands when facing the other way on a steep slope.

Should you slip and land on your butt or back, simply roll over onto your stomach in the direction away from the spike of your axe. This will prevent the spike from catching in the snow as you roll over. If you are right-handed, you would roll to your right.

The PCT hiker's ice axe

Today's hiker does not use the ice axe as a walking cane. A waist high shaft would be unnecessarily heavy and bulky, and the constant clanging with every other step would blunt the spike, to say nothing of frightening away the Hobbits. In actual use on steep snow, the shorter ice axe performs just as well. My axe is 25 inches long, and 9 inches along the head.

The ice axe is normally stowed outside the backpack, in such a way that it won't snag overhead branches, and that it won't injure the hiker in the event of an accidental slip, for example when tip-toeing on rocks crossing a creek. And ideally the axe should be accessible without having to unharness the backpack.

Finally, I recommend attaching a lanyard, about 3 feet in length, to the head of the axe for securing to your wrist when in use. Use cord or thin webbing. On a steep slope you should be mentally prepared to fall, and to self-arrest immediately. But if you fall unexpectedly, your uncontrolled reflex could toss the axe into space.

For information about crampons, rope and snowshoes see "Special equipment for snow travel," page 254.

Partners

The Lord knows what we may find, dear lass,
And the Deuce knows what we may do –
But we're back once more on the old trail,
Our own trail, the out trail;
We're down, hull down, on the long trail –
The trail that is always new.

– R. Kipling

Many hikers prefer going solo for the simple freedom and spontaneity. But that doesn't mean they live in solitary confinement. They meet other hikers along the way, and sometimes they may hike with them a ways. If the arrangement is amenable then a loose partnership can form and can continue, on and off, for weeks or even months. Or the solo hikers might simply stop and talk with the others awhile. And of course they meet townspeople when detouring from the trail to collect their resupplies, which, on the average is every three or four days. So actually a solo hiker is not really living solo as it might seem.

As Fred Coleman noted: "Those of us who go alone do so of necessity, or perhaps because we enjoy the solitary pleasures of thinking our own thoughts, adjusting to our own schedules and needs, and having total, silent connection with the nature which surrounds us. The price we pay is a slightly heavier pack and perhaps an additional element of risk. But hiking alone also carries with it more excitement and less adjustment to the moods and needs of others."

Most hikers enjoy the steady company of one or more partners. With them they can share their thoughts, feelings and anxieties. They can also share the journey's delights as well as its decisions. But how to find such a partner, and what are the pitfalls?

Before you start looking for a suitable partner it might be a good idea to think about what qualities you are looking for, and about what qualities you have to offer.

The American Heritage Dictionary defines the word "partnership" as *a relationship between individuals or groups that is characterized by mutual cooperation and responsibility, for the achievement of a specified goal.* The achievement of a specified goal is the key here. Prospective partners must understand what each other's objectives are, while at the same time allowing for personal differences in style and character.

Are you willing to make the compromises necessary to accommodate another hiker into your game plan? Are you a natural leader or a natural follower? Which is more important to you, the goal or the relationship? If your partner decides to quit the hike, would you be prepared to continue without him or her?

One of the best places to find a partner for the PCT is on the Internet. Here, as anywhere, enthusiasm is your greatest asset. People are attracted to those with genuine plans of action. Before making definitive plans with someone on-line, though, get to know each other better by swapping pictures and talking on the telephone.

Partnerships made or broken along the way

If you would like to find a partner but haven't succeeded, don't dismay. Even though you may be alone during the planning stages, rest assured that you are likely to meet other hikers in the same predicament, once you have begun. And if you find that you share common interests, hiking styles, and goals with someone, then you may decide to travel together a ways. Many lasting partnerships have been formed in this manner. So don't be reluctant to start out on your own. And remember that action is a great opener of doors.

At the same time, many partnerships have split due to incompatibilities which were not apparent until put to the test. So don't lose heart if your partnership dissolves somewhere along the way. Once again, you are quite likely to meet others.

Many hikers have traveled the full distance solo, and virtually anyone can do it. Yet if you feel that you absolutely cannot go without a partner, you might consider hiking the Appalachian Trail. The AT is so popular with long distance backpackers that your chances of finding partners for it, either before or during the hike, would be excellent. Contact the friendly folks at the Appalachian Trail Conference, P.O. Box 807, Harpers Ferry, WV 25425-0807; (304) 535-6331. Ask to subscribe to their newsletter, and about placing an ad in the "Public Notices" section.

A close friend

If you and a long-time friend plan to spend the summer on the trail, consider yourself fortunate. Both of you are probably aware of each other's strengths and weaknesses, and with a little luck and a lot of effort you should be able to forge a favorable hiking relationship.

Pigs in a poke

If you have arranged a partnership with someone who plans to hike the PCT same as you, but whom you haven't met in person, the chances of this working out can be quite good. The fact that both of you want to hike the trail suggests a great deal in common. Still, you might want to exercise a certain amount of caution when it comes to sharing equipment in order to save weight. Should differences arise, a few days or weeks into the journey, both of you will need sufficient gear to carry on. Give yourselves several hundred trail miles together before you start sending home redundant gear.

Your spouse as partner

Jenny and I always enjoy meeting other hikers on the trail, particularly other couples. One summer we ran into Garrett and Leisha Holmes, who had recently been married. In fact, their summer's journey on the PCT through Oregon and Washington was their honeymoon. At the conclusion of their journey they wrote:

"If you have a new spouse or a long term friend, go on a long distance hike with them! Our relationship's strength grew tremendously during our trip. Together we endured snow, rain, sleet, bugs, forest fires, and all the "ups and downs" a trail like the PCT can dish out. When the going was exceptionally tough due to minor injuries or other "inconveniences" we could always hold hands and know that with each other and God's help we would persevere. And we did!"

Spouses can make excellent hiking partners. I suppose some hikers enjoy getting away from theirs on occasion, but as Garrett and Leisha pointed out, the rigors of the trail can do much to strengthen the bond, as mates learn to work together, solve the problems, and go the distance. Sharing the beauties of wilderness trekking with the one you love can be a real joy. And in fact, long distance hiking is usually so all-encompassing that the two of you are actually sharing a big part of your lives.

More commonly, one mate enjoys hiking while the other views it with certain misgivings. I imagine that such trepidation could be based on unpleasant past outings. The fact is, most *genuinely* skilled outdoors-people can easily teach beginners how to enjoy hiking and camping. They do this by ensuring the experiences will be pleasant. This is a skill that reflects competence in the wilderness setting. The person with this skill will foresee and avoid unpleasant incidents, such as exhausting the partner, or allowing them to be drenched in a midnight downpour. And the skillful will be able to lend gentle encouragement and extend illimitable patience. These hiking and partnering skills can be developed together, years in advance of a thru-hike or during its training stages.

Staying together

As an instructor for Outward Bound, one of my jobs was to keep my group of 10 students together. Naturally, some of them preferred to hike fast, and some slow. Losing someone, either ahead or behind, was a constant concern, especially considering that we rarely followed trails, and even then that trails have a way of branching and branching again. A lost student constituted a major disruptive event. All course activities had to suspend while we searched; and this was a good way to lose someone else. So although it may seem overly regimented, I had to teach the students to stay together from day one.

Initially, I would discuss the problem with the group. This often went ignored, so I would resort to the technique of "roped travel." If nothing else it was good practice for hiking on glaciers, I would remind everyone as they struggled along the trail, each secured with harness and carabiner at regular intervals along one of their climbing ropes. But if the rope did anything it emphasized the differences in hiking style and amplified them all out of proportion. Choreographed hiking is not ingrained in anyone, especially with ten different people from ten different parts of the country pulling in ten different directions. But the students soon learned that if they were to make any forward progress at all, they had to hike together. One session of maybe fifteen minutes usually illustrated the concept of individual compromise for the benefit of the group; that a group travels at a different speed than the majority of its individuals would prefer.

PCT partnerships are not Outward Bound patrols, and there is no instructor to threaten you with roped travel. But you may face exactly the same problems of staying together, and face the same emergency if, and when your partner goes astray. The fact is, you and your partner(s) will likely want to travel at different speeds. As often happens, the partnership may split during the day and reform again each evening at camp. Outwardly, this system might seem to afford everyone the needed freedom. But it can also greatly increase the chances of not finding each other that evening.

Back in the late 70's I was sea kayaking with two friends along the coast of Baja. One late afternoon two of us stopped for spearfishing, and our third partner decided to press on to camp. We reconfirmed where that camp would be – on a prominent finger of land five miles ahead. Late that evening the two of us arrived there, but could not find our friend. Fortunately I had specified a contingency plan, so we all knew where our next camp would be, 50 miles farther along, and we all understood that if we didn't meet at that camp, then we would wait one full day for any stragglers.

The two of us paddled the 50 mile stretch, thankful that from the start we had insured that each person carried his share of the food and community equipment. Our third partner still didn't show up, so we waited at that next camp all the next day, again to no avail. Considering that our misplaced friend was the independent sort, we decided that rather than return to look for him we would continue to the next town, five days ahead. Four days later we were resting ashore when our friend came paddling past. After a happy reunion we compared notes, and discovered that we had camped nearly together on the first finger of land, him on one side and we on the other; that all three of us had waited the full day within a quarter mile of each other; and remarkably, that we had been leap-frogging all the way along the coast without seeing each other.

This scenario can happen anywhere, not just in kayaks along a coastline. Whether you and your partners plan to hike together or not, realize that you may lose track of one another. Before starting out each day, make sure that everyone knows the day's objective. If actually planning to lose sight of your hiking companions, agree on a place and time to meet next. And agree where to camp that night. Also, have a mutual understanding of what to do if someone doesn't show up. Will you wait? And for how long? Or will you continue ahead to your next resupply station? As a contingency, always make sure that each person has the resources (food, equipment, map, etc.) and the wherewithal to carry on alone.

Jenny and I always stay close together when "on journey." The only exception is when one person detours to the bushes to answer the call of nature; and even then the other person will continue ahead no more than 100 yards before sitting down and waiting. We know that the chances of losing each other are genuine, and the consequences would far outweigh any inconveniences caused by staying together. And besides, we rather enjoy each other's company.

Packweight

On a long journey even a straw weighs heavy.

– Spanish proverb

As an ultra-long-distance hiker, every additional ounce on your feet and back will magnify itself against you two and a half thousand times. Don't try to conquer Nature by dragging along items of luxury and comfort designed to resemble what you are leaving at home. They will only subtract from your comfort while on the trail. And remember that the trail is long. Make it easier on yourself by carving your packweight. Start during your training hikes and continue right on through to your final resupply package pick up.

Ray's myth-busters

Myth: The longer the hike, the more gear it requires.

Fact: The longer the hike, the *less* gear it requires. This is because the more weeks and months you spend on the trail, the more efficient your methods will become, and the more confidence you will gain. A month into the hike you will begin to rely more on your skills rather than purely on your equipment.

Myth: According to tradition, the backpacker needs a comprehensive load of equipment for a safe, comfortable, and enjoyable trip. "It's better to have something and not need it," the saying goes, "than to need it and not have it."

Fact: A comprehensive load of equipment is extremely heavy. Carrying a heavy load for two and a half thousand miles is neither safe nor enjoyable. The gear might provide comfort once you reach camp, but if you are trying to hike long distances, then by the time you reach camp you are likely to be beyond needing comfort. All you will need is a place to collapse from exhaustion.

Myth: Tradition also holds that this equipment must be rugged and durable.

Fact: For the person prone to dropping it off cliffs, yes.

Myth: The backpack may feel very heavy now, but it won't be so bad once you get in shape.

Fact: Initially, a 60 pound pack feels merely heavy, including when training with it at home. After the first 100 miles of actual PCT hiking it will feel more like a crushing burden. If you are striving for high mileage days, the heavy pack will steepen every hill, magnify every mile, and drastically reduce your daily mileage while making you far more prone to injury. And in the process it will sap your enjoyment. Never will you accustom to it, and always will the act of taking it off bring immense relief.

Why, then, do hikers carry heavy loads? Generally, I imagine it is for these reasons:

✗　They are trying to be prepared for any and all unforeseen occurrences, falsely imagining that great quantities of equipment will provide greater margins of safety.

➠ This rationale generally stems from a lack of knowledge regarding human ability, adaptability and the environment. Heavy-duty, superfluous gear can actually subtract from the hiker's safety.

✗　They may be easily persuaded by advertising.

➠ One ploy with advertisers is to obscure the relative heaviness of their products. For example, they will describe an item weighing 8 ounces as "featherweight." Imagine a bird having feathers weighing half-a-pound each. The poor creature would weigh about 400 pounds. Who benefits from this nonsense – the backpacker struggling along under a ponderous load of "lightweight" gear, or the manufacturers selling it?

✗　They may be dragging along as many creature-comfort impediments as possible, trying to simulate the comforts of home.

➠ Those who demand the comforts of home might prefer staying at home.

✗　They learned their methods from people and organizations they respect, such as from their parents, the Boy or Girl Scouts, or the military.

➠ Were these "authorities" proficient long distance hikers?

✗　They might be trying to impress others.

➠ Are we to take backpackers lumbering beneath 60 pound packs as macho and experienced, or as comically (or sadly) uninformed?

When Jenny and I set out from Campo on our second PCT hike, our packs weighed 22 pounds each. This included a 2½ day supply of food, and all the clothing and equipment needed for the first month. The gear list on page 131 reflects the same level of expertise for one person hiking autonomously. The packweight in that chapter is also 22 pounds. This does not include food or water, but it does include the clothes and shoes the hiker would be wearing.

When used with more efficient hiking and camping styles, lighter weight gear and the minimum of it is of tremendous benefit. So let's take a look at how you can go about carving your packweight.

Reducing packweight

Typically, hikers will cut half the handle off a ½-ounce toothbrush, trim the margins off their maps, combine all their candy bars into a single bag and dispense with the individual wrappers, and with sense of accomplishment call the job done. The result? The 64 pound pack is reduced to 63.9 pounds.

When trying to reduce packweight, we benefit the most by concentrating on the heavier items first. Buying a 3½ pound backpack rather than a 7½ pound one saves a whopping 4 pounds. Buying a 3½ pound tent rather than a 6 pound one saves another 2½ pounds. Of course, we don't want to compromise function. A tent which is too light could also be too flimsy. But consider the tarp that Jenny and I carried on our third PCT. It weighed 1¾ pounds and was capable of withstanding gales that would have blown most tents away. This was because when necessary it could be pitched low lying, and because the support sticks chosen can be far stronger than the flimsy aluminum poles that come with most tents.

The second most productive weight savings measure comes in resisting the temptation to indulge in superfluous gear. Obviating a piece of equipment reduces its weight by a full 100%.

The third phase entails selecting the lightest and most useful of the usual profusion of small items, such as the compass, knife, flashlight, and so on. Each fractional ounce saved is not much, but in quantity they can add up fast.

The fourth stage takes place in the field. It is the mailing home or ahead of any and all gear which is proving unessential. Even if we think we might need an item someday, this is no justification for carrying it. If we are not using it then we should consider ridding our pack of it. If we will not be needing it we would send it home. If we might be needing it farther along, we could place it in our drift box and send it ahead.

There are, however, a few emergency items that hikers should always keep with them. First and foremost is a set of storm clothing. This would include an insulating sweater, a waterproof/breathable parka, shell pants of breathable nylon, and hat and mittens. Even if the weather has been mild for weeks on end, it could suddenly deteriorate. Hikers should also carry an emergency fire starter kit in a waterproof container. This kit would include stick matches, birthday candles, and some dry tinder. A small knife is also essential for fire starting in rainy weather, for making fuzz sticks and stripping off wet bark. In addition see the "ten essentials" footnote page 32.

Daily mileage versus packweight

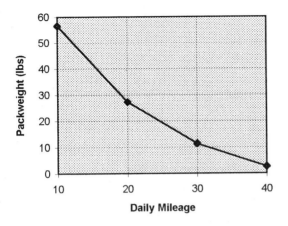

Daily Mileage

Traveling the PCT in both directions, Jenny and I kept careful track of our hiking time between camps. While hiking southbound and nearing a resupply station with packs empty of food, we far outdistanced our northbound mileages coming out of those stations loaded with supplies. This provided some very interesting information regarding daily mileage versus packweight. I extrapolated the data and plotted the results to show the correlations. This graph might also give you an indication of your daily mileage capabilities in regards to your overall packweight. Remember, though, that it is only an indication, due to the great many variables in terrain, physical conditioning, motivation, type of footwear, and so forth.

Tabulate your gear

Most hikers grow fond of their gear after using it a few seasons. And the marketer's hype only further saps their objectivity. During the planning stages, then, it is a good idea to weigh every piece of your intended gear, and to tabulate the items and their weights in ounces and tenths of an ounce. Examining your gear in letters and numbers can help you see it more objectively. Items which are heavier than necessary, and those which are non essential might become more apparent. And incidentally, while perusing gear both in the stores and in the catalogs, don't trust the published weights. Some are so inaccurate they cannot be used even as guidelines. When entering weights in your own gear tabulation, weigh each item on a kitchen scale.

Sharing gear with a partner

One excellent way to reduce packweight is to share some of your gear with a hiking partner. Obviously, which items you can share will depend on the nature of the partnership. Discuss how tolerable each of you are to encroachment of personal space, and to what extent each of you is willing to rely on the other.

Even the closest alliances can separate, whether intentionally or not. For some reason partners that habitually venture ahead or lag behind are prone to selecting the wrong fork in the trail. So with this in mind, each member of a group should maintain a certain amount of autonomy by carrying various items essential for personal safety and well being. At the minimum these would include some type of shelter, a sealed packet of matches, food, cookpot, water, map and compass, money, and ID.

Tuning in to the environment

Hikers going into the High Sierra early in the season might carry a magnum load of fuel to melt snow for drinking and cooking. And they might carry climbing ropes, crampons, snowshoes, expedition tents, and heavy mountain boots – as though they were storming Annapurna. If they are looking for that type of adventure then that's one thing. But instead of entering the Sierra in its early season they could start their hikes according to one of the itineraries in this book. That way, when they reach the Sierra they should find that most of the snow has melted. A certain amount of gear is needed to handle adverse conditions, but the hiker's timing can often obviate those conditions altogether.

Avoiding adverse conditions also entails foresight and prudence: leave the trail and descend to lower terrain when a storm threatens, or refrain from climbing over a high pass when the clouds start spitting lightning.

By tuning into the environment we can greatly increase our safety margins, and thus do away with much of the more traditional backpacking gear. For example, most backpackers carry self-inflating mattress. Why?

✗ To cushion compacted ground at the designated campsites where thousands of campers have scraped away not only the pine cones and sticks, but also the forest litter and duff, and where both people and beasts have compacted the soil.

✔ Instead, they could stealth camp on soft and insulating ground, where the natural forest litter and duff provide perfect bedding, insulation, and drainage. A stealth camp normally requires only a minimal pad or a few spare clothes to lie upon.

✗ And as insulation from the snow.

✔ During all five of our mega-hikes Jenny and I did not camp on snow – even though we traversed the High Sierra twice in very early season, the North Cascades once in early season, and the northern Continental Divide in early season. All of these were extensively snowbound. In springtime, pervasive snow exists only at the higher elevations, and even there you can find the occasional patches of bare ground. By working with Nature and camping on bare ground you can do away with a thick sleeping pad and the extra 1½ pounds.

✖

The type of gear you need on your PCT trek will depend largely on how well you can duck Nature's salvos, and to what extent you react to those you cannot avoid. But whatever your level of expertise and foresight, remember never to set off from a resupply station carrying spare change. It's too heavy. Spend it on snacks.

Equipment

Those who prepare for all the emergencies of life beforehand
may equip themselves at the expense of joy.

E. M. Forster

*Emma "Grandma" Gatewood
(1888-1975) did not look like much
of a hiker. But sometimes looks can
be deceiving. During an illustrious
hiking career that spanned 18 years
she thru-hiked the Appalachian
Trail, not just once, but twice; and
she section-hiked it a third time.
She also hiked the Chesapeake and
Ohio Canal towpath from Washington, DC to Cumberland, Mary-
land, the Long Trail in Vermont, the
Baker Trail in Pennsylvania, and
the Buckeye Trail in Ohio. And on
the 100th anniversary of the historic Oregon Trail she walked its
entire 2,000 mile length in 15 days
less than it had taken most of the
wagon trains.*

Grandma Gatewood started hiking at
an age when most ardent backpackers retire to their armchairs.
And even then her performance was
amazing. During her second thru-
hike of the AT, a 2,000 mile journey of over 4½ months, and completed just a
few days before her 70th birthday, she took no rest days. Her secret? "I had
always lived on a farm and was used to hard work," she said. "I was in good
physical condition, so I decided to hike that Trail, and I just started out." And
in her spunky style she quipped, "Most people are pantywaists. Exercise is
good for you."

What set Grandma apart was her disdain of contemporary equipment.
Backpackers wore sturdy boots to protect their feet. Grandma wore Keds™
sneakers. They used expensive parkas and "lightweight" and bugproof tents.
She used a rain cape and a plastic shower curtain. They carried expensive

frame packs which distributed their heavy loads evenly. Grandma didn't carry heavy loads. Her items of extra clothing and gear were few, and she carried them, and her food, in a bag of her own making and simply draped over one shoulder.

Grandma's legacy reminds us of our own abilities, and of the excesses of today's high-tech paraphernalia. She was obviously a strong woman, but I doubt whether she would have hiked a fraction of those trail miles while lugging the standard elephantine load. And what's more, I cannot think of a single item of modern clothing or gear that would have added to her success.

I am not suggesting we need to abandon our gear and adopt the minimalist approach. But I do think that the bulk of today's trendy gear is not essential to hiking and camping enjoyment. The type of equipment each of us needs depends almost entirely on what we believe we will need. So before discussing our equipment, perhaps we should discuss our equipment beliefs.

Make no mistake about it. Our beliefs are influenced very strongly by the propaganda of marketing and advertising in books and magazines. Let's look at how this operates.

The deluge of hype

As today's society finds itself with more leisure time, more people are becoming interested in outdoor activities. Accordingly, the marketplace is responding to the profit potential with clothing and equipment of higher technology. And indeed, the profits can be quite high for the companies which minimize overheads, pay relatively low wages while expecting high output, and which purchase raw materials in great bulk. Naturally, many manufacturers have been lured into the arena. Several are reputable and careful not to copy the ideas of their competitors. But others have found themselves generally unable to design gear that distinguishes itself from among the competition. So they have simply copied. As a result, much of today's merchandise is adrift in a sea of "sameness."

This sameness is no obstacle to the marketeers[1]. They need only make the customer feel attractive and invincible while using the company's products. They know that what today's moneyed customer wants is trendy, outdoorsy costumes with all the right brand names conspicuously evident. And they know that it is not the gear that makes the customer feel successful, but the association with its advertising.

---

[1] I coined the word "marketeer" as a combination of marketer (one who advertises, promotes, and sells commercial goods) and racketeer.

Advertising so pervades our culture that virtually every one of us is susceptible to it. Some is beneficial, but I take exception to the type which attempts to imbue the products with magical qualities. People are so accustomed to seeing this propaganda that they hardly take notice. Yet it sinks in, subconsciously. Look inside any popular hiking magazine at the full page ads, then look inside the typical backpacker's backpack. The contents of each are bound to be strikingly similar.

Fanning through a magazine you are subjecting yourself to subliminal advertising. As each corporate logo and each repetitive advertisement flashes into your eyes, it refreshes your memory and works its way deeper into your subconscious mind. Try examining some of the advertisements and ask yourself what is the reality and what is the attempted magic. Seeing advertising objectively is a skill, and once you develop it you may be surprised at what you see.

Grandma Gatewood disassociated herself from the glossy marketing mainstream, yet she enjoyed a lengthy and successful backpacking career on par with the best of them. How? By exercising her strong will to succeed, and by practicing her skills of self-sufficiency. "It's about as nice a thing as anybody can do – walking," she said. "And it's cheap, too!"

Reassuring guarantees

Some companies today are producing cheaply made equipment. And in order to compete they must guarantee their products like their more reputable counterparts. But there's a catch. Their guarantees do not necessarily attest to the quality or durability of their products. Instead, they simply assure the customer that should problems arise they will be rectified. But what good are such guarantees to the hiker whose pack strap rips out miles from the nearest trailhead?

When an equipment failure occurs, the novice distance hiker will usually hitchhike out to civilization, make the appropriate phone call to heaven, as it were, ordering the replacement, then wait for days – complaining, and of course resting and feasting all the while. In truth, if the backpack or any other item of gear fails, the hiker is the one accountable. The industry thrives at the expense of the consumer, but the consumer is the one responsible for recognizing hype, for considering any ill advice from salespeople, and finally, for exercising judgment when deciding to buy a product. Even gear made of heavy materials can be cheaply put together. So if anything breaks down, try to improvise the repairs yourself. If a strap rips off, tie or hand-stitch it back on. If a bag rips, sew or duct-tape it back together. If a frame breaks, temporarily splint it with a stick, tape and lashings.

Why is today's gear so heavy?

The concept of guaranteeing equipment works against the long-distance hiker who knows how to treat the equipment with care. Let's say that a customer buys an expensive backpack, first making certain that is fully guaranteed. If a seam rips out or a straps tears off, the disgruntled customer will return the product for repair or replacement, not only suffering the loss of valuable time but paying the postage. This is bad news also for the manufacturer, who thinks in terms of profit margins and public images. Especially for those who import their products. So the manufacturer responds by enhancing the design, not by reinforcing the over-stressed area, for that would be too labor intensive, but by increasing the weight of the affected component: the fabric, fastener, etc. In time, after scores of backpacks have come back for repairs – each with a different problem – the manufacturer has made the product massively stronger, and of course heavier. This ultra-durability might be ok for expeditionary use, but it is outright overkill for long distance hiking in relatively accessible areas, particularly for hikers who know how to take care of their gear.

We make our own

The packs that Jenny and I carried on our most recent PCT trek weigh 13.5 ounces each. They worked great, and because we knew how to reinforce the stress points, and because we took care of them during the trip, they returned home in like-new condition.

We make most of our hiking clothing and gear because we can also tailor it to our needs. This saves us lot of money, but more importantly it saves us a lot of weight.

✔ Compare one of our backpacks, weighing 0.8 pound and costing $10.40, to a store-bought model weighing 6.0 pounds and costing $275.00. Our pack is 13% of the weight and 4% of the cost.

✔ Compare our two-person sleeping quilt, rated at 20°F, weighing 3.1 pounds and costing $34.00, to a pair of commercial sleeping bags costing a total of $600.00 and weighing 7 pounds. Our quilt is 44% of the weight and 6% of the cost. (Compare our equivalent of 1½ pounds per person bag with its 20°F rating to *any* commercial sleeping bag. It's no contest.)

✔ Compare the tarp we used on our southbound PCT hike, weighing 1.8 pounds, costing $15.00 and taking us 5.0 hours to make, to a commercial tent weighing 4.3 pounds and costing $350. Our tarp is 42% of the weight and 4% of the cost.

These three items alone save us 16.9 pounds and $1,430.

Learning to custom make your gear will usher you into the inner sanctum of the ultralight arena. I discuss the matter in more detail in the "Advanced Techniques" section. Still, I realize that most hikers lack the time and inclination to learn the skills of sewing, simple though they are. Which takes us back to square one.

Examining new gear

As an experienced backpacker, no doubt you own a fair amount of equipment. Yet again, you might feel that your upcoming PCT trek will require a more specialized selection of the finest equipment available. So you might pore through stacks of backpacking equipment catalogs, and study magazine advertisements and equipment reviews. In addition, you might visit the local shops to examine and try on loaded backpacks, compare sleeping bags, and to crawl into tents.

Sales pressure

Enter the sales clerks. By the nature of their jobs these people must appear enthusiastic and knowledgeable. And indeed, many are genuinely capable. Of those who are less so, they can still meet the needs of most backpackers. As an aspiring distance hiker, though, your requirements are unique. So beware of any off-the-mark advice. Rely on your own thinking, augmented with the parameters in this book.

Shun bold logos

Never mind the high profit margins. Forget the ubiquitous hype. But when it comes to big, bright, brand-name logos affixed to the products themselves and designed to seize our attention, we have a problem. Granted, we can flee to the primeval regions seeking freedom from the distractions of commercialism. There we find no advertisements – until Hapless Hiker pulls out his water bottle emblazoned with the bold logo. Wham! The advertisement smacks you in the face. Then he slips on his jacket. Pow! The bold logo on the sleeve socks you again. Reeling, you reach for the fuel bottle. Bap! The logo covers the whole thing. Disgusted, you retreat to the tent. Smash! The bold logo above its doorway sends you straight back to the dirt. As you lay there, bleeding, beaten, consider yourself fortunate. Future generations of hikers are likely to have it far worse.

Gear emblazoned with bold logos advertises itself. And those who carry it are marketing it. If the company wants to give us their logo-emblazoned products, and pay us for acting as their walking, camping billboards, then we might consent. Otherwise, I don't think it's our responsibility to provide free services, nor to taint the wilderness experiences of the other hikers. Edward Abbey suggested the benefits of sawing billboards down, but I favor attacking the problem at its root. Curtailing the demand might be our best method of affecting the supply. Don't purchase any item of clothing or gear which has a bold logo that you cannot remove.

Modifying your equipment

Most commercial products come with guarantees that forbid you from modifying the products. This leaves you feeling that the company still owns the products long after you have paid for them and brought them home. But the truth is, your purchases belong to you, and you may modify them any way you like. And by doing so, they are far more likely to serve your specific purposes. For many people, the idea of taking a knife to a newly purchased backpack or pair of shoes is unthinkable. But the PCT hiker-in-planning *should* think about it, and think about it very seriously. Use imagination and flare, and remember that if you whack too much you can always sew it back together. In the following sections I give a few suggestions.

The backpack

The backpack is the hiker's most important piece of gear. Come to think of it, though, Grandma Gatewood didn't carry one. She used a home-made bag, as we saw, rather like a pillow case and closed at one end with a draw cord. It had no straps, but was simply draped over one shoulder. With it she hiked many thousands of miles. Contrast her bag with the modern, massively built techno-backpack found in every backpacking store and catalog. Complicated, gaudy, unwieldy, and very expensive. In my opinion such gimmickry doesn't address the needs of the long distance hiker very well, and it adds unnecessary weight. A lot of weight. Perusing today's market we find internal-frame packs listed at 6 and 7 pounds. And the actual weights can be as much as two pounds over the listed weights – such are the "variations in manufacture."

The distance hiker is trying to carve fractions of an ounce from the gear, and the backpack manufacturers are adding them back in pounds. How do they get away with this? By assuring us that their high-technology backpacks carry heavy loads comfortably. To the long-distance hiker such hype is about as beneficial as a trail full of rattlesnakes and poison oak. The truth is: the heavier the load, the more work is required to transport that load. The best way to make hiking more efficient is not to design a backpack to carry the load more comfortably, but to reduce the load. And by far the most effective single measure in reducing the load is to reduce the weight of the backpack itself.

If you have ever imagined that some of this high-technology is merely high-hype, consider that even a $550 backpack pack will require a separate rain cover, and I have yet to see a rain cover that didn't leak profusely. The best way to keep one's gear dry is to insert a plastic garbage bag inside the backpack, and to load everything into that. Imagine a $550 backpack requiring a garbage bag liner to make it work properly!

For best results choose a smaller backpack of the lightest weight and best construction available, then modify it to suit. Not only will the reduced weight of the pack save you two or three pounds (not just ounces), but its smaller size will limit the amount of gear you can cram into it. A smaller pack requires more forethought about one's equipment inventory, and this is exactly the type of thinking that makes for a more refined wilderness experience.

Of course, one must be careful not to compensate by lashing things all over the outsides. This reminds me, humorously, of Jenny and me walking out of grocery stores near the Appalachian Trail with bags of groceries suspended in our hands. Instead of heading for a car like everyone else we headed for the trail and resumed our journey. We were using small home-made backpacks that summer and were not resupplying with more compact foods. The store-bought groceries which wouldn't fit into our backpacks? Invariably within the first few hours of hiking we had eaten them all.

Pack capacity

Assemble all your clothing and gear before you buy or make your backpack, so that you will know how large the pack will need to be. Here is my method of determining pack size: Select a cardboard box of a size and shape resembling a backpack. Carefully pack your summer's selection of gear into it. Measure the box's length and width. And with all your gear carefully packed in the box, slide a yardstick down the inside of the box and measure how many inches high your gear is. Multiply these three numbers together to obtain your gear's volume in cubic inches. Keep in mind that the volumetric figures given for various commercial packs often include the volume of the extended collars. With the collars loaded, however, the backpacks can be unwieldy.

If you would like to know the capacity of your present backpack, visit your local shipping store and ask to borrow a large box of recycled plastic "peanuts." After filling your pack with them, pour them into an empty box. Once again, measure the width and length of the box, and slide a yardstick into the box and measure the height of the peanuts. Multiply the three figures to obtain the cubic inch volume. And don't forget to return the peanuts.

Cut and whack

If there is one modern innovation which we might call breathtaking, it is the sternum strap. This constricts us where we need it the least, directly across our lungs. If you find that your shoulder straps slide off your shoulders, then maybe you do need one of these chest corsets. Otherwise, prune it. Ditto the compression straps. Cut away all but the ones on the sides, which can serve as clotheslines. To fashion a clothesline, remove the compression-strap buckle, cut the straps just long enough so that they overlap one inch (while the pack is fully loaded). Then pin the straps to each other and sew them together.

Prune all plastic lashing pads. Insert a knife blade beneath the lashing pad and carefully slice the stitching. Use the gizmos as little Frisbees.

The infernal frame pack

Internal and external frames, hip belts, and their myriad adjustments are contrivances designed to accommodate heavier loads and the different sized hikers who carry them. I find that with a load of under 30 pounds I do not require a frame, or any of this gadgetry. This is merely a preference, but I recommend that you experiment with carrying your pack with its hip belt unfastened. Or at the very least that you prune any hip belt stabilizing (read: pelvis immobilizing) straps. You will walk more efficiently without the restraint.

As we walk, our pelvis moves in three ways: It swivels as though we are dancing the "twist," opposite the arms as they swing forward and back. It seesaws, one side up, the other down, then visa versa. And it shuttles side to side as our body weight shifts from one leg to the other. The motions of our shoulder girdle are similar to those of our pelvis, but in opposite phase. Our spine connects the two, and accommodates the opposition by bending and twisting. A backpack with its hip belt cinched acts as a brace, resisting these opposing motions. Over the long haul this saps energy. Furthermore, by restraining our spine, which was designed for suppleness in absorbing shocks, the frame also increases the chances of an injury.

Shoulder strap adjustments

Many commercial backpacks feature complicated arrangements for adjusting the upper shoulder strap attachment points. Once adjusted, though, these features are of no further benefit, even though they must be carried throughout the journey. A backpack lacking in these features, but which fits to begin with, could be lighter and more reliable.

Compartments

Some backpacks have partitions between the main loading area and the lower sleeping bag compartments, accessed externally by zippers. This arrangement allows for better weight distribution by locating the heavier food items higher. However, the weight of the food and gear constantly compressing the sleeping bag can gradually compromise its loft. I recommend cutting the shelf out and placing most of the heavy food items into the cavernous hold. The load might not balance as well, but as the journey progresses into autumn you are likely to sleep a lot warmer. Place much of the food into the backpack first, then the sleeping bag. On top of the sleeping bag stow extra clothing and any remaining items, such as empty water bottles, breakfast, and that magnum-size coulter pine cone you've been lugging the past few days as a present for Mum. But try to avoid packing heavy items above where the shoulder straps attach to the pack, as this can compromise the pack's stability and affect its maneuverability.

External pockets

The distance hiker's pack should have three external pockets made of mesh. One on one side for the water bottle, for accessibility. One on the other side for the fuel bottle, for ventilation. And one on the back, a larger mesh pocket, for the tent fly or tarp for stowage when wet. Back in the days when I carried a backpack heavy enough to warrant a hip belt, I sewed a home-made camera bag to my hip belt for easy access. This kept my rangefinder camera out of the way when not needed, but very handy when it was. Now I simply carry the camera in one of the backpack's elasticized mesh pockets, and swing the entire pack around into my reach when needed. This works because my pack is small and mobile, and I carry it on one shoulder only.

Donning the backpack

Backpackers carrying massive loads usually try to find rocks or logs to rest on. After seating themselves they unlatch the hip straps, then remove their arms from the shoulder straps. Starting out again they reverse the process. This is easier on the back, but chair-high, trailside objects are not always where they are needed.

Normally, PCT hikers would not need to carry such ghastly loads. But sometimes our packs can be quite heavy, for example when loaded with a week's food to see us to a distant resupply station, or several gallons of water to sustain us along a dry stretch of trail. When the pack is heavily loaded we must take particular care in shouldering it, to prevent back injury. And remember that our spinal disks are even more susceptible should we be dehydrated. If we are hiking with a partner, and if each of us is traveling with a heavy load, then for safety's sake we might help each other shoulder them. Otherwise, we would grasp the pack by its haul loop and one shoulder strap; hoist it to bended knee, and support it momentarily there; then heft the pack to shoulder height and quickly turn our back into it, inserting an arm into its shoulder strap. The pack is now hanging from one shoulder. As we walk away with it, (turning around and checking for anything left behind) we insert the other *elbow* into the other strap loop, then shoulder that strap, bringing the arm through at our convenience.

The tent

Many of today's backpacking tents are modern marvels. Even though comparatively light in weight, most are capable of offering excellent shelter against rain, wind, insects, and cold. Most are also high-profit items, and naturally not all manufacturers have acted with conscience when designing them. Imitations are commonplace, and in many cases these imitations seem cheaply made. Let the buyer beware; especially when selecting a tent for its lightness as well as its function.

Free-standing

The free-standing tent tends to be heavier than its non-free-standing counterpart, but it does look nice on the showroom floor. And granted, in benign conditions the hiker can merely toss a few weighty items inside to secure the tent in place. This can lessen puttering about camp, and can be an advantage on pumice or sandy soil in which the usual types of stakes are ineffective. However, imagine that the wind is blowing and that you have to answer the call of Nature in the middle of the night. Your free standing tent could become a free flying one. All tents must be anchored to the ground. This not only keeps them in place, but it helps distribute the loads of a suddenly developing storm. For more information about tent stakes, see that section, below.

Here's my method of determining the relative strength and stability of a tent. Press down on its high point, and move it side to side, and front to back. How well it resists your hand indicates how well it will resist the wind. If you make this test with various models you may find considerable differences.

Tent size

The hiker going solo should try for a tent weight of 3 pounds or less. Add another pound for a second person. And remember that the accommodations need not be commodious. The smaller the tent, generally the stronger and warmer, and the less space it will need on the ground. You might be surprised at the number of stealth sites that will accommodate only a small tent. Having said that, I must caution against tents so small that they restrict ventilation. Over the long term, many bivy bags, for example, are said to be "sweat sacks."

Ventilation

During the night each of us exudes several pints of moisture. Some is from our breath, which is always saturated. And some is from our skin, in the form of insensible perspiration. The warm, moist air from our breath and bodies rises to the tent's ceiling where it collects. Most tents have separate flies that stop short of the ground. These peripheral gaps supposedly provide ventilation. But consider that the hot air balloon also has a large hole in its bottom. Like the tent, the balloon is full of warm air, and because warm air rises, the hole at the bottom does nothing to ventilate the interior. Ventilation ports must be located at the top to expel warm, moist air, and at the bottom to intake fresh, drier air. And to be effective these vents need to be huge. Instead, most tent designs compel us to keep the doorway open. Wide open.

Examine a particular tent or a picture of one, and consider whether rain would fall directly into its interior if its doorway were open, or if rain would at least drip into its open doorway. If so, then you are looking at a tent designed by some "expert" who had very little experience camping in rainy weather for extended periods. While thru-hiking the PCT you will probably find yourself sleeping with your tent fly's doorway open for ventilation most nights. But of course, you will probably keep the netting doorway closed for protection against mosquitoes and so forth. If rain forces you to close the fly's door, then you are likely to awaken the next morning in a very damp interior. And this dampness will have pervaded your clothing and sleeping bag, adding packweight and decreasing insulation to such an extent that after several days of this you might find yourself facing a survival-type situation. This is not a weather attack, but an equipment failure.

Condensation

Back to the interior of a poorly ventilated tent. Some of the moisture exuded from the occupants condenses on the fly's inner surface. If the fly's walls are steeply inclined, then the beads of condensation will run harmlessly down them. Otherwise, they will drip onto the tent, soaking the fabric, and eventually dripping onto the occupants and their belongings. This further wets the sleeping bag and clothing. And here is another problem with condensation: Sometimes heavier drops of rain striking from outside will knock drops of condensation loose from the inside, making the rain seem to be passing through the fly unimpeded.

Along the PCT, hikers can expect this condensation to form on the inside of their tent flies, most nights. So before setting off early they will often be packing a wet fly. For best results they would stow the wet fly in a mesh pocket external to the backpack. There it would be handy for drying at the first or second rest stop.

The Jardine Tent Awning

Jenny and I lived with extremely poor ventilation with one of the more popular tent designs during our first PCT hike. Preparing for our second hike I sewed a simple awning to the tent fly which extended over its doorway. The awning allowed us to sleep with the doorway fully open, even during the heaviest of rain. And in fine weather it protected our back-packs from the night's dew.

The awning worked so well that while preparing for our CDT hike I cut away the entire vestibule from the tent fly. This left a huge open doorway, which greatly enhanced ventilation. And the subtracted weight of the vestibule actually compensated for the added weight of the awning. During stormy and blustery weather we tried to pitch the tent in the protection of sheltering trees or boulders, and with the foot pointing into the wind and the doorway facing away from it. When this was not possible we lowered the awning so that its front edge was close to, or against, the ground.

The old timers used tents of less flammable materials and with open, sheltered doorways. In rainy weather they built campfires nearby, and the heat radiated into the tent and dried the damp belongings. My awning design can provide much the same benefits, when used with great care. Admittedly, Jenny and I have used it this way only once. Nevertheless it was a time of need, and it greatly improved our comfort and possibly our safety. If you build a drying fire in front of your tent-awning, keep it distant and keep it small. A tent catching fire would be a disaster.

Clotheslines

Every tent should have a clothesline running along its interior. Our tents had clotheslines beneath the awnings also.

Eyeglasses holders

If you wear eyeglasses, consider attaching a small loop of cord to the tent fab-ric somewhere over your head. Hang the eyeglasses from this loop, where they will be out of harm's way but handy when needed. To attach the cord you could sew it to the fabric, or you could simply use a hot nail held with pliers to pierce the fabric in two places, ½ inch apart, run the cord through both holes, and tie the cord on the outside of the tent where the knot will be out of the way. Fogged glasses in the mornings is a predictable problem in cold climates. When first awakening, place your glasses next to your body to warm them before putting them on.

And by the way, make sure to tighten the little screws on your eyeglasses or dark glasses before leaving home. I recommend also applying Locktite® Threadlocker 242 to prevent the screws from working out. Otherwise, if and when your eyeglasses fall apart during the journey, you could improvise a temporary repair with duct tape.

See my comments about a wristwatch holder on page 76.

Tent color

When camping near the outreaches of civilization, for example when laying over near a resupply station, for safety's sake, try not to attract attention to yourself. This would be difficult in a brightly colored tent designed to attract attention. Where possible, choose a tent color which blends in more with the environment.

UV deterioration

After one or two seasons of hard use, a tent can become far less water repellent. The fly's coating can begin breaking down from exposure to the sun's ultraviolet radiation, and the floor's coating can abrade away. Such a tent will leak during every rainstorm, but you may be unable to locate exactly where. Re-coating is possible, but it adds weight and is prone to flaking away. For those of us who spend most of every summer in the wilds, buying an new tent every season can add up to a lot of money and a lot of time spent sealing the seams and making all the modifications. This is one reason I now use a tarp.

Seam sealing

Sealing the seams of home-made gear is part of the process. But when sealing them on a commercially made item I sometimes feel like an unpaid employee of the company. This is a time consuming and sometimes tedious job, and one that is best done correctly the first time. Oddly, some widely distributed seam sealing compounds harden and begin flaking away within a few *weeks* of application, especially when exposed to strong sunlight. Even some of the more reputable tent manufacturers supply this junk with their products. Why? Because it is easy to apply. However, viewing the results of your ten hours work exfoliating away of its own accord is not a pretty sight. And speaking from experience, the act of removing the inglorious mess in order to repeat the job can be even more dispiriting. So before you begin, test your compound on a few less conspicuous places on the item to be sealed. Expose these tests to sunlight for several days, then try to scrape the cured compound away with the blade of a knife. If you find that the compound has hardened to the extent that when you fold the material you crack the compound, or if you can flake the compound away, don't use it.[2]

Before seam sealing a garment or tent, wipe away any residues of manufacture using a damp cloth. Otherwise they could prevent your sealing compound from bonding properly. And let the item dry thoroughly afterwards.

---

[2] I have had good results with sealing products from McNett Corporation.

Also, try to avoid sealing seams indoors. The vapors can make you quite sick. Even outside, work only in 10 or 15 minute intervals. This allows your respiratory system to recover and the compound's solvents to evaporate. The more you try to seal in one session, the more the newly sealed seams will tend to fold back onto the material. This damages the sealed seams and smears the compound.

When it comes to sealing seams, two people are better than one. As one person applies the sealing compound, the other stretches the seam as though trying, halfheartedly, to pull it apart. This exposes more of the stitching to the compound brush. If working alone you can place one knee on the material, or use a heavy weight, and stretch the seam with one hand while applying compound with the other. Use a small bristle brush to apply the compound. If the bristles are not stiff, trim them short. And don't try to make a neat job. Neat jobs are far more prone to leaking. Smear the compound on the seam half-an-inch wide. This prevents water from wicking laterally through the fabric. Usually, sealing the seams only on the outside of the item is sufficient.

After you have sealed the last seam, allow the sealant to cure undisturbed for a day or two. Then before you wad the finished product into its stuff sack, rub talc onto the sealing compound. This will prevent the seams from sticking to themselves and pulling bits of compound away later. The final step is to test your garment in the shower or your tent under a garden hose, and correct any leaks. On humid days, though, the cold water from a hose could cause condensation to form inside the tent, making it appear to be leaking. Look carefully for beads of water actually coming through a seam.

In camp, you can improvise sealing compound with lip balm, sap, or even peanut butter in a pinch. For more lasting repairs, include a tube of seam sealing compound in your drift box. Use it to repair small tears also. Tape them closed from one side, and apply compound to the other. Before starting, de-grease the area with a solvent or accelerator[3]. And to greatly shorten the setting time, mix a little accelerator with the seam sealing compound before application.

Ground sheet

The function of the ground sheet is to protect the tent floor from abrasion, soiling, and from picking up globs of sap. When breaking camp, fold the ground sheet in half, bottom sides together. I recommend the All Weather Blanket, manufactured by Metallized Products. It is a four-layer laminate, consisting of a plastic film, a thin sheet of aluminum, a fiber scrim, and another plastic film. One side is a reflective silver color, and the other a ripstop-

---

[3] For example the Cotol-240™ accelerator for Aquaseal®

like plastic in various colors. If you chose the bright orange, you might refrain from airing it orange side up. Otherwise an aviator could misconstrue your "signal" as a summons for help.

At home, spread your ground sheet on the floor, pitch your tent on it, then draw a line on the ground sheet around the tent's perimeter. Then cut away the sheet's extraneous material outside the tent footprint. This extraneous material is not just dead weight. It would collect rainwater running off the fly, and channel it under the tent.

In short order, pine needles and cone shards will probably riddle your ground sheet in pin holes. But these do not seem to lessen the sheet's performance. If so motivated you might repair any larger holes or tears with duct tape, which you could use also to mend mosquito netting, the tent fly, and waterproof bags.

Tent stakes

Along the PCT the skewer type stakes generally work well. These are made of hardened aluminum alloy, 2024-T6 rod, 3/16 inch diameter, and bent nearly into a ring at their tops.

Regardless of your tent's make and model, I recommend that you permanently fit 3½-foot lengths of parachute cord to its fly, one at each of its stake loops. In ground so loose that the stakes won't hold, you can lead these guy lines out to bushes, limbs, rocks, or sticks weighted down with rocks. For rocks use heavy ones with flat bottoms. If using logs, position them endwise to prevent them from rolling toward the tent. If using bushes, wrap the guy lines around them at their bases twice, to prevent the lines from sliding upward, then bring the ends back toward the tent and tie taut line hitches.

The sleeping bag

The colder the weather, the heavier the sleeping bag needs to be. At least that's the present myth. But consider that when Robert Peary and his small band of hardy adventurers marched to the North Pole, they did not carry sleeping bags. They slept in their clothing after pulling their arms inside their parkas.

Most hikers set aside their warmer clothing before crawling into their thick, heavy sleeping bags. This is quite an inefficient system in regards to weight and bulk – the enemy of every distance hiker. Then why is it so common? Force of habit perhaps, but in many cases it is because the hikers were wearing too many clothes during the day, and they soaked them with sweat. If they were more careful to remove extraneous layers while hiking, then they could wear these garments inside their sleeping bags to augment insulation.

This is not an advanced concept, but it might as well be as far as most hikers are concerned. So let's go back to square one and discuss the sleeping bag by itself.

Regardless of the type of fill material, the warmth of a sleeping bag depends primarily on its loft (thickness). Design indiscretions such as sewn-through seams can reduce a bag's effective loft. Absorbed moisture can reduce it, as can wind. And so can excessive porosity of the bag's outer layer, allowing vertical convection. (Warm, more buoyant air seeping upwards through the sleeping bag.) One way to increase the effective loft would be to use vapor barrier materials to reduce convective losses. Another way would be to use reflective layers both inside and out.

Concerning the insulation itself, the tiny fibers capture the air in boundary layers, restraining its movement. And it is the air, not the low-density material, which insulates. Equal thickness layers of 700 fill prime northern goose down, PrimaLoft,® shredded and crumpled newspapers, and #000 steel wool would all provide about the same insulation. As long as the fill fibers themselves are very small, they neither conduct nor insulate appreciably. Their only function is to trap the tiny pockets of air.

The temperature rating formula

Everyone reacts differently to night-time temperatures. Some don't mind being a little chilled, while others prefer incubation. To quantify the matter in general terms, though, we use the "temperature rating." The thickness of the sleeping bag above the body determines its temperature rating. My formula is:

$$100 - (40 * T) = TR$$

T is the sleeping bag's thickness, in inches, covering the person. Multiply this by 40, then subtract the result from 100. This gives TR, the temperature rating in degrees Fahrenheit.

Here is how to measure the bag's thickness: Lay it on a hard floor, opened so that it is not doubled. Lay a yardstick gently on the bag. Stand a ruler on the bag, and press it to the floor. Read the thickness on the ruler at the yardstick.

I usually ignore the manufacturer's temperature ratings because they are rarely accurate. Instead, I look at a bag's thickness. For PCT hiking I recommend 2 inches of insulation covering the person. Plugging this 2 inches into the formula: $100 - (40 * 2") = 20°F$, the bag's temperature rating.

In the same way that a chain is only as strong as its weakest link, a sleeping bag's temperature rating must be measured at its thinnest section on the parts covering the person. If the bag's thickness is two inches in one place and only one inch somewhere else, then the bag's temperature rating would be only 100 - (40 * 1") = 60°F. Beware of such design oversights.

Leaving one's face and neck exposed can degrade the temperature rating of an otherwise effective sleeping bag. During cold weather the hiker should sleep in a warm hat that can be pulled down over the face. Such a cap can be sewn together in just a few minutes from two identical halves of wicking material.

Loss of loft

Another factor to consider, of course, is the bag's loss of loft over time. This is not readily quantified. Jenny and I used down bags our first 3 thru-hikes, and found that after each journey each bag lost over half of its loft.

Uninformed hikers can greatly accelerate the process. The first time they ram-pack a new sleeping bag into its stuff sack it loses about 8% of its loft. Forever. Those imprudent enough to use a compression stuff sack can bid an additional 10% good bye on the first hyper-compression and another 2% for each subsequent one. However, sitting on the sleeping bag when it is contained in its stuff sack is the most damaging. Distance hikers must be extremely careful to preserve the loft of their sleeping bags. After all, the journeys are long and the early-winter nights can be frigid. For best results use the largest stuff sack practicable, refrain from stowing heavy gear or provisions on top of the bag, and do not sit on it, for example when resting alongside the trail.

The down-filled bag

Although technology is closing the gap, high-fill goose down continues to offer the least weight and greatest compressibility for the greatest warmth. And even the slightest weight savings is of considerable importance over the course of the summer's journey, especially considering that the extra weight of the synthetic insulation gains the hiker nothing 97% of the time. It is that other 3%, however, which can turn the tables. When goose down gets wet it loses most of its loft. Ringing it out rids it of much of the water, but does nothing to restore its loft. So once a down bag becomes soaked its ability to insulate is drastically compromised. It must be dried, for example in front of an emergency campfire, and this can be slow and risky. When synthetic insulation becomes soaked, it, too, loses much of its ability to insulate. Ringing it out not only rids it of excess water, but in most cases also restores a fair percentage of its loft, so no emergency campfire is needed.

For these reasons I would not recommend a down bag for the novice hiker, nor for someone hiking in humid climates such as those usually encountered along the Appalachian Trail. Quality goose down is also quite expensive, as are the sleeping bags made to accommodate it, due in part to their complex baffles.

I see three prerequisites for using a down bag along the PCT. First, one's tent must have an awning. This enhances ventilation inside the tent during rainy weather, and keeps the down drier. Second, the hiker must know how to dry the sleeping bag, and must do so daily – even in inclement weather (see directions, below). And third, when not in use, the down-filled sleeping bag must be protected in a waterproof stuff sack. The synthetic filled bag must also be protected in the same manner, but the down bag must be protected as though your life depends on it.

Internal Baffles

Most down-filled sleeping bags contain lateral baffles that lack side-to-side compartments. Some manufacturers would like us to believe that this is an asset. They suggest that on warm nights we can shake some of the filler from the top to the sides, and on cold nights visa versa. Yes, but what happens on cold nights after the down has lost some of its loft through time or dampness? When we remove a down bag from its stuff sack, the semi compressed down roves about the insides, as pulled by gravity. Crawling into the bag and settling down for the night, we may discover that much of the insulation has shifted uselessly to the sides. So before retiring we will have to shake the bag laterally, trying to coax more of its insulation to the top where it will do the most good. The more the loss of loft, the less effective this chore becomes.

The stuff sack

Whatever type of bag you choose, carry it in a waterproof stuff sack. A typical down-filled sleeping bag rated to 10°F fits into a cylinder 8" in diameter by 20" in length, without compromising its loft appreciably. Synthetic filled bags require larger stuff sacks, some much larger than others. Waterproof stuff sacks are available commercially, but I recommend making your own. The ones Jenny and I make are half the weight and a fraction of the cost of the commercial types. Failing that, you could simply place a plastic trash bag inside your stuff sack, and after stuffing the sleeping bag carefully into it, you could squeeze some of the air out, then twist the plastic closed. The plastic would add some weight, and it can tear if not well cared for. But it is easily replaced if you throw a few spares in your resupply parcels.

Drying the sleeping bag

Weather permitting, the wise hiker will air his or her sleeping bag every day, ridding it of the insensible perspiration absorbed during the night. Down bags benefit the most from airing, as they need to be kept dry to preserve their loft.

But even synthetic fill bags will shed a pound or two as their entrapped moisture evaporates.

The sun does not have to be gleaming from a cerulean sky in order to dry the gear. The clearer the sky the better, of course, but we distance hikers are not always afforded such luxuries. Even beneath a fully clouded sky we can spread our gear just about anytime between mid morning and mid afternoon, in the absence of rain, of course. Much of the sun's energy penetrates the clouds, and will dry our gear nicely. As a general rule, though, the cooler the day, the more we would avoid spreading our gear on vegetation. On dank days I look for patches of rock or gravel that face into where the sun should be.

If the ground everywhere is wet from recent rain, we can drape our sleeping bag over ourselves and carry on down the trail like emperors in luxurious robes. This will not dry the bag completely, because our body will be pumping moisture back into it. But it will help a great deal.

In periods of heavy rain, if the synthetic fill sleeping bag becomes quite dank it will still perform adequately. And this is why I recommend it for novice distance hikers. If you choose a down bag you might have to dry it in front of an emergency campfire, built at a safe distance from your tarp or tent awning. In such conditions, while hiking along the trail you would be wise to watch for bits of dry tinder beneath the occasional tree, and after collecting some, to carry it in a plastic bag for use at camp. And indeed, in a survival situation one must never underestimate the benefits of a hearty campfire.

The sleeping pad

Backpackers usually carry as many items of creature comfort as possible, oblivious to the contradiction that carrying them is extremely uncomfortable. And if there's one item that is almost ubiquitous among them it is the self-inflating mattress. Granted, these pads are ideal for camping on snow. Chris Townsend tells me that he uses two of them on his ski trips to the far north. But the PCT is not the far north, and its thru-hikers will rarely, if ever, need to camp on snow. During our five mega-hikes Jenny and I did not camp on snow a single time, as I mentioned back on page 48. One might imagine that we had toughened ourselves to the cold. Quite the contrary. Distance hiking depletes a person's metabolic reserves and ability to maintain body warmth.

The self-inflating mattress is very heavy, very bulky, and very expensive. It is susceptible to damage, and it cannot be customized to fit. Instead, we use pads of 3/8 inch thick closed-cell polyethylene foam, of the type commonly available in the sporting goods sections of variety stores. Each season we buy a new pad and cut it in half. Each of us gets one half, and we trim each one here and there to eliminate unnecessary weight and bulk. It need be only as large as a "torso print." On journey we place these pads on the ground sheet. For pillows we use our empty packs, or our shoes placed under the ground sheet. And for insulation beneath our legs and feet we use our spare clothing and stowbags.

The reason we slept comfortably warm on our thin foam pads is that we were selecting campsites that featured:

☑ Good drainage, so that in the event of rain our camp-site would not become a camp-pond. This means that we avoided camping on dished ground, however attractive it might have appeared. Remember: the occasional presence of standing water is what prevents brush from growing at these places.

☑ Natural ground insulation: soft duff of the forest floor, carpets of pine needles, and so forth. This means we never camped on compacted sites. And even in the Sierra, and even in early season, we always managed to find snow free, well drained ground to sleep on.

☑ Protection from the wind, usually in the form of trees. We climbed high and camped low. But not so low that we were in the katabatic zone of cold air, which often acts like rivers and lakes up to 100 feet thick above the drainages and basins.

The umbrella

I first saw the idea of carrying an umbrella as hiking gear in Peter Jenkins' book *The Walk West: A Walk Across America II* (Morrow, 1981). He and his wife had attached umbrellas to their pack frames, and used them for shade in the hot and arid southwest. Jenny and I adopted the idea for our second PCT thru-hike, and found the umbrellas so valuable that we continue using them to this day.

Whether rain or snow is falling, or wind is driving it sideways, the umbrella offers excellent protection for the hiker on the move. Most experienced hikers know the feeling of crawling into a tent at day's end, after hiking all day in stormy weather. An umbrella offers much the same comfort without having to wait for day's end, and without having to stop. To me, the umbrella is a half-a-tent on the move.

As we hike in cold rain the umbrellas keep the frigid water off our parkas, where it would conduct our body heat away. It also shields our backpacks to quite an extent. When we need to stop and withdraw something from the packs, the umbrellas held overhead prevent rain from pouring into the packs' open accesses. On a rainy day the umbrellas provide shelter at the rest stops. On a rainy and blustery day we can rest beneath a sheltering tree, where the ground is often drier, and place the umbrellas close in front of us to block the wind. And in the late afternoon we can cook dinner using the umbrellas to shield both us and the stove.

In rain or snow on a windless day we hold our umbrellas upright. But if the wind is blowing then we point them into the wind. If the wind is rain laden, the umbrellas block both. When hit by stronger gusts we partially close the umbrellas. This protects the umbrellas structurally, while they protect us. In strong headwinds we hold the umbrellas in front of our faces, peering over the tops. This provides almost full-torso protection, yet it allows us to see where we are going.

Jenny and I have carried our umbrellas some 12,000 miles with few problems. Nevertheless, any umbrella will blow apart in a vicious gust, as mentioned on page 218. Even if strong wind is only threatening, prudence would suggest stowing the umbrella and donning the back-up waterproof-breathable parka. Use the umbrella to make high mileage in normal-to-mildly-stormy conditions, then switch to the W/B parka should a storm intensify.

While desert hiking, the umbrella shields us from much of the sun's harmful ultraviolet radiation. It also blocks a great deal of the sun's heat. And it will block a great deal more if covered with a film of reflective mylar. See page 234.

If the days are continuously fine, then you might view your umbrella as so much useless weight. But when the rains come you will pull out your "brolly" – rather ceremoniously if anyone is watching – and continue ahead lightheart-edly.

If I have been hiking through exceptionally rainy weather, at day's end I will still be wet. The umbrella doesn't keep me perfectly dry, but it does keep me perfectly happy. I wouldn't think of setting out on a long hike without one.

Modifying the umbrella

The type of umbrella I use has a 21-inch radius, and weighs 14½ ounces new. I select the type with the fewest complexities, in particular with no joints mid-span in the tines. Then I modify the umbrella extensively – primarily to reduce weight. To begin, I saw off the J-shaped plastic handle, leaving a 3½-inch stub. This is just enough to hold on to. Next, I discard the plastic top cap, then hack-saw the excess metal shaft to within ¼-inch of the top of the fabric. And of course I file the shaft's new end smooth.

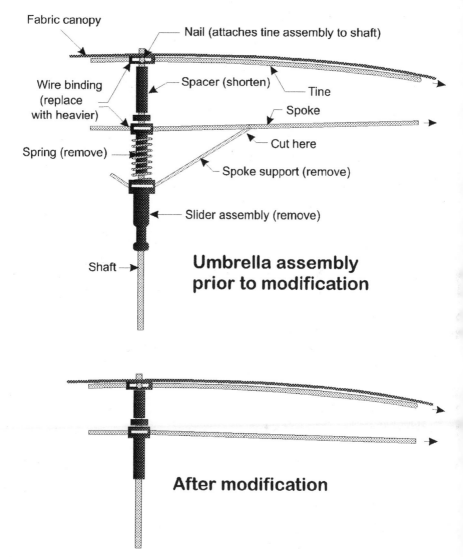

Umbrella assembly
prior to modification

After modification

I then remove the springs and other nonessential components. Here's how: The metal rib-like pieces are called "tines." Each has a plastic end-cap, to which the fabric is sewn. Pull 3 adjacent end caps off their tines, then cut the thread holding the umbrella fabric to these tines. Do not cut the thread off the end-caps. You should now be able to slip the umbrella fabric over the top of the umbrella assembly, just enough to expose a small nail head at the top of the plastic assembly. This nail secures the assembly to the shaft. Pry it carefully out, and save it for later replacement. Now lift the assembly off the shaft.

At the bottom of the shaft, just above the plastic handle, is a slot with a trigger piece inside. Remove the trigger unit by depressing its anchor point, a few inches above the slot. Discard the trigger piece.

Refer to the illustration to see what other components to remove. Then reassemble the unit, replace the nail, and seal the fabric top by gluing on a piece of coated fabric, 1½-inch diameter.

Fire starter kit

The fire starter kit is not for everyday use, but for survival in case of a major storm. Every distance hiker should always carry one while on journey. Keep the kit small and lightweight, and keep it absolutely dry.

The kit should contain

- Kitchen stick matches in a plastic bottle with a screw-on lid and proper gasket, such as a pill bottle
- A few birthday candles
- A small handful of dry tinder

Buy the matches new at the start of each season. Check the bottle's gasket by screwing on the lid, dipping it into water, and squeezing. Any bubbles indicate a defective seal. If you have ever tried to start an emergency campfire when the woods are drenched, then you will understand the importance of dry tinder. This tinder is best collected when the woods are dry, and carried as an emergency item. It weighs only a fraction of an ounce, but it can make a ton of difference when needed.

To start an emergency campfire, begin by picking kindling sticks from the lower branches of the trees where they are somewhat sheltered from the branches above. Also, you might look for kindling beneath leaning or fallen trees. Prepare your fire sight by scraping away the pine needles and duff. Lay down two short sticks, ½ inch in diameter. Lay a few pieces of kindling across them, then lay on a bit of dry tinder. Onto this place more kindling, laying each piece carefully. The ½ inch space beneath provides air circulation. Remove one match from its bottle and replace the lid. Strike the match with your thumbnail, or on the dry bottom of a rock. Hold the match under your materials until it starts threatening to burn your fingers. Remove the nearly spent match and insert it into the materials, where it will assist the wee flames and act as dry kindling. Put your head near the ground and blow *gently* into the fire to feed it more oxygen, adding more kindling between breaths.

If the fire dies, remove your materials and discard them. Build a new pile of materials as before. Strike a second match and ignite a birthday candle. Hold the candle over the materials and drip the wax onto them. The wetter the materials, the more wax required. Then hold the burning candle under the materials. The flame should ignite the melted wax, which should then dry and ignite the tinder.

Stove

When selecting a stove from among the bewildering variety, consider the fuels in common use.

◗ White gas or Coleman™ type stove fuel[4] is not always available along the way. And the US Postal Service and the United Parcel Service do not normally handle these volatile liquids. Stoves designed to operate on these fuels operate best on them. But they also might operate on unleaded gasoline; meaning that you could refill a fuel bottle at any gasoline station. Unleaded gasoline contains various additives which can clog the jets of many types of stoves, and this can require disassembling the stove at regular intervals and cleaning its jet. Some types of stoves are designed to use unleaded gasoline, and with care you can modify your stove to do the same. Simply place a small piece of aluminum foil over its air intake, closing off about 25% of its area. Even so, of the resupply stations listed in the Resupply Stations chapter, 11 of them lack gasoline stations in their areas.[5] Still, one can anticipate these and carry additional fuel from the previous stations.

◗ Kerosene might be legal to mail, depending on who you talk to, but many stoves that use it are heavy and known for producing soot and consuming time and patience.

◗ LPG canisters are not legal to air mail. And most mail now travels by air. And as yet the empty canisters are not refillable and I recommend against using them for this reason. Otherwise, if you pack in LPG fuel canisters, it's your responsibility to pack them back out.

◗ Stoves that burn wood are illegal to use in some backcountry areas and in my opinion they are unsafe in most others. This is because while breaking camp in haste, hikers might carelessly dump the smoldering shards onto the forest litter. Wood burning stoves and stealth camping do not mix. It is no joke that PCT thru-hikers have started major forest fires.

---

[4] White gasoline does not contain anti-knock additives, nor the red coloring agent eosin (ê-e-sen). Coleman™ fuel is basically white gasoline with a blue die additive.

[5] The stations that presently might not sell unleaded gasoline are Campo, Mt. Laguna, Vermillion Valley Resort, Reds Meadow, Echo Lake Resort, Burney Falls Camp Store, Hyatt Lake Resort, Crater Lake Village, Cascade Summit, Olallie Ranger Station, and the Timberline Lodge.

Jason Ontjes notes that "despite claims to the contrary, fuel bottles do leak." And he goes on to suggest wrapping the fuel bottle in a plastic bag and carrying it below the food. This would be the best method for the hiker whose backpack lacks the appropriate external, open mesh pocket. Such a pocket allows any leakage to evaporate. If your pack does not have one you could easily sew one on.

NEVER use a stove inside a tent

I consider it insanely stupid to use a stove inside a tent. It could explode. (I've heard of it happening first hand.) It could ignite a nearby article of clothing. It could topple and spill scalding hot liquid. Or it could fill the tent with deadly carbon monoxide. Even if the edges of the tent fly are set above the ground, theoretically allowing for ample ventilation, the tent could become like a hot air balloon filled with poisonous gas. And even if the stove is placed at the tent's open doorway its fumes can drift inside and collect. Carbon monoxide has no odor, and its asphyxiation produces only very slight symptoms. Stefansson[6] wrote: "If you watch carefully, a feeling as of pressure on the temples can be detected for some little while, perhaps only a few moments, before you keel over."

Using no stove

Jenny and I have hiked a great many miles without a stove. And we've experimented with many types of non-cook foods. Other than dehydrated corn pasta, we haven't found any foods that provide much energy. And the dehydrated corn pasta was not very appetizing. Our present feelings are that the energy which fresh-cooked corn pasta provides, more than compensates for the weight of the stove and fuel needed to cook it.

If you decide to hike without a stove, remember to sterilize your utensils regularly. You could put your plastic spoon and water bottle into a microwave oven at a resupply station, or you could include a small bottle of chlorine-based laundry bleach in the occasional resupply parcel. Or if you are carrying water purification chemicals you could use those.

Cookpot

Carrying a minimum of cookware reduces packweight, pack volume, and the continual fussing about while washing up. One person hiking alone could carry a cookpot of 1½ quart capacity and its lid, a plastic drinking cup and its tight-fitting lid, one small folding knife, and a spoon made of high-impact

---

[6] *Arctic Manual* by Vilhjalmur Stefansson, 1944 by The Macmillan Company.

plastic. Two people cooking together would each need their own spoons and perhaps drinking cups, but they could share the knife and a two-quart cookpot.

The cookpots made of titanium are an interesting option. They are far lighter than their stainless steel counterparts, and stronger than their aluminum ones. Cooking with aluminum pots has been frowned on, due to the risks of contracting Alzheimer's disease; but to date this has not been even remotely proven[7]. Titanium cookware costs more, but should give a lifetime of service. Some models have bold names on them. Abrade them off with sand paper, finishing the job with increasingly finer grit. And while you're at it, sand the bottom of your pot, whatever its type, with coarse sandpaper so that it will not slip as easily when perched atop the stove.

Knife

Jenny and I were talking with three hikers near the base of a beautiful waterfall in the North Cascades. As they swung the conversation to packweight and daily mileages, one women happened to withdraw an astonishingly large folding knife, with which she then sliced a small chunk of cheese. "We don't hike very far each day," she said. And then, unthinkingly, "We're carrying heavy packs, and we just take it easy."

Myself, I carry the diminutive Victorinox Classic. With it's tiny blade I sever cord, slice vegetables, and cut packaging tape to length. I use the scissors to cut adhesive tape, 2nd Skin, and to trim finger and toenails and the occasional hangnail. I round my trimmed nails with the knife's file. And I use the tweezers to remove any slivers or ticks. All this utility costs me a mere 0.8 ounces.

To the knife I fit a 7 inch doubled length of bright orange parachute cord. This makes the wee tool more conspicuous within the confines of the ditty bag, and less likely to get lost among the pine needles at camp.

A small blade can dull very quickly, especially when used to cut cardboard, which is very abrasive. Yet this task is required at most resupply stations when making boxes smaller for returning items home in. For this job I use a disposable-blade utility knife, included in the drift box (page 292). These cost only a few dollars, and a single, multi-segmented blade lasts several seasons.

---

[7] "The cause is unknown, although there appears to be a genetic component. The excessive beta amyloid proteins and traces of aluminum found in the brains of victims are being studied as possible contributors." The Concise Columbia Encyclopedia

Wristwatch

If you decide to wear a watch, its band must be long enough to accommodate your wrist as it swells while you are hiking. The difference in the size of my wrist, from when I rise in the mornings at home, to when I retire at night during a thru-hike, is 4 holes on the watch band. Also remember that a plastic watch band can restrict ventilation and irritate the wrist. Consider replacing the standard band with one perforated in holes.

Wristwatch holder

During a long hike I like to rise at the first hint of dawn. And I have found that I sleep better knowing that an alarm will wake me at that time. In the pre-dawn darkness, if I am wearing the watch on my wrist, then the chances are that I will miss its alarm. So each evening when retiring I unclasp the watch and place it near my head. For this I have sewn a hook-and-loop tab to the tent wall. A loop of cord, as described for the eyeglasses, would work about as well.

Self-timer

During your training hikes you could use the stopwatch feature to time the duration of your forays. This data you could enter into your training log. Also during the training hikes you could use the watch's countdown timer, set at 10 minutes. At each rest stop you would activate the timer. When the watch alarm sounds you know it's time to be moving along. This is an excellent method of conditioning yourself against dithering at the rest stops.

Dead reckoning

One of the more important uses of the wristwatch is for dead reckoning. This term comes to us from the days of the square-rigged sailing ships, and the method was an important component in any navigation scheme. It works on the concept that distance equals speed multiplied by duration. If we hike at 3 mph for 2 hours, we travel 6 miles. I try to look at my watch at each known point, such as a signed trail junction, a high pass, a lake, or a road crossing. If later I become confused as to my whereabouts on the map, I look at my watch again, and DR my distance hiked from the last known point. On the PCT I have found that a hiking speed of 2¾ mph in my calculations yields the best results.

Summary of desirable features in a wristwatch

- Waterproof to at least 6 feet.
- Shows date and day of the week (very important for planning to not arrive at a resupply station on a Sunday when closed).

- An alarm and a night light.

Compass

I prefer the types with only the features I need. These are two: a rotating housing and a sapphire jewel bearing.

Here's how to determine whether your compass has a quality, minimal-friction bearing. Lay the compass on a table. After the needle has settled, with almost imperceptible slowness rotate the compass base. Determine at what angle the bearing releases and allows the needle to return to magnetic north. Repeat the test in the other direction. If the discrepancy is more than one or two degrees in each direction, consider buying a compass with a higher quality bearing.

The person adept at taking field bearings by hand can achieve an accuracy of ±1½°. Those who are not adept might be wise to carry a compass that has a sighting mirror. Granted, the PCT hiker rarely needs much accuracy in field bearings, but there are times when monkeying around with sloppy navigation can cause unnecessary confusion, which could lead to a dangerous situation.

Some types of compasses feature a built-in adjustment for the local magnetic declination. But this is of little benefit to the person who cannot remember whether the adjustment is supposed to be set to the left or right. The problem is that most hikers are never quite sure whether to add or subtract the declination. My mnemonics should settle the matter:

> Along the PCT and the CDT, the compass needle points a little east of true north, as though honoring the AT. Along the AT the needle points a little west of true north, as though honoring the others.

Now that we know which way the needle points, we need to know whether to add or subtract declination:

> ### Field-to-Map – Add.
>
> ### F–M–A
>
> ### First Man Adam.
>
> When taking a bearing from a distant mountain, then setting the compass down on the map, we are going from field to map. First Man Adam. F-M-A. Field to Map, Add. We *add* the declination before setting the compass onto the map.
>
> When reading a bearing on the map, then raising the compass and pointing it to where we want to go, we are going from map to field. M-F-S. Map to Field, Subtract. We subtract the declination.

This is for use in the western states, but it also works in the eastern states by adding a negative declination. (When the compass needle points to the left of true north, the declination is negative.)

The local magnetic declination is given on most maps. Along the PCT it varies from 13E in the far south to 20E in the far north. You can measure it directly by taking a bearing on the north star (Polaris).

Experiments have proven that a blindfolded person trying to walk from point A to point B will only wander around in errant loops and circles – believing all the while that he or she is traveling in a straight line. None of us is blessed with an innate sense of direction, and many people have perished who thought otherwise. Imagine the trapper lost in the far north, coming upon a set of day-old tracks (his own) and following them for help. It has happened. Along these lines, a climbing partner and I were descending one of Colorado's 14,000-foot mountains in whiteout conditions. We came to a drop-off, rigged a rappel sling, and used our rope to get down. Continuing for another three hours, we eventually came to something that stunned us momentarily senseless. Our rappel sling! There was nothing for it but to use it a second time. In another hour the sky cleared and we eventually found our way down to camp. Our only guess was that somehow we had walked all the way around the mountain, but this was incomprehensible as we felt we were descending diagonally.

When walking beneath clear or partly cloudy skies, we can remain aware of the sun's position, and far more significantly, of the direction of shadows as the day waxes and wanes. This is my method for cultivating a "sense" of direction. I frequently look up and locate the sun, think about the approximate time of day, then look at the direction of the shadows. This is just another aspect of my anti-passive hiking style.

Water bottles

Water bottles and bags of all sorts are well known for cultivating stubborn splotches of mold, the darker molds being the more obvious. These are known as "water mold," and comprise various fungi. They may or may not be harmful, but they certainly can impart an unpleasant musty taste to the water. This can be particularly so with the type of waterbags designed to be carried against the hiker's back, which warms the water and encourages microbiotic growth. At any rate, this foul taste can be difficult, if not impossible, to remove.

Water bottles can be scoured by filling them half full of treated water and adding a scoop of dry sand. Take care to keep the sand off of the threads, to prevent scoring the seal. Screw the lid on and shake the bottle vigorously. Then dump out the mixture and rinse vigorously with more treated water. The threads inside the lids can be partially cleaned with a small, pointed twig.

Water containers of all types can be treated with a fungicide, for example by filling with a solution of iodine or chlorine bleach, and letting stand overnight. Or they can be zapped in a microwave oven, under a watchful eye.

Despite the durability of the wide mouth Nalgene™ bottle, many hikers consider it unnecessarily heavy. And due to the design of its neck, the bottle seems to have an annoying tendency to dribble when the lid is removed. But more to the point. When the manufacturers implemented the bold logo a few years back I wrote to them, objecting that such blatant commercialism does not belong in the otherwise pristine backcountry. A representative replied with a personable letter, saying that the logo had increased their sales and was there to stay.

Many hikers, myself included, now use soda bottles, usually available in the stores along the way. Some types have fairly wide openings, which I prefer, but the narrow mouthed bottles serve just as well, as long as they come with screw-on caps. After drinking or dumping out the soda, and stripping away the paper or plastic label, we have a water bottle that is very light and surprisingly durable. And should we somehow damage it, we can usually repair it with duct tape, and at the next store probably buy a new one. Most importantly, by changing bottles every few weeks we are discouraging the invidious microbiotic growth, mentioned above.

The PCT hiker should carry 1 or 2 one-liter (or quart) water bottle(s), and in the drier regions such as southern Oregon and some parts of southern California, each one or two person party might carry a water bag with a capacity of two or three gallons. Use the bottles to contain treated water, and the bag for untreated. Test your water bottles and bag for leaks. Fill them to capacity and apply pressure. Even the slightest leak can be a source of trouble.

When hiking long waterless stretches, do not trust in a single, large water container. If it should start leaking you could lose your entire supply.

Flashlight

Despite my quest for packweight savings, I consider a small flashlight essential for making higher daily mileages. This is because Jenny and I often hike well into the nights. And we usually spend 45 minutes each night chronicling the events and observations in our trail journal.

I like the waterproof flashlights that use either one or two AA or AAA batteries, and which use krypton bulbs. In my experience the krypton bulb is good for about 5 battery changes. I always keep a spare bulb inside the flashlight, and from experience I know how to replace a burnt-out bulb by feel, in the dark. If and when your flashlight bulb burns out, you too will learn how to change the bulb in the dark. But it's easier to figure it out ahead of time, in daylight. Currently, lithium batteries cost twice as much as alkaline ones, but they last three times longer, they are much lighter in weight, and they a have much longer shelf life, meaning that what you don't use this summer you can use the next. One must never dispose of batteries in the wilds, of course, but with lithium batteries this is even more so, as they are said to be far more environmentally harmful.

When hiking along the trail at night, hold the flashlight as close to the ground as you can comfortably reach. This produces the best shadows and therefore the best definition. Holding it at eye level washes out almost all detail. Headlamps and hiking don't mix.

If your last battery is dying, but you have not yet reached camp, turn the flashlight on to illuminate the way ahead, then turn it back off. Do this repeatedly and only as often as necessary. You can also use a disposable butane lighter, even one that has run out of gas. Flick the Bic® and memorize the terrain ahead in its sudden flash. I once found my way out of a mile-long cave that way when my lamp ran out of carbide.

Sun hat

The umbrella is our best defense against intense sunshine, but in benign hiking conditions I use a hat instead; one with an extra wide brim. Before leaving home I insert a length of wire around the brim's perimeter to stiffen it. This keeps it from flopping down into my line of vision with every gust of wind. I also sew on a chin strap fitted with a cord lock.

On the PCT in '94 I had set my hat down at a road junction and gone off in search of the trail. Returning, I found that someone had taken the hat! I couldn't believe it! Fortunately I found another one on the trail a few days later. It had obviously been there awhile, but it did keep the sun off my head. That reminds me of the time in Glacier National Park when Jenny discovered that she had left her spoon back at camp. She happened to find a similar spoon on the trail, a few miles farther along. And that, in turn, reminds me of the time we were resting alongside the CDT and found an old metal kitchen fork; something a prospector from a century past might have left behind. Picking it up for closer examination Jenny said, "This means something." We continued on our way, and eventually discovered that we had passed our intended trail junction. Backtracking, we searched for the junction to no avail, but finally discovered it while thrashing through the brush. We returned to the trail to mark the fork in the path, as a service to future hikers. And there was our rest spot.

Lidded drinking cups

Each hiker could use a small, plastic bowl with a lid as a drinking cup. They could also use it to contain food or drink, and to carry cooked food, or food emptied from tin cans at the previous resupply station. In times past we favored the ones made by Rubbermaid,™ cylindrical in shape and having a 3-cup capacity. Now we go without them, eating cooked foods and drinking hot beverages directly from the pot, to save weight and space.

Repair kits

To keep your stove operating efficiently you will need a wrench with which to unscrew its jet assembly. For the stove lacking an internal jet-cleaning needle, you will also need a special jet-cleaning needle. A stove jet (orifice) is tiny, and its cleaning needle is much thinner than an ordinary sewing needle.

A large sewing needle and length of heavy thread can come in handy for making repairs to backpack stress points, etc. Press the needle into the material with a rock, and pull it out the other side clasped between two pieces of adhesive tape. Carry the sewing needle with your stove jet cleaning needle, duct-taped to something flat and hard, such as your fuel bottle.

Rips in the parka, sleeping bag, mosquito netting, etc., can be repaired with duct tape. And again, this can also work well on a leaking water container.

Ditty bags

These are small bags that contain all the knickknacks. They should be bright in color so you don't accidentally leave one behind, as should the knickknacks themselves. As anyone who has done much camping can affirm, to leave little things lying about camp is to lose them. After using any item, stow it in its proper bag. And when setting off from camp or a rest stop, walk a few paces then turn around and inspect the area for anything you might have left behind.

Ice axe

Every PCT northbound thru-hiker should carry an ice axe at least through southern and central California, and then through northern Washington. The southbounder would carry an ice axe at least through Washington, and depending on the amount of snowpack that particular year, perhaps through the Three Sisters Wilderness in Oregon.

Journal

The hiker who fails to keep a trail journal is bound to forget a great many interesting details of the trip. When filling your resupply boxes, be sure to include journal writing paper. I write about 3 pages (both sides) a day. Multiplying that by the number of days' travel beyond that resupply station tells me how many pages to place in that resupply box. We cut them from a pad (6-inch by 9-inch), then staple or stitch them together at their tops and bind them with adhesive tape. Adhesive tape alone will allow the inside pages to slip out, hence the stapling or sewing.

We carry the journal in a resealable plastic bag, along with our maps and any other paperwork, minimized because of its weight. And usually we send each section's journal home from the resupply stations.

As PCT hiker Mike Anderson points out: "The more you put into your journal, the more you will get out of it." And as Oscar Wilde quipped: "I never travel without my diary. One should always have something sensational to read on the train."

Pepper spray

Recommended defense against aggressive bears, dogs, and people, these canisters contain a 6% to 10% mixture of oleoresin capsicum, a natural derivative of hot peppers. See page 204 for where you can mail order it. If you live in a state that restricts its purchase, you might be able to mail order it through an out-of-state friend.

The canister can be clipped unobtrusively to the clothing or backpack strap by day, and kept within easy reach during the nights. It might not be legal to carry into Canada.

Jenny and I carry a large capsicum canister in the Arctic as protection from grizzly and polar bears. Recently, here in our community I decided to try it out on a particular dog fond of disrupting our daily walks. I sprayed the gnarly creature in the face at a distance of about 10 feet. The dog's only reaction was a small sneeze.

Zippers

Frequently used zipper sliders on pack pockets and tent netting-doors should be made of stainless steel or nickel plated sliders, as they last a lot longer. Otherwise, the sawing action of zipper teeth can wear out a coated aluminum slider in a single season's use. A worn slider will slide, but it will not zip. To temporarily cure this malady, reduce the size of the zipper slider's aft-end by crimping it *slightly*. In lieu of pliers, try using a couple of rocks.

In closing this chapter on equipment, remember that our gear is only a means of enjoying the end; and that there are many means to many ends. A hiker planning to tackle the PCT should not become obsessed with whether he or she has all the right gear. I have seen all sorts of equipment travel the full length of the trail. The important thing is simply to *go*, and to enjoy the trip for all it is worth, which will surely be a great deal.

Modified umbrella. See page 71

Clothing

Good weather, cold weather, hot weather, snow, intense sunshine, insects, wind, rain, and brush. Welcome to life on the PCT! These are the conditions you will be hiking in, and which will challenge your clothing. But if you are like most hikers you will over-protect yourself by wearing too much. This will cause you to overheat and to sweat, even in the coldest temperatures.

A sweat-soaked garment is a misused garment. Sweat greatly reduces its insulating value. It also clogs the fibers and makes the garment far less breathable, and it increases its transparency to ultraviolet radiation. Wet polyester or nylon, for example, has a Sun Protection Factor of nearly zero.

While on the trail you should remain aware of the changing conditions, and of how your body is reacting to them. Wear your clothing dynamically. The minute you start to sweat, remove a layer or two.

Trail life can be extremely hard on clothing. So while putting together your wardrobe, steer clear of the psycho-glitterosis of high wilderness fashion. Less expensive garments can be just as serviceable. In the following paragraphs we look at what clothing is best for PCT hiking, and in which conditions it is most suitable.

Clothing for use in fine weather

In any kind of weather, clothing made of 100% synthetic materials is best. For those days on the trail when the weather is "just perfect," select the lightest weight, fastest drying, and most comfortable clothing you can find.

Clothing for rain

The type and amount of clothing you wear when hiking in the rain will depend on the ambient temperature and the frequency of your rest stops. In all but the warmest rain you will need to remain aware of your body temperature and sweat factor, donning or removing layers as necessary. For best results when hiking high mileages in heavy rain, carry an umbrella and be careful not to overdress.

Clothing for cold weather

Hiking briskly in cold weather (as opposed to hiking leisurely, resting, or sitting around camp) does not require being bundled in heavy clothing. What it does require is drinking plenty of water, eating lots of high-energy foods, and staying alert to your body temperature and to your degree of sweating. If you saturate your clothing it will not serve you very well once you stop.

Clothing for wind, mosquitoes, ticks & brush

The shell jacket and pants, described below, offer protection, and I recommend you carry them throughout your trek.

Clothing for use in intense sunshine

There seems to be two schools of thought here. Both have their merits, and the individual must decide which is the most appropriate. The first approach is to use full-coverage clothing to shield against the intense solar radiation. As we learn in the "Hot!" chapter, most lighter weight clothing does not have a very high Sun Protection Factor. So the full-coverage clothing in this first approach would have to be of a much heavier and tighter weave. The second school of thought, and the one to which I am presently leaning, is to provide as much protection from the sun as practicable using a mylar covered umbrella, and to dress very lightly. The mylar covered umbrella blocks 100% of the sun's harmful radiation, as long as it shades the hiker's body, which is not always possible in the early mornings and late afternoons. It also provides maximum ventilation, allowing the skin to cool itself naturally through perspiration.

Garment Descriptions

Umbrella, mylar covered (See pages 69 and 234.)

Wide-brimmed sun hat: Used in mild weather when the mylar covered umbrella is not needed, and in strong sunshine when the wind is too gusty for the umbrella.

Insulating hat: Made of fleece or other synthetic fabric, preferably covered with a waterproof/breathable shell. Used on cold days, and while sleeping at night.

Head net: Made from no-see-um netting. Used when the mosquitoes are swarming – on the trail, at the rest and meal stops, and at camp.

Parka, waterproof-breathable: Most backpackers and hikers wear waterproof-breathable parkas during stormy weather. Jenny and I used to, until we discovered the benefits of umbrellas. Still, I recommend that every PCT hiker carry a W/B parka for use in conditions too strong for an umbrella. The parka should have a full-length front opening zipper to aid ventilation and to permit the garment to be worn backwards, the advantages of which are described on page 221.

Shell jacket and pants: Loose-fitting, lightweight, and highly breathable, these nylon garments are extremely versatile. They thwart mosquitoes and biting flies. They block the wind. They protect the arms and legs while thrashing through brush. They provide surprising warmth for their weight. And they are very quick drying.

Shells are fairly easy to find commercially, although you may have to shop around for ones made of single-layer, lightweight materials without all the frills. Avoid those made of coated fabrics or W/B membranes. And steer clear of extraneous zippers, flaps, and designer features, which only add weight and bulk. For the jacket you would need one large, zippered pocket on each side, a full length front-opening zipper, and elasticized arm cuffs. Lacking an elasticized waist you could simply tuck the shell jacket into your shell pants while in mosquito country. For the pants you would need an elastic or draw-string waistband, and elastic leg cuffs.

You can make your own shells quite easily from 1.9 ounce breathable nylon. Look for patterns in the fabric stores, and modify them to suit. The emphasis with these, as with all your sewing projects, should be on simplicity.

Jacket, fleece: Features a full-length front-opening zipper for ventilation, and zippered side pockets. This garment is not used while hiking, but while resting alongside the trail and lounging around camp. It can also be used as a pillow, or under your legs at night as ground insulation. More advanced hikers might not carry this item. Instead they would keep moving on chilly days and retire straightway into their sleeping bags at camp.

Shirt, polyester: Short-sleeve, full length front opening for maximum ventilation when needed, this shirt would be made of polyester, which is easy to launder and dries marvelously fast. Worn in cool to warm weather, and used as an inner layer in cold weather. Is also the garment of choice when hiking in very hot temperatures in situations where going shirtless and hiking beneath an umbrella might not be socially sensible.

Shirt, wicking: Long-sleeve, made of a wicking fabric such as Polypropylene or Thermax. Reasonably fast drying, yet because it is thicker than polyester it is considerably warmer.

Mittens, fleece: Mittens are much warmer than gloves. Made of fleece they are reasonably fast drying. In the unlikely event of a lost pair of mittens, a few layers of socks might suffice.

Shorts, nylon : Or Lycra® tights if your inner thighs are prone to chafe.

Pants, wicking: Made of Polypropylene, Thermax, or other wicking fabric. Worn under the shell pants while hiking in cold and windy conditions.

Socks, thin nylon: For hiking in warm weather. Sold in department or variety stores, these socks are inexpensive, light in weight, and highly breathable. They are easy to wash and quick to dry. In fact, they can be simply rinsed in cold water, rung out, and put back on. They seem to perform just as well as expensive sports socks. And the right ones can be extremely durable. Thin nylon socks typically last me thousands of miles, but the ultra-thin ones can wear out in a single day. I test them for durability during my training hikes.

Socks, medium weight, wool-synthetic blend: For hiking in cold and wet weather. Double up on them in very cold weather. Wool can provide warmth when it is wet. But it is poorly resistant to abrasion; thin socks of 100% wool can wear out very quickly. For longer trail life, choose wool socks with a blend of synthetics; preferably with more wool than synthetic. Even then, if you hike in sandals or running shoes, the wool socks will probably have a relatively short trail life due to the dirt-crusting factor. Mine typically last about two weeks, which is one reason I prefer thin nylon socks in all but the coldest climes. Another is that the thin socks are far easier to hand-launder and faster to dry.

Shell booties: When the mosquitoes are particularly numerous, these boo-ties will allow you to rest and to cook your meals unmolested. They are also very handy for use on a buggy night too warm to remain inside your sleeping bag (if you are using a tarp instead of a tent). Not avail-able commercially, but easy to make. Use 1.9 oz *uncoated* nylon, from scraps leftover from your shell jacket and pants projects. Make the booties baggy, and long enough to tuck up into your pant legs. A pair of shell mitts would also be quite useful.

Shower booties: To keep your feet free of athlete's foot when stepping into shower stalls, whether in a campground or motel room. These are easy to make out of lightweight *coated* nylon, with elastic around the top edges much like an inverted shower cap.

All of these garments are listed in the Gear List on page 137. As you compile your clothing for the summer's trek, remember that it will wear out. You might need two or three shirts and pairs of shorts, and many pairs of socks.

Cotton and hypothermia

Cotton garments are comparatively slow to dry. This is because the individual fibers absorb moisture. This moisture conducts heat away from the body, which is why the hiker imprudent enough to wear cotton garments, and to sweat-soak them during cold weather, will be socializing with hypothermia at every rest stop. Certain synthetic fibers (polyester, polypropylene, etc.) ab-sorb far less moisture, so clothing made of them are faster to dry. They are just as cold when wet, but they are more likely to dry, at least partially, during the rest stops. Still, hypothermia will be lurking over the shoulder of anyone in wet or damp clothing. It's just that synthetic materials are a little more for-giving. Which is why every hiker should always choose garments of 100% synthetic material – with one exception: wool blend socks which can still re-tain warmth when wet.

Colors

The heavier the clothing and the more of it, the more it hampers the body's ability to dissipate metabolic heat. The color of the clothing also plays a sig-nificant role. Light colored clothing absorbs less of the sun's radiation. This is important when hiking in direct sunshine, for example in the lower regions of southern California. Also, flying and biting insects are less attracted to light colored clothing. And ticks, which are a light brown color, are more easily noticed on light colored clothing. At times, however, dark colored clothing might be of benefit. It radiates excess metabolic heat better, and would therefore be a good choice for hiking in shaded forests on hot days, for example in northern California and southern Oregon.

Clothing stow bag

After a full day of hiking in the rain, you would normally make camp and slip into a dry set of clothes. To insure these will be dry when needed, carry them in a waterproof clothing bag. If nothing else, use a plastic garbage sack. And while you're at it, use a larger plastic garbage sack as a liner inside your backpack as well. This would give your spare clothing double protection.

Sock considerations

Most socks feel great when fresh and clean, but when caked in dried sweat mixed with trail dust they can become hard and abrasive. Enter the expensive socks advertised as blister-free, or providing moisture-control systems, shock absorbing cushioning, and a host of other claims. Wear them for half-a-day in sandals or running shoes on a hyper-dusty trail and you may feel like you are hiking in 30-grit sand paper. What is most needed in a distance hiking sock is its ease of laundering and drying. This is a strong case against complexity, which makes for deeper soiling and slower drying. I prefer thinner socks, doubled or even tripled when extra protection is needed, which when hiking high mileages is rarely the case.

You can launder your socks, and other items of clothing in a tub filled with water, with or without soap. You can make such a tub by cutting the top off a 2½ gallon collapsible water jug (Reliance,® six-liter capacity for example). Such a tub is reasonably lightweight, and because it folds nearly flat it appropriates very little space in the pack. Use it also to pour water onto yourself, dundo-style, when bathing. Lacking a tub you can wash your garments dundo method (page 180) using your cookpot or water bottle. Washing garments in a creek is not recommended. Those who choose to do so should be sure to hike far downstream from the trail and any campsites, and to use no soap.

Whichever types of socks you choose, buy a good supply and place a few pairs in each of your resupply parcels.

Footwear

It is better to wear out one's shoes than one's sheets.

– Genoese proverb

As a distance-hiker in the planning stages, you must choose your footwear with great care. For after all, it will be the link between your feet and the ground, and every step of the way, 46,000[1] steps each day, month after month, that link will be tested.

Our feet are naturally light in weight, flexible, and full of sensory receptors and transmitters. As we walk barefoot, the nerves in the soles of our feet provide our brains with a wealth of tactile information. This sensory data helps augment our sense of orientation and balance, and as a bonus it brings us more in tune with the environment. In fact, there is something Neolithic and sensual about hiking barefoot in a quiet, needle-carpeted forest, on a trail of soft dirt, or on glacier-polished and sun-warmed granite. Those who have not tried it are missing a great deal.

Unfortunately, most of the earth's terrain is not so accommodating. On a PCT hike, our toes require protection should we accidentally kick a rock, root or pointed stick. The soles of our feet need protection from sharp rocks, cactus spines, needle-tipped pine cone scales, and even some types of pine needles. And they need to be insulated from snow and frozen ground, and from the searing desert. And no doubt they benefit from barriers against parasitic microorganisms that could auger into the soles of our feet, for example when we unavoidably step on manure.

The PCT hiker must avoid a stubbing or puncturing injury at all costs. But the main drawback of walking barefoot is how it reduces the pace. The barefooted hiker must place the feet very carefully, and with much less force – almost daintily. Footwear allows us to tromp along with great vigor. And although this is beneficial from the standpoint of speed, it is very questionable from that of stress-related injuries.

Aside from the possibility of injuries, hiking long distances barefoot can be done, but depending on the climate and the individual, it can also be quite hard on the feet. Mainly, this is due to excessive ventilation. A certain amount of ventilation is both desirable and necessary, but too much can dry the skin

---

[1] 22 miles per day times 5,280 ft/mi. divided by 2.5'/step.

of the feet, particularly the soles. The thick calluses of barefoot walking must be kept moist or they will crack. As long as the barefoot walking continues, these cracks will never heal because calluses are essentially dead skin. Nevertheless, they can be very painful because the callus is attached to the underlying live tissue and the cracks penetrate this also.

Many hikers enjoy traveling the trails in sandals, without socks; and so do I. But here again, the excessive ventilation can cause cracked calluses. I'll delve more into this later.

Despite the hazards, hiking barefoot for short distances – say, half an hour a day – can be therapeutic, especially for the blistered hiker in the early stages of a long journey. It's a great way to toughen ailing feet, both internally and externally. Leg pains can disappear after walking only a short distance barefoot – a fact which points to the footwear as the culprit. I consider regular but brief stints of barefoot hiking both a preventative and something of a cure.

Footwear restrains natural walking motion

Each of our feet contain 126 ligaments which interconnect 26 bones. These interconnections act like working, flexing joints, and are designed to help accommodate irregular terrain. Footwear protects our feet and allows us to hike at a higher pace, but it also restrains much of this beneficial flexing inside our feet. The stiffer the footwear is, the more it restrains, and therefore the more inefficient it is for ultra-long distance hiking.

A personal choice

Most backpackers[2] wear stout boots. Talk to any of these traditionalists, young or old, and you will probably find they have rather strong opinions pertaining to these clunky devices. It's one thing to have strong opinions, but another to base them on sound reasoning. If they wear boots for fear of twisting an ankle, or to protect the bottoms of their feet from sharp rocks, then that might be sound reasoning. Maybe they lack the time and inclination to go out and toughen their feet and strengthen their ankles in lighter weight shoes. And maybe they are not concerned with hiking higher daily mileages, and of doing so with greater safety and enjoyment. If they wear boots because they are reluctant – or afraid – to try new ideas, then that may not be very logical, but still there is nothing wrong with it. If looking the part of the boot-clad hiker bolsters their image, then that is their prerogative. If their belief in heavy,

---

[2] The term "backpacker" brings to my mind the traditional style of wearing big boots and lugging a massive pack. I use the term "distance hiker" to denote someone using a more modern, lighter weight and efficient approach.

stout boots stems from the propaganda of the boot industry, then so be it. The bottom line is that each of us is free to enjoy ourselves on the trails, and to select whatever clothing and equipment best facilitates this.

Experimentation and experience

I am continually examining my own equipment-related beliefs, and tempering them with experimentation and experience. Growing up in the foothills of the Colorado Rockies I hiked a great many trail miles and climbed scores of peaks – all in heavy, leather boots. In my late twenties I began instructing for Outward Bound, and proceeded to hike hundreds of miles each summer – again, in heavy, leather boots. However, at this point I also carried a pair of running shoes in my pack for use around camp. Eventually, I found myself hiking in the shoes and carrying the boots in my pack. Such an arrangement was practically unheard of at the time. People imagined that their ankles would immediately buckle under the load of a backpack. Mine didn't, and I found that with less weight on my feet I could cover the miles easier and faster. Granted, such a discovery would not be terribly significant for the person hiking only a few dozen miles, but it makes a tremendous difference for someone hiking many hundreds.

When Jenny and I hiked the PCT the first time, the snowpack in the High Sierra happened to be 120% deeper than normal. We spent the entire month of May wallowing from Kennedy Meadows to Tuolumne Meadows, wearing heavy boots. In so doing we learned two important lessons. First, don't start the hike too early in the year. This was impressed on us by thru-hikers coming along later in the season and walking on bare trail. And second, we learned the futility of wearing heavy leather boots. Once they became saturated, which was practically at the outset, they stayed that way. And each time we applied waterproofing compound we only made them heavier still. Reaching Tuolumne Meadows we sent them home (never to wear them again). I switched back into my running shoes, and Jenny her lighter-weight fabric boots, and we continued to Canada.

During our second PCT journey we again went through the High Sierra too early in the season, but not so early this time that the snow had not consolidated. Snow covered the ground most of the way, but we walked mainly on its surface and traveled from Kennedy Meadows to Tuolumne in 12 days. During this time we both wore lighter-weight fabric boots on the steeper sections, and running shoes on less steep snow and occasional stretches of bare ground.

On the CDT we wore running shoes the entire way, and with mostly excellent results. "Mostly" because we did experience one problem among the prickly weeds of New Mexico. The stickers pierced our shoes and socks, and made walking painful. Duct tape solved the problem.

On our third PCT hike we wore lightweight fabric boots in the snow during the initial three weeks of the journey through Washington. In weight, these "boots" were only a few ounces heavier than a pair of lightweight running shoes. The specific make and model is no longer in production, but I mention them to illustrate the possibilities. Once out of the snow we switched to running shoes and sandals, and wore them the remainder of the way.

Kinetics of the footstep

Heavier footwear resists forward motion. Let's examine the kinetics by imagining we are sitting at a rest stop watching a hiker striding past. The hiker is moving ahead at a steady pace – say three miles an hour. But if we could watch the movement in slow motion we would see that each foot is starting and stopping with every step. When a foot is on the ground and the hiker's weight is on it, that foot doesn't move relative to the ground. Its forward speed is zero for that moment. Then as the hiker takes weight off the foot, the leg muscles accelerate it quickly ahead, in the process of taking the next step. This quick acceleration requires muscular exertion. How much depends on the mass of the leg, the foot, and the footwear. We can't reduce the mass of our legs or feet, but we certainly can select the lightest footwear possible. The lighter it is, the less energy we will expend while taking each and every step forward. To the long distance hiker, the importance of this energy savings is not to be ignored.

More miles with no extra effort

More specifically, I estimate that each 1¾ ounces removed from a shoe or boot (3½ ounces for the pair) will add about a mile to the day's hiking progress. 1¾ ounces is not much weight. It's about the same as a sleeping bag stuff sack. Or a pair of Spenco™ insoles. But it's enough to degrade progress by one mile each and every day.

The lighter the footwear, the less strenuous the hiking. Let me put this into perspective: Replace a pair of medium-weight leather boots weighing 3 pounds, with a pair of medium-weight running shoes weighing 1 pound, 5 ounces, and with *no extra effort* find yourself hiking 7½ *more* miles each day.

As a hypothetical but entirely representative example, two hikers start from Campo together, equally trained, carrying equal packs and eating the same kinds of food. But one wears stout boots and the other lightweight running shoes. The first day, the boot hiker travels, say, 11 miles. With no extra effort the hiker in running shoes walks 18½ miles. The running shoe hiker reaches the first resupply station - 43 miles into the journey - 1½ days ahead of the other. And he reaches Canada 1¾ months[3] ahead of the other.

All other factors being equal, that thru-hiker in running shoes covers the trail in **seven weeks** less time. But of course, all other factors are not likely to be equal. The hiker in running shoes places more emphasis on traveling with greater efficiency, and will therefore carry a much lighter pack as well. This will further reduce the journey's duration.

Higher daily mileages are important to the thru-hiker because of the huge distances to be covered and the comparative brevity of the hiking season. But far more importantly, lighter-weight footwear allows us to cover those mega miles with greater safety and enjoyment.

Ankle support

But aren't stout boots required for ankle support? No, and I think this is another myth perpetrated by the boot industry and widely accepted by traditional backpackers. In my mind, the best, and perhaps the only viable type of ankle support is the internal type. I'm referring to strong muscles, ligaments and tendons.

Weak ankles are a result of walking mostly on the flat floors, stairs and sidewalks of the cities. By design these level surfaces do not stress our ankles in a sideways direction. Civilized, yes, but they leave our ankles unprepared to handle the irregular surfaces of the natural world. Boots attempt to rectify this, but I maintain that the real solution is to strengthen the weak lateral muscles and ligaments of the ankles and feet. Our ankles were meant to sustain the weights of our bodies and loads, without external support, and to carry us over rugged terrain for hundreds and thousands of miles. And in every probability they will do so, if first strengthened during a pre-hike training program.

The prerequisite to hiking in lightweight shoes or sandals, then, is to first train in them, preferably on uneven ground.

You are likely to hear experienced backpackers objecting to the notion of hiking in running shoes and sandals. Such complaints are usually based on conjecture rather than personal experience with the alternatives. If a hiker plies the length of the PCT mainly in running shoes and sandals, and then comes back and tells us the disadvantages, then we will listen and listen well. Meanwhile, I am more impressed by Grandma Gatewood who hiked the AT three times in Keds.™

---

[3] 2,700 mi. in 5½ months = 16.1 mpd. Add 7.5 mpd - 23.6 mpd. 2,700 m @ 23.6 mpd = 3¾

Problems with stiff soles

In addition to degrading forward progress because of their greater mass, heavy shoes or boots also interfere with the hiker's economy of motion due to their stiffness.

A boot's longitudinal center of effort is the effective point about which its sole pivots with each step. The stiffer the boot sole, the further forward its center of effort, and the more effort will be required to walk in that boot. As an extreme example, imagine trying to walk with boards strapped tightly to your feet and extending in front of your toes. The farther the boards extend forward, the harder your calf muscles have to pull in order to lift your heels.

A boot with a stiff sole places unnecessary demands on the muscles, tendons, and ligaments. Not only does this increase fatigue, but over the long haul it also increases the chances of pulling a muscle or tendon, and of stressing the tendons and cartridges within the ankles and feet. Therefore, when trying on a shoe or boot prior to purchase, test it's center of effort by grasping the toe in one hand and the heel in the other, and bending the shoe or boot lengthwise, as though simulating a step. Compare it to your everyday street shoe or trainer. If the shoe or boot you are testing is very stiff, do your legs a favor and give it a miss.

Kicking steps in steep, hard snow

But don't we need stiff soles in order to kick steps in steep, hard snowpack? Yes, and this is why we travel through the alpine regions equipped with two types of footwear: One, a slightly stiffer boot for trouncing steps in steep snow; and two, a softer shoe for making miles along open ground. But the snow boots need not be board-stiff. I recommend lighter-weight fabric boots that feature a good toe-bumper for kicking steps, and sturdy edges for biting into hard, steep snowpack. The skier on steep, hard snow digs in with the metal edges of the skis for purchase and security, and the hiker does the same with the boots. It is the edges which provide the security, much more so than the lug soles. When the snow is frozen too hard to kick steps with our lighter-weight boots, we chop the steps with our ice axes.

Keep in mind, though, that the same qualities in a lightweight boot which enable security on steep snow can cause a lot more damage to the sensitive soil and plants of the alpine regions. When descending out of the snow, change into your softer soled running shoes right away.

---

months. 5½ - 3¾ = 1¾ months.

Tread softly for minimum impact

Hiking and backpacking are gaining in popularity, and the impact of lug-soled boots is becoming far more pronounced. This is particularly apparent in places where the ground is soft or moist, such as the delicate springtime meadows or the alpine trails. Softer-soled running shoes and sandals cause significantly less damage to the trail and its surroundings, and I think this reason alone would prompt the more conscientious hikers to give them a try.

Renowned climber and mountaineer Steve Roper originated the Sierra High Route, one of the most rugged and challenging hikes in America. In his guide book for this route[4] he recommends wearing running shoes to reduce the impact on the fragile alpine ecology. To me this is a strong statement in favor of both wilderness preservation and the suitability of running shoes for negotiating rugged terrain.

Protecting the bottom of the feet

But don't we PCT hikers need stiff soled boots for treading on sharp rocks?

Many backpackers assume that hiking in running shoes while carrying a heavy pack would bruise their feet, mainly when stepping on sharp-edged rocks and kicking pointed rocks and roots. Yes, massive boots protect the feet from these things, but they also cause the clumsy style of hiking responsible for treading on and kicking the rocks.

During one of our PCT hikes, Jenny and I walked a short ways behind a fellow who hiked with a most peculiar style. Several times a minute he kicked rocks or roots, slipped on mud, or skidded recklessly down intervening snowbanks. But with each blunder he would immediately correct and throw himself adroitly back into balance, as a matter of course and apparently without giving it much thought. Pondering this curious behavior, I concluded that because he was accustomed to wearing heavy boots, he was not in the habit of watching where he was placing his feet. Jenny and I were wearing running shoes at the time, and these necessitated our stepping more carefully. Just as subconsciously, we were avoiding those rocks and roots, and treading the mud and snow more deliberately so as not to stumble and slip.

So yes, stout boots do protect the bottom of the feet more when stepping on sharp-edged rocks. But running shoes allow us to avoid stepping on most of these objects. When we switch from boots to shoes, we need to refine our walking style, making it more deliberate and graceful.

---

[4] *Timberline Country; The Sierra High Route*, by Steve Roper; published 1982 by Sierra Club Books

One might argue that hikers in running shoes spend more time watching where they are stepping, and therefore that they enjoy less time admiring the scenery gliding past. This is backward logic. Boots do not exempt the wearer from maintaining vigilance, especially in southern California where the on-going danger of a snake bite requires the hiker to watch every step. And it is this same attentiveness that will prevent the hiker from kicking and stepping on obstructions. With practice the hiker becomes adept at moving the eyes constantly from the foreground to the scenery.

Of all the long trails, the Appalachian Trail has the greatest reputation for terrain so rugged that it requires stout boots. Jenny and I hiked its full length in running shoes. Yes, we found it's terrain extremely rugged in many places. In particular, veteran AT hikers told us that we would never make it through the notoriously rocky sections of Pennsylvania in our running shoes. But in fact, we had no problems with the rocks there, or anywhere else. Picture the difference between sports cars and dump trucks. To me, that is the difference between running shoes and boots. The more rugged the terrain, with rocks and roots and steep slopes and difficult tread, and with boulder hopping, the more maneuverability it requires. The lighter the shoe or boot, the more maneuverability it provides. Most AT hikers wear boots, but in my estimation those boots greatly magnify the difficulties.

Hiking rugged terrain safely

I'd like to spotlight the often advertised claim that hefty boots allow the hiker to negotiate rugged terrain safely. Is this true? Maybe we should ask some of the hundreds of hikers who have injured themselves in boots. I know several who have broken legs or sprained ankles while wearing sturdy boots. The summer that Jenny and I hiked the AT, four people suffered serious mishaps on the slopes of Mt. Moosilauke alone, all in stout boots. In my mind, boots actually encourage these accidents by decreasing the hiker's dexterity and tactual awareness of the terrain underfoot, the accuracy of foot placements, and the speed of reaction to imbalances. To the long distance hiker, these are not favorable trade-offs.

Safety aside, another reason I hike mainly in running shoes is the heel and mid-foot cushioning they provide. I find this decidedly lacking in most boots, despite manufacturer's claims to the contrary. And the running shoes are a lot easier to break in.

The person fresh from the city with plans for a short overnight hike, carrying a big pack loaded with all manner of creature-comfort paraphernalia, will usually wear stout boots. If the boots are new, then they will usually start "breaking in" the feet. For after all, they are tough and durable, just like the advertisements claim. After several such trips, the pain and discomfort will probably lessen. And this is when the hiker believes that his or her feet have "broken in" the boots. To a certain extent, perhaps. But more likely, the feet have merely adapted, as much as possible. This weakens the feet. And while such an arrangement may be tolerable on shorter trips it can create real problems on a journey of several hundred miles.

Rattlesnake protection

Well, aren't boots good protection against rattlesnakes? For the feet, yes; for the legs, no. Rattlesnakes use their infrared (heat) sensors to decide where best to strike. Legs which are bare or covered with thin pants would constitute equally suitable targets.

Boots in rainy weather

But aren't boots the footwear of choice in rainy weather? For the long distance hiker, emphatically, no. Leather boots might deter the pervading wetness for a day or two, depending on their quality and the amount of sealing compound recently applied. But eventually they will become waterlogged, and when they do they will be that much heavier. This is not much of a problem for the weekend hiker who can take the boots home, place them in a back room to dry, and be rid of them. Nor for the person hiking hut-to-hut, who might be able to dry the wet boots and socks, at least partially, overnight. But for the long distance wilderness hiker it means having to walk and camp for days with the sopping things.

Even in dry weather, waterproofing compound applied to leather boots greatly restricts breathability. This prevents the sweat from evaporating and can result in dank, uncomfortable feet. This is of particular concern for PCT hikers descending from the many snowbound mountains of southern California and crossing the wide deserts. And lack of comfort aside, sweaty, boot-bound feet are much more likely to blister.

But what about boots laminated with an inner ply of waterproof-breathable material? Don't they permit the moisture to escape while holding the water at bay? In theory, yes. But in fact the breathability of these membranes is minute, compared with the breathability of the permeable fabrics commonly found in running shoes. And the high-tech membrane in leather boots only *seems* to obviate the need to apply sealant. The problem is, the outer boot material will soak water like a sponge, gaining weight as it does. Then the membrane only inhibits drying by restricting cross ventilation. The user who applies a sealing compound in order to reduce external absorption nullifies the membrane's function, and the intervening sandwich of leather will only retain the entrapped moisture almost indefinitely. Such dilemmas can only be justified by daubing them liberally on both sides with hype. Anyway, waterproof-breathable membranes are very susceptible to chafe, and I suspect that when used in a leather or fabric boot they break down rather quickly.

But here's the good news: Our feet are waterproof, and they really don't mind being wet while we are hiking vigorously and generating plenty of heat – as long as they don't become too cold, and as long as they spend the nights comfortably warm and dry inside our sleeping bag. What we need, then, is not boots to keep our feet dry, but shoes and socks that will dry reasonably quickly once the rain has stopped. With these we will spend far less time wet footed.

Footwear for cold and rainy conditions

Most backpackers worry about being caught in extended periods of wet, cold weather. I used to, until I discovered that I was mainly worried about keeping my heavy boots and socks dry. The prospects of "bad" weather left me feeling vulnerable because I knew that once my boots and socks became wet they would stay that way for days. I imagined that this could freeze my feet and launch me into hypothermia. When I started leaving my heavy boots at home, I found that I was also leaving the anxiety they were causing.

Wearing wool-blend socks and running shoes can engender newfound confidence in wet weather hiking skills. Thus attired, we don't need to worry when our shoes become soaked. We know they are not going to grow massively heavy like boots, and we know that they will dry fairly quickly. This leaves us squishing along feeling almost impervious to the rain, sloppy snow, and wet brush.

During our CDT thru-hike Jenny and I endured a month of frigid rain in Montana. We figured this was a good test of our running shoes, particularly because in addition to the rain and sopping wet bushes we often forded dozens of creeks a day, without bothering to remove our shoes or socks. The water was only momentarily numbing; our feet re-warmed after walking only a short ways. The prolonged wetness and low temperatures did not affect us, mainly because during the days we ate plenty of energy-providing food, and we kept moving. And during the nights we slept warm and dry.

Wool has the marvelous ability to retain body warmth, even when wet. It gains considerable weight when waterlogged, though, which is why we ultra-hikers don't use it for shirts and pants. And it tends to wear out rather quickly, which is why we choose wool socks blended with synthetic yarns for their durability and ability to hold shape. I normally choose a blend with about 70% wool. And I try to avoid the heavily marketed and expensive types.

Wool blend socks and lightweight shoes work extremely well in cold, wet weather, but only for the hiker who is consuming ample calories and hiking briskly, and therefore generating ample heat. As the muscles of the feet and legs flex and relax with each step they help the heart pump blood. If the legs and feet are cool, then they will help cool the blood also, which in turn helps mitigate the over-sweating problem.

However, once the hiker stops, the situation begins to reverse. The muscles are no longer generating heat, so the wet feet may begin to chill. When hiking in wet, cold weather we must strive to keep our rest stops brief. Ideally, we either hike, or we make camp and crawl into the sleeping bag.

How to deal with wet shoes and socks in camp

Reaching camp after a long wet day on the trail, we pitch the tent or tarp and immediately remove our wet clothing – outside. Ducking inside, we hastily dry ourselves with a small towel, don dry clothing and crawl into the sleeping bag. This is a good time for a high-energy snack, which will help us regain warmth more quickly. Once comfortable, we reach outside and wring our socks, and hang them under the tent's awning if it has one, or on the clothesline rigged inside the tent or tarp. If our socks freeze they will not be usable in the morning. If the night will be very cold then we place our socks somewhere under our foam pad. In the morning they won't be dry, but in all probability they will be just as functional as before.

If we expect the night's temperature to plunge we place the shoes under our tent or ground sheet, close by, where our warmth will prevent them from freezing. Otherwise we leave them outside the doorway, under the open awning or within the vestibule. By morning we will find them probably much less wet. And if the day's weather proves fine, and if the dew is not on the meadow grass, then our shoes will dry within a few short hours of tramping.

Gaiters

Trudging through snowpack we would normally wear gaiters over our boots. Otherwise, snow could cram itself down inside and chill our feet. However, neither the gaiters nor the footwear need to be the expensive variety because once again, with wool-blend socks we hardly mind that our feet become wet – as long as we keep moving. Satisfactory gaiters for distance snow-slogging are short, breathable anklets that cover the inviting gap between the boot and sock. Their only job is to prevent snow from entering the gap. The hiker needing to improvise might follow Jenny's example by cutting the toes off an old pair of socks and slipping the resulting "tubelet" over the ankle and shoe.

Creek fording footwear

One of the hallmarks of the backpacker is the boot prints which course directly through easily avoidable puddles of water and mud. The hiker in running shoes is usually careful to avoid stepping in such places. Wet shoes are entirely permissible, but dry ones are even better.

For this reason, when it comes to creek fording I normally prefer to remove my shoes, and wade across in a couple of pairs of dirty socks. This gets me across in reasonable comfort, and it helps wash out the socks. Sitting down at the far bank I wring out one pair of socks and hang them on my pack to dry, then wring out the other pair and put them on.

If the water is flowing strongly, and if it is no deeper than what I can handle safely – which is well below the knees – I wear my shoes for better traction and maneuverability. In fine weather they will dry quickly enough. In wet weather they don't need to.

Shoe requirements

The variety of running, hiking and cross-training shoes on the market is astounding, and in response to the competition the manufacturers are continually shelling the market with new models. I can't recommend the ones that have worked well for me because without a single exception they are no longer made. Such is the price of progress. But the fact is, I don't need to. All I have to do is categorize the distance-hiker's qualifications. A suitable hiking shoe would therefore:

☑ Be of moderate cost (in the $25 to $50 range at the time of this writing).

☑ Be relatively lightweight – 10½ oz. each, or less (average weight for men's size 10½; proportionally heavier for larger sizes).

☑ Afford ample (not massive) tread for traction.

☑ Provide adequate heel (not ankle) support (which keeps the shoe centered under the heel).

☑ Offer excellent cushioning beneath the heel and mid-foot.

☑ Be constructed with breathable uppers, allowing perspiration to evaporate.

And a few qualities to steer away from:

✗ Visible cushioning device molded into the sole. These are known for bursting on contact with sharp rocks. I've had this happen more than once, but found that the punctures didn't affect the performance of the shoes. (Which says something about the effectiveness of these gizmos to begin with.)

✗ Irregular soles having indentations and gaping holes. These increase the ground pressure and decrease the stability.

✗ Stiff, or extra wide, soles.

✗ Foam linings, which over-insulate and restrict ventilation.

✗ Built-in elastic sock, which greatly restricts ventilation.

Shoe construction: lasting

Before you buy any type of hiking footwear, remove the sock liner (insole) and inspect the lasting. This will not be possible with cheaply made shoes that have the liners glued in place. Nevertheless:

• Inside a *board lasted* shoe or boot we find a foot-shaped piece of cardboard or other stiff material, glued in place.

• In a *combination lasted* shoe, a piece of cardboard covers only the rear half of the foot area.

• Inside a *slip lasted* shoe or boot we see fabric joined by a hand-sewn seam running the length of the shoe.

Cardboard lasted shoes and boots are less costly to manufacture. The cardboard last adds stiffness, and naturally it comes in various qualities. Some, such as are found in many types of boots, merely abrade and roughen when wet. Others, such as those found in some cheaply made running shoes, actually begin disintegrating when wet. And the glue securing the boards in place sometimes dissolves. Bereft of its last, a board-lasted or combination-lasted shoe can be unwearable. Given the choice, I usually select slip-lasted footwear.

Insoles

The sock liners that come with today's running shoes and boots are designed to be extremely lightweight and disposable. I trim mine in the area of the toe and heel to provide more space for my feet.

In my earlier hiking days I fitted Spenco™ insoles beneath the sock liners for added cushioning. Eventually I realized I needed the extra cushioning only because I was walking with too hard a footfall, carrying too heavy a load, and because I was also hiking too many miles in the shoes before replacing them with new ones. They were breaking down internally and losing their built-in cushioning. The problem with trying to extend the life of any shoe or boot is that sooner or later it can begin causing various pains. These can surface suddenly and without warning, for example, in the middle of a long section between resupply stations. These are the pains of a budding stress injury, and I discuss them in the "Leg and Foot Pains" chapter, page 177.

Orthotics

Years ago I sustained a karate-sparring injury that resulted in an over-pronating ankle. So before embarking on the PCT for the first time I consulted a sports podiatrist. He cast a plaster mold for each foot, and supplied me with a pair of custom orthotics. Invented by the late Dr. George Sheehan, a well known running advocate, these are removable plastic inserts which fit inside a pair of shoes or boots. My orthotics provided support, not beneath the arch, but just behind the arch on the forward part of the heel. I wore them during the pre-hike training, and eventually determined that the non-injured foot was gaining no benefit. I wore the orthotic in the other shoe the full distances of our first two PCT hikes, and with good results. The more thousands of miles I hiked, however, the stronger the injured foot became, until eventually I no longer needed the orthotic.

Pronating ankles are not necessarily incapable. But they can cause pain in the ankles, the knees, or alongside the kneecap. Here's how you can test your feet as to whether they might benefit from orthotics. Place a sheet of paper on the floor. Wet your foot and step naturally onto the paper. The moisture should leave a foot print. If most of the foot area is visible, but a small area is scooped out at the side, then your arch is probably normal. If the entire outline of your foot is revealed, your ankle might be over-pronating. Also, ask someone to stand behind you and watch as you walk away from them bare-footed, and bare-legged from the knees down. They should be able to tell if your ankles are flexing inward.

The hiker with over-pronating ankles would do well to pay particular attention to the calf-stretching exercises, as described on page 170. And to prevent the ankles from flexing inward during the stretch.

Heel support

Most hikers have "normal" feet, and do not require orthotics. But almost everyone needs good heel support, which helps keep the shoe centered under the heel. The problem is, most shoes made for good heel support are also fairly heavy. Eleven ounces (average for a men's size 10½) is getting up there, and many shoes go into the 12 ounce category. Ugh! Study the running shoes catalogs, and pay attention to the weights and the touted degree of support provided. Better yet, visit a shoe store and examine the models personally. To test a shoe, squeeze it laterally at the heel area. The stiffer it is, the more heel support it provides. It's that simple. What is not so simple is finding shoes that have good heel support, yet which are light in weight and easy on the wallet. They do exist, but sometimes it takes a bit of searching to find them.

Wide soles

Earlier I discussed the longitudinal center of effort. We can also talk about a shoe's lateral center of effort, or that in the sideways direction. The stiffer and wider a shoe or boot is, the greater its chances of spraining an ankle. I prefer shoes that have narrow and flexible soles. Sometimes I will buy shoes that have a number of other desirable qualities, but an unnecessarily wide footprint. I simply grind the excess off with a high speed belt sander. A sharp knife would also do the job.

Reflective material affects photographs

The reflective material used in many running shoes is designed to alert any night time motorists. However, it can also wreak havoc with the hiker's photography. In any situation where the fill-in flash is used, day or night, the burst of luminescence can rebound from the reflective material of the subject's shoes, and over-expose that part of the photo. The same can happen with the sun's reflection when the subject is hiking away from a sunset or sunrise. Cover the reflective material with paint. Otherwise, photographers will need to remember to point the camera a little higher, keeping the reflections from the shoes out of the picture. And once home they could carefully dab any "arc-welding" spots on their transparencies with a fine-tipped permanent marker.

The proper fit

Selecting the proper size of footwear is comparatively easy for city dwellers, but for long distance hikers it can be a real challenge. In the *Handbook's* first edition I emphasized the need to buy the footwear much larger than normal, to accommodate the feet as they enlarge to their proper hiking size. Granted, selecting shoes which fit extremely loosely is difficult, particularly in the presence of a "helpful" salesperson. But I've received scores of letters from hikers who didn't take my advice seriously, and who affirmed that once they had been on the trail a few weeks they could no longer wear their shoes or boots, and had to buy new ones.

Enlarging feet are not an indication that the continual hiking is wearing the person down, but that the feet are strengthening to the task. The muscles are growing in size and the blood vessels are expanding. If you are going to be covering higher daily mileages, then you are likely to need shoes that are 1½ to 2½ sizes larger than usual. If you set off from Campo wearing shoes that fit, then as your feet begin swelling they will become very cramped. This is likely to blister your feet so painfully that it might force you off the trail. Consequently, you **must** plan for expansion.

However, unless your feet are naturally very wide, I don't recommend buying EE or EEEE shoes. No matter how enlarged your feet become, these extra wide shoes will be far too roomy in the mid-foot and rear-foot areas. Even when swollen, your feet are likely to wallow in them. Conversely, some brands of shoes are very narrow in the forefoot. These are best avoided also, even if your feet are quite narrow. Once on the trail you may find the extra space to your advantage. For the same reason, for women I generally recommend men's shoes because they tend to be considerably wider in the forefoot, where that extra space will be of benefit.

Hot spots

During the initial stages of your journey you must remain aware of your feet. As they enlarge they may begin chafing the inside of your shoes or boots. An increasing pain warns of a blister in the making. Stop when you feel one of these "hot spots," and try to remedy the problem. And even if you don't detect a hot spot, stop every hour, and more often in very hot weather. Remove your shoes and socks, and examine and massage your feet and toes. Tape any hot spots with <u>breathable</u>-fabric adhesive strips, such as Band-Aids®. And change into fresh socks.

Modifying your shoes

If the hot spots are multiplying out of control, consider that the time is ripe for surgery. Not on your feet, but on your shoes.

First, cut out their tongues. You accomplish this by cramming the tongue deep into the shoe's toe box, then carefully slicing the tongue-to-uppers stitching. With the tongue done away with, you would then slit the upper forefoot, down its centerline an inch toward the toe of the shoe. This slit allows the shoe's forefoot to expand laterally, creating a little more forefoot space. After hiking in the shoes awhile, should you feel the need to elongate the forefoot slits, by all means do so, but only in ½ inch increments. Think twice before slitting all the way to the vicinity of your toe nails, which might begin snagging the slit with every step. If you slice too far, though, you can always break out the sewing needle and thread, and stitch a cross-hatch pattern back along the full length of the slice, leaving it plenty wide. No matter how far forward the slit extends, the cross-hatch back-stitching will prevent interference to your toes.

Removing the tongues and slitting the upper forefoot areas greatly increases the shoe's ventilation, and this can help your feet stay cool and dry. It also admits a lot more dirt, yet even this might be an advantage because the dura-dirt probably helps toughen the feet, as long as it is washed off near the end of each day. These extra gaps also admit the occasional bit of gravel. I handle this by lacing my shoelaces so loosely that I can slip out of the shoes without having to untie the laces, and slip back into them the same way. But of course I tighten the laces for steep terrain and the more serious creek crossings.

Don't be afraid to modify your shoes. They may have cost you a lot, but that doesn't make them your master. In reality, the footwear is only a tool to help you get down the trail. In the past 10 years I've worn out scores of shoes; and I don't recall a single pair that I didn't modify for improved fit and function.

So if your shoe is chafing your feet in other areas, pull out your pocket knife and attempt to remedy the problem. Slice the shoe or boot to make it larger, or cut out a hole where the material is causing a persistent blister. Another common problem with some shoes is that they rub the Achilles tendon, making it increasingly tender. You can relieve the pressure by slitting the shoe an inch or so down the back. If you slit so far that your heel tends to slip out with every step, just cross-stitch it partially closed.

Protecting the stitching on footwear

All exposed stitching on a store-bought shoe or boot is vulnerable to abrasion. I recommend coating it with fast-setting (3 to 5 minute) epoxy, which after it hardens is much more flexible than the slower setting types. While mixing the epoxy you could add an equal amount of rubbing alcohol. This acts as a thinner, encouraging the mixture to soak into the fabric and stitching better. Either way, use a toothpick to dab it on. And smear some also wherever you wish to protect the uppers from abrasion, for example where the shoes might chafe against each other near the ankles. Mix your epoxy in small batches on tin can lids.

Problems caused by improper footwear

Compared with stout boots, running shoes are much more efficient for long distance hiking. And even though they are not designed to handle scree slopes and other types of rough and rugged terrain, they often withstand the punishment surprisingly well. However, they are not a panacea. Like boots they are fully capable of injuring the hiker's lower appendages. And this can happen anytime during the journey, from the first day to the last. I've even heard of the symptoms surfacing a few weeks after journey's completion.

I discuss this in "Leg and Foot Pains," page 177, but the matter bears looking at in a different light here. Let's consider the mechanics: With each footfall, the irregularities of the terrain apply unbalanced pressures to the sole of the hiker's foot. These are transferred into the ankle, leg, knee, hip, and on up into the lower back. Walking barefoot, these unbalanced forces are accommodated by the twisting and sliding of the many cartilaginous "joints" of the feet and ankles. And because the irregularities of the ground vary with each step they tend to nullify one another. A shoe or boot restricts the foot's natural give and take, and it transmits a fairly unchanging irregularity with every step. This subjects the foot to the same unbalanced forces, step after thousands of steps. If the unbalance is pronounced and incessant, and if the affected body parts are unable to accommodate them, a stress injury could ensue.

The degree of this injurious imbalance depends on the design of the shoe or boot, its age measured in trail miles, and its fit. Let me give an exaggerated example. Suppose you buy a pair of shoes or boots that, due to a quality control problem, has a big lump under the ball of one foot. It could be a glob of glue or a fold in several layers of material. You notice something a little odd, but decide to break in the shoes gradually over a few week's time. Later, you embark on the PCT in these shoes and for the first few weeks all seems well. What is happening is that your foot is adapting to the lump as best it can. But as your foot works like a valve tappet, hammering incessantly against this irregularity, eventually you start feeling a nagging pain at that spot – or perhaps somewhere in your leg or knee.

Every shoe, boot, and sandal contains irregularities. They are not normally as pronounced as in my example, and they might not be lumps, but parts of the shoe which twist or cramp your foot in some unnatural way. You will probably not feel them, and if these irregularities are minor and your feet manage to accommodate them, you may experience no problems. But from what I have seen and experienced, the chances are about 70% that your foot will not manage to accommodate them, and that - shoes, boots, or sandals - sooner or later they will begin causing a stress injury.

Traditionally, hikers have tried to ignore the pain of budding stress injuries. And finally when these grew so painful that they could hardly walk, they quit their hikes and returned home. But I offer a different solution. What causes the problem is the repetitious application of the same unbalanced forces. Solving the problem is a simple matter of taking off the shoe, boot, or sandal at the first hint of pain, and not putting it back on. Ever. And, of changing into a different pair, of a different make, and hiking on. Why of a different make? Because the company that made the original shoe or boot probably uses the same size and shape last to make all their models. The irregularities that caused trouble with the original pair could easily be present in a new pair.

Generally, running shoes have far better sole cushioning than boots. This is extremely desirable for the long distance hiker, but it comes at a cost. With the passing of many miles this cushioning begins breaking down. The problem is, the cushioning doesn't break down evenly. This greatly magnifies the imbalances, which again can cause a stress injury. The clue is an increasingly sharp or burning pain with each step which manifests itself for no apparent cause. The pain can be anywhere from the foot up to the lower back.

Hiking pains can stem from other problems, such as a lack of pre-hike training, too heavy a load, severe and prolonged dehydration, inadequate nutrition, lack of calf-limbering exercises, and of course, from stepping down crooked when hopping across a brook or slipping off a wet log. Most often, though, they are caused by wearing the wrong footwear. If you begin experiencing a pain that stabs with every step, suspect your footwear.

Spare Shoes

Incapacitating pains can develop rather suddenly. One minute all is fine, and the next minute you may find yourself hobbling. At times like these, ten miles to the nearest trailhead can be a considerable distance. For this reason I recommend that you carry a spare pair of footwear. This could be a pair of very lightweight running shoes or lightweight sandals. If nothing else, these would allow you to change back and forth several times a day, for variation. And far more importantly I suggest that as you pack your resupply parcels, you include a variety of shoes. Think ahead and know that your feet will be closer to the center of your personal universe than they are now. Give them plenty of choice in footwear types all along the way. Wear one pair to the next resupply station, then send them ahead in your drift box. Think variety!

I received a letter from a PCT thru-hiker-in-planning who wrote:

"The main issue I'm looking at is economics. I would believe that shoes not designed for a lengthy trek would break down more rapidly causing you to have to purchase more and more pairs. Why not buy just one pair of boots that will last the whole way?"

I suggested that the fellow overlook the expense of the footwear for a moment, and that he consider the costs of the journey as a whole. First, there's the value of his time spent planning, preparing, and training, and of lost wages during the actual journey. Then there's the cost of equipment, provisions, postage on the resupply parcels, transportation to the start and from the finish, and groceries, meals, and perhaps a motel room or two along the way. Altogether, the summer's endeavor is going to cost a bundle, and the price of the footwear, be it one pair of boots or half a dozen or more pairs of running shoes, is a small fraction. Now let's look at cost effectiveness. The success of the journey will depend, in its entirety, on the footwear. I suggested that the fellow consider the consequences of those boots failing him. And I didn't suggest that they might fail him, but that they probably *would* fail him. Again, the chances are about 70%. Trusting in a single pair of boots, or shoes, is like playing Russian roulette with the journey.

Also, I pointed out another factor: Switching from boots to running shoes would allow him to travel more efficiently, and he might therefore find himself reaching the end of his summer's journey much sooner than anticipated. The lost wages this would save could pay for all his shoes several times over.

Sandals

I first saw hikers wearing sandals on the Appalachian Trail in '93, but it wasn't until my friend Chris Townsend recommended I try a pair that I actually did. Chris was using them on all sorts of hiking endeavors and raving about them.

That next summer Jenny and I wore sandals for about 500 miles on the PCT. In California we met Ted Derloshon, a northbound thru-hiker who had worn sandals since the start of his trip. He had even worn them through the snow of the High Sierra, in combination with neoprene socks. For safety reasons I would not recommend this.

In my experience, strapping on a pair of sandals after hiking a few hundred miles with a persistent blister can feel heavenly. The ventilation is sensual. The foot room is divine. The cushioning in some types of sandals is quite good, but in others it is not. But with almost any type of sandal the heel support is practically non-existent, and this requires strong ankles – especially when humping a relatively heavy load of supplies. Sandals expose the feet to dura-dirt, and this has to be vigorously scrubbed off near the end of each day. With the straps well secured, sandals work great for creek crossings. Some sandals have a raised lip around the sole, and this helps protect the toes when stumbling or inadvertently kicking rocks or roots. The straps can chafe, but I found that a piece of adhesive tape will take care of that problem, and the feet will toughen after a few days anyway. In fact, all the skin of the feet will toughen, due mainly to the improved ventilation. The fungus responsible for the infection of athlete's feet doesn't stand a chance in this kind of ventilation, although the mosquitoes certainly do.

Hiking in sandals requires a few novel techniques. Pebbles tend to work themselves under the sole of the foot, but can usually be removed with a few shakes of the foot. The more obstinate pebbles require a few well placed kicks against a rock or log. Bits of gravel will also tend to work into any small hole in a sock, requiring that you sit down and remove both sandal and sock to expel the pebble. And one must be particularly careful of those ornery sticks lying on the trail. You know the kind. Not noticing, you step on the far end which raises the near end, and when your other foot swings forward it is speared by the near end. Ouch! I remember one that put me down for 15 minutes of first aid. That was a good lesson in treading more carefully.

One day during that hike I noticed what felt like a sliver in the sole of my foot. Closer inspection showed it to be a crack in the callous. I applied triple antibiotic ointment and carried on. Nevertheless, every day the crack grew larger, even though I applied the ointment regularly. Then other cracks began appearing. I tried grinding the callous down with sand paper, but that didn't work. I would have applied a callous-dissolving solution, but didn't have any. So on the theory that the sandals were providing too much ventilation, I started wearing more layers of socks. Three pairs of thin nylon socks solved the problem. The cracks didn't go away, but at least they quit hurting. Because of this problem I went back to wearing running shoes, and wore the sandals only occasionally.

Future technology in trail footwear

In the future I'm sure we will continue to see new types of footwear designed for the strenuously active outdoor enthusiast. I can't predict what's up ahead. But to reiterate this important matter, I can give a few guidelines to help you select among the options. The desirable features in the running shoe, which I mentioned earlier, would apply equally to any newly designed piece of trail footwear. Of all the criteria, weight is the most important. If that new model which has attracted your interest weighs much over 11 ounces (men's size 10½) give it a miss. Another criteria is heel and mid-foot cushioning. Another is adequate (but not excessive) breathability. And until someone figures out a way to make the shoe mold to your foot and *stay* that way, don't forget to buy several pair, of different makes and models.

Ordering footwear by mail

While hiking the trail, should you need a new pair of shoes, sandals or boots, and if you haven't included a pair in an upcoming resupply parcel, then at your next waypoint you might telephone your home base and request that a pair be express mailed to you there, or to your next stopover. Or if you have a credit card you might be able to mail order them direct from Road Runner Sports (800-551-5558), or Eastbay (800-826-2205). Before making the call, though, you might arrange with someone locally to receive your package. These companies usually won't ship to General Delivery. If all else fails you might have to hitchhike to the nearest city and buy a pair. But consider that the problem of needing fresh footwear is very common, and that it is so much easier solved ahead of time by including spare shoes in your resupply parcels. And rest assured that what shoes you don't use on the trail you can mail back home for use on your next hike.

Appropriate footwear for the High Sierra passes

If you reach the base of Forester Pass in June or July, you might as well chuck the foregoing discussions on running shoes and sandals into the nearest moat. Shoes and wool-blend socks perform well on compacted and gently inclined snow slopes, but when the snow steepens and hardens they are out of their intended territory. Running shoes and sandals do not edge well, nor do they kick adequate steps into hard crust.

On the steeper, snow-clad slopes you will need boots, preferably of the lighter variety, but with ample tread and stiff toe-bumpers and edges. And remember to go easy on the ecology by changing back into your soft shoes when you reach bare ground.

For northbound thru-hikers, Sonora Pass usually heralds the end of the technical snow in California. So during a year of normal or below-normal snowpack you might safely send your snow boots home from your next resupply station. Beyond, the trail will probably be free and clear all the way into central Washington. So you might ask your home-base person to send your boots back to you at Snoqualmie Pass or Skykomish.

✕

The technology represented in today's running shoes is vastly superior to that of Grandma Gatewood's Keds. Today's shoes offer improved cushioning, stability, and motion control. I'm not suggesting they are the ultimate in long distance hiking footwear. But I do think that by following the guidelines in this chapter you will find that they can help you enjoy a trouble free journey.

Food

Time-Tested Recipes, by Mice and Men

> Part of the secret of success in life
> is to eat what you like,
> and let the food fight it out inside.
>
> *– Mark Twain[1]*

For the long distance hiker trying to maximize performance while living at the highest levels of awareness and enjoyment, diet plays a key role. Quality foods provide long-term energy and vitality, but more importantly they provide maximum regeneration from the previous day's fatigue. This helps insure that the hiker will awaken each morning with vigor and anticipation for the new day.

Freeze-dried foods do not seem to impart these qualities. Nor do many types of dehydrated foods. Fresh, wholesome foods would be best, but of course they are not usually available along the way, and they would spoil in the resupply parcels. In this chapter we look at a variety of foods which I feel do indeed meet our requirements.

Unwrapping the freeze-dried fallacy

During my first summer as a professional wilderness instructor I subsisted on a diet mainly of freeze-dried food, as supplied by the company. My second year I began to suspect that these meals were not providing adequate go-power, so I experimented with more nutritious foods from the supermarket. The job entailed backpacking almost continuously throughout the summer and I found that despite the heavier load of fresh food, my energy levels and hiking enjoyment increased dramatically.

The immunity of the weekend hiker

Freeze-dried foods are generally light in weight, appealing, tasty, available in all the right backpacking stores and catalogs, and expensive. Therefore, they meet the trendy weekend hiker's every requirement – save one, which is how to dispose of the flagrantly counter-ecological packaging. Nevertheless, during even a week of strenuous activity these backpackers can gormandize on these nutritionally "empty" foods without noticing too many ill effects. But in

---

[1] Mark Twain was not a distance hiker. ☺

reality they are relying instead on the reserves stored in the cells of their own bodies. They are eating freeze-dried foods, but they are feeding, literally, off their own bodies.

Burning the reserves

Distance hikers starting out on their long journeys burn these reserves during the initial week or two. And if they don't compensate by eating quality food in quantity, they *will* begin experiencing more and more fatigue. This will prompt them to take longer trailside rests, to spend more time lounging around camp, and take more layover days. Eventually, if the trend continues they may quit their hikes altogether, feeling – wrongly of course – that they are simply not cut out for long distance hiking.

Aside from the fatigue, poor nutrition coupled with extended and strenuous exertion can also cause very pronounced mental effects. Recognizing these may help alert you to the problem, and knowing what is causing it may allow you to rectify it.

In the second or third week of the hike, as the reserves start bottoming out, the brain senses that survival is at risk. It knows what it needs: quality food. And it knows where to get it: in the kitchen cupboards back home. The conscious mind is told that hiking is no longer the right thing to do. It, in turn, starts prompting the hiker to go home. And when the hiker shrugs it off, the mind starts suggesting various excuses designed to convince the hiker of the need to quit the journey. Generally, these excuses have nothing to do with the real problem, which is the dehydration and profound nutritional deficit. Instead, some external aspect becomes the scapegoat, and soon grows intolerable. The hiker imagines him or herself dying a slow death, roasting in the hot sun like a desert survivor or freezing in the pervasive snow like a member of the Donner party. Blisters might seem to be destroying the feet. The trail's propensity to wander might seem more outrageous with the passing of every mile. There might be too much sun and not enough rain, or too much rain and not enough sun. Or perhaps the hiker develops a rekindled passion for a former hobby, such as stamp collecting. These are mental ploys, contrived by a brain struggling subconsciously to direct the body to the supply of nutrients it so desperately needs.

The problem might seem enigmatic at the time, but the solution is very simple. The successful distance hiker must drink plenty of water throughout the day, and eat quality foods in fairly large quantities.

Stoking the boilers with quality fuel

Of those hikers who persist beyond the first two or three weeks, many will continue trying to hike great distances while subsisting on nutritionally deficient foods. In effect they are like steam locomotives burning rubbish. The result is abbreviated mileage and forfeited enjoyment. This is regrettable because, once again, were they to stoke their boilers with quality fuel, in quantity, they would almost certainly become vastly more energetic and enthused. I believe that with adequate pre-hike training, lighter-weight packs and the skills to use only the basic gear, most distance hikers have about the same potential. But it is only by eating properly that any hiker can even begin to realize that potential.

Pack weight and food weight

I think of packweight in terms of the total load, minus the food and water. To some this may seem strange, considering that it all has to be carried. But I make this distinction for two important reasons. First, the food and water are expendable. Heading out from a resupply station we will be carrying perhaps 2½ pounds of food per day. Along the way we eat most of the food. But as the food weight drops from dozens of pounds to nearly zero, our basic packweight remains more or less unchanged. More importantly, I make the distinction because even though reducing our packweight is extremely important, reducing our foodweight is equally counterproductive. Long distance hikers must never scrimp on quality food. Ultralight (and nutritionally empty) meals are about as useless to them as pogo sticks would be to astronauts. Neither provide enough usable energy to get them where they want to go.

Continuing with the analogy, rocket fuel is extremely heavy, but it is also packed with enough energy to propel the rocket skyward. Take it from me: rocket engineers work only with those fuels capable of delivering the most payload the highest and farthest, in the most practical manner. And wise distance hikers do exactly the same.

The weight of an item is important, but its function is far more so. Hikers who carry and eat heavier but more nutritious foods are capable of traveling farther each day than those who carry slightly lighter packs while subsisting on empty foods. Moreover, they are likely to travel with more enjoyment, they will probably reach the distant objective in much better condition, physically and mentally, and they are likely to need less layover time. And because quality food can empower them to the next resupply station in fewer days, they don't need to carry as many days' supply.

So back to the original question: what kind of trail foods pack this kind of energy?

Fresh foods would be best, despite their weight. But of course while traipsing through the backcountry we lack daily access to well stocked supermarkets. And for the most part we cannot place fresh foods in our resupply parcels because they would spoil. So we have to compromise.

Corn pasta – the distance hiker's power food

While training for our first PCT trek, Jenny and I sampled a variety of processed foods and evaluated the resulting energy boost, if any. Every other day we trudged up the snow covered flanks of Colorado's Pikes Peak, testing our food experiments to the max. One day we found ourselves covering the miles far more easily and buoyantly, and we thought back to our previous dinner: corn spaghetti. This was the first time we had tried it, and naturally we thought the energy boost was coincidental. However, the more we experimented with corn pasta on subsequent hikes, the more we began to realize that its energy boost was genuine.

During our first PCT trek we ate corn spaghetti twice a week. This proved so successful that on our second PCT hike we ate it two out of three dinners. Not once did it fail to provide the energy we needed, and never did we tire of eating it. Had we included more in our resupply parcels we would have eaten it. In fact, during the latter stages of that hike we were actually rationing our supply, eating the corn spaghetti only in the late afternoons when we needed major energy boosts for the day's remaining several hours of hiking.

During our CDT thru-hike we ate corn spaghetti two out of three dinners. On our AT hike we went without it, as an experiment in saving weight by not carrying a stove. We bought our food at stores along the way. This didn't work well because many of these stores were very small and sold only snack items. Then on our third PCT hike we reverted back to corn spaghetti, and ate it for almost every dinner.

Since the first edition of this book, hundreds of other long-distance hikers have eaten corn pasta, with equally favorable results. Like ourselves, a few have reported eating it for almost every dinner, all summer long, and never tiring of it. Currently, I recommend eating an average of two servings every three days. Seven ounces, dry weight, per meal should satisfy the hiker of average appetite. Higher-mileage hikers have said they eat as much as ten ounces per serving.

Weight for weight, all forms of corn pasta would provide equivalent energy and nutrition. In the package, corn elbows are half again as bulky as corn spaghetti. But more importantly, our recent experiments have indicated that corn elbows require about 20% less fuel to cook. Because of this, and because they are easier to cook, I now recommend corn elbows, perhaps with the occasional meal of corn spaghetti for variety. Whatever your choice, apportion the corn pasta meals by weight, not volume. Again, seven ounces, dry, per meal, per person, should be about right.

What is corn pasta, and where is it sold?

Corn pasta looks like the more usual wheat pasta except that it is yellow. It is manufactured in much the same way, but it consists only of corn flour. It is reasonably inexpensive, simple to cook, and even though it contains no additives or preservatives its shelf life is measured in years, as long as it is protected from sunlight and moisture.

Corn pasta is sold in most health food stores and some supermarkets. If your grocers do not stock it, they might be willing to order it for you, especially if you want to buy one or more cases[2]. Failing that, you can probably mail order it from either of these two companies:

Westbrae Natural Foods, Carson CA 90746; (800) 776-1276 should be able to direct you to an outlet for their products in your vicinity (in the US and Canada). According to the representative we spoke with, the company uses organically grown corn, harvested from small farms mostly in the Midwest. It has processing plants throughout the US where the corn is ground into flour, mixed with water, put through pasta machines, and dried. The company makes corn spaghetti, elbows, shells, garden twists, and angel hair.

DeBole's Nutritional Foods, Inc., 215 Hillside Ave., Williston Park, NY 11596; (516) 742-1252. This company distributes its corn pasta and other products to supermarkets and health foods stores, and it sells direct to the customer.

Cooking corn pasta

While preparing for your trek you might cook a few corn pasta meals in your backyard or on a few of your training hikes, for practice. This will insure that your cookpot is the right size, and that you understand the use of your new stove. However, don't dismay if you find the taste and texture of corn pasta a bit strange. In every likelihood you will grow to like it once you have been on the trail a week or two, and have experienced the energy boost and sense of well being it can provide.

Corn pasta is cooked much like wheat pasta, with one exception for long distance hikers: Normally, when the pasta is finished cooking, one would pour off as much of the starchy liquid as possible, then rinse the pasta prior to serving. This is wasteful of treated water and valuable nutrients and vitamins.

---

[2] A ten pound box yields twenty two 7 oz. dinners.

Those hikers new to corn pasta might cook it this way initially. But once accustomed to it they would proceed to the more pragmatic method:

Assuming we are cooking for one person, we would pour 1½ cups of water into the cookpot. This should be sufficient to cook 7 ounces of corn elbows without having to pour any of the starchy fluid off afterward. Cover the pot with a fitted lid or a sheet of aluminum foil. This helps conserve fuel and prevents any flying insects from sacrificing themselves into the cookpot. If your stove has a separate fuel tank, don't forget to place a windscreen around the stove. This conserves fuel by blocking the heat-robbing wind and reflecting some of the radiating heat back to the pot. (Never place a windscreen around a stove with a built-in tank, for obvious reasons.) If you blacken the bottom and sides of the pot the water will come to a boil a little faster. Campfire soot works well, and the blackened cookpot can be packed inside its own stowbag.

If you are cooking spaghetti, use two cups of water, and while waiting for it to boil break the spaghetti into pieces three or four inches long.

When the water boils, remove the lid and place a handful of the pasta into the pot. Allow the water to resume boiling before adding more. Stir, and repeat until you have dispensed the full 7 ounces. Bring the water back to a boil, then shut off the stove and fit the lid. The hot water will continue cooking the pasta nearly as fast. No sense in wasting fuel.

If you're cooking spaghetti, lift the lid occasionally and stir the spaghetti. The corn elbows normally don't need to be stirred. Corn pasta is fairly delicate and must not be overcooked. When the time is about right, five or ten minutes after shutting off the stove, fish out a few pieces and sample them. When the pasta has reached the *al dente* stage, firm and not yet mushy soft, it's time to add whatever seasonings you prefer, (see below) and eat – directly from the cookpot. And once again, don't discard the starchy liquid. It contains a lot of energy and nutrition and is part of the meal. What pasta you can't finish that afternoon, save for the morning's breakfast, cold.

Incidentally, the higher the altitude, the lower the water's boiling temperature. Yet even in the High Sierra we have experienced no problems with cooking these meals.

Sauces and seasonings

Just about anyone can make a good pot of corn pasta *al dente*. But it takes a real *chef extraordinaire* to concoct just the right sauces which bring out its best. And I've met plenty of these people along the full length of the PCT. Jonathan Jarvis, who hiked the trail in '94, says that his favorite "gravy" is powdered milk and peanut butter, Thai style, with crushed red peppers. Denny

Fixmer, PCT thru-hiker of '94, uses catsup, carried in a plastic bottle. Admittedly a little heavy, but worth it he says.

Jenny's Spaghetti-Sauce Leather

My favorite sauce is Jenny's tomato leather. You can make this on your home food dehydrator. Begin by mixing a small can of tomato paste and one of tomato sauce. Add Italian seasonings, or a store-bought packet of spaghetti seasoning – selecting the type that contains the fewest chemicals. Chop and sauté a few mushrooms if you like, or onions or bell peppers, and blend into the sauce. Another option altogether is to dehydrate ready-to-heat spaghetti sauce, which usually comes in jars.

First, cover the food dehydrator tray with a sheet of plastic wrap. Use enough so that the ends overhang the sides of the tray an inch or two. Then tape the plastic's four corners to the tray, to prevent the plastic from curling back onto itself. Spread the sauce with a spatula to about ¼-inch thick.

When the leather has dried well, you can either freeze it and shred it in a blender, or you can leave the plastic wrap adhered to its backside and roll both in the shape of a tube. A piece of "leather" about eight inches square will season one serving of corn pasta. Either way, package the sauce in resealable bags to protect it from moisture.

Add your blender-shredded leather or your torn-into-small-chunks leather to the pot as your pasta returns to the boil. You could also add any embellishments such as dry salami or cheese, or dehydrated items such as meat, tomato, mushroom, onion, or bell pepper.

If you happen to find pre-packaged, dehydrated spaghetti sauce in a supermarket, you could use that instead. I've seen it in other countries but not in the US. Still, I have seen some interesting package mixes available here. Who says you can't put Pesto sauce, chili seasoning, or chicken Dijon on your corn pasta? Just remember to select the types containing the fewest chemicals.

To any and all of the above we add liberal quantities of powdered milk. This helps round out the essential amino acids. Sometimes we also sprinkle on some parmesan cheese.

The missing amino acids

The protein content of corn ranges from 8½ to 10½ per cent. However, it lacks two essential amino acids (tryptophan and lysine). Therefore, hikers who rely on corn as a primary source of energy and nutrition should augment it with legumes and dairy products. In order to reap the benefits of complementing amino acids, the foods have to be eaten at the same meal. As mentioned, I recommend adding powdered milk to the corn pasta.

Other corn-based products

Jenny and I avoid eating corn nuts for fear of breaking a tooth. But we do snack on corn chips and popcorn. These are sometimes available at the stores along the way, but more usually we include them in our resupplies. Most types of corn chips are high in fat. In cold climates, fat can help keep the hiker warm. In warm climates, foods high in fat can rob the body of go-power by requiring more energy to digest. Some types of corn chips are made without oil, baked rather than fried, and when available they might make a better choice. Bean dip would round out the corn chip's amino acids. This usually comes in a can, so we could either eat the chips and bean dip at the resupply station, or we could empty the bean dip into a resealable plastic bag and dispose of the can before heading off into the hills.

Studies with rats have shown that instant oatmeal is about as nutritious as the box it comes in. I think that is a bit of an exaggeration, but either way, why mess with it when wholesome corn meal mush cooks just as quickly? With powdered milk it is a complete protein, and with a little brown sugar Jenny and I find it makes quite a satisfying breakfast or lunch. To cook it, add the corn meal to cold water, then stir occasionally as the water comes to a boil. Once it boils, remove it from the heat, put the lid on the pot, and allow to cool a little.

Wheat pasta

I've seen long distance hikers go for months on wheat spaghetti instead of corn spaghetti, thinking that the magic is in the spaghetti making machine rather than what type of grain went into it. But I have yet to see anyone do it successfully. Three months is about the average fuse time until burn out. I met one fellow who had been eating mainly wheat spaghetti for 4½ months. The reason, he said, was that he wasn't using resupplies but was buying his food at the stores along the way. None of them sold corn pasta but most sold wheat spaghetti, and he figured that was close enough. I asked how he was enjoying his trip. He said he hated hiking! I mention this only to illustrate how a poor diet can affect the summer's enjoyment.

Marathon runners dine on wheat pasta the night before a race. "Carbo loading" they call it. In my opinion this works only because they have plenty of nutritional reserves to help process the meal. Distance hikers long on the trail lack these reserves. For them, wheat spaghetti can make a nice change of diet on occasion, but they should not use it as a mainstay. I would also discourage eating a lot of wheat based macaroni and cheese. It may be filling and satisfying, but its energy boost is miniscule.

Once I met a fellow who said that he had "a bad case of the trudges." I asked what he was eating for trail food. "Oh, I'm eating good," he answered. "I eat lots of Top Ramen noodles." (!)

Variety

Corn pasta makes a great mainstay, but it must be augmented with other quality foods. In the Bibliography you will find my recommended list of books giving hundreds of suggestions for trail foods. There is a lot of variety there, but unfortunately not all that much go-power. We all have different food preferences and tastes; but the fact is, we all have basically the same nutritional and energy requirements. Different personalities but similar bodies, which is where the corn pasta comes into its own. Still, we need a certain amount of variety to round out the shortcomings of the corn pasta and to brighten our mealtimes. So let's look at a few more items which in my opinion provide good nutrition and usable energy.

Wholesome, commercially available foods to place in the resupply parcels

Powdered milk

Powdered milk is an excellent source of protein and calcium, and it is packed with usable energy. I recommend powdered *skim* milk for use in warm climes, and powdered *whole* milk for colder ones, where the extra fat content will help keep you warm. Either way, this staple is loaded with nutrients, it has a long shelf life, it is light in weight, and it tastes pretty good too. Place a large bag of powdered milk in each resupply parcel, and use it to augment your corn pasta meals, your grain breakfasts, and to make hot and cold drinks.

Whole potatoes

Potatoes can be an important source of nutrition for the distance hiker. Prior to departing on a big hike Jenny and I place a couple of them in each of those resupply parcels going to a place where there is no store. Previously, at the supermarket we selected them individually for robustness. Usually the potatoes arrive at the resupply stations, months later, in fine condition. Some will have budded, and these buds we discard because they are said to be toxic. I should note, however, that potatoes require a certain amount of ventilation during storage. If packaged in plastic they can quickly spoil.

How to cook them on the trail? Dice and boil them. Otherwise, eat them raw. "New potatoes" taste the best this way. These are not a separate variety, but are merely harvested early. They are small, usually reddish in color, and have thin skins.

Instant mashed potatoes

One of the easiest of all trail meals is a pot of instant potatoes. Before buying, examine the list of ingredients for extraneous chemicals. Jenny and I have sampled many brands, but always revert back to Barbara's® Mashed Potatoes, sold in the health foods stores. They are wholesome and chemical free, which is important when eaten regularly throughout the summer. And we prefer their flavor and texture. The company also makes great tortilla chips (my favorite is their Multigrain Pinta Chips, made with organic yellow corn, pinto beans and brown rice) as well as crackers, bar snacks, and so forth.

Whichever brand of instant potatoes you choose, ignore the directions on the box and simply mix the product in cold water and stir in some powdered milk. Mix them very watery, though, and let them stand a few minutes to thicken. And as with any dehydrated foods, be sure to drink plenty of water with them.

V8® juice

V8 juice is a superb distance-hiking food. It is easily digestible and absolutely packed with nutrition. Some of the stores near the trail carry it. Otherwise, you could include a large can in the occasional resupply parcel. Drink it at the resupply station so that you won't have to carry the can into the woods.

Three-bean salad

Another excellent choice is canned three-bean salad. It is a great source of complex carbohydrates and usable longer-term energy. Open the can and pour the contents into a resealable plastic bag, or lidded bowl if you are carrying one. Either way, place it inside your upright cookpot and dispose of the can in the store's trash container. Include cans of three-bean salad in your resupply parcels going to those stations that lack stores.

Wholesome foods sometimes available along the way

Restaurant meals

Many resupply stations have restaurants nearby, and I strongly recommend that you take advantage of them. Just be sure to follow the sanitary precautions on page 184. And try to order wholesome meals rather than junk food.

Meat

Beef is sometimes sold in the stores along the way, usually frozen. It is another great source of nutrition. To cook it, simply cut it into small pieces and boil. But keep the boiling very brief or you will destroy most of the vitamins. Cook only until the pieces are brown on the outside and still somewhat rare on the inside. Drink the broth as well, as it is full of vitamins and makes a satisfying hot beverage.

A few words about the ethics of eating meat: Many vegetarians believe that our digestive systems – all the way from our tooth structure to our long intestinal tracts – were not designed to process meat. I don't relish the killing of animals for food, but I do have to agree with Tom Brown, Jr. when he wrote: "Vegetables scream just as loudly when they are killed." I think what he meant was that both animals and vegetables are alive, each in their own ways, and that we are being discriminate in condoning the killing of one while forbidding the killing the other. The famous Arctic explorer Vilhjalmur Stefansson considered meat to be the adventurer's ultimate food, and the higher the fat content the better. He based his theories on the diets of the Eskimo. I have experimented with prolonged vegetarianism during strenuous undertakings, and can report that typically all went well until I ate my first fresh meat and experienced a genuine increase in vigor. And granted, we have all heard about the abominations of steroid laced meats, usually from people selling vegetarian products. I don't care for cold cuts and the processed meats containing nitrates and nitrites, which are said to be carcinogenic. For the most part, though, I think the fresh or fresh-frozen meats we see in the groceries are wholesome.

Fresh fruits and vegetables

Where you find meat for sale you might also find vegetables. These are well worth their weight in terms of the restorative effects and sense of well being they provide. They can be boiled alone or in a stew, but they are far more nutritious when eaten raw. Corn on the cob is particularly so. And you don't have to eat the fresh vegetables and fruits at the resupply station. You can load them in your pack, and if well cared for they will keep for several days. Cabbage is particularly long lasting.

Sandwiches

Sandwiches are somewhat nutritious, and although they are not particularly high in energy yield they can help round out the hiker's bill of fare and reduce mealtime monotony. Jenny and I eat them frequently while on journey, buying the materials wherever available. If given the choice we buy 100% whole wheat bread. Usually, though, the only option beyond white bread is "wheat bread," which is white bread disguised with molasses coloring. About 75% of the time we eat sandwiches of peanut butter and jam, which we carry in plastic jars. The remaining time we make them with cheese, lettuce and tomato where available. Along with our sandwiches we often snack on tortilla chips, potato chips, pretzels, and so forth.

Cheese

Cheese goes well on sandwiches, but it lends itself exceptionally well to a pot of corn elbows. It rounds out the corn's amino acids, it adds protein and vitamins, and it makes a very satisfying meal. Once the corn pasta is nearly cooked, simply dice in the cheese and stir in some powdered milk. Voila! Corn macaroni and cheese.

Fresh milk

Fresh milk is also an excellent sustenance item. Drink it during your layover days.

Home-blended foods for the resupply parcels

Ray's Way-Of-Life grains

Jenny and I originated the "Way-of-Life" cereal recipe while preparing for our first PCT hike. We eat it both on the trail and at home, to this day. It has become, indeed, our way of life.

Our basic Way-of-Life mixture contains equal portions of barley, oats, millet, and corn grits. We buy only grains that are organically grown. Most health food stores stock them. And we make sure the whole grains are in their sproutable condition, meaning that they are "alive" and waiting for the right conditions for germination. Most types of processing kill the grains and reduce their long-term nutritional value. The best way to check is to try sprouting a small handful of kernels. Soak them in water overnight, drain them, and place in a well ventilated container in a dark place. After that, drench and drain them once a day. In two or three days you should see the initial stages of growth. This indicates that you have the genuine articles. And incidentally, when germinated they are even more nutritious.

To speed cooking time and to reduce fuel consumption we crack the grains in an old-fashioned hand grinder. This reduces long term value, granted, but still we are way ahead of the packaged mixes whose ingredients were processed long ago. Here, the idea is to split each kernel into just a few pieces. A blender will grind some of the grains to powder and leave most others intact. Most motor-driven grinders impart too much heat, which affects the grain's ability to retain its nutritive value over the long term.

To discourage repetition we add smaller amounts of enlivening ingredients such as triticale, rye, buckwheat, rice, sunflower seeds, sesame seeds, chopped almonds, or pecans. And we might further differentiate the breakfasts with cinnamon, nutmeg, or almond or vanilla extract.

After bringing 3 cups of water to a boil we cook 1 cup of the grain mixture (for two people) for 15 minutes, or 10 minutes if we had soaked the cracked grains in cold water overnight, or even less time if we had placed them under the quilt with us at night, sealed in a water bottle. And like the corn pasta, the grains must not be overcooked. Slightly chewy is preferable to glutinous.

Our usual sweeteners of choice are liberal quantities of powdered milk and a handful of raisins. Sometimes instead of the raisins we use home-dried fruits such as apple, pear, peach, apricot, pineapple, or papaya. And when on the trail we sometimes add jam, honey, or our favorite trail-side delectable in northern climes: huckleberries. We always add the sweeteners after the grains have cooked. Otherwise they can scorch the bottom of the pot.

When on journey we usually cook the following morning's breakfast immediately after eating dinner. We leave it in the cookpot, place it carefully in a backpack, then carry it for the remainder of the day, and for a few hours the next morning until stopping for a cold breakfast at eight or nine o'clock.

Grain and legume dinners

Cracked grains can also be used for dinner, in combination with cracked peas, beans or lentils to round out their amino acids. These legumes cook in the same manner and length of time. Our favorite is short-grain, brown rice in combination with black-eyed peas. For seasonings we use salt, beef jerky, and dried herbs.

Whole grains

Whole grains make a good cooked breakfast, lunch or dinner. Most natural foods stores carry a selection, which might include oats, rice, corn, wheat, barley, millet, triticale, buckwheat, sorghum, amaranth, and quinoa. You can cook just one type, or combine as many as you like. The fastest cooking is millet and quinoa: three minutes after the water reaches boiling, with an additional 5 minutes off the stove while covered with a lid.

Nutty muesli

Granola has been a standard breakfast item with hikers for years. Jenny and I don't care for the commercial varieties because they seem highly processed and sometimes repulsively sweet. And when purchased in bulk they can be rather stale. Making granola at home is not difficult, and many cookbooks give recipes for doing so. Jenny always makes a quantity for our hikes.

She also makes muesli, which is easier and does not require the several hours of baking. Mixed with powdered milk and water, muesli is quite nutritious and it makes an excellent lunch. The following recipe yields about 20 cups:

Combine 4 cups each of rolled oats, barley flakes, and triticale flakes, or whatever combination of grains you prefer. Chop them in a blender, 1/2 cup at a time, until the flakes are smaller but not powdered. Toast them in a large, dry skillet (or in a smaller skillet, working with half the batch at a time) until slightly brown. Stir frequently so as not to burn them. When they are nearly toasted, drizzle on 1/4 cup of vegetable oil. Remove them from the heat, stir in 1 cup of wheat germ or oat bran, 1/2 cup of brown sugar, 1 tsp. of almond flavoring, 1/3 cup of shredded coconut, 1 cup of date crumbles, 1/3 cup of sunflower seeds, 1 cup of chopped nuts, and one 20 oz. store-bought box of corn flakes. Mix thoroughly and package. And incidentally, you can also add 1/3 cup of dry powdered milk to each 1 cup of muesli before packaging, so that your milk is already in the bag with the cereal.

Other dehydrated food

For the carnivores, beef jerky is a great snack. It can also be added to your cookpot along with the rest of the meal. Store-bought jerky is expensive and usually loaded with nitrates, nitrites and MSG. Jenny buys lean steak, not necessarily a tender cut, and slices it in ¼-inch wide strips, across the grain for tenderness. She marinades the slices in a mixture of ¼ cup Teriyaki Sauce, 1 tsp. brown sugar, ½ tsp. salt and ¼ tsp. pepper. Or she might simply use a store-bought BBQ sauce. When the strips of meat are well coated she spreads them on the food dryer rack. She also makes fish and poultry jerky.

Fruit leathers are easy to make, and their flavors and texture are excellent. Place the fruits into a blender and distress them to capacity. Pour the resulting mash onto a plastic coated drying rack, and place in the food dehydrator. You can also dehydrate fresh, canned, or frozen fruits and vegetables.

In fact, you can dehydrate entire meals. Chili works particularly well. Simply prepare it as you normally would, then spread it out on the plastic-coated drier rack. On the trail, rehydrate it by adding water and allowing to stand for 3 or 4 hours. Normally you would place it in your pack, inside a resealable plastic bag or lidded plastic bowl, and safe within your cookpot, and hike with it for that period of time. Leave plenty of space for expansion, as the rehydrating food will swell to perhaps double its volume. At dinnertime, cook the meal for 10 or 15 minutes, or simply eat it cold.

When Jenny and I hiked the CDT we did not carry a stove for the first two weeks through grizzly bear territory. We ate home-dried meals that required only soaking in cold water. Predominant among these was home cooked and dehydrated corn spaghetti. It seemed to impart about the same energy, but it lacked its unique texture and most of its flavor, and was therefore rather uninspiring. We were glad when we reached our resupply parcel containing our stove.

Snacks: the day-long lunch

Regular meals are of primary importance, but except for corn pasta most foods don't contain enough usable energy to fuel five or six hours of continuous hiking. That is why most hikers, Jenny and myself included, snack at virtually every rest stop.

GORP

During our first few mega-hikes we ate a lot of gorp[3]. In the preparatory stages we mixed various ingredients into bags – two cups of gorp per person, per day – and loaded these into our resupply boxes. These ingredients included dried fruit, chopped dates, shredded coconut, raisins, salted peanuts, almonds, cashews, walnuts, and sometimes small candies. For even more variety we added chips, crackers, and dry breakfast cereals made from corn.

The reason we paid such attention to variety was that we were growing increasingly tired of eating so much of what seemed like the same old gorp. We tried making it an art form. We tried making it colorful to look at and fun to eat. We avoided items laden in chemical additives. But no matter how varied and rich with myriad ingredients, half way through the hikes we found ourselves picking through the bags and slinging various undesirables to the imaginary chipmunks. During our third long hike this intolerance grew so acute that we stopped eating gorp altogether.

I have a theory about foods which become intolerable. It is not merely a matter of taste; rather the body is rejecting them because they are not wholesome in the long term. I have no theories as to why gorp falls into this category. Maybe there is some combination of gorp ingredients that can be tolerated in quantity year after year. But I have yet to discover it.

Energy bars

Jenny and I have a tradition: we rise early, pack quickly, and set off with a small "energy" bar each in our pocket. It isn't that these bars yield much energy, but they are handy to carry and they make a suitable early morning munchie. Something to heighten the enjoyment of the morning's rambling.

I avoid the various Power-Techno-Wonder-Bars, in their many makes and models. Primarily, I object to the heavy marketing exerted by some of these companies. Full page, monthly advertisements are phenomenally expen-

---

[3] Good Ol' Raisins and Peanuts. Also known as "trail mix."

sive, and they are paid for by the unsuspecting customers who fall for this kind of hype. The advertising works by imparting magic-like qualities to very ordinary products, emphasized with the endorsements of superstars who are paid mega-bucks. Ignore the high prices and catchy names and examine the list of ingredients on the packages. Usually they are nothing out of the ordinary. Sometimes they consist of long-named chemicals reputed to produce astounding results. Baloney. These products are nothing but glorified Fig Newtons.™ Save your money and buy Fig Newtons instead, and if you're concerned about vitamins and minerals, take a vitamin pill every few days.

Jenny makes our snack bars at home. She examines the list of ingredients on the wrappers of various commercial "nutrition" bars, buys those ingredients at a health food store, mixes them imaginatively, and bakes them. The results are nothing like the commercial products because she is always experimenting with different ingredients and proportions. I think her culinary productions are superior, and I encourage hikers to experiment with their own ideas.

Hot and cold drinks

During our self-propelled journeys we typically forgo the morning hot drink ritual. But a hot "cuppa" at day's end can provide a welcome ambiance for journal writing. Our hot beverages include Cafix with milk, sweet-milk, hot chocolate, or plain powdered milk.

I make a batch of "sweet-milk" mix by blending 1 cup dry powdered milk, ½ cup sugar, and a pinch each of cinnamon, nutmeg, and cloves. This also works great as a milk shake when mixed with ice-cold water and shaken vigorously.

Filling the resupply boxes

Line your resupply boxes along a wall – and out the door and along the adjacent wall. Then refer to your chosen itinerary (See the chapter beginning on page 283). Your itinerary tells you the number of days' food needed between each of your resupply stations. Onto each box tape a temporary label specifying its destination. Into each box place the corresponding number of days' provisions. If you are using the above types of foods, as a general guideline you might plan on 2½ pounds of food per person, per day. But remember that you will probably be buying some food along the way.

Home packaging

Strive to minimize the food packaging materials. Otherwise you can find yourself carrying large, heavy bags of trash for days at a time. To package your pasta, weigh each seven ounce serving on a kitchen scales, then place on a sheet of brown paper, such as that cut from a grocery sack. Roll the paper to envelop the contents, fold in the ends, and tape everything closed. Then write the contents on the wrapper. Once you arrive at the station and open your re-supply box, load all these packages together in a single, larger plastic bag to keep them dry. A spare trash bag liner for your backpack would work fine. Then you can incinerate the individual paper wrappers along the way. Please refer to page 183 for details on how to burn your trash properly.

Junk food

An all-too-common mistake with distance hikers is the failure to distinguish between the needs for calories and nutrients. Calories represent the *potential* for energy. Nutrition, on the other hand, represents the capacity for growth, strength, cellular repair and reproduction, and mental acuity and stability. In short, the basis for the continuance of life itself.

So if the hike becomes a battle it is probably because your body needs quality fuel. When you go inside a store for refreshments, think about the quality of the food and beverages you are buying. This is where your battles will be won or lost.

Candy bar lust

Myth has it that the calories in candy can supply energy to our hard working muscles. If this were true then all weight lifters, football players, and mara-thon runners would gorge themselves on candy prior to every competition. The fact is, candy is quite useless when it comes to supplying energy. And it is also useless at promoting mental acuity and encouraging what is perhaps the journey's most vital ingredient: a positive mental attitude. Nor does it en-courage recuperation from strenuous exercise, or cleanse our muscles of their byproducts. It does not help repair micro-damaged muscles fibers, nor will it help strengthen our muscles and increase their stamina.

I'm not saying we should avoid candy. I'm merely suggesting that it won't bolster us. Eat all you like, but be prepared for the resulting *collapse* of energy, both physical and psychological, as the pancreas over-reacts by se-creting a lot of insulin, which, in turn, reduces energy levels.

One step at a time

The task of preparing the summer's food is a major one. Yet like the hike it-self, it is considerably facilitated if approached one step at a time. Having read and studied this chapter you might begin experimenting with some of these ideas at home, well in advance of your journey. Remember, though, that your tastes will probably change dramatically once you've been on the trail a few weeks, as your needs for metabolic fuel begin to spiral.

First Aid

A Few Items Carefully Chosen

Some of the more prevalent first aid books are extremely well done and I recommend you study at least one of them. My favorites are listed in the Bibliography. Be careful, though, about projecting yourself into the material. Always maintain a "clinical perspective," lest one day you find yourself afflicted with a few of the more "interesting" maladies.

The PCT thru-hiker's first aid kit is a little more specific, so I'll give a few suggestions pertaining to its contents.

Prior to embarking on a long hike, you might do well to have a physical exam. In addition to alerting you to any potential problems, the physician can also prescribe any medication you might need, (such as medication for giardiasis and poison oak) and caution you about its use. Make it known that you will be hiking in the mountains for a few months. Some types of medication can lessen a person's capacity for strenuous exertion. And some types can cause photo-sensitivity of the skin.

The first aid kit is not meant to handle every contingency. Such a kit would be enormous. So instead, we have to compromise by including only the basic items needed to handle only the more possible situations. My first aid kit contains only a few items, but each is carefully chosen. Certainly you may find the need for other items, but it is up to you to anticipate those needs.

- **Dr. Bronner's Pure-Castile soap,** used mainly as an antibiotic scrub for the reduction of giardia protozoa on the hands after eliminating. It also works great in a dundo shower for shampooing the hair in cold water. Carried in a small vile, replenished from the resupply boxes.

- A small vial of **hydrogen peroxide,** (3%) used as an antiseptic. This is an excellent infection preventive for superficial cuts and abrasions. Again, replenished from small bottles in the resupply parcels.

- **Betadine,**® for use in deeper lacerations, where hydrogen peroxide would "burn" the tissue.

- Hydrogen peroxide is a flash sanitizer. Betadine is the same but it also leaves a protective film. Use either when you want the wound to breathe. For more lasting protection use a **triple antiseptic salve.** This works especially well on callused feet. We have tried most brands, and recommend Campho-Phenique® Antibiotic Plus Pain Reliever.

- Small vial of **antifungal solution** for the periodic treatment of athlete's foot. Use also as a preventative after showering in a motel or campground.

- A few **Steri Strips**, and a 5-inch by 9-inch **combine dressing**.

- A full course of **one of the "cillins"** as an antibiotic. For example Amoxicillin.®

- Prescription hydrocortisone ointment, for the treatment of poison oak rash.

- Metronidazole (generic equivalent of **Flagyl**) for giardiasis.

- And always a supply of **aspirin** and **vitamins**.

In addition to our first aid kit we carry a foot-care kit, accessible in an outside pocket of one of our packs. It is nothing more than a resealable plastic bag containing a few breathable adhesive strips and a packet of 2nd Skin.™

PCT and AT Comparisons

For the Benefit of Seasoned AT Hikers

In many ways the Appalachian and Pacific Crest Trails are quite similar. Both have lush, expansive forests, beautiful wildflowers, deer and bear, the evening chortle of birds, and the friendly hikers and townsfolk along the way. But in many ways the two trails are very different. Each has its own tempo. Each can be strewn with "obstacles," both natural and man-made; although we tend to over-dramatize the harshness of environments unfamiliar to us. Each trail has innumerable merits, but by and large these merits differ almost completely from one trail to the other. Yet despite the differences, each can provide an exemplary and highly rewarding distance-hiking experience to the hiker with an open mind.

Jenny and I thru-hiked the AT and PCT in successive summers and in much the same style, wearing running shoes and carrying about 8½ pound packs, not including food and water. The AT, at roughly 2,200 miles, (including trips out for resupplies) took us 89 days overall. Of these, 87 were hiking days, full or part. The PCT, at about 2,700 miles (including side trips), took us 96.5 days, of which 92 were hiking days.

Trail	Miles hiked	Total hiking days	Daily average
AT	2,200 miles	87 hiking days	25.3 mpd
PCT	2,700 miles	92 hiking days	29.3 mpd

From this table we might expect the experienced AT hiker to cover 16% more miles each day on the PCT. The PCT is 23% longer, but far more gently inclined. And its humidity is much lower and doesn't interfere with the body's evaporative cooling, meaning that its hikers can travel it more efficiently. But of course the snowpack can certainly hamper progress.

Karl Diederich, who has thru-hiked both trails, wrote a sensitive commentary describing the plights of two accomplished AT hikers who quit their PCT hikes prematurely.

"Ray, your attitude is to take the trail on its terms, rather than to try to force the application of one's ideas. I'm not a mind reader, but in my opinion and perception of their attitude, this is the mistake Burt and Brad[1] made. For both of them the AT had been one of the greatest things in their lives. I feel they were both looking for an encore in the PCT. That's fine. I would too. Their error was in looking for a repeat of the AT, rather than a new adventure. So they showed up on the PCT looking for the social community of hikers, the camaraderie they had experienced, the canopied trail, and the shelters where hikers gathered and shared. These elements were missing. Although the PCT has plenty to offer, the things of the PCT were not what they were searching for, and so Burt and Brad never saw them. So it was not the trail, but the pre-conceptions they had, that left them unfulfilled. And I suppose that is what ends the adventure for many through-hikers."

Jerome Richard hiked both trails, and wrote a very useful comparison: "The AT is a cultural experience and the PCT is a wilderness experience. The humidity is really high on the AT, and the PCT is very arid in comparison. The AT is by far steeper, because there are no grade limitations like on the PCT. All day long it is up and down, and it really wears you out. The AT is like a rain forest with a lot of dense vegetation. The PCT is very open, with fewer trees and a lot more views. On the AT you can obtain water from good springs most of the way with no long distances between them. The PCT has fewer springs but a great many nice creeks, a few questionable ponds and lakes, and sometimes great distances between sources. The AT has a lot of hardwood trees, where the PCT has almost all conifers. The AT has very organic soils for the most part, except for some glacial till near Pennsylvania and New Jersey. The PCT has a lot of granite in the south and volcanic soil in the north. I am sure that if the winter's snowfall on the west coast was severe the PCT would be a lot tougher than the AT. Typically, on the AT you don't need an ice axe. The AT is better maintained, better marked, and has many more places to resupply. The people along the AT are more trail conscious and take a lot of pride in the trail and in helping thru-hikers. On the PCT hardly anyone along the way knows much about the trail and there is a lot of apathy in the communities, towns and the National Forest and National Park Services."

To these I would add a few comments of my own:

---

[1] Not their real names

Compared with the steeply inclined AT, the PCT tends to be extremely gradual. The main reason for this is that it was built to stock standards. It is not that stock can't climb steep hills. They can. But the steeper the slope the more they tear it up, because of the way their hooves pivot and gouge with each step. But if the AT can test the knees, then the PCT can test the feet. Shoes for AT hiking must provide stability, while those for the PCT need to provide more cushioning, and they need to be longer and wider to accommodate swelling of the feet.

The PCT covers a greater spectrum of temperature zones, so its thru-hikers need to carry a wider variety of clothing. But contrary to myth they need not worry about the effects of altitude. The trail begins at lower elevations and gradually works its way upward, allowing hikers to acclimatize.

Preeminent among the climatic variations is the snowpack. Because of the possibility of PCT hikers encountering lingering patches of steep, hard, and slippery snow, each hiker needs to carry an ice axe and know how to use it. Like a parachute, the axe may never be needed – particularly in years of drought. But when suddenly the axe is needed it can be life saving. Several PCT hikers have injured themselves on steep snowfields, and in every likelihood these accidents could have been prevented with proper use of an ice axe.

Another environment unique to the PCT is the torrid deserts of southern California, sandwiched inescapably between snow-clad mountain ranges. The thru-hiker descends from winter into summer, then climbs back up into winter. This presents some marvelous contrasts.

I think it would be fair to say that both the AT and PCT can be very challenging. Both can be difficult, but neither more so than the other. No long trail is perfect, but the experiences it can provide *are* perfect. A perfect blend of frustration and gratification, of solitude and friendships, of mini-failures and profound accomplishments. These await the long-distance hiker willing to try a new trail. With an open mind you are sure to find new and wonderful qualities that you had not realized existed. And that is what trail magic is all about.

Financing The Journey

Men for the sake of getting a living forget to live.

— *Margaret Fuller*

Distance hikers are a select and hardy band of individuals. They are pioneers, of sorts, who temporarily leave the civilized world behind to immerse themselves in the natural world. Experienced hikers usually find that the hardships and occasional privations pale in light of the ineffable rewards. But to be quite honest, the novice can find the rigors of extended trail life quite tough. To succeed in the multi-thousand mile wilderness quest, the novice hiker has to want to succeed very seriously. For without an uncompromising sense of motivation and perseverance, a checkmate is practically inevitable. This is true no matter how much money a person has, no matter how much spare time, and no matter how much fancy equipment. Put the other way: money, time, and equipment are not the essential ingredients. The key ingredient is the will to succeed. Once a person sets his or her resolve, he or she will earn and save the money, buy or make the equipment, and allocate the time.

Life is a matter of priorities, in that most of us anchor our lives to whatever things are important to us. Adventure is more important to many distance-hikers than extravagant, comfortable lifestyles. So they organize their lives in ways that allow them to pursue their wilderness adventures, and they consign the rest to the back seat. To others, it might be the career and family that imbue life with meaning. And of course for many it is the quest for so-called financial security. Whatever is important to a person, that is what he or she usually focuses on. So when someone says to me that they would give *anything* to hike the PCT, but that they just couldn't leave their antique collection (I am not making this up) then they are describing their priorities quite clearly. To thru-hike a big trail one must sacrifice just about all else during the months of preparations and actual journey.

I believe virtually anyone can latch onto a dream and carry it through. Granted, in our western culture money tends to rule the game. But not every player uses all the rules to best advantage. For example, regardless of a person's income, his or her financial situation is affected mainly by the "outgo." Money in the bank depends on the deposits, granted, but it can depend far more on the expenditures. Most distance hikers finance their multi-month excursions by working long hours during the winter months, while spending the absolute minimum. Even though their income is not great, their expenses are minimal so their savings grow. For younger people this is generally easier to do because they have fewer responsibilities, and far more importantly, because they have fewer misconceptions about the way they spend their money. Mature individuals often buy items of luxury and consider them essentials. And they tend to view the monthly payments as necessary payments. They are necessary only because of the debts incurred. Consider that the monthly payments and insurance premiums on a newer model automobile, for example, could grubstake a more frugal thru-hiker for many years.

Our lives are made expensive by the many debts we enter into. Typical expenses might include supporting a family, house payments, furniture payments, insurance payments, repair bills and property taxes, utility and telephone bills, health and life insurance, luxury-car installments and the associated insurance premiums, licensing fees, and gas and maintenance costs. And then there are entertainment expenses, vacations, credit card interest, and so forth. Money in the bank equals deposits minus all these expenditures. And people wonder why money can be such a problem.

Most people could easily afford a summer's journey by eliminating, or at least minimizing, some of these expenses. One way to do that would be to move to a less expensive part of the country. Granted, the job might not be as glamorous nor pay as well, but the costs of living would be far less. And I think that those people with their sights set beyond the ostentatious amenities of our culture might be just as happy, and that their savings would grow. Frankly, without the frills, the human body is quite economical to operate. And on the trail this is particularly true. So let's examine some of the costs of hiking the PCT, or any other trail.

Trail expenses

Obviously, these costs vary widely among individuals. At one extreme we might have someone sinking a fortune into a big load of all the latest equipment. I have seen it done many times. And at the other end of the spectrum we have the hiker who shopped at the army surplus store years ago. One of the happiest hikers I ever met was a fellow carrying an odd array of old equipment lashed haphazardly to his pack frame. For a hiking stick he was using an old mop handle. Even more frugal was the PCT hiker we met who was eating mostly rice cooked over a fire, and making bracelets to sell along the way. So the style you choose will have great bearing on the costs of your journey. The trip does not have to be terribly expensive, but it certainly can be if you let it.

Scrimping on the footwear can be false economy. You shoes or boots will be your *modus operandi*. On them will hinge your entire journey, along with the bulk of its associated costs in money and time. I recommend buying at *least* five different pair, including 3 pairs of running shoes, 1 pair of sandals, and one pair of lightweight fabric boots for the snow.

Buying a four or five months supply of food can seem like a big expense, but only because you buy it all at once. If you stayed home all summer you would still have to eat. Granted, hungry hikers eat a lot more than they would at home, but their food tends to be less extravagant. So I don't think it costs any more to eat on the trail than it would at home – unless you eat freeze-dried food, perish the thought. But of course mailing the boxes of food to the resupply stations is a consideration, and this is particularly true the farther from the west coast you live.

Travel to and from the trail, by airline, train, or bus, can be another cost factor. This can be avoided by hitchhiking, of course, but for safety's sake I recommend strongly against it. "Standby" air travel is still a great way to travel. This works only when the next plane to your destination has an empty seat, which is usually the case, and when you tell the counter clerk that you will fly *only* standby. You can purchase a legitimate ticket at an equally deep discount, and with very short notice, from a ticket consolidator. Look for them in the phone book. It's best to stop by their office and pay for your ticket with cash.

The occasional wholesome restaurant meal should also be planned for, as the extra nourishment will do you a lot of good. These meals will probably not be extra expenses, as most likely you would eat in a restaurant a few times had you stayed at home. Also, I recommend planning for the occasional motel room. The largest expense of the summer will be the forfeited wages. But to the hiker who also cuts off the monthly costs of living that went along with those wages, this loss should not be of any great consequence. At the same time, however, I recommend against burning all your bridges, in case you decide to return home early.

Gear List

A lower packweight is no accident. Instead, it is the result of a great deal of forethought, research, and trial and error. To give you a few ideas I've compiled a list of equipment and clothing that the hiker of modest experience might carry on a thru-hike of the PCT. It is not for beginners who lack an understanding of the principles in this book, or who are not willing to adopt any of them. Nor does it represent any kind of definitive selection. Use it only as a catalyst in your thinking. Then make a list of your gear and study it carefully for any problems and areas of potential improvement.

Most of the gear in this table is commercially obtained, representing the approach of the typical novice distance hiker. For a list of what the more advanced hiker might carry, much of which is home-made, see the tabulation beginning on page 358.

SAMPLE INVENTORY

Backpack, and plastic garbage sack as waterproof liner	3 lb	11.0 oz
Ice axe with lanyard	1 lb	3.0 oz
Tent, poles, fly, stakes, repair sleeve, and stowbag	3 lb	0.0 oz
Ground sheet: Sportsman's Blanket™ cut to tent floor size		6.5 oz
Foam pad (3/8-inch thick closed cell, 40 inches long, 18 inches wide at the top and 14 inches wide at the bottom)		4.8 oz
Sleeping bag, stuff sack, and trash bag liner for stuff sack	3 lb	4.5 oz
Guide book section		1.0 oz
Journal pad and two ball point pens		1.0 oz
Bag of valuables (resealable plastic bag) includes driver's license, paper money, travelers checks, credit card		4.0 oz
Camera, 1 roll film, bulb brush, spare battery, and stowbag		7.9 oz
Water filter and stowbag		8.5 oz
Water bottle (empty soda bottle) 1 quart		1.6 oz
Water bag, empty (2½ gallon capacity)		3.5 oz
Stove, windscreen if any, stowbag, fuel bottle if separate, ½ liter fuel	1 lb	9.8 oz
Cookpot (aluminum, 2 quart capacity) with lid and stowbag		7.2 oz

Spoon (high-impact plastic)	0.2 oz
Dish towel (1/2 bandanna, cotton)	0.4 oz
Stowbag for food items with P-51 can opener attached to drawstring	0.3 oz
First Aid kit, in resealable plastic bag, includes: hydrogen peroxide in plastic vial, Kenelog™ (for poison oak), Betadine™ (antiseptic), triple antibiotic ointment (antiseptic), Amoxicillin (antibiotic), Flagyl (giardiasis), lip balm, antifungal solution, etc.	2.0 oz
Aspirin and vitamins, in resealable plastic bag	0.5 oz
Sun screen	0.5 oz
Foot-care bag (resealable plastic bag) contents: Adhesive strips, packet of 2nd Skin™	1.3 oz
Ditty bag, with draw string and cord lock	0.3 oz
Emergency whistle, with lanyard	0.4 oz
Comb, toothbrush, dental floss	0.8 oz
Shampoo (in plastic packet)	0.3 oz
Deodorant (for use at resupply stations)	0.2 oz
Toilet kit: TP and Dr. Bronner's™ soap in plastic vial	2.0 oz
Sunglasses, in protective pouch	1.4 oz
Windex, in plastic bottle (for cleaning eyeglasses and camera lens)	0.7 oz
Half a bandanna (for cleaning eyeglasses and camera lens)	0.4 oz
Flashlight with two AA lithium batteries	1.5 oz
Knife, with lanyard	0.8 oz
Compass, with neck lanyard	0.7 oz
Duct tape, 5 foot roll, flattened, for repairs	0.3 oz
Parachute cord (15 feet, nylon) for clothesline	0.4 oz
Sewing kit: includes needles, safety pins, and heavy thread	0.3 oz
Emergency fire-starter kit in resealable plastic bag, contains small lighter, stick matches in small plastic bottle, and birthday candles	0.9 oz
Insect repellent in small pump spray bottle, carried in resealable plastic bag in case of leaks	1.0 oz
Umbrella (modified), with mylar covering for desert travel	10.0 oz
Sun hat with chin strap	2.2 oz

Insulating hat (waterproof / breathable shell with fleece lining)		2.1 oz
Mosquito head net (no-see-um netting)		1.2 oz
Parka, rain (waterproof / breathable)		15.9 oz
Shell jacket (lightweight breathable nylon)		5.2 oz
Jacket (fleece)		14.5 oz
Shirt, lightweight polyester, short sleeve, button down front		4.0 oz
Shirt, long sleeve, wicking (polypropylene or etc)		8.0 oz
Mittens (fleece)		1.3 oz
Mittens, mosquito (breathable nylon)		0.2 oz
Shorts, nylon jogging, or Lycra tights		4.3 oz
Shell pants (lightweight breathable nylon)		5.7 oz
Pants, wicking (polypropylene or etc)		6.9 oz
Socks (nylon, lightweight) 3 pair		2.3 oz
Socks, (wool/synthetic) 2 pair		2.4 oz
Shell booties (breathable nylon) for mosquitoes		0.2 oz
Booties (coated nylon) for showers		0.8 oz
Spare sandals	1 lb	4.5 oz
Towel (cotton, 12"x12")		1.7 oz
Clothing bag (plastic trash sack, or waterproof nylon stow-bag with drawstring and cord lock)		1.5 oz
Total	22.0	

Part 2
The Journey

Reaching The Trail's Beginning

Again let us dream where the land lies sunny
And live, like the bees, on our heart's old honey.
Away from the world that slaves for money –
Come, journey the way with me.

– Madison Cawein

Starting out on your long hike you will probably find yourself bristling with excitement and anticipation for the summer's adventure. And rightly so; for you have placed yourself here, by work, sacrifice, and commitment, and you deserve the richness of this moment. Just think of all those empty journal pages, both in your pack and in your resupply parcels. Each evening you will be writing the chronicles of your journey as it unfolds. If you could only read them now!

Starting at the PCT's south end

The PCT begins near the town of Campo, California, about 50 miles east of the San Diego airport via Highway 94. To reach Campo from San Diego, ride the trolley 15 miles to El Cajon (EL-cuh-HONE), then the Southeast Rural Transit van to Campo.

The details:

- From the airport, board the #2 bus headed for downtown San Diego. Ask for a transfer, which may serve as your trolley ticket. And ask to be let off at the Broadway and Kettner stop.

- Those arriving downtown San Diego via Amtrak train or Greyhound bus would walk to the same corner of Broadway and Kettner. There, they would buy a trolley ticket from one of the vending machines.

Board the trolley marked "El Cajon and Santee." Hang on to your ticket because it counts also as partial fare for the van ride to Campo. Ride the trolley to it's final stop, the El Cajon Transit Center. Disembark and walk across the street to the bus terminal area. Look for the sign reading "Southeast Rural Transit."

For information regarding the city bus and the trolley, telephone (619) 233-3004.

At the time of this writing, the Southeast Rural Transit van departs the El Cajon Transit Center bound for Campo once a day at 3 pm, seven days a week. The company asks that you telephone a week before your expected travel date to confirm this information and to place your reservation. (619) 478-5875. Mention that you will be carrying a backpack, as they sometimes need to plan ahead.

Once in the van, show the driver your trolley transfer. The ride from El Cajon to Campo is about 2 hours, so you'll be arriving at Campo about 5 pm. The driver will let you off probably in front of the Campo store. If you haven't brought your water with you, you'll need to get enough for the evening's camp, and the 15 miles of hiking beyond Campo to Hauser Creek. Stash your water as soon as you reach the trail, for pick up later that evening on your way back from the border.

The Wilderness Press guide book recommends checking in at the US Border Patrol Station. Why, I'm not sure, especially considering that finding someone there is unlikely, except at the changing of the guard, which occurs daily at 7:00 am, 3:00 pm, and 11:00 pm.

As you hike south along the dirt road 1.3 miles to the border, keep in mind that this region between Campo and the Mexican Border is not a good place to camp. Nighttime games are sometimes played here, and I don't think any of us would want to participate. The problem is not so much with the illegal aliens sneaking across the border, but with the Border Patrol officers who have a reputation for treating transients with aggression. They will not hassle you, of course, but they might inadvertently catch you in the crossfire, so to speak. On a similar note, I might mention that some of the locals view pedestrians with suspicion. Make it easier on their nerves by not stopping for a rest in sight of their houses.

After snapping a few inaugural photographs it's time to shoulder your pack and begin. I recommend you forget the road leading back to Campo, and that you follow the trail to the letter. Yes, it winds in and out, up and down, tempting you to follow the road. But the road has nothing to do with the PCT, and it is here that you will probably set the trend of your entire summer's journey.

Collecting your water where you left it, continue along the trail, up and away from Campo, across the highway, and as many miles beyond as you can manage that evening. Then look for a likely place to make a pleasant stealth camp, hidden from the trail.

The end of the northbound hike

Finishing your journey at Manning Park, you could detour to the Visitor Center and sign the trail register. Farther west, Manning Park Lodge has showers, saunas, a restaurant, and a small store. The Greyhound Bus stops in front of the lodge office twice daily. For information about the Canadian Greyhound bus, call 604-662-3222. The bus will take you to the Vancouver airport, or the Vancouver bus terminal where you could board another bus for Seattle.

Beginning the hike at the PCT's north end

The PCT's northern terminus is in Manning Provincial Park, Canada. To get there you can ride the Greyhound bus 215 miles east from Vancouver along Highway 1 and 3, or 180 miles west from Osoyoos (oh -SOY-yohs).

To reach Osoyoos, take the bus north along Highway 97 to Ellensburg, Washington. There, transfer to the Empire Line, and ride its bus to Osoyoos. From there take the Greyhound to Manning Park. Entry permits are not required of American citizens traveling into Canada by bus or auto. At the border crossing the customs inspector will probably ask whether you have any weapons, including Mace® and pepper defense spray canisters.

Once at the Manning Park Lodge, a few minutes' hike east along the highway will take you to the Visitor Center at the Park Headquarters, which has a PCT register. Continuing east, you will soon reach the trailhead, which is actually the road climbing Windy Joe Mountain.

The end of the southbound hike

Southbound hikers ending their trips at Campo can ride the Southeast Rural Transit van to El Cajon, and the trolley to San Diego. See the above information and apply it in reverse. Presently, the westbound van departs from the Campo store at 8:20 am, 7 days a week. Try to phone the company a week in advance to confirm this information and to make your reservations. Failing that, you can call from Campo and take your chances.

※

As you ride the bus taking you away from the trail, you might almost glow with the satisfaction of a summer's adventure rightly lived. All those journal pages which were empty and waiting expectantly at the start of your trip are now full with the story of your journey as it unfolded day by glorious day. The moment is yours and yours alone. Savor it richly.

Hiking Enjoyment

Nature has given the opportunity of happiness to all,
knew they but how to use it.

— Claudian

The hiker starting out on a long trek undergoes an abrupt change in lifestyle. The exertion levels skyrocket, launching the nutritional requirements right into orbit. Yet the types of food eaten default to the usual trail-food variety, causing the nutritional intake to plunge. And the excitement of having finally started the trek, coupled with the anxieties of dealing with the great unknown, usually reduces the appetite. So rather than eat greater quantities of higher quality food to satisfy the soaring needs for energy and nutrition, the hiker usually eats less food of lower quality.

Food plays one key role, and water another. For the hiker starting at the Mexican border in late spring, the days can be quite warm and the humidity low. The hiker will sweat, and this can lead to dehydration. Water sources will be somewhat sparse, and the mineral and bacteriological content may differ from what they are back home. And during those first two or three days while making way from Campo at 2,600 feet, to the summit of Mt. Laguna at 5,900 feet, the atmosphere may be a little thinner. This may further upset the body's fluid balances by increasing the rate of sensible and insensible perspiration.

Trail shock

Blend in a bit of fatigue from the hectic last-minute preparations, from traveling, and the weariness from the actual hiking with a few stiff, aching muscles and maybe a growing collection of blisters, and we have a recipe for a crash somewhere up ahead. The problems can suddenly become so great that the journey loses every hint of its former luster and the prospects of continuing suddenly seem impossible. The result is a feeling of depression, as the mind struggles to accept the reality of "failure" and its myriad and unthinkable consequences.

I call this "trail shock" and recommend that every hiker plan for it. Basically, the newer the person is to the long distance hiking game, and to the particular environment, the sooner and harder the shock may hit. The more out-of-shape, and the more the hiker over-exerts, the harder it is likely to hit. But take heart. Trail shock is not a sign of failure but of adaptation. In every likelihood the journey is not at risk. We are merely going at it too hard, and need to throttle back for a day or so, to help our bodies and minds adjust to the difficult transition. All caterpillars metamorphose into butterflies, and although this is an awkward process it is necessary for growth. And personal growth is a requirement for almost any successful adventure.

Jenny and I have experienced trail shock in the initial stages of each of our journeys, to greater or lesser degrees. But we have learned to recognize it for what it is, and have been able to minimize it. We do this by training well ahead of time, by not over-exerting, particularly during the first few weeks of the journey, and by paying careful attention to our nutrition and fluid intake.

Happiness in the wilderness experience

In his book *Flow, The Psychology of Optimal Experience*, Mihaly Csikszentmilalyi[1] details his "…principles to transform boring and meaningless lives into ones full of enjoyment." Happiness, he says, does not just happen, nor is it the result of money, power, good fortune, or chance. Instead, happiness must be cultivated from within. And he goes on to say that "the best moments usually occur when the body or mind is stretched to its limits in a voluntary effort to accomplish something difficult or worthwhile."

Happiness in the wilderness experience doesn't just happen either. Nor is it the result of high-tech equipment, favorable weather, or a properly graded trail free of brush. Yes, Nature has the capacity to enrich our lives, but only the capacity. We ourselves must create any meaningful experiences from within. When it comes to distance hiking, we can do this in two ways. One, by developing the skills necessary for safe and efficient and therefore enjoyable travel. And two, by fueling our minds properly so that they are capable of interpreting external events in a positive way.

The human brain is a machine, in the sense that it requires proper fuel to operate at peak efficiency. It is extremely sophisticated and capable of emanating the full spectrum of emotions, but it will emit positive emotions only when well nourished. Staying positive, then, is first and foremost a matter of eating properly. As I mention in the chapter on food, if distance hiking can be thought of as a battle, then that battle is fought, not on the trail, but in the grocery stores along the way. Show me someone who is not enjoying their hike, and I will show you someone who is eating nutritionally deficient foods. Foods loaded with chemicals, when consumed in quantity, can be particularly onerous. I've known people who drink diet sodas by day and take antidepressant drugs by night, without seeing the connection.

---

[1] See Bibliography.

Once the brain is well nourished and capable of emanating positive emotions, it is up to us to direct our thoughts in positive ways. In one respect our minds are like radios. When they start playing unpleasant music we can change the channel. Assuming we are well nourished and chemical free, we don't have to entertain negative thoughts. Negative thoughts can be especially detrimental to long distance hikers who have so much time to dwell on them. Detrimental, because they can escalate, and if allowed to run rampant they can ultimately destroy the journey by sending the hiker home, terribly upset at some trivial concern.

I've seen many examples of this. I remember one fellow who quit his hike because he had become horribly disgusted with the bushes growing on the trail. Bushes growing on the PCT are a fact of life, as are buzzing mosquitoes and falling rain. These are not genuine obstacles, but minor inconveniences calling for an abandonment of our unrealistic expectations.

If you find yourself grumbling about the way some hiker did something, change the channel. Concentrate instead on the way *you* are doing things. Remember that we are all kin of the mega-trails. Each of us is an individual, and thank God for our own individuality. Each is pursuing a dream, however he or she interprets it. And like everything in life, a positive attitude toward our fellow outdoor enthusiasts engenders far more energy and determination within ourselves.

Dealing with external negativity

Negativity can also come to us externally, for example from "friends" and possibly even relatives at home. Make it easy on yourself: share your plans only with those who comprehend or at least accept them without retort, not with those who would criticize them and dissipate your energy. Perhaps your best resources for support are those who have hiked the trail. They will understand your problems and share your enthusiasm, and in most cases they will be happy to offer a listening ear and perhaps a few words of encouragement.

On the trail you might meet a few negative-minded hikers. The mind fed a constant diet of low octane fuel is bound to cause a lot of smoke. If you can think of a tactful way to recommend a more nutritious diet, you might do so. Either way, remember that attitudes are infectious. On the trail or off, choose friends who add to your life, and, in general, steer clear of people who would subtract from it.

Personal Security

Adventure is the result of incompetence

– *Vilhjalmur Stefansson*

The more time you spend on the trail, the more you will hone your skills and build the kind of competence that will prevent you from suffering mishaps at every hand. Snow travel will become something to look forward to instead of something to dread. You will feel confident about crossing waterless, hot stretches of trail. The so-called hazards of the natural world will become surmountable, although they will never lose their potential to develop into dangerous situations. The same holds true with your personal security. Both on the trail and off, the potential for vandalism, personal threats, harassment – or worse – is real, and you will need to remain alert.

The way to attract disaster is to imagine that it could not possibly happen to you. The way to reduce it is to realize specifically what could happen, and take the appropriate defensive measures to prevent it from happening. And the key to happiness is, after having taken these measures, to carry on enjoying your trip. Keep your eyes open to potential trouble, and plan ahead, but don't become obsessed with what could happen.

Personal safety

For the experienced hiker, the dangers in Nature pale in comparison with those in the concrete jungles. And fortunately for us all, the desperadoes from the cities rarely venture into the natural world. As far as the PCT is concerned I know of only two incidents where dubious characters were associated with hiking. One was a trio of fugitives posing as PCT hikers, camping near the trail and raiding a few near-trail rural communities. The other was a pair of fellows hitchhiking from one PCT resupply community to the next, posing as hikers and taking full advantage of the hospitality extended them, and then some.

The trail itself is virtually free of miscreants, but some of the road crossings along the way could be potential sources. In general, troublemakers travel only by vehicle and they tend to remain near the roads. So the first rule of hiker safety is: don't camp near a road. If sometimes you want to camp near a resupply station or trailhead, move well away and make a stealth camp where you will not be noticed.

For your own safety, don't linger at the road crossings, and in particular stay away from the 4WD crossings, especially on weekends. If someone comes along and asks what you are doing, say that you are waiting for your friends who will be along shortly. Don't tell a stranger where you are going or where you will camp. If you are traveling solo, consider carrying pepper spray. Even so, always use avoidance as your first line of defense.

Hitchhiking

PCT thru-hikers on a 4¾ month or shorter itinerary would not need to hitch-hike out for supplies during the full course of their journeys. The itineraries indicate hitchhikes to Independence from Kearsarge Pass, and Skykomish from Stevens Pass. Both stations can be skipped. And they indicate a hitch-hike to Tehachapi. Instead, hikers could leave the trail at Highway 58, hike 2 miles along the highway, turn left onto Tehachapi Boulevard, and hike west 7 miles to town. All other resupply stations associated with these itineraries are well within walking distance of the trail. Many carry basic supplies, and all can receive packages – meaning that the hiker's home-base helper can send a needed item by Priority Mail, and that it should arrive in a few days.

There may be occasions, however, when the hiker will want to go out to a larger town, for example to buy an urgently needed pair of shoes, or perhaps to get medical attention. In the right company, hitchhiking can be easy and enjoyable, and a great way to meet friendly and interesting people. In the wrong company it can be disastrous. The lone hiker is especially vulnerable, and the lone woman is all but asking for trouble. One of the most sobering incidents in my experience came after an Outward Bound course, when one of our students was hitchhiking home from her month in the mountains. She never made it.

The safest way to hitchhike is to choose your drivers, rather than to sub-mit yourself to their choice like a cow at an auction. Wait where cars are parked, preferably well off to one side, then approach any likely looking mo-torists and ask for a ride. This is particularly effective at popular trailheads. You may see backpackers loading their cars and preparing to drive out of the hills. If they appear to have room, introduce yourself and tell them of your needs.

If the trailhead has several parked cars but no people in evidence, then you might wait a while and see if any hikers return. If not, or if the parking lot is empty, you might decide to start walking the road in hopes of hitching a ride farther along. Be advised, though, that in walking along the road with your thumb out you are relinquishing much of your control. Be wary, and don't be afraid to make quick decisions. Even though you may have been trying to hitch a ride for hours, if someone pulls to a stop who looks or acts peculiar, leave the area. Remember that in the woods the advantage is yours.

Signs can work well, and large, black letters on a white background work best. Write something catchy that will let the motorists know that you are not a threat. Lyle Langlois, section hiker and computer professor, writes the math symbol "≈" (approximately equal to) in front of his destination. He figures that this distinguishes him from the usual derelicts, and he reports positive feedback from motorists who have stopped for him.

One eye for your pack and hang onto those valuables

During your summer's journey, carry your valuables – money, credit card, identification, journal, camera and exposed film – in a small, unobtrusive bag. Make it look like an uneaten sandwich or something which no one would be tempted to steal. And carry it with you whenever you must leave your backpack, for example when going into a post office to pick up a resupply box, or into a store to buy groceries.

When I say "leave your pack," I am not suggesting that you should leave it unattended. Several hikers who have done so have been ripped off. When going into a post office, leave your backpack *inside* the door where you can keep an eye on it, and again, carry your bag of valuables with you.

When entering a restaurant, ask if you may bring your backpack with you. If the answer is "yes," ask to be seated near the door, sparing you from having to lug your pack through the restaurant and possibly bumping into tables and other patrons. If the answer is "no," ask to be seated by a window, then place your backpack outside that window where you can watch it. And once again, keep your bag of valuables with you.

When entering a grocery store, leave your pack just inside the door, again where you can keep an eye on it while you shop. And yes, carry your bag of valuables with you. It helps if you greet the cashier and ask if it's ok to leave your pack there, and to show them your bag to allay any suspicions of shoplifting. Most clerks will appreciate this gesture. In rare instances the store will have a "no backpacks or bags inside" policy. If you are with hiking companions, then one of you might have to wait outside with the packs. The hiker who leaves a backpack outside a store is tempting some motorist to grab it and speed away, safe in the knowledge that you lack a car with which to give chase.

When showering in a public stall, leave your backpack just outside your shower stall, and part the curtain just enough so that you can keep an eye on things. Keep your bag of valuables inside the stall, out of the spray and away from where someone might reach over or under the partitions.

It's all a matter of common sense, really. And of maintaining a certain amount of vigilance.

Vicious dogs

I love dogs, and even though I feel they don't necessarily belong in the back-country, I don't mind seeing them there on occasion, as long as they are well behaved toward the wildlife and other hikers. And as long as the owner is carrying the dog poop 100 feet from the trail and water sources and burying it. Unfortunately, though, not all dogs encountered in the wilds are friendly, and while I would not intentionally hurt someone's pet, I feel that the hiker's safety comes first. My advice is this: Whenever you see *any* dog at a distance, pick up a few hefty rocks just in case. Ninety nine dogs out of a hundred are well mannered, and you will know by the way they approach you. The bark means very little. Look at the ears, lips, and tail. If the ears are upright and the tail is wagging then the dog is probably friendly. If the ears are pinned back and the teeth are bared, get ready to protect yourself with a well-aimed salvo or two. One connection is usually all it takes to inform a vicious dog that – surprise, surprise! – you can defend yourself.

Hiking Pace

Walking with Lightness and Economy of Motion

When I was on the Yukon trail
The boys would warn, when things were bleakest,
The weakest link's the one to fail—
Said I: "By Gosh! I won't be weakest. "
So I would strain with might and main,
Striving to prove I was the stronger,
Till sourdough Sam would snap: "Goldurn!
Go easy, son; you'll last the longer."

– R. Service, Take It Easy

Top runners may cover 20 miles a day when training for competition. But even backpackers can equal those mileages while carrying heavy loads over rugged terrain and gaining and losing thousands of feet in elevation. During our southbound PCT trek Jenny and I hiked from Elk Lake to Kennedy Meadows averaging 33.9 miles a day, unsupported for 39 consecutive days.

We once met a fellow who said he was running the trail. Receiving extensive assistance from load carriers, shuttle drivers, and resupply people, he and his companion carried no packs but wore a few extra garments wrapped around their waists. They were the epitome of fitness and almost military organization; however, they seemed to require one or more days of recuperation between nearly each day's travel. Because of the required recuperation time, perhaps, these fellows were actually among the season's slowest travelers. I don't mean to take the gentleman's approach out of context. His goal was to "run" the trail. But I do feel that the other hikers passing him demonstrated that the slower but steady approach gains the better overall mileage.

So the question is, what is the optimum hiking speed that maximizes the day's, and the week's mileages? Naturally, this depends on the terrain and the load carried. But I think we can quantify the matter by simply striving for the optimum cardiovascular rate.

Power-hiking

Running forces the cardiovascular rate far above its optimum, hence its inefficiency. The same is true of power-hiking. Jenny and I were introduced to power-hiking during our trek of the Appalachian Trail. We began on the 8th of June, far behind about 1,500 other thru-hikers. After our first month we started catching up with them, and for the remaining distance we passed dozens each day. We reached Katahdin behind only about 25 others, most of whom had been on the trail six months and longer.

I mention all this merely to describe the benefits of hiking more efficiently. We passed AT thru-hikers by the hundreds, yet I cannot recall a single instance where we actually passed someone on the trail. Invariably, they were resting or camping when we happened by. However, we were passed time and again by power-hikers. Why were they trying to hike so fast? Competition, it seemed to us. Whenever we would come to a thru-hiker resting alongside the trail, we knew we would soon be passed. Then maybe an hour after the sweating, laboring dynamo had sped past us, we would catch up to him or her resting beside the trail again. Or more likely we would come to a trail junction where the power-hiker had powered out of sight, as indicated by the boot tracks. We passed these people only because we continued hiking long after they had stopped for the day. Why did we continue? Because we were not tired, even though we were more than doubling their mileages.

I look at it the other way. By hiking too fast while carrying heavy packs they were cutting their distances by half – with no extra enjoyment, it seemed to us.

Whole-body control

My definition of "power-hiking" is this: striving for maximum leg rate while disregarding heart rate. Instead, for best performance we need to tune in to our hearts and keep them beating at their most efficient levels. We regulate our heart's beats per minute by slowing or speeding our pace. This is a conscious exercise in whole-body control, not merely in leg control.

Whole-body conditioning begins at home, not during the training hikes but on the floor or ground, with contemplative exercises in deep breathing and body awareness. These teach us to listen to the beating of our hearts. Find a quiet place, sit on a special mat reserved for these exercises, block out the world and concentrate on the inner workings of your body. Feel the blood surging through arteries in your neck and upper arms. Feel your heart beating and your lungs expanding and contracting. Practice this every day during your training period.

Once you have learned this cardio-awareness at home, you can start practicing it on the trail. By focusing inward and paying careful attention not to over-exert or under-exert, even for a moment, you will hike the farthest each day for the least expended energy.

Going uphill and downhill

The gang buster's pace is counter-productive, but there are times when the circumstances might behoove us to hike at slightly elevated pulse rates.

Let's imagine we hike 10 miles on level ground at 3 mph. Except for periods of rest we would cover the distance in 3.33 hours. Now instead of hiking level ground, let's say that we have a hill to surmount. We hike slower uphill for 5 miles, and reaching the top we hike faster 5 miles down the other side. Will we still travel the 10 miles in 3.33 hours? For an answer, let's examine the following table. In each case, a certain speed is subtracted from the 3 mph going uphill, and then added back double on the descent.

Steepness of hill	Speed while hiking 5 miles uphill	Speed while hiking 5 miles downhill	Time required to hike the 10 miles
flat	3 mph	3 mph	3.3 hours
moderate	2 mph	4 mph	3.8 hours
steep	1 mph	5 mph	6.0 hours
craggy	0.5 mph	5.5 mph	10.9 hours

So we see that scurrying downhill at a fast clip does not even begin to recoup the time it takes to hike slowly uphill. This is because while hiking uphill we are traveling slower for a longer period of time, and the two effects multiply against each other to our disadvantage. This demonstrates the benefits of hiking uphill at a slightly elevated heart rate, and the futility of trying to make up for lost time by surging downhill.

Tight calved hiking

The steepness of the slope, the ruggedness of terrain, and the weight in your pack will all affect your uphill and downhill speeds. And they will affect how tight your calves become as well. But more importantly, so will your gait. If you pull your heels off the ground prematurely with each step, and if you shove off too hard with the ball of the foot and toes, then you are overworking your calves. These exaggerated motions waste precious effort, stiffen the muscles, and increase the chances of injury. For the hiker in the journey's early stages they can even create blisters on the ball of the foot and on the toes.

Critique your tracks. Craters at the ball of the foot and toes indicate you might be pushing off too hard. When walking on soft sand or crusty snow, the toe push will actually retard progress. In this case practice *lifting* the toes at the end of the stride, rather than shoving ahead with them. Walking on firm ground, a certain amount of toe push is beneficial. How much is a matter of terrain and personal style. Also, when looking at your tracks, look for duck walking: toes turned out. For the most efficient stride, keep your feet tracking generally in line with your direction of travel.

Hiking with the brakes on

Another factor that can contribute to an inefficient stride is unnecessarily tensing muscles that are not being used for forward progress. During each step, the leg's anterior, or forward muscles draw the leg quickly ahead. Then they must quickly relax to allow the posterior, or rearward muscles to draw the leg back. If the forward muscles fail to relax fast enough they resist the rearward muscles. This inadvertent braking action holds true with a multitude of opposing muscle groups in the body and lower extremities. On occasion you might practice what I call the "robo meltdown." Without breaking your stride, tense all your muscles like a robot, then slowly decrease the tension until you achieve the bare minimum of stiffness required to carry on.

The rest step

I learned the rest step at a Sierra Club climbing class back in 1964, and have used it ever since for climbing steep slopes, particularly those that are snow-packed. The idea is to rest momentarily on the back leg with its knee locked, then take the next step by leaning forward while bending the forward knee. As the weight comes onto the forward leg, straighten its knee. This uses an entirely different set of leg muscles than normal walking, and is an excellent way to moderate the pace when climbing a steep slope.

Cruising

In his book *Maximum Performance* (Simon & Schuster, 1977), Laurence E. Morehouse describes a technique he calls "walking in cruising mode," which in my opinion is quite similar to the rapid walk / slow run technique used by South American natives for many hundreds of years. The method is to walk with the knees slightly flexed and the head held steady without bobbing up and down. Crouch a few inches lower than you normally walk, and pretend you are carrying a jug of water on your head. Start slowly, then build a little speed. Once skilled at this you can cover the miles more quickly and with less effort. It requires an ultralight backpack, and it is, incidentally, a good way to pull a hamstring or give yourself shin splints if you are not well conditioned for these type of movements. Jenny and I use the method on occasion when we want cover a few quick miles. And I mean very quick miles.

Thumb loops

While hiking, our arms dangle and swing like pendulums in cadence with our step. But because the arm muscles are not being used, the vessels enlarge and the blood tends to "pool" in the fingers and hands. Several hours of this can stiffen these extremities. To counteract this we can elevate our hands occasionally and hook the thumbs inside the backpack's shoulder straps, at chest height, or into special thumb or wrist loops tied to the shoulder straps. Not only will this help reduce the swelling in the fingers and hands, but it will relieve the shoulders and help ventilate the lungs by encouraging the chest cavity to expand a little more efficiently.

Interludes

To break a monotonous rhythm we might turn and walk several steps sideways, or turn completely around and walk a ways backward. I know this sounds ridiculous, but try it. Remember that we are not soldiers or hiking droids. Be creative with your hiking style. Strive for efficiency but season it with a little variety. Variety is the spice of life. And it is also the spice of long distance hiking.

Divide the day in thirds

Here's a technique that Jenny and I use when adhering to a higher mileage itinerary: Let's say we want to hike a 33 mile day. We divide the day into three sections of 5½ hours each. During each segment we need to cover 11 miles. Thirty three miles in one day might seem like a lot, but it requires averaging only 2.0 miles an hour. We consider this a very reasonable average, mainly as it includes the rest stops. But of course it also mandates that the rest stops be fairly short.

Daily Mileage	Hours hiked	Segment Mileage	Segment 1	Segment 2	Segment 3
24	12	8	6 am – 10 am	10 am – 2 pm	2 pm – 6 pm
27	13.5	9	6 am – 10:30	10:30 – 3 pm	3 pm – 7:30
30	15	10	6 am – 11 am	11 am – 4 pm	4 pm – 9 pm
33	16.5	11	5:30 – 11 am	11 am – 4:30	4:30 - 10 pm

The table summarizes the triple-segmented day for various daily mileages, at an average hiking rate of 2.0 mph. Select a daily mileage and divide it in thirds, and divide your day in thirds.

Optimum resting

As we hike along the trail, the muscles in our legs actually help pump blood back up to our heart. That is why doctors call our legs "our second heart." Also, the leg muscles keep their blood vessels properly sized. When we stop and rest, our leg muscles relax and allow their vessels to enlarge. This is called "vaso-dilation." As a result, the blood drains down into the lower legs and feet.

The restorative effects of a rest depend almost entirely on ample circulation supplying nutrients and oxygen to the tired muscles, and removing the waste products of metabolism. Sitting down to rest on a log or rock at chair height is an extremely inefficient way to rest. It pools the blood into the lower legs and feet, and hampers circulation enormously. Hikers who rest this way are squandering precious resting time. A much better resting position is to sit on the ground with the legs extended, preferably with the legs also elevated a few inches. But by far the best resting position is to lie on the back and elevate the legs and feet to heart level by resting them on a log, rock, or backpack. Jenny and I often carry our foam sleeping pads secured to the outside of one of our packs, specifically to use as resting pads. The pads serve mainly to keep the backs of our shirts, pants, and heads out of the dirt.

A good night's rest

Optimum circulation is equally vital for a restorative night's sleep. For the same reasons as above, the conscientious distance hiker sleeps with the legs slightly elevated. The greater the fatigue at the end of the day, the more the blood will pool in the legs and feet during the night if they are significantly below heart level. This restricts circulation.

In his book *Walking My Way*, (Hogarth Press, 1984) John Merrill writes: "Use your evenings to recover. At the end of the day's walk, after installing myself in my tent, I remain lying down until the next morning. This is essential for one's legs. After twelve hours' rest, one's tiredness has gone and one's vitality has been restored."

Water

We'll never know the worth of water till the well goes dry.

– Scottish Proverb

Backpackers often suffer the notion that they must stay dry at all costs. They imagine that if their clothing becomes wet it will be useless, and if their bodies become wet they will plunge into hypothermia. Their view of water as a nemesis affects their drinking of it also. They fear the harmful microbes it may contain, and they are reluctant to drink water in the evening because it will prompt them to get up in the middle of the night. As a result of these fears they spend $350 on a waterproof parka, and consider drinking water a sign of weakness.

Thirst is mainly psychological, as we shall see in this chapter. But it is not a human weakness. Nor can hikers condition their bodies to needing less water. The simple fact is, the dehydrated hiker is far less capable.

On any hike, long or short, the higher altitudes and greater levels of exertion can sap water out of the hikers' body like a sponge. The ensuing dehydration robs them of energy and vitality, gives them headaches and constipation, and leaves them vastly more susceptible to stress injuries.

Water as an anatomical lubricant

We are essentially walking waterbags. Our bodies are 70% water; our brains are 75% water, and our blood is 90% water. As we hike along the trail we lose some of this through respiration, sweat and insensible perspiration, and through urination. We must replace these losses by drinking plenty of water at regular intervals.

This is particularly important for us hikers because water lubricates the joints in our hips, knees and ankles, just as oil lubricates machinery. Dehydration increases friction, and this, too, increases our susceptibility to injury.

Moreover, as our blood dehydrates it thickens and decreases in volume. This slows circulation and increases blood pressure. Fuel and oxygen delivery to the muscles decreases, as does the removal of the by-products of metabolism. Thus, we tire sooner and more profoundly. Thicker blood also impedes the brain's activities, leaving us less capable in our mental and emotional processes.

Water is the best re-hydrator

People are often deeply dehydrated without realizing it. They may drink plenty of fluids, but usually very little pure water. For all practical purposes, H_2O is the only fluid capable of rehydrating the high-mileage hiker's body. Soda pop, sports drinks, powdered milk, and flavoring crystals (if mixed strongly) add very little to the body's fluid balance. And of course coffee and beer are all likely to cause even deeper dehydration.

Thirst is mainly psychological

Strive to stay well hydrated, but don't panic when confronted with the occasional and unavoidable period of thirst. You can safely hike for many hours feeling terribly thirsty, and you can even make camp feeling the same – as long as you re-hydrate yourself thoroughly at the next water source. While driven in thirst to that next water source, remember that thirst is greatly intensified with incessant thoughts of cold drinks. Force your mind away from the water that you do not have. Once you learn to live more in the present moment your psyche will no longer work so hard against you. And thirst, in this instance, will no longer be such a tormenting influence.

Because thirst is mainly psychological, we distance hikers must never rely on it to tell us when we need to drink water. For one thing, by the time we feel thirsty we are already dehydrated. For another, drinking even a small amount of cold water often satisfies the psychological need, yet drinking even an entire stomach-full would not satisfy the physical need. Those who rely on thirst are likely to walk away from the water sources still deeply dehydrated.

Don't wait for thirst. Drink large quantities of water as often as your system can tolerate. Monitor your urinary output. If it diminishes in quantity and darkens in color, you are deeply dehydrated. Guard against that by planning for your fluid needs ahead of time. Carry enough water so that you can drink freely all the way to the next source. But at the same time, don't waste energy by carrying too much. As a rule, when you reach the next source your bottles should be empty.

Water sources

According to conventional backpacking wisdom, virtually all wilderness water sources are contaminated with giardia, and we hikers and campers need to purify every drop that we drink, as well as what we use for cooking and brushing our teeth. You can read this in hundreds of magazine articles and books. Jenny and I followed these rules faithfully during the first four of our five mega-hikes. And I was sick with giardia-like symptoms many times.

Obviously, something was wrong. If I was treating the water, then why was I not staying healthy? Jenny was staying healthy, and she was drinking the same filtered water. Apparently my immunities were lower than hers. But the fact remains that somehow I seemed to be contracting parasites despite my assiduous use of the water filter. The filter cartridges we were using were common, brand-name varieties, and we had no reason to suspect they were not working properly.

I decided to test a few theories, on the basis that I didn't have much to lose. While training for our third PCT journey we drank from natural sources, just a few sips at first, then gradually increasing the intake, allowing ourselves to adapt to the water's flora. Then during the actual journey we drank all our water straight from the springs, creeks, and sometimes from the lakes. And for the first time on any long trail I suffered no giardia-like symptoms. Nor did Jenny.

My theory, and it is only that, is threefold:

- Presently, many water sources along the PCT are as pristine as any bottled water sold commercially. Water from them does not need to be treated.

- But of course, many other sources are polluted, some to the extent that no water treatment system available to backpackers is capable of making water from them safe to drink.

- Another primary source of pathogens is fecal contamination, however microscopically.

Based on these theories, my advice is this: Learn to recognize pristine water, and treat it if you prefer. Learn to recognize contaminated water, and realize that it can be extremely virulent. Don't filter it or chemically treat it. Don't boil it or cook with it. And don't wash with it. And finally, after eliminating, sterilize your hands.

One of the most common contaminants in backcountry water is giardia. So let's have a look at what it is and what it does.

Giardia

Occurring worldwide, Giardia[1] lamblia, the protozoan, causes giardiasis, the intestinal infection. When giardia cysts are ingested by animals, including humans, they metamorphose into trophozoites and attach themselves to the

---

[1] Gee-ARE-dee-uh Lam-BLEE-ah (after Alfred Mathieu Giard (1846-1908), French zoologist). Gee-are-DIE-uh-sis. Protozoan: an animal-like, single cell organism. Tro-pho-ZO-ite: a protozoan in the active stage of its life cycle.

small intestine. Once there, they can begin interfering with the host's diges-
tion. Later, the trophozoites encyst, and after the millions of new cysts travel
down the colon they are excreted. Thus, the host acts as a reservoir. And if
infected stools contaminate a water source, the disease can spread to those
mammals later drinking that water. Thus, the cycle repeats.

Biologist, research physiologist, and long-distance hiker Chris Oswald
and I have had some interesting discussions about the topic of giardia and its
transmission. She notes that, "The cysts of Giardia lamblia can survive at
least 2 months outside of a host. So it is quite a simple matter for the parasite
to be transmitted from one host to another via water (or soil or plants) contaminated by the feces of an infected animal."

I imagine that parasites of giardia have existed as a normal part of the
intestinal flora in mammals for millennia. Giardiasis, the infection, however,
is another matter altogether. Previously, people and animals were reasonably
immune to it. Their defenses produced antibodies that fought off the microbes
and stayed their effects. But within the past few decades, three factors have
probably contributed to the increased risks of contracting giardiasis.

- Being chemically, electrically, and mechanically treated, our municipal
  water is practically devoid of giardia. Because at home these microbes
  are no longer entering our digestive tracts, our bodies have generally quit
  producing the necessary antibodies.

- Medicinal antibiotics have expunged pre-existing parasites from our
  bodies. Again as a result of living in such civil sterility, we have relinquished much of our natural immunities.

- Giardia cysts might be far more numerous in the backcountry than in
  years past, perhaps because humans and livestock, including cattle,
  horses, mules, and llamas in escalating numbers are polluting the water
  sources.

Regardless of the cause, when we venture afield and drink the water, we risk
becoming sick. I say "risk" because giardiasis ordinarily does not produce
symptoms. Many hikers, if not most, who remain afield for extended periods
become unknowing parasitic hosts without showing significant ill effects.
Staying healthy is mainly a matter of ingesting a minimum of pathogens,
while developing immunities to those which cannot be avoided.

When symptoms occur, they might do so only weakly or intermittently.
Or they might be quite pronounced. They would range from flatulence to
malabsorption, and include diarrhea, nausea, and abdominal pain. Hikers who
begin exhibiting these symptoms have every chance of producing the needed
antibodies. Those who choose to ride the symptoms out, as I have always

done, would do well to increase their intake of water in order to reduce the malady's dehydrating effects. Those who find themselves with increasing symptoms should visit a doctor in case the ailment is not giardiasis. Dr. Forgey (see Bibliography) recommends carrying Diasorb, in tablet form. This is one of the more powerful non-prescription anti-diarrheal medications. Otherwise, you might plan ahead and carry a prescribed medication such as metronidazole (the generic name for Flagyl). But use it only as a last resort, as it could reduce your natural immunities further.

Treat your water

As I mentioned, Jenny and I were testing my theories on water contamination and avoidance during our most recent PCT hike, and not treating our drinking water. And because we were trying to go ultralight, a 7.5 ounce water filter seemed prohibitively heavy. As our journey progressed, and as we drank of the many springs and creeks along the way, we found ourselves drinking maybe three times as much water as we had when using a filter. It was that much easier and more convenient, and we feel that this extra intake benefited us greatly.

If you are accustomed to drinking "bush water," if you can recognize pristine water when you see it, and if you are hiking higher daily mileages – allowing you to bypass suspect sources with impunity – then you might not need to treat your water. Even so, consider that your summer's journey may not be the best occasion to experiment with your digestive tract's vitality. I recommend you play it safe and treat your drinking water.

Water treatment options

Boiling

When using the boiling method you can turn off the heat after the water reaches a rolling boil. Because of the time required to boil and cool the water, however, and because of the fuel consumed, this method is not so expedient. It is, however, effective at killing viruses, but I've not heard of viral infections, such as hepatitis, affecting PCT hikers.

Adding chemicals

The backpacker's usual water treatment chemical is iodine, in its many commercial forms. In this application I think iodine has a few advantages and a host of disadvantages. One advantage is that it is lightweight and compact.

One disadvantage of using iodine to treat all drinking water is the large amount that the thru-hiker would ingest during the full course of the summer. Two tablets, for example, for each quart of water, perhaps six quarts a day, for months on end. That would be a huge amount of chemical coursing through the system, and to a certain extent iodine is cumulative, which is why the municipal treatment plants don't use it.

Hikers could use it only occasionally, to treat water of suspect quality. But again I recommend against trying to treat obviously polluted water. The label on one product states "all waters can be made bacteriologically suitable for drinking when treated with [the product.]" This is very loose wording, so let me tighten it somewhat: hikers who rely on any product to treat genuinely polluted water are taking enormous chances.

Besides the large quantity of the chemical ingested, another disadvantage of iodine treatment is its required 20 minute soak-time with cold water. And most water along the PCT is indeed cold. Imagine hiking most of the day between distant water sources in very hot weather, arriving at a water source at long last, and having to wait 20 minutes to take a drink! What usually happens is that the hiker adds the chemicals and waits only a short while before drinking. Microbes don't die that quickly, and when the dehydrated hiker drinks the solution, the walls of the stomach and intestines act like water filters, absorbing both the water and the iodine, leaving the microbes to seek their niche in the digestive tract.

Chlorine is the treatment of choice in most municipal facilities. The Sierra Water Purifier® uses a very strong solution of chlorine to kill the microbes (strong enough that the solution has a very strong smell of chlorine), then an equally strong solution of hydrogen peroxide (H_2O_2)to remove the chlorine. The chemical reaction of the two yields water, salt, and oxygen. That is: calcium hypochlorite + hydrogen peroxide = calcium chloride + water + oxygen. Or in more technical terms: $Ca(OCl)_2 + 2H_2O_2 = CaCl_2 + 2H_2O + 2O_2$ I consider this treatment, when used intelligently, superior to iodine treatment.

Filtering

Filtration units with maximum porosity of about two microns will catch most giardia protozoa. The finer the filtration, the more resistance to water passing through it, and the slower it operates and the less water it can treat before clogging. Improved models are becoming more available, and I would recommend them as the water treatment of choice. Their disadvantages are their weight, expense, and the effort to pump the water through them, unless gravity fed. The advantages are that they treat the water very quickly, and they prevent the vast majority of critters from entering the digestive tract.

Even so, no filter can keep the hiker's body free of pathogens. It might be misused or defective, or a few protozoa might slip through regardless. And the microbes can enter the hiker's body in other ways, for example when bathing or moping the face with a wet hand towel. Or when washing the hands in untreated water, wiping them on a pant leg, then reaching into the bag of gorp for a snack. Giardia is ordinarily a water-borne parasite, but it does not need water to survive. After you wash the cookpot, cup and spoon in untreated water, and towel them dry, the giardia might cling to them. We can also be our own source of protozoa – remember that bag of gorp and our not so clean hands.

I mentioned earlier that contaminated water can be far more virulent than commonly believed. As long-distance hikers, then, we can greatly benefit in the ability to judge the degree of contamination of the natural water sources.

Judging the quality of a water source

Judging the purity of water is a wilderness skill. The more we practice, the better our accuracy. The general method is this: First, we look at the water. If it contains a lot of decayed plant matter, then it is probably unsafe to drink. This organic matter usually harbors bacteria and fungus, working to decompose it. And it probably contains other adverse microorganisms as well. All of these can infect the human digestive tract. However, if you find only a few bits of plant matter, and if there is no chance of livestock upstream, then you might treat it safely by one of the above methods.

Water that appears clear is not always reliable. After all, most pathogens are invisible to the human eye. So we need to ask ourselves where the water is coming from. If it is flowing as a small brook, then we would consider the terrain upstream. We look at the map and see if there are lakes or ponds upstream. If there are chances of meadows and cows, better give it a miss. Otherwise, it's probably ok. If the water is emanating from the ground as a spring, then the water is probably safe to drink, as is. I say "probably" because we must also examine the area above the spring. Infrequently, we might find a pond or boggy area from which the water is percolating into the earth and resurfacing as our spring. This water would be subject to contamination. Let's look at these considerations in more detail:

Creeks

The "average" creek along the PCT contains good water. How do we know? We don't, but again we can make a good guess by examining where the creek is coming from. If from the high country, the water is probably ok. Generally, the higher in elevation, the better the water. (Before descending into a valley, then, it's often a good idea to fill our bottles.) But if we are in low country and the creek is wending along a valley bottom, beware. It might be polluted by beaver, or far worse, by cattle.

If we find animal feces in the water, then that water is obviously contaminated and should be categorically avoided. Horse and mule feces are the most commonly encountered form of pollution along the PCT. Cow manure is next, followed by that of domestic sheep. In my 35 years of hiking I don't recall seeing wild animal dung in a water source; but of course I don't discount the possibility. Some wild animals live in the water and we can assume that they pollute it. If we come to a creek with signs of beaver, such as beaver dams or food sources like willow and aspen growing alongside the banks, then we can assume the water is polluted, particularly if it is not flowing swiftly and voluminously.

More significantly, though, if we come to a creek in a broad valley where cattle could be grazing upstream, then that water is almost guaranteed to be contaminated. Grazing livestock is the thirsty PCT hiker's nemesis. Pollution aside, I have found it amazing how just a few cattle can destroy an otherwise pristine water source. Deer, elk, bear and all the wild animals will drink from a pristine spring without harming it in the slightest. And they have obviously been doing this for eons. But the first cow that comes along can decimate it. Suddenly it is little more than muddy ground and dung – rendered useless to hikers and our wild animal friends. Horses can do the same.

Standing at a creek, water flowing cold and crystal clear, judge for yourself as to the possibility of cattle grazing upstream. I have seen strong evidence of how cattle pollution has made hikers very sick, regardless of how they tried to purify it.

Springs

I consider springs to be the PCT hiker's ultimate sources of water. In fact, since discovering how important they are to good health, I've come to think of them as sacred – as did many of the native Americans. They are not sacred to modern hikers who rely on so-called purification methods, and who are often sick, just as I was. One of our tactics on that southbound trek, then, was to bypass open water sources in favor of more distant springs.

How much water to carry

A liter of drinking water carried in the backpack increases the load by approximately 2½ pounds. To the packweight-conscious hiker, that is the equivalent weight of 5,000 trimmed map borders, 3,763 sawn-off toothbrush handles, and 3 extra tent stakes. Why do we carry the water? We need it, of course, unlike all those toothbrush handles. But we do not need to carry too much.

My technique is to rest near a water source, while drinking of it copiously ("super-saturating," I call it), then to press ahead to the next source while carrying a minimal supply. Where the next source is distant I carry enough to drink freely every hour, but not so much that I would have some left over. This is not difficult to plan, thanks to the information on maps or in guide books. In rare instances when my water bottles become depleted, due to an oversight on my part, and when the next water source is yet distant, I accept the ensuing thirst and carry on as usual.

If you are filtering all your water, you might think about carrying your filtered water in quart or liter bottles, and during the long, waterless stretches, carrying your untreated water in a two- or three-gallon waterbag. Drink the filtered water from your bottles, then as they become depleted, stop and filter more water into them from the bag. That way, should the bag develop a leak, you won't lose as much water.

Collecting water from seeps

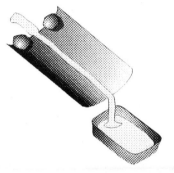

To fill a bag or bottle from a seep, use a piece of aluminum foil as a collection trough. Assuming the seep is flowing slightly, place the foil in it, then weight it down with a pair of stones at its up-hill end. Dig a small hole downstream, under the trough where the water is dribbling off. Place a small container in the hole as a catchment. Jenny and I once bought a single-serving box of corn flakes in a café on the AT. The cereal came in a little plastic tub, which we have used ever since for collecting water from shallow sources.

When filling a bottle from a deep but slow-moving source, submerge it before unscrewing its lid. This will prevent any floating debris from entering the bottle.

Hiking between distant water sources

Nature does not always place water at intervals convenient to us. But she does give us the intelligence and strength to travel from one to the next. Let's look at a few techniques.

The twenty mile waterless stretch

Let's suppose that water sources "A" and "B" are 20 miles apart. We reach point A in the mid afternoon, and there we cook dinner, but do not eat it. Instead, we stow it carefully in the backpack. Each of us fills a pair of one-liter or quart water bottles with treated water. Also, each pours a few quarts into a water bag. We also fill our stomachs and enjoy dundo showers (described on page 180). Setting off, we hike a few hours, then sit down and enjoy dinner.

Refreshed and revitalized, we continue with a will another several miles into the evening. There, we leave the trail and make a pleasant stealth camp. Next morning we rise at dawn and hike to water source B, where we will probably arrive mid-day and not long after having consumed the last of our water.

Twenty mile waterless stretches are fairly common along the PCT. Hikers using the above technique should be able to traverse them with no problems whatsoever.

The thirty mile waterless stretch

Now let's suppose that water sources A and B are 30 miles apart. Reaching point A mid morning, we each fill our pair of quart or liter bottles and load our water bag with another gallon per person. We drink our fill and bathe dundo-style nearby. Pressing on, we hike until late afternoon, then cook and eat dinner. Then we carry on determinedly into the evening and make a stealth camp away from the trail. Early morning we set off once again, and hike without dallying to water source B, arriving there perhaps in the afternoon.

Of course it is not often practical to time our arrivals at point A according to the above scenarios. In any case, the basic idea is to hike as far beyond water source A as possible before retiring for the day.

The sixty mile waterless stretch

During years of drought, hikers would of course bypass any desiccated or obviously polluted creeks. Using the above techniques and carrying more water, they should be able to hike much farther than 30 miles between viable water sources. The secret is to carry a lighter pack to begin with, so that the combined load does not become a crushing burden.

During our third PCT trip, Jenny and I hiked through southern California late in the summer. The days were broiling and often we had to carry water for 40 and 50 miles between sources. Our loads of water slowed progress, but otherwise they did not bother us. Our longest stretch was from Barrel Springs, over the San Felipe hills, bypassing trickling San Felipe Creek (of suspect purity that time of year) and continuing to the settlement at the summit of Mt. Laguna. We arrived with 2 quarts remaining in our bottles, having hiked about 60 miles. Had we needed to, I am sure we could have hiked much farther.

Survival time

How long can a person survive without water? According to contemporary medical knowledge, a person can walk without water in 90°F temperatures for five days. At 60°, survival is reputedly extended to eight days if the hiker is active, or ten if inactive.

But consider that in 1941 Slavomir Rawicz (RAW-witz) and six other escapees from a Siberian prison, plus one acquired along the way, walked across the Gobi Desert. Their story is described in Slavomir's book *The Long Walk*, (see Bibliography). Carrying neither food nor water, they walked 6½ days to the first oasis. With only a small mug to carry a pittance of water, they set off again and walked 13 days to an almost dried out creek. From there they began eating the occasional snake, and walked another 9 days to a trickling spring at the edge of the desert. Two of the party perished, but the others endured, and they taught us a great deal about the psychology of thirst, the effects of extended dehydration and starvation, and about the power of one's will to survive in the face of impossible odds.

Coffee & Alcohol

To be a successful distance hiker you must first be a successful athlete. Respecting your body is prerequisite, and that respect starts and finishes with proper nutrition. Feed and hydrate yourself properly, and not only will you feel and perform better, but in every probability you will experience a noticeable decline in your cravings for junk food, caffeine, and alcohol.

During our first PCT hike, my wristwatch alarm sounded at 5:30 am, and Jenny would reach out and ignite the stove and set on the coffee pot. We would rise, pack our gear, then hastily chug two cups of cafe-campo before shouldering our packs and setting off, usually by 6:15.

I had been drinking coffee all my adult life – ostensibly to stimulate alertness. In reality I was addicted to it, as indicated by the ensuing couple of months of low-level headaches when I quit drinking it. Jenny quit also, and before long we both began to notice an increased mental acuity.

During our second PCT hike, the alarm sounded at 4:40 am. We would rise, pack our gear, and set off typically by 5:00. Whereas breaking camp used to take 45 minutes, now released of the coffee rites we were afoot in 20 minutes, with vascular systems delightfully liberated of caffeine.

But by drinking the morning's coffee, weren't we helping to re-hydrate ourselves? No, coffee is a diuretic. We drink it brown, our kidneys filter out the particulates and solvents, and we pee it clear. Then begins the work of flushing the excretory organs, with water stolen from the cells. The result is a net loss of fluid. By refraining from the morning coffee, not only were Jenny and I able to maintain better fluid balance, but we also gained an extra 25 minutes every day. We used that time for hiking, but could have used it for sleeping, journal writing, or just relaxing and enjoying the surroundings. The fact is, boiling the water, infusing the (expensive) coffee grounds, letting the concoction steep, cool, and then drinking the brew like addicts was wasteful of both time and stove fuel.

A good substitute

We still enjoy coffee-like beverages at our evening camps and at home. Cafix® is my favorite, made from roasted grains and figs, and I also enjoy an occasional evening cup of Pero® Cappuccino; both sweetened with powdered milk.

Alcohol

Hikers who fail to eat adequate portions of corn pasta and other nutritionally beneficial foods can find themselves constantly driven by hunger. Almost every thought is focused on food, and the urge to reach the next waypoint of civilization can be almost overwhelming. And typically during the stampede into town they will not drink much water.

So they arrive at the store profoundly depleted. And it is here that they are most vulnerable to the sudden shock of junk food binge. They imagine these powerful cravings are the normal result of hard work, rather than the abnormal result of poor nutrition. So they celebrate their "success" with a six pack of beer.

Alcoholic beverages are powerful diuretics. They deepen the discharge of urine and leave the body severely dehydrated. In fact, the effects of a hangover are mainly those of acute dehydration. If you find that you must drink beer during your journey, then for your body's sake drink an equal amount of water along with it. For best results, though, drink just the water.

For refreshment I recommend V8® juice. Plan ahead by sending yourself cans of it, at least to those locations where there are no stores.

Stretching

Avoiding Muscular Brittleness

Long distance hiking places extraordinary demands on the leg muscles. In fact, it causes microscopic tears in them. In an attempt to guard against this damage, these muscles tend to stiffen. And this only leads to more damage. Regular, gentle stretching encourages these muscles to relax, and can do much to prevent the tears from growing larger and leading to a bona-fide injury. And I should note that drinking lots of water also encourages suppleness. If you know you have not been drinking enough water, stretch only with extreme gentleness.

In his *Yoga 28 Day Exercise Book*,[1] Richard Hittleman writes, "[Stretching] requires a minimum of effort to attain maximum results." In other words, stretch only until you feel a slight pull, and no more. Otherwise the muscles being stretched can actually shrink, again in an attempt to guard themselves. I have gone through Hittleman's 28-day program many times and recommend it highly. But I would caution the high-mileage hiker against working the joints away from the axes in which they are daily being used. Out-of-axes *exercising* strengthens the ligaments; out-of-axes *stretching* tends to weaken them. So for example, hikers should refrain from practicing the lotus position, which can weaken the knees laterally.

Before we can stretch a muscle we must relax it. Otherwise, it will probably stiffen and might even tear. Relaxing a muscle is not easy, especially after it has been propelling us along the trail for several hours. It can be done, but it takes practice.

One of the first mistakes novice hikers make with their calf stretching exercises is to practice them while standing upright and without the aid of a balancing object. The reason they are balancing upright is that their calf muscles are subconsciously and continuously flexing and relaxing. To relax those muscles would be to immediately fall over. So, in order to relax a calf muscle you must lean against a tree or rock, and use your arms for balance instead. Let's look at the specifics:

---

[1] See Bibliography.

The hiker's leg stretch

This is a most important stretching exercise for the distance hiker. Practice it not only during your hiking hours, but in the morning before setting off, and in the evening before retiring.

The hiker's leg stretch is a modification of the classic runner's calf stretch. Perform it by standing face to a rock, embankment, or tree, with your feet positioned a yard or more out from it's base. Lean in and brace your hands against it, elbows locked straight – as though about to do a push up.

Stretch one leg at a time. Let's stretch the right one first: Lock the right knee straight, heel flat on the ground. Cross the left leg in front of it, toe on the ground and heel slightly elevated. The back of the left knee is pressed against the front of the right knee for support. This helps the right leg relax by preventing its knee from buckling, and it shunts most of the balancing mechanisms that would interfere with the relaxing. Don't let your right ankle pronate, or roll inward, as this would place great strain on the ligaments. If your ankle naturally pronates, which most do to some extent, place the inner edge of your right foot on a small rock or stick for support.

Once in position, slowly bend your elbows, bringing your body closer to the tree while stretching the right calf. Relax, feel the stretch, push away slightly, and hold for 20 heartbeats.

Lift the right leg and let the foot hang limp. If you have been hiking vigorously you might feel an increasing throbbing, caused by the muscle relaxing, the blood vessels dilating, and the blood pooling. This throbbing is a sure indication that you need to give much more attention to the stretching exercises, and to keep them gentle. When the dangling calf has relaxed as much as it's going to, and the throbbing has eased, place the foot back down gently, and repeat the stretching procedure with the other leg.

For the second leg stretching exercise, it helps to have a small platform, such as a rock, log, or sloped embankment, on which to rest the foot. Something no more than 6 inches high. Leaning forward against the tree, the right foot back, heel flat on the ground but without locking the knee, bring the left foot forward and place it on the object. Without placing body weight on the forward foot, rock it up onto the ball, flexing the toes back gently. Do not pivot the ankle and stretch it out-of-axis. Now, relax the leg and allow it to sag, such that its weight flexes the ankle. Hold that position for 20 heartbeats. The forward calf should be feeling a nice stretch. Repeat with the legs reversed.

✖

Regular calf stretching will do much to keep you injury free on the trail. Make these exercises a part of your everyday routine.

Foot Care

Why is it that we often neglect our feet during regular personal hygiene? Perhaps because they are so far away. Out of sight, out of mind, as it were. Still, for the long distance hiker these distant relatives deserve our very best care and attention.

———————

Imagine the complexity: each of our feet have 250,000 sweat glands, which altogether exude ½ to 1 pint of sweat per day. And this is when we are at rest – the sweating is far more profuse while we are hiking, especially in hot weather. So keeping our feet ventilated is a major concern, and one that is not well addressed by heavy socks, shoes, or especially boots. For best results wear thin socks, and change and wash them often. Unless the weather is frigid, avoid heavy socks, which act like ovens. In torrid climates those double layer, padded "blister free" socks can actually be "blister makers." In desert climes you might try placing a pair of foam insoles in your shoes for added insulation from the hot ground. Choose lightweight shoes that breathe. Buy them at least 1½ or 2 sizes larger than usual. They will not feel like clown shoes once your feet swell to proper working size, after you have hiked a few hundred miles. And split them open when they start feeling a little tight. Also, remove your shoes and socks at each rest stop, and in camp. Rest with your feet and legs elevated. Consider further toughening your feet by walking a short ways barefoot each day – just watch where you step. Try to wash your feet at least once a day, using the "dundo" technique. Dry them thoroughly and apply antifungal solution, particularly between the toes and around the toenails. Blister prevention starts by attacking your athlete's foot fungus with a vengeance – even if you don't know you have it. Be sure to wear your sandals when in public places. When necessary, trim your toenails in a slight curve, and not too close.

Ok, you didn't do any of that, and now your feet are blistered.

Blister first aid

The first step in the treatment of blisters is to determine what caused them, and to try to remedy it. Otherwise, it will prevent the blisters from heeling. If your toes are covered in blisters, they are probably infected with athlete's foot, and your shoes are probably much too small. If the side of your heel is blistered, then your shoe is rubbing at that spot. Try cutting that part of the shoe away. Cut a small hole initially, hike a ways and feel for any difference, then enlarge the hole in stages, making sure the shoe still performs well. Maybe you were wearing too many socks. These can take up valuable space inside your shoes.

Regardless of where and how large your blisters are, they were caused by your footwear. Remove the footwear, and all the tape you may have applied, and the blisters will immediately begin to heal. Three days of this and your feet will be practically as good as new. Keep this in mind the next time you imagine that your blisters are threatening to send you home. Two or three days respite is all you need, and that is a tiny fraction of your summer. So don't despair, and remember that even one full day completely off your feet can work wonders.

When the pain of walking on blistered feet becomes unbearable, remove your socks and all the dressings and tape, wash your feet and put them back into your shoes naked. Then head for civilization for a few rest days. And remember that when you start out again your feet will be subject to the same ol' blisters if you didn't change what caused them in the first place. So during those days of rest, keep your feet clean, aired, and well coated in antifungal liquid. And buy a larger pair of shoes and a few thinner pairs of socks.

Now let's talk about how to treat a single blister on your foot or toe, while on the trail.

If the blister is not too pronounced, wash and dry it, and cover it with a *breathable*-fabric adhesive strip: a Band-Aid® or its generic equivalent. Avoid applying the adhesive part to the blister, because it might worsen the injury when being removed. If the adhesive strip doesn't stick, you could coat the skin with tincture of benzoin, and after it dries, apply a new bandage. This is how I taped my fingers and hands against abrasion when climbing in Yosemite. However, you will probably not be carrying tincture of benzoin. And I don't recommend it as a skin toughener – that is just another myth – but you will probably be carrying a few patches of moleskin, and this sticks extremely well to *clean* skin. Too well, at times, which is why I use it only rarely. When being removed it tends to pull up some of the good along with the bad and ugly.

Also, you might carry a partial roll of white adhesive tape. This is useful for bandaging blisters, and is the recommended first aid treatment in the unlikely event of a sprained ankle, although a properly tied bandanna would also suffice. However, avoid applying too much tape to your blisters. It can actually worsen their condition by increasing the crowding that caused them, by restricting mobility, and by reducing the ventilation and heat dissipation.

If you find that the adhesive strips and tape are not helping, it's time to get serious.

If the blister is bloated with fluid, dab the area with antiseptic – I recommend hydrogen peroxide – and lance it with a flame-sterilized needle. Blot the fluid with a square of toilet paper dabbed in hydrogen peroxide. Then apply a layer of Spenco 2nd Skin.™

2nd Skin is expensive but so valuable that I recommend you include a few packages in your resupply parcels and drift box, and that you carry a full package in your first aid kit. I also recommend that you carry extra 2nd Skin Adhesive Knit patches. The ones included in the kits always seem to run out long before the gel sheets. If you find that you are not using your 2nd Skin, count your blessings and dispense it to any blister-footed hikers you meet along the way.

Start by cutting out a piece of gel only as large as the blister you are treating. This gel comes sandwiched between two layers of plastic. Remove the cellophane on one side, apply the raw gel to the blister, then remove the cellophane from the outside. Then secure the gel in place with a larger strip of the adhesive knit.

The gel is 96% water and must be kept hydrated. Add half a spoonful of filtered or treated water to the bag containing the gel sheets every few days. Also, apply a few drops of treated water to the patches on your feet, once or twice during the day. At day's end, remove the dressings and dispose of them in your litter bag. If needed the following morning, apply fresh ones.

Burn first aid

Say you knock a boiling hot beverage onto your foot, like I once did during a sea kayaking expedition, and you watch in dismay as a large patch of skin shrivels and sloughs away. 2nd Skin is also an excellent dressing for first, second and third degree burns. Wash the area gently with non-medicated soap. Then apply the 2nd Skin gel and adhesive knit. Keep the dressing hydrated by applying sterile water once in awhile. If the skin later becomes red and swollen, this may indicate an infection – apply a triple antibiotic ointment.

The ravages of athlete's foot

This topic is so important that it warrants a more detailed discussion. I estimate that athlete's foot is a key factor in 95% of all hiking-related blisters. This parasite is ubiquitous, and although most people don't realize they have it, it is always present on everyone's skin. Nevertheless, the surest indication of the infection is underfoot dead skin that you can scrape away with your fingernails after soaking in a hot bath, or a lack of foot and toe callous. And these are the malady's most debilitating features. Too much callous is detrimental, but because the fungus consumes all callous, it is the scourge of the distance hiker, whose battle against it should be never ending. I recommend that whether you think you have the infection or not, at the onset of your training program, five months in advance of your hike, you start treating your feet daily. Apply a *liquid*, or liquid spray antifungal solution. The powders and spray powders are not nearly as effective.

Never step barefooted into a tub or shower, or even onto dry concrete, tile, linoleum or carpet. This applies not only when in motels, but even in your own home. While on journey, protect your feet with sandals, home-made shower booties, or simple plastic bags secured with rubber bands or cord. Or wear your thickest socks and wash them in soap and hot water afterwards. At home you can wear beach thongs, disinfected occasionally in a microwave oven. After showering, dry your feet well and apply the anti-fungus medicine. On the trail you can carry this medication in a small vial.

Another hazard with showering *barefooted* in public stalls is the danger of contracting a plantar wart. Once the wart develops it feels like a sharp pebble on the bottom of your foot. It is caused by a virus which can be transmitted by someone else with such a wart.

Foot care at the rest stops

A big part of foot care is ventilating, cooling, and resting the feet properly at the rest stops. When hiking in hot and dry weather, during the morning rest stops you might place your bare feet flat against a shaded rock, which can impart a wonderfully cooling effect. Another option is to place them in the dirt, which in many places can act like a powder in absorbing heat and perspiration. Sometimes you can dig them in a ways, reaching the cooler soil beneath.

Before setting off again, secure your recently removed socks to the outside of your pack, where they can air. Brush the dust and debris from your feet, massage them encouragingly, and put on a fresh pair of socks. Stretch the toe area of the sock lengthwise and widthwise to give your toes a little more space. And check for wrinkles, which can induce a blister in short order. Lastly, if the weather is particularly hot, change into your second pair of shoes or sandals.

Leg and Foot Pains

The Agony an De Feet

Many of us distance hikers experience occasional stress pains of the feet, ankles, legs, knees, hips, or lower back. These almost always signal a problem, but they don't always point to it. For example, a severe pain in the knee can stem from a problem in the foot. But one thing is for certain: If we don't stop the pain, it is likely to stop us. This is one instance where determination is practically guaranteed to cause a debilitating injury. I know runners who tried to run through various pains, only to end with multiple surgeries that left them permanently *injured.*

But the good news is that normally we don't have to endure these pains. A few minutes is about my limit. How do we stop them? By stopping what is causing them.

I estimate that 99% of all hiking pains in the lower extremities are caused by four factors. In order of priority they are:

✦ Lack of pre-hike training (and carrying too heavy a load).

> The body is stressed, not by the distance-hiking, per se, but by too rapid a transition from a relatively sedentary lifestyle to an extraordinarily active one. The body will easily adapt to the rigors of the trail if conditioned to do so gradually. Pushing the body far beyond its present abilities, while disregarding the necessary time for adaptation, is an open invitation for a stress injury. By "adequate" training I mean: carrying a gradually heavier load over gradually longer distances, on irregular terrain, three times a week, for five months prior to the actual hike. Read more on this in the "Training" chapter, beginning on page 30.

✦ Lack of calf stretching during the training and the actual journey.

> Strenuous and prolonged hiking places great demands on the calf muscles. Once these muscles grow accustomed to the exertion they are likely to perform their tasks capably and efficiently. Before then, if the exertions are prolonged, as distance hiking tends to be, then the calf muscles will begin to tighten and lose much of their elasticity.

Gentle and regular calf stretching encourages suppleness. For the details, refer to the "Stretching" chapter, page 170.

✦ Chronic and prolonged dehydration.

All of our joints are lubricated and cushioned with water. The hiker is most concerned about the joints in the toes, feet, ankles, knees, hips and spine. Our muscles, tendons and cartilage are lubricated with water. Deprived of adequate moisture these become somewhat brittle. And this can happen with our bones as well, increasing their susceptibility to stress fractures. When dehydrated we are like machinery badly in need of oil – eventually things may start breaking down. Severe and prolonged dehydration almost ALWAYS figures into the pain/injury equation. Read more on this in the "Water" chapter, page 157.

✦ Ill-fitting or broken-down footwear.

I estimate the chances are about 70% that *any* pair of shoes or boots will eventually cause pain, whether sooner or later. If this pain and the problems causing it are not rectified, a debilitating injury can, and probably will, result. One reason might be that the shoes or boots don't fit correctly. Another is that they may begin breaking down internally and start creating unbalanced forces with every step, even though they may look fine on the outsides. Refer to the "Footwear" chapter, page 90.

Simply put, a pain that stabs with every step is a signal of a budding injury. The alarms are sounding and the red lights are flashing – it's time to take prompt action.

First, we say requiem for the shoes or boots we are wearing. It doesn't matter how many miles we have hiked in them, or how few. It doesn't matter how heartily the manufacturer advertised them, how much we paid for them, or how attached to them we have become. They are now threatening our health *and* our entire summer's adventure. We remove them and place them in our pack, with plans to carry them out to civilization where we will either send them home or leave them for someone else to try.

We then change into our spare pair of shoes or sandals, and hike to the next water source. There, we start drinking water by the liter. Remembering that our bodies take two or three days to re-hydrate, we continue our rehydrating efforts for that period of time.

If we are not carrying a spare pair of shoes or sandals when the injury strikes, then we will have to experiment. We might jam a bandanna or wad of grass into the shoe of the hurtful leg, placing a sizable wad under the arch. Then we would walk a ways and see if this helps. If not, we would move the wad under the heel. Also, we would rest often with the feet uphill, and perform *gentle* but frequent stretching exercises. And another consideration: Over the many miles we might have developed a habit of stomping: of setting our feet down with too much force. A lighter foot fall might help.

If none of these work, we would haul off the trail and make camp, and try these remedies again in the morning, but not before stretching – very, very gently – after awakening. And again we would drink water copiously to help rehydrate ourselves.

Upon reaching the next resupply station, if we find that we had neglected to place a spare pair of shoes or boots in our parcel, we might mail-order a pair from one of the national outlets and have them sent express. Or we may have to hitch to the nearest town and buy a pair.

Lastly, I should note the folly of replacing a pair of shoes or boots with those of the same brand, let alone of the same model. Once again, most companies use the same "last" to construct their different models, as well as the same types of materials placed at the same strategic locations. If the originals caused problems, their cousins are likely to do the same. As with nutrition, the key word with footwear is *variety*, and plenty of it.

Hygiene

Backcountry Practices
for the Promotion of Good Health

One of the joys of a long summer on the trail is its freedom from many of society's obligations. Incidental niceties - hair styling, the use of deodorant and toothpaste, etc. - are not necessary when we set out on our simpler life-style. Still, that does not mean we should ignore certain hygienic practices. Regular hygiene on the trail and in camp go a long way in discouraging various intestinal disorders. It can promote a sense of well being, which in turn can lead to a more positive attitude. And it is a sign of respect for one-self and others. I've seen hikers walk in to resupply stations looking and smelling like three day old fish, and criticizing townsfolk for not being friendly. Becoming a trail tramp is not a mandatory part of the summer's freedom, but a sign of laziness, plain and simple.

Bathing in the wilds (the dundo shower)

Swimming or dipping in backcountry creeks and lakes is becoming an increasingly controversial issue. Most hikers, myself included, take pleasure in the occasional dip, especially in large lakes and the very occasional hot springs. But I feel we need to consider the adverse ecological impact on many of the smaller sources. Particularly as the residues washed from our bodies are far more polluting than most of us would imagine. Stop the drain and take a quick shower, then examine the water and you'll see what I mean. The "dundo" method is more effective than dipping or swimming because it allows the use of soap. And it is almost as convenient and refreshing.

Jenny coined the term "dundo" shower during our AT hike. A passage from our trail journal describes how this came to be: "After a day of crossing the Skyline Drive, climbing the next hill, thrashing through brush, and descending to the road again, ad infinitum, we passed the turnoff to the Black-rock Shelter and continued a few miles to the Dundo Picnic Area. The place was deserted, so at a drinking fountain we stripped, and ignoring a light rain we filled our water bottles and poured the contents over ourselves while hastily rubbing on a bit of soap. We had not been long re-dressed when a car drove slowly past, its 3 women passengers gawking at us. Never mind the publicity, one cannot describe the wonderful feeling of the chilly splashes embellished with a small bar of soap after a long, hot, and sweaty day." Jenny started referring to this type of bath as a "dundo," and the name stuck.

Regardless of the type of container you use, dip it into the water source and carry it to your shower area. In this way you can use a small amount of soap without polluting the water source. For best results, scrub vigorously with a wet hand towel. Collect more water, back well away, and rinse yourself. Repeat as necessary. Wring out the hand towel and use it to dry yourself, wringing it a few times again. Shampooing the hair can be done in the same manner.

A shortage of water or a blustery day is hardly an obstacle to bathing. You can sponge bathe while wearing your clothing by reaching under and scrubbing your body with a damp hand towel. Also, you can sponge bathe while inside your tent or under your tarp, again using a damp hand towel.

Off the subject a moment, but a few words about the Deep Creek hot springs might be in order. PCT hiker Ryan Christensen reports that he considers the ominous warning in the W.P. guide book to be overstating the case. "The springs are really too special pass up," he says, "especially for the dusty, weary PCT hiker." After looking into the matter, I agree. Apparently a 19 year old died of an amoebic disease back in 1971, and a 9 year old contracted a similar ailment but recovered. Both cases were attributed to amoebas found in the Deep Creek hot springs. The source of these was traced to the soggy ground above the springs. While it is true that these two illnesses *could* have originated at the hot springs, (and that the patients could have been suffering severe immunity disorders) and that similar illnesses could occur, I don't think we can discount the fact that untold thousands of people have soaked in the Deep Creek hot springs with no apparent ill effects. But I will say that due to the large number of people frequenting the area, and to its lack of restroom facilities (because of past vandalizing), PCT hikers should not collect drinking water downstream of the hot springs.

Oral hygiene — Can you say dental floss!?!

Hard work and good nutrition promote healthy bodies, and the teeth and gums are no exceptions. Generally speaking, distance hikers suffer very few dental problems. Nevertheless, every hiker should consider brushing and flossing on a regular basis. Some dentists suspect that tooth paste actually complicates various gum problems. Tooth paste is an abrasive, and it is loaded with chemicals (so-called natural ingredients), most having nothing to do with oral hygiene. I feel that brushing without these agents makes better sense in the wilds. If you brush while you hike, though, breathe through your nose. Brushing creates a fine mist, which you would not want to inhale while breathing hard. And of course you would be careful not to stumble with a toothbrush in your mouth. Remember that rinsing the toothbrush in suspect water could introduce giardia into your system the next time you use it. Rinse it in treated or spring water instead. And at some of the resupply stations you would do well to soak your toothbrush in hydrogen peroxide as a disinfectant.

The primitive privy

On your way to the "bushes," collect a bit of natural toilet paper: a few handfuls of snow or smooth stones, leaves, evergreen twigs, or Douglas fir cones. If you prefer, you can finish the job with a few sheets of toilet paper. The idea is to minimize the use of toilet paper because it can remain intact for a long time, particularly in the drier regions.

At the selected site dig a "cat hole" about six inches deep, using the adze of your ice axe, a stick, or in soft soil simply with the heel of your shoe. If stooping is painful to your swollen knees, try sitting on the edge of a log or rock, or even the edge of your backpack.

In his book *Chips from a Wilderness Log,* Calvin Rutstrum writes: "You also need to train your evacuation organs. Once trained they will respond by reflex. Don't sit on the seat for long periods straining. Watch an animal. He does it as you should, in one fell swoop. Forget what you can't readily evacuate with the first generous effort, and proceed with the cleaning process. In time you will have trained the bowel to give forth a stool in one single release."

On your return from the bushes, wash your hands with an antibacterial soap, such as Dr. Bronner's. Not in a creek! but dundo style – pouring water from a container, well away from the water source. Sterilizing your hands will greatly reduce your chances of introducing microorganisms into your body the next time you dip into that bag of gorp. Lacking antiseptic soap you might try the method used by Asian cultures for thousands of years: left hand wiping and right hand eating and shaking hands. And remember that not all hikers wash their hands after elimination.

Buried tampons and sanitary pads are invitations for odor-sensitive animals to dig them up. Burning them requires an extremely hot fire, inconsistent with today's no-trace ethic. Perhaps the best method is to double bag the materials and carry them out. As an option, consider the use of a natural (and reusable) sea sponge. Carry water away from the source, and pour it on the sponge to rinse it, and to wash yourself.

Washing dishes

Washing dishes with soap and hot water is a carry-over from home, and that is a good place to leave this practice when venturing into the backcountry. This is not to suggest that we should ignore the job altogether, but normal dish washing soap, although it will cut some of the grease, will not sterilize the dishes against harmful microorganisms. And the soap residue left on the dishes can cause diarrhea (and soap left in camp-laundered clothing can irritate the skin). Scouring dishes with a nylon scrub pad is particularly unhygienic. The pad collects bacteria and allows it to multiply, then actually contaminates the dishware it is supposed to be cleaning, to say nothing of the water sources when being rinsed out. If our camp dishes are greasy or oily, water by itself will clean them very little, particularly if the water is cold. And unless that water has been treated, it can introduce giardia and other undesirable protozoa. Even after the dishes have dried, a percentage of the microorganisms can remain active.

I recommend a different approach. Jenny and I eat directly from our cookpot. Leaving the plates and bowls at home obviates the incessant chore of washing them, and of having to sterilize them on a regular basis. After eating from the cookpot we clean it of scraps. One way is to pour water into it, then after scraping and stirring with a spoon, to drink the resulting gruel if we are low on water, or simply to disperse it far from our stealth camp and away from any water sources. We then wipe any remaining residue using a handful of weeds, bracken fern, leaves, or pine needles. Any persistent spots we scrape with a stick, which is less likely to scratch the metal. After use, these materials, too, can be dispersed, leaving hardly an indication of our presence.

The next time we cook with the pot we are effectively sterilizing it. And we are also disinfecting the spoon used to stir the meal. For the hiker carrying a cup, pouring boiling water into it for a hot drink sterilizes it. And stirring the brew treats the spoon once again.

Sterilizing water bottles

We must also sterilize – or replace – our water bottles on a regular basis. This is particularly so if the bottles are used for mixing flavoring powders. (And while on the subject, it is not a good idea to mix powdered milk in a water bottle. Not only can it engender bacterial growth very quickly, but it can sour the bottle and make it almost impossible to freshen.) To sterilize our water bottles we can zap them in a microwave oven, found at some resupply stations (zap your plastic spoon at the same time). Or we can soak them overnight in a strong solution of water purification chemicals or household bleach included in the resupply parcel for the purpose. As mentioned on page 79, I much prefer the use of recycled beverage containers as water bottles. Renewing them often obviates the chore of sterilizing them.

Incinerating trash

When finding bits of trash along the trail, consider picking them up – if for no other reason than the next hiker coming along will think they were yours.

Plastic in any form should be carried out of the woods and deposited in a proper litter bin. Most plastics emit toxic fumes when burned. Breathing these fumes can make you ill.

On a windless day, paper, cardboard, and cellulose (a wood product) can be burned during a rest stop. Here's how: Select a place on bare dirt or sand. Make absolutely certain it is not humus or duff, and stay away from tree roots, as a smolder could work its way underground, consuming the sap-rich root as it goes, until eventually reaching the tree. Build a tiny fire, no bigger than 4 inches diameter at the base and 4 inches tall. Use match-stick size twigs. Into this, feed the paper and cardboard, small bits at a time. Occasionally add more kindling. As the ritual is winding down, place the unburned shards of wood into the little fire. When the flame self-extinguishes for want of fuel, don't simply bury the ashes. Instead, stir them into the earth. The more you stir them, the more you grind them into powder, and the more the admixture of dirt cools the particles and distances them, rendering them incapable of rekindling. Sufficient stirring will erase the little fire site altogether. Lastly, "monster mash" the embers, as described on page 355.

Restaurant sanitary measures

Restaurants are perhaps our best sources of nutrition. But they can also be our best sources of colds and flu, caused by germs left behind by infected customers. We distance hikers are particularly vulnerable because we tend to lose some of our immunities while living in the wilds, which are relatively free of these types of germs. The trek can lose its luster while these ailments run their course. So, unlike the average city person, we need to take definitive precautions when visiting unsanitary places.

Our best defense is in keeping our hands off the usual infectious objects – doorknobs, table tops, etc. – and by eating with our own spoon instead of the house silverware. Forks are particularly susceptible because the spaces between the tines can harbor microorganisms. Nevertheless, we should view all house tableware with great suspicion. The laws pertaining to sterilizing dishware are often vague and rarely followed.[1] And remember that the table top is almost never sterilized. Refrain from eating bits of food which you might have dropped on it. Also, you might drink water from your own water bottle, and consider asking the waitress to serve the meal on a paper plate. (And while you're at it, order a second meal "to go" and carry it with you to your next camp. It will make a great dinner.)

---

[1] According to FDA Model Rule, which most states follow, (but few restaurants do) the rinse cycle of a dishwasher must reach 160°F. Dishes washed by hand must be by the 3-sink method: wash, rinse in 160°F water, and sterilize in 75°F water and chlorine bleach @ 50-200 ppm.

If you wish to take further precautions you could use your table napkin to open the restroom door. Women could stoop over the toilet without touching it. All could flush with the shoe. You could turn on the lavatory's spigots with the napkin or a paper towel, and wash some of the trail dust from your hands and face with soap and hot water (taking extra care not to leave a mess for someone else to have to clean up). Then you could use the napkin to turn off the spigots and to open the door. Stop the door with your foot, then turn and toss the napkin into the trash container before returning to your table.

Enjoy those restaurant meals; they are few and far between. But don't forget to take your spoon with you when you leave. And don't touch that doorknob!

Stealth Camping

> The wanderlust has blest me;
> In a ragged blanket curled,
> I've watched the gulf of Heaven foam with stars.
> I've walked with eyes wide open,
> to the wonder of it all;
> I've seen God's flood of glory burst its bars.
>
> — *Robert Service*

Imagine that one midsummer's night, every camper in the Sierra Nevada shines a flashlight into the sky, and that a passing satellite photographs the scene with a powerful lens. The picture would show, not randomly distributed pinpricks of light, but circles delineating the lakes, and linear clusters depicting the trail-side creeks. Otherwise, it would show vast areas of blackness. This blackness would indicate that despite the crowded campsites, the overwhelming majority of the area is vacant.

Hikers who learn how to camp away from water sources are at a wonderful advantage. For them, that expanse of blackness on the hypothetical satellite photo becomes the potential for virtually unlimited camping.

I coined the term "stealth camping" to denote camping in these empty areas, far from the established campsites. Because it is not common practice, the concept provides us with an entire chapter full of advantages.

Stealth derives from the word steal: in the sense of moving or behaving inconspicuously. Most wild animals live by stealth. They move and act with quiet caution intended to avoid notice. No doubt our predecessors camped quietly to avoid danger, and they must have moved covertly in order to locate and approach their prey. The stealth ethic is more aligned with their ways. Sometimes we may experience danger, mainly when near roads. And we try to approach animals, not with spear and atlatl, but with camera and appreciative eyes. To understand why I prefer stealth camping, let's take a closer look at the concept of today's established campsite.

The peculiarities of established campsites

Camping near water is an unfortunate and almost universal rite that has been practiced by outdoor enthusiasts for generations. In the process of preparing their tent sites and making them more "comfortable," they have scraped away the beneficial layers of duff and forest litter. The result is a pervasive dirt-ash mixture that blackens the ground sheet, and a dust that penetrates the nostrils, food, tent, and gear. And I might note that the ground is not only dirt and ashes. Some of it is desiccated stock manure. And even though it has dried, the pathogens and coliforms it contains can remain virulent for years. Nevertheless, the incessant trampling of boot and hoof compacts this "ground" as though it had been run over by a steam roller. Thus, it requires the use of a foam mattress for sleeping on. This compacting also represses the area's regeneration enormously. Bits of rubbish often litter these sites, particularly in the ugly and deeply-scarred campfire sites with their blackened rocks. And small wads of TP might be hidden in the crannies of nearby rocks and beneath fallen trees, marking buried feces, teeming with coliforms.

Rodents usually maraud these established campsites nightly, chewing into gear and eating and contaminating campers' food. Worse, the equestrians allow their stock to drink from the nearby water sources, turning blind eyes when their animals urinate and defecate in them – as long as their stock is downstream of *their* camps. And stock is not the only problem. Both backpackers and equestrians are well known for leaving scraps of food – remnants of dish washing – in the water and its proximity.

If these widely practiced camping methods teach us anything, it is how they are degrading the ecology. Grouping together, trammeling the earth, building large campfires, making noise, and broadcasting litter are but a few of the unfortunate ramifications of contemporary camping practices. By my way of thinking, they are inappropriate in the wilds.

The long distance hiker has even more important reasons for avoiding established sites:

Where the mind reaches, the body follows

For the backpacker out for a 15 mile weekend loop, the usual objective is to reach the established camp of choice early, and to relax there until time to return to the car the following day. Traditionally, distance backpackers have followed suit, segmenting their journeys into daily objectives. But in deciding ahead of time where they will camp each evening they are shackling their minds to that objective. So when they arrive at their chosen campsite, most likely they will consider the day's hiking a success and pitch the tent. Never mind that several hours of enjoyable progress might remain in the day, and that they are forfeiting several miles – for no reasons other than psychological ones.

There is nothing wrong with relaxing in camp and smelling the proverbial flowers. But in terms of hiking the entire PCT in a single season, more effi-

cient methods are in order. One of the more advantageous methods is to continue hiking well into the evenings, then to take the occasional layover day
near the resupply stations.

The campless dinner, the dinnerless camp

With little more than a mental adjustment we can expedite our journeys considerably. If we arrive at the last creek for several miles in the late afternoon,
then indeed we would stop for a relaxing and refreshing break. Naturally, we
might be tired from the day's exertions. But much of that tiredness stems from
lack of food. If we are in shape and traveling light, then at this point in our
day we probably need a hearty meal more than a prolonged rest. So almost as
though we were making camp, we cook and eat dinner, we gather and treat a
supply of drinking water, and we wash our pot and spoon. Then we might
dundo shower or at least sponge the day's dust and sweat from our bodies.
But instead of pitching the tent we re-load our packs and press on. If the meal
was nutritional, and particularly if it was corn pasta, then in every likelihood
it will re-energize us and we will find ourselves hiking buoyantly a few more
hours. Much farther along we leave the trail and walk a distance into the forest or desert, and establish a dry camp. Our arrival here can be quite late because the camp chores will be mostly done. About all we will have to do is
pitch the tent or tarp and crawl into the sack.

This technique is extremely effective at extending daily mileages. And
nowhere is this more important than when hiking between distant water
sources.

Eluding bears

Another major advantage of stealth camping is that it obviates 99% of the
bear problem. Bears concentrate mainly in the more fruitful areas: namely the
human congested ones. So to elude the bears we need to avoid sleeping at, or
near, established campsites. This is discussed more fully in the "Bear" chapter, beginning on page 213.

Climb high, camp low

Stealth campers can greatly reduce weather-related problems according
to their knowledge and experience. In boisterous weather they will normally
avoid camping in the high, exposed areas. Instead, they would descend and
look for small tent sites protected by foliage, trees, or rocks.

During our CDT hike Jenny and I happened to meet another hiker (the
only one of the summer) in the remote mountains of western Montana. The
day was late and after an enjoyable conversation, this fellow resumed his ascent, and we, our descent. A short ways farther along we made a comfortable

camp nestled in the pines. Our evening was a pleasant one, highlighted by a pair of owls which flew round the tent and landed on a branch within a few yards of our open doorway. In the morning we awoke to find the mountain enveloped in cloud, and we worried about our friend who had camped up there. And indeed, after his hike the fellow sent us copies of a few pages from his journal describing how he had endured that harrowing night on top of the peak, hanging onto his tent in a savage, freezing gale.

The three of us had camped only half a mile apart; our camp protected snugly in a vale and his fully exposed to everything the elements could hurl at it. We were following the time-honored adage "climb high, camp low." And this was one of many instances in my experience where it made a world of difference.

Avoiding katabatic air

Stealth camps can often be 15° to 20° warmer than established campsites in the general area. This is because they can be located above the katabatic zones. These are rivers of cold, heavier air flowing down from the alpine heights in the late evenings and nights. These "rivers" follow the drainages and pool in the valleys. So where we find water we usually find frigid, katabatic air hanging over it. And of course adjacent to water we also find the established campsites.

As you hike into the late evenings, watch for, or rather, feel for katabatic air and avoid camping in it, especially if you are lightly equipped. Collect your water, cook and eat dinner, then move out of the drainage. I have rarely seen katabatic air more than a hundred feet thick. Most often it is more like 20 or 30, and the trail usually climbs that high in only a short distance.

So to the adage "climb high and camp low" I would add: but not too low.

Better bedding

The ambient air at the stealth sites, out of the katabatic air, is warmer. And so is the ground. And that ground is normally covered in forest litter and duff, which provides excellent bedding and insulation. This is extremely beneficial to the hiker traveling lightly, but it also mandates extreme caution with fire.

The surface layer of a typical forest floor is called litter. It comprises recognizable needles, leaves, cones, sticks, and other natural materials. Beneath the litter is a layer of decomposed and compressed litter called duff. Unenlightened campers commonly mistake duff for dirt, and build fires on it. Even if they recognize it for what it is, they might imagine it is non-flammable, particularly when wet or very moist. What they don't imagine is that their campfire will dry it.

Speaking of unenlightened campers, on a winter mountaineering trip in the Colorado Rockies back in the '60s, my partner and I skied in to "base camp" and pitched our tents. Digging through several feet of snow to the ground, we built a modest fire and cooked dinner. Afterwards we buried the fire under what seemed a ton of snow, and packed it down with our boots. The following morning we left camp and climbed our chosen mountain. Returning in the late afternoon, we were aghast to find a small hole in the snow bellowing smoke. For an hour we dug the smolder, following a few spreading arms. One was headed for a nearby tree. This was an unforgettable lesson about the flammability of "wet" duff.

Nature uses fires to maintain her ecology, and most are started by lightning. Decades ago the Forest Service deemed wildfires detrimental to their timber "harvesting" and declared war on them. As a result, the downed kindling is not regularly burned away, and our second and third growth tree farms have become immense tinder boxes. Policies are beginning to change, but it is still true that campfires can start colossal forest fires. And when it happens with PCT hikers, the trail receives a flood of bad press. Witness the Clover Meadow fire, started by a PCT hiker reputedly burning toilet paper.

So when it comes to building the traditional evening campfire, the stealth camper should forget it. Granted, there might be a time or two when you need the warmth of a campfire to dry wet clothing. You would do this at an established site. But if you meet PCT hikers who are building *nightly* campfires at established sites, then you are meeting people who are out of line with today's no-trace camping ethic. The campfire scorches deeply into the subsoil, much more so than a forest fire, sterilizing the subsoil's micro-ecology. And it leaves an ugly pile of spent coals, usually surrounded with blackened rocks. Building a campfire in an established site only impacts that campsite further.

Sleeping on a slope

Most backpackers prefer to camp at established sites, which in fact are about the only open, level places with good access to water. Note the word "level." Most campers insist on sleeping on level ground. Which is why they sometimes find themselves in ponds after a hearty rain. Many, if not most stealth sites, however, are on sloped ground. If forced to sleep on a slope, the novice tends to do so with feet downhill. As we learned earlier, this pools the blood into the lower extremities, which drastically restricts circulation, and which in turn curtails the restorative effects of an otherwise good night's rest. Or the novice might try sleeping laterally on the slope, only to discover something called gravity.

We stealth campers don't balk at gradually sloping tent sites. We search for them. Our blood doesn't pool in our legs and feet because we do not sleep with our feet downhill. We don't roll downhill in the night because we do not sleep laterally on the slope. Instead, we sleep with the feet uphill, a position which obviates pooling and even draws the day's swelling from the extremities. This is good therapy for hard working extremities.

The ability to spend the night on sloped ground has many other benefits. During rainy weather the ground water will likely run off, rather than collect beneath the tent or tarp. If rain is falling hard, and if you are camping beneath a tarp, you might scrape a V-shaped gutter a few inches deep, pointing uphill and centered above the foot of your tarp. The trench will channel away the runoff from the ground above you. Just make sure to eradicate all signs of your excavation before moving on. I should note, though, that the necessity of trenching a site is extremely rare. I have done it only on two occasions.

Which way is down?

Judging which way is downhill is a simple matter when the ground is considerably sloped. But not when the ground is barely sloped, or when you are fatigued after a long, hard day on the trail. In such cases you might pitch your tent or tarp in what *seems* the correct orientation, only to spend the night trying to prevent yourself from rolling to one side.

The solution is twofold. First, walk around your potential site and examine it from all directions. While you look at the ground from one vantage it might appear sloped toward you. But when you view it from the opposite side, again it might appear tilted toward you. Chalk it up to fatigue. Nevertheless, this walk-around routine is the first method of determining which way is *probably* down, and it should be followed at every prospective stealth site. Second, spread your ground sheet and lay on it with your feet pointed in the direction that seems uphill. If the slope feels uphill toward your feet, then it most likely is, and you can pitch your shelter with assurance.

Incidentally, this inability to judge slope manifests itself on the trail as well. When fatigued, the hiker often gauges downward slope as being far more gradual than it is. Jenny and I hiked the trail northbound twice, and were quite familiar with certain areas where the trail's downward gradient seemed almost moronically gradual. I was surprised, during our southbound journey, to find those same slopes amply graded, hiking them uphill rather than down. It was yet another lesson in how the fatigued mind can misinterpret reality.

How steep a slope can you sleep on? Generally, don't balk at a steeper sloped site until you have checked it for feel, lying on your ground sheet. My rule of thumb is this: If I awaken the following morning and discover that I have slid out of the tent or tarp, then the ground was a little too steep.☺

If the area of your stealth-site is hardly sloped, choose a place on a slight rise which would provide run-off in the event of rain. Partly for the same reasons, stealth campers would refrain from digging hip and shoulder holes beneath their beds.

New worlds of possibilities

Stealth camping heightens the wilderness experience and opens new worlds of possibilities to distance hikers. In the National Parks and congested wilderness areas, the main impact is at the camping sites. We stealth campers have virtually no impact on these sites because we don't use them. Nor do the rangers have to worry about us impacting our impromptu campsites, because the vast majority of us will practice no-trace methods. For after all, our love and respect for Nature is why we enjoy stealth camping in the first place.

Of course we would refrain from altering the natural setting while establishing these impromptu sites. We might hand-preen twigs, pine cones, and sharp-pointed cone scales, but we would not brush away the forest litter, break away green limbs, or yank out saplings that might occupy the prospective site. If we find such obstructions in the way, we simply search elsewhere for a place naturally free of them.

A part of stealth camping is in maintaining a low profile. We avoid attracting unwanted attention by talking softy and not clanging spoons against pots, and so forth. This way we are not degrading someone else's wilderness experience while enjoying our own. And in so doing we are far more likely to see and hear wildlife at closer range. In short, we respect the quiet of the wilderness as though inside a church, if you catch the connection.

A good night's sleep brings the dawn of a new day. The early morning is my favorite time of day, and I find it incredible that most backpackers sleep through it. In pilot training we learn to take off from the beginning of the runway. "The runway behind you does you no good" is a flight instructor's saying. And so it is with the hiker's day.

Photography

Camera, Contrast, and the Art of Seeing

A man must carry knowledge with him
if he would bring home knowledge.

– Samuel Johnson

Most hikers like to take photographs during their treks. For some, pictures are a way of sharing the summer with family and friends back home. Some might want to give more formal slide presentations to groups. A few will need pictures for articles or books. And almost every hiker enjoys reminiscing over his or her pictures, refreshing the memories and reliving the experiences.

The hiker interested in high quality, professional images must be willing to carry more expensive (and usually very heavy and bulky) camera gear. But the cameras, lenses, tripods, flash attachments and reflectors are only half of the equation. I've seen scores of hikers make the mistake of thinking that a high quality SLR camera will guarantee them high-quality photos. It can, but only for someone well versed in the art and science of photography. Despite its complexity of computerized components, the camera is little more than a box which holds the film and lets a little light in when its button is pressed.

In my opinion, the distance-hiking photo-novice is likely to obtain better photos with a quality point-and-shoot camera. Why? Mainly because these cameras are so much simpler and handier.

Regardless of your reasons for taking photographs, you can greatly improve their quality with an understanding of the basics of photography. Excellent books on the subject abound, and the more you read and study some of them, the more your skills will improve. One of the best I know of is *The Backpacker's Photography Handbook,*[1] written by Charles Campbell, who happens to be a friend of mine. Like most how-to photo books this one presupposes the use of complex equipment, a fact which excludes us weight-

----

[1] Published 1994 by Amphoto, an imprint of Watson-Guptill Publications. Campbell also offers seminars and video training tapes on nature photography. Highly recommended. PHOTOnaturalist, P.O. Box 621454, Littleton, CO 80162. Ph 303-933-0732.

conscious ultra-hikers. Even so, it describes the basic concepts with clarity, and I feel that many of these concepts are equally important for those of us who use lighter and less complex gear.

The distance-hiker's camera

I recommend a rangefinder, (as opposed to an SLR) autofocus camera with a high-quality lens (very important), a self-timer, and a built-in flash. The model I've used for years weighs 6.2 ounces.

Several of today's point-and-shoot cameras are weatherproof or weather resistant. These features can extend the life of the camera, and they permit taking pictures in inclement weather, allowing the hiker to capture a more realistic impression of the expedition. Still, one must be careful not to introduce moisture and grit into the camera when changing film. Water can damage the electronic and mechanical components. And just a single particle of dust can scratch the film acetate or its emulsion when the film is later advanced, and again as it is re-wound. The result is what appears to be one or more telephone wires traversing each scene. To minimize the problem, clean the camera's interior with a small blower brush before inserting each roll of unexposed film. And be sure to brush off the film canister before placing it into the camera. For convenience you might carry your bulb brush with your spare film.

The human camera

As we gaze at a scene to be photographed, our eyes constantly adjust focus as we look from one part of the scene to another. Our pupils constrict and dilate, adjusting to the varying intensities of light coming from objects in sunlight and shade. And most importantly, our brain interprets the image by automatically compensating for harsh contrast and filtering out extraneous detail. The result is a pleasing rendition, perceived via an unimaginably complex battery of faculties.

Even the most technologically advanced camera and lens is severely limited when registering the same image. Therefore, the photographer must select scenes that lie within the capabilities of camera and film.

Shadows: the photographer's nemesis

The term "high contrast" denotes the harsh differences in light, for example between objects in direct sunlight and those in shade. Today's cameras and film generally are not capable of accommodating high contrast. And the hiker-photographer who ignores this problem is all but asking for a number of substandard photographs.

Looking through the viewfinder, examine the scene carefully for shadows. Think of even the mildest shadow as a patch of photo blackness. It does not appear black to your eyes because your brain and eyes are working to smooth the contrast. A photo taken mid-day in the forest, in which shadows from the trees are falling across a hiker, is unlikely to turn out well. Depending on how the camera adjusts its settings, the areas in sunlight might be properly exposed, but those in shade are likely to be very dark, almost black. The same is true of a photo of people wearing shading brim hats in direct sunlight. The hats might look great but the faces will be lost in darkness. The hiker in the forest is best photographed early or late in the day, or on a cloudy day when the light is diffused and the shadows are subdued, or when fully illuminated in a patch of sunlight. Just don't snap the photo if shadows are falling across your subject. On sunny days, portraits and close-ups are best taken using a manually-activated fill-in flash. However, if your subject is wearing eyeglasses, these can reflect the flash. Ask the subject to turn away slightly, or to remove the eyeglasses. And remember that although the flash on a small camera seems extremely bright, it is not capable of reaching more than six or eight feet. Use it only within that range, even at night.

Most point-and-shoot cameras do not give direct control over the f-stop and shutter speed settings. And this is one big reason that photo buffs avoid using these cameras. However, you can gain some measure of control by centering the viewfinder on darker or lighter areas, depressing the shutter release half way to lock the settings, (in cameras that have this feature) and then framing the photo the way you like and snapping the picture. Nevertheless, you will still need a basic understanding of photography to use this method to best advantage.

The self timer

I have seen many hikers' slide shows, and by far the best were the ones in which the photographer took the trouble to set up the camera, activate the self-timer, and move back into the picture. Scenery shots can be extremely pleasing, but to capture the essence of the journey you will need to impart a sense of presence: a hiker walking along the trail with an interesting view in the background, for example; or a hiker at camp. Both are quite effective at drawing the audience into the experience.

A tripod allows a variety of shots, but again due to its weight and bulk few hikers carry them. Instead, you can place your camera on rocks, tree stumps, or the occasional fence post. You can even tie it to a tree with a length of cord. And for an interesting angle try placing the camera directly on the trail.

Photography can be a great means of exercising creativity. And while thinking of the possibilities, remember that hiking is not *all* serious. Be sure to include some humor. The funniest hiking slides I've seen were by Jeff Robbins, who has a penchant for making his audiences laugh uproariously. One of his slides shows a hiker ambling along a logging road with a massive sign, six feet wide, lashed to his backpack. "OVERSIZE LOAD," the sign reads: it must have fallen off a truck. Another of Jeff's pictures shows a group of hikers imitating a rock band, but in a snowy, alpine scene. They carried toy instruments and strange costumes just for the occasion. Another time he had placed a plastic golf club in the hands of the Walt Whitman statue on the Appalachian Trail. The fit was perfect. "Look for humorous situations," Jeff advises, "and you'll find them just about everywhere."

The film

Whether you use slide or print film is a matter of choice. Most photographers striving for quality use slide film. Color photos for magazines or books are best made from transparencies (slides). Color prints can be compiled into photo albums, and these are quite handy for casual viewing. Print film is also much more accommodating to differences in contrast, meaning that the camera's metering does not have to be as accurate.

Jenny and I normally use ISO 100 color slide film. During the journey's preparations we decide how much we will need, then we telephone a few firms advertising in the national photo magazines. We find out how much they charge for the amount of film we need, for the same number pre-paid processing mailers, and for the shipping and handling. Armed with this information we then telephone the local photo shops, and tell them what we need. We also mention the mail order price, saying we would rather do business locally if their price is reasonably competitive.

At home we include the film and pre-paid processing mailers in our resupply parcels. On the average, we shoot a roll of 36 exposure film every 3½ days. So for example if we are planning for a 7 day stretch between resupply stations A and B, we place two rolls of film in box A, and two processing mailers in box B. Once we have reached resupply station B we mail the exposed film to the processing plant, using our home address as the return address. Processing the film right away insures the best results. As a further precaution you could use the address of a relative or close friend as your return address, and ask them to examine the photos and alert you to any problems with your camera.

Spare battery

I've met hikers unable to use their cameras because of dead batteries – casualties of the high altitudes and cold temperatures. I once improvised a battery replacement on my own camera by wiring a couple of AA flashlight batteries to it. For electrical hook-up wiring I used a pair of plastic-bag twisties stripped of their insulation. Flashlight batteries are normally 1.5 volts, so wiring two of them in series supplied the needed 3.0 volts. My camera looked like some sort of an amateur-built bomb, batteries taped to its exterior. But it worked fine and took some great pictures which otherwise I would have missed.

Save yourself the trouble by always carrying a spare battery. And leave a few extras with your home-base person, or place them in your resupply parcels or drift box. And speaking of spares, be sure your slide projector has a spare bulb. I buy mine from the Bulbman (800) 648-1163.

✖

When photographing the magnificent forests of the PCT, consider yourself recording the scenes for posterity. Many outdoor enthusiasts imagine that the national park and wilderness designations will protect the enclosed land and forests forever. But an increasing demand for timber and other resources is likely to breach those legal barriers as though they never existed. It's all a matter of time, big money and politics. Do your part by joining a few conservation groups.

Poison Oak

Itching for Knowledge
or Lack of It

Some plant species along the PCT are equipped with measures designed to protect them from animal browsing. And as anyone with the misfortune of coming into contact with those plants can affirm, we're better off not touching them. Many examples are based on the cactus theme. Fiddleheads come equipped with hair-like prickly spines that inflict discomfort to those wading bare legged through patches of these otherwise attractive annuals. Stinging nettles thrive near some creeks, their tiny needles taking the concept one step further by injecting a toxin which inflicts intense but temporary pain. But of all these, poison oak can cause the PCT hiker the greatest discomfort.

Native Americans were immune to the irritants in poison oak. They even made baskets of its vines. As for PCT hikers, about a third would remain unaffected by an "average" brush with this plant. But almost anyone would suffer severe skin irritations of a massive exposure.

And indeed, every year a number of hikers do just that, with patches of dermatitis characterized by oozing blisters and a rash that itches like fire whenever touched. [1]

Poison oak was a common affliction with us Yosemite climbers, mainly as the result of thrashing through brush while scouting for new routes. Initially I was reluctant to spend the money for prescription medication. But I learned the hard way that a rash could grow far more intense, and that it could last for several months.

The poison

Poison oak contains a toxic, oily juice[2], which combines with the proteins in human skin immediately on contact. Once it has combined it cannot be washed away. The toxin pervades all parts of the plant, including the leaves,

---

[1] A note for hikers from the eastern states: The poison oak found in western climes is much more pernicious than that found, for example, along the AT. The same is true with western nettle, what little of it there is along the PCT.

[2] urushiol (ou-ROO-she-all)

stems, berries, and roots. Dead stems are equally pernicious, as is the smoke of the burning plant.

The menace of bare stems

Along the Pacific Crest, poison oak is found in the lower and montane elevations throughout much of California, and farther north in the Columbia River Gorge. In the arid climes of southern California it grows mainly along creek banks, whether water is flowing in them or not. It prefers shade more than moisture, though, and can flourish high above the drainages.

Poison oak can be a particular menace to northbound PCT thru-hikers because they are likely to encounter the plant in early season when it is still leafless. When in the proximity of creek beds, then, watch for small communities of widely scattered bare stems standing one or two feet tall. The hallmark of these stems is their characteristic curve. And often each stem will be capped with a small, pointed bud – the coming season's new growth.

If you have not identified these bare stems well before reaching Hauser Creek, you would do well to avoid touching, setting on, or placing your clothing or equipment on *any* little bare stems, especially those found along natural drainages. In a few places you might encounter bare stems reaching out across the trail. Shove them aside with a stick as you pass by.

As spring gives way to summer the bare stems develop leaves. Normally in groups of three, these are shaped somewhat like oak leaves, hence the name. But unlike oak leaves they are greasy or shiny, and usually vibrant in color. During the summer they are green, tending to bright reds and yellows in the autumn.

Mistaken identity

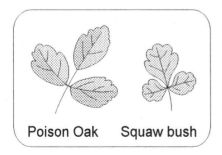

Poison Oak   Squaw bush

The center leaf in each three-leaf cluster of poison oak has its own stem. The center leaf of squaw bush lacks an individual stem. Squaw bush is almost universally mistaken for poison oak, but in fact it is quite harmless. It is fairly widespread, but is particularly abundant in the vicinity of Baum Lake, north of the Hat Creek Rim.

The stems of poison oak are not thorny, as are those of the raspberry, which again the novice might mistake for poison oak – for example while hiking along Grider Canyon near Seiad Valley.

Contact

Occasionally you might find poison oak growing lavishly on both sides of the trail, and sometimes directly on it. If you accidentally brush against it, proceed to the nearest water source, and using the dundo technique[3], well away from the water source, wash the affected area repeatedly with soap. Fels-Naptha® soap if you happen to have some. This will eliminate much of the *remaining* transmissible toxin.

If you are sensitive to poison oak, then a few days after the encounter you may notice a small, itchy rash resembling a mosquito bite. If touching it causes a fiery sensation, it's probably poison oak. Experts tell us that scratching a poison oak rash will not spread it. But I can assure you that it will greatly aggravate it.

Over-the-counter cortisone preparations are ineffective in this application. So unless you know for certain that you are immune to poison oak, I recommend you carry prescription medication.

I might mention another common disorder which resembles a poison oak rash. This is photo-toxic dermatitis, caused by mild sunburn in combination with a skin allergy to a soap or cream, or to some type of food or drink. It usually affects the backs of the fingers and hands. See page 235 for details.

Parked on trouble

During our first PCT hike Jenny and I met a fellow who said that he had recently hitchhiked out for medication. The doctor treated him for a severe case of poison oak, yet this fellow claimed not to have touched the plant. I explained how virulent the leafless twigs can be, and pointed them out all around us, including where he happened to be sitting.

[3] Described on page 180.

Mosquitoes

It has long been an axiom of mine
that the little things are infinitely the most important.

– Sir Arthur Conan Doyle

*Venturing into the wilds, we need to carry – and wear – clothing that pro-
tects us from whatever adverse elements we encounter. For cold weather we
carry insulating garments; for desert travel, clothes that protect us from
intense ultraviolet radiation; for rain, rainwear; for wind, wind proofs; and
during those seasons when the mosquitoes and biting insects are particularly numerous, we need to wear bug-proof clothing and head netting.*

Just as some years bring more rain than others, and some more snow, some
years bring more bugs. Most types of mosquitoes hatch in water, so their
populations vary according to the precipitation of the previous winter and
spring. But some types hatch on the underside of branches, for example on the
buck brush of central Oregon. These pests can be numerous during the height
of the season in any year, and are found both near water and far from it.

DEET

For the distance hiker plying the trail for months at a time during a particularly buggy year, insect repellent, even with DEET, is not adequate protection. This chemical seems to work, not by repelling the bugs but by hiding us
from them, or at least what parts of ourselves we have treated with the chemical. I've had them squeeze under my watch band to get at the untreated skin
there. But more importantly, large and prolonged applications of DEET can
be unhealthy, particularly as it does not stay put. Purportedly, six hours after
application about half of it will have absorbed into the skin, and most of that
will have entered the blood stream. Ten to fifteen percent of each dose can be
recovered from the urine. Most weekend hikers can use the product with impunity. But after several weeks of application, distance hikers can experience
various mental effects. They will begin to loathe the repellent; and this is good
because it limits the applications. But also they may begin losing their toler-
ance of the mosquitoes themselves, making the buzzing hoards *seem* far more
tormenting.

I use DEET, but only sparingly and when the bugs are not too numerous.
A 35% solution seems to work best, and I avoid the "long lasting" types
which can be uncomfortable on the skin. I use a spray pump applicator, which

distributes a thinner and more even coating. But to apply repellent to my face I spray it on my palms then rub it on my face. And at day's end I always try to wash the repellent off, at least what remains, using the dundo method away from the water source so as not to contaminate it.

DEET dissolves many types of plastic, such as that of the eyeglasses and wristwatch. According to the manufacturer it will not harm Gore-Tex® fabrics, but I do not know whether this is true for other waterproof / breathable membranes.

Psychological?

We have all heard the philosophy of mosquito forbearance. "Just ignore them. It's all psychological." I admit that in small numbers they can indeed be ignored. A few bites probably won't hurt anything, at least here in the US. Try this in tropical climes, though, and you could contract one of the dreaded mosquito-borne diseases which altogether kill some two million people every year. However, even along the PCT, hoards of mosquitoes are not to be ignored, as evidenced by the early natives covering themselves with clothing and sometimes with mud.

Protective clothing

We distance hikers would do well to emulate those natives, who in some ways may have been fortunate in lacking modern chemical repellents. We do this by wearing clothing that physically barricades the insects from biting our skin.

My recommended bug-proof wardrobe is made with two fabrics:

➤ Tightly woven nylon, 1.9 oz/yd^2. Because mosquitoes cannot pierce it, it may lie safely pressed against the skin, for example at the shoulders, elbows, and knees. The material should be breathable, but not overly so. Test it by pressing it to your lips and sucking air through it. If it breathes quite easily then it is probably not mosquito proof.

➤ No-see-um netting for the head. This must fit very loosely. Otherwise the mosquitoes will insert their probisci through it and into your skin.

My bug-proof wardrobe consists of these items:

✔ Jacket shell – made of tightly woven nylon, used also to block the wind. The waist and wrists are fitted with elastic.

✔ Shell pants – of the same nylon material, with elastic waist and pant cuffs.

✔ Shell mittens – of the same nylon material extending half way up the forearms. Elastic cuffs hold them in place. The mitts can be large, loose-fitting cylinders with no thumbs. Used mainly when hiking and sleeping.

✔ Shell booties – of the same nylon material, covering the feet and lower legs, and worn when resting or cooking, and while sleeping beneath a tarp on nights too warm for a sleeping bag.

✔ A loose-fitting head net of no-see-um netting that extends below the shoulders. One flap extends 18 inches down the back, and one down the chest. The flaps tuck inside the shell jacket.

The trail registers of central Oregon are loaded with woeful remarks of PCT hikers who lacked appropriate bug wear. So why not prepare yourself ahead of time? The garments I recommend are light in weight, and very serviceable in times of need.

Color

The nylon garments should be light in color. These absorb less solar radiation, so they are cooler and therefore more tolerable to wear. This is a genuine consideration on a warm day. Moreover, flying and biting insects seem to be less attracted to lighter colors. I have noticed this many times as Jenny and I have sat together, one of us in light colored clothing and the other in dark.

The head net, however, should be dark in color. Black netting absorbs more of the scattered light reflected by its fibers, and is therefore a little more transparent when close to the eyes.

Jenny and I make all of our bug wear. And even the novice should have no trouble doing the same. Those not so inclined can buy commercially made shell jackets and pants of breathable nylon, and head nets. Commercial netting jackets and pants are ineffective. Where they press against the clothing or skin the bugs can bite through them.

Revenge

As we hike from place to place during the height of mosquito season the bugs are likely to buzz around our heads for endless hours. If we swat at them they will retreat, only to attack again later. Or they might ride on our backpacks or clothing, waiting for better opportunities. I often stop and flatten the blood-thirsty buggers to the last one, then hike on in peace. Their replacements are often surprisingly slow in coming. For a weapon I use a damp hand towel. Another method might be to spray Permethrin on the clothing and backpack. See page 204.

Ticks

In parts of southern California ticks can be quite abundant along the PCT, mainly in the springtime. Hikers must inspect their clothing after scraping through each section of brush. Light colored clothing greatly facilitates this, due to the tick's contrasting darkish color. But clothing of any sort provides concealment for ticks. Very important when in tick country, then, is to inspect your bare skin every few hours, and particularly before you retire at day's end. If hiking with a partner, inspect each other's underarms and backsides. If hiking alone you will have to inspect yourself, by sight where possible and by feel otherwise. Before crawling into your sleeping bag, run your fingers over every square inch of your body. A tick feels like a little mole which you did not know you had.

Virtually the only ticks discovered by sight or feel are the adults, generally measuring ¼-inch across, a little smaller than the one crawling around on this page. But the pin-head sized nymphs are equally capable of transmitting disease. For this reason, hikers need to physically protect themselves with special clothing and repellents. Back on page 202 and also in the previous chapter I discussed the shell jacket and pants. Ticks seem to find these garments very slippery, and in fact Jenny and I have never found a tick on ours. Temperature permitting, we always wear these shells when in tick country. And we protect our ankles and feet with DEET. This is important because a tick can chew through a sock. And it can also crawl underneath a pant leg, even one with an elasticized cuff.

Tick poison

Another way to deal with ticks is to poison them. Permethrin is a potent chemical designed to do just that. It is strictly a clothing treatment and is not to be used on the skin. It comes in various forms, including Duranon,™ and Permanone™ in 6 ounce aerosol cans containing 0.5% Permethrin. Two mail-order sources are: Cabela's (800)237-4444, and Leonard Rue Enterprises (800)734-2568. Rue also sells snake-proof chaps, pepper spray (page 82), and a good selection of photography accessories and wildlife books. I suggest that if you want to use Permethrin you do so only at your resupply stations. Spray it on your shoes, some on your clothing possibly, your backpack, and maybe even certain areas of your tent. But remember that the fumes can be quite strong (which is why I don't use it). Then after checking with the postal clerk about the current legalities of mailing pressurized aerosols, you could place the can in your drift box, along with other items not presently needed, and mail it two weeks ahead.

Tick removal

If you find a tick embedded in your skin, grasp it with tweezers as close to your skin as possible. If you lack tweezers, cover the tick with a piece of plastic bag to protect your fingers from infection. Pull *very* gently and steadily, without twisting, until the tick lets go. Take great care not to crush or puncture the tick, or to contaminate your skin with its fluids. If you pull too abruptly the tick's mouth parts can break away and remain embedded, possibly causing infection. After removing the tick, disinfect the bite site, for example with hydrogen peroxide, and scrub your hands with an antibacterial soap such as Dr. Bronner's.

Tick related disease

Presently, most ticks along the PCT do not carry the dozen known tick-borne diseases. Still, because these diseases can be serious, and because time is of the essence, hikers would do well to recognize the early symptoms of the three most prevalent types.

Rocky Mountain spotted fever

Endemic throughout the continental US, this is perhaps the most serious disease transmitted by ticks. Most often the initial symptoms are: high fever, headache, chills, muscle pain and deep fatigue. Four days later a spotted rash often develops – hence the name – initially on the hands and feet, but spreading. This disease is considered a medical emergency. If you begin experiencing these symptoms, head for the nearest doctor.

Lyme disease

The earliest evidence of infection in most cases is a skin rash at or near the bite. The rash is most likely to appear about a week after the bite. In the next several days it might expand, growing into an ever-widening red splotch. However, there are many variations. Along with the rash, or sometimes in its absence, the patient might experience flu-like symptoms: fever, malaise, headache, and possibly a profound sense of fatigue. Even if not treated, these symptoms usually disappear within a week or ten days. But the disease generally progresses unperceived until it resurfaces later and possibly causes serious health problems.

Doctors can treat Lyme disease at any stage, but the earlier, the better the patient's outlook for a full recovery. The diagnosis is usually based on the symptoms, because in the disease's early stages blood tests rarely confirm the presence of Lyme. Antibiotics are the treatment of choice.

HGE

HGE (Human Granulocytic Ehrlichiosis). Similar to Lyme disease but more sudden in onset and without the telltale rash. Symptoms include sudden high fever, severe headache, vomiting and abdominal pain. Like the others, HGE is treatable with antibiotics.

Snakes

Travel teaches toleration.

– Benjamin Disraeli

Up to seven or eight feet in length, but harmless to hikers who leave it alone, the gopher snake can be found along the PCT throughout much of California. Normally it behaves passively, but if confronted it might hiss, flatten its head, and vibrate its tail. And if molested it is likely to bite. Due to this behavior, and to the patterns of darker blotches on its back, it is regularly mistaken for the rattlesnake and killed. This is unfortunate because like rattlesnakes they are extremely beneficial to the ecology, but unlike rattlesnakes they are non-poisonous.

I remember one time while hiking through the Tehachapi Mountains, Jenny and I came to a shading tree and were about to sit down, when we noticed a gopher snake about six feet in length. Over the years we had seen many, often stretched across the trail like sticks, but we had not seen one quite this large. Leaving it ample room we sat down anyway, and soon it slithered behind us, only inches away, before continuing on its way.

The rattlesnake

PCT hiker Dan Herold was resting with his wife beside the trail in the San Gabriels, reading his guide book section when a rattlesnake crawled out of the brush next to him. Perhaps he had not heard that a rattler can strike in $1/100^{th}$ of a second, for he swatted it with his reading material. The result was a bite on the back of the hand. Fortunately for Dan the snake injected little, if any, venom. I have heard of only one other rattlesnake bite to a PCT hiker. Scott Williamson reported that he was hiking briskly through the desert when a small rattlesnake snapped the toe of his running shoe. The snake's fangs did not penetrate his skin.

I asked Dr. Anthony Manoguerra, Director of the San Diego Regional Poison Center, about the incidence of rattlesnake bites to hikers. He said they are fairly common. How serious are they? He explained that the damage is proportional to the amount of venom injected and the elapsed time between injection and receipt of antivenin. The patient may spend a couple of days in the hospital, or a week at most.

First aid

Dr. Manoguerra said that the most important thing to do if bitten by a rattle-snake is to stay calm. In roughly half of the cases the snake injects little or no venom. The victim will usually know within about 5 minutes. The poison causes severe pain and swelling, and with more serious bites, discoloration and a tingling sensation.

A rattlesnake which is greenish in color could be the Mojave Green rat-tlesnake, an exceptionally venomous species. In the unlikely event of being bitten by one of these, send someone out for help right away, or walk out yourself. If bitten by another type of rattler you might wait a few minutes to see if signs of envenomation manifest themselves. Remember that weakness, sweating, nausea, and fainting are not signs of poisoning, but simply of the trauma of being bitten.

How to recognize a rattlesnake

The rattlesnake has small pits on its head, between its nostrils and eyes. These house its infrared heat sensors, which are so acute that they allow the snake to follow the heat signatures of its prey long after the animal has passed, and straight into its nest or den. Interesting, but if you are close enough to see the pits, and to see that the pupils are elliptical instead of round, then you are much too close. What you will notice from a safe distance is the flattish, tri-angular-shaped head, wide in the jowls and fashioned improbably onto a thin neck. This is the viper look. And you will probably see and hear the tail rat-tles, although in some cases these might have broken off.

Of the dozen or more snake species along the PCT, only the rattlesnake is venomous. It is found throughout much of California, and rarely in the Co-lumbia River Gorge. Otherwise, it is almost unknown along the trail through Oregon and Washington.

The snake will probably detect you first

Being exceptionally sensitive to ground vibrations, the rattlesnake can sense your approach from quite a distance. It may slither for cover, but only if this will increase its chances of not being discovered. Otherwise, its primary de-fense is to remain inconspicuous and motionless. And this is exactly what makes it dangerous to hikers, especially as its camouflaging helps it to blend in with the shrubbery. The hiker can easily and unknowingly approach within striking distance, and only after the snake's primary defense has failed will it buzz a warning.

The reason the rattlesnake must remain inconspicuous is that it is not de-signed to flee. A human can throw a rock and kill it with a single, well-aimed blow. Or, more commonly, a bird of prey can attack silently from behind, or the bird may fluff itself up and allow the snake to strike it repeatedly and harmlessly, before commencing its counter-assault.

In our three PCT hikes Jenny and I have seen dozens of rattlers. And no doubt we and most other PCT hikers have walked past many without realizing it. I once stopped to drink from my water bottle, and a rattlesnake buzzed me from behind. I turned and saw it lying at the edge of the trail. I had walked right past it, but the point is, the snake didn't buzz until it figured I had seen it. It interpreted my stopping as a threat.

Hiking in snake country

In snake country walk attentively. Scan the trail eight or ten feet ahead. Where the trail is overbrushed, probe ahead with a long stick. Those hikers wishing to take every precaution could wear snake chaps.[1] A more economical option would be to wear pieces of cardboard wrapped around your feet and lower legs, and taped together. Otherwise you could wear whatever clothing you have that might help protect your feet and legs. The more layers, the better, but still this would not constitute adequate protection.

I have inadvertently come well within striking range of several rattlesnakes, and several other hikers have reported doing the same. This demonstrates that rattlesnakes don't always strike when presented the opportunity. But it also illustrates the difficulty of avoiding snakes and keeping a safe distance.

Every time we encounter a rattlesnake Jenny dashes away. And every time I assure her that a couple of snake-lengths away from the creature's head is perfectly adequate, as long as she remains on guard and leaves plenty of room for a quick retreat. It wasn't until the final stages of our third PCT hike on the northern flanks of Mt. Laguna, when she was buzzed by a large rattler that she merely moved aside, and studied the area for the snake's whereabouts. I was coming along behind at the time, and heard a terrible shriek. The lesson: don't stand a couple of snake-lengths away from where you *think* the snake might be. It could be much closer.

Camping in snake country

A tent with its netting doorway zipped closed would offer excellent protection, especially if the occupants kept away from the walls. One hiker told me of sitting beside his tent and watching a rattlesnake crawl under it, only to reappear on the far side and continue on its way. I imagine that most rattle-

---

[1] See page 204.

snakes are wary of large mammals, awake or asleep. Jenny and I have slept under the stars in the mountains and beautiful deserts of southern California a great many times, and have not had a rattlesnake bother us.

Snakes for dinner or decoration

Graham Mackintosh[2] ate quite a number of rattlesnakes during his hike around Baja California, and I asked him about this.

"My procedure for eating rattlers," he replied, "was generally to: 1. Kill with rocks at a safe distance. 2. Cut off the head to prevent an accidental bite - they tend to squirm and twist long after they're dead. 3. Rip off the skin. 4. Pull out the innards which are neatly packaged in a visceral sac. 5. Take the white tunnel of meat that's left, chop it into manageable lengths then boil or fry. 6. Maybe the easiest way to eat them is to "comb" the cooked meat off the ribs with your teeth. Fried in bread crumbs they're pretty good, certainly when hungry. As for conservation, I believe rattlesnakes are an important and fascinating component of any wilderness ecosystem. Since the completion of my round Baja trip, I have seen scores of rattlesnakes and apart from taking a few photographs, I have left them alone. Today, I would only kill a rattlesnake if I felt it was essential for safety reasons."

If you decide to eat a rattlesnake, you might also want to save its skin. Lay the skin on a rock or log, inside up, and scrape away any extraneous tissue with a knife. At your next resupply station, rub salt generously onto the skin as a preservative, then roll it tightly, place it in a few plastic bags, and mail it home. Once home, rinse and soak the skin in water to soften it, and tan it with a commercial fluid, available at leather tanning outlets. Once dry you can either shellac the skin, which brings out the colors for wall mounting, or rub glycerine (available in drug stores) on it for softening.

---

[2] Author of *Into A Desert Place; a 3000 mile walk around the coast of Baja California.* See Bibliography.

Cougar

Like winds and sunsets,
wild things were taken for granted
until progress began to do away with them.
Now we face the question
of whether a still-higher standard of living
is worth its costs in things natural, wild and free.

– Aldo Leopold

*Early American settlers tried to eliminate the cougar, mainly out of fear.
And of course they were trying to protect their livestock, which they were
importing into the cougar's domain. But despite the onslaught, the cougar's
power, stealth, and adaptability has enabled it to survive. More sensible
management is emerging, and today the cougar is reasonably protected in
most states and fully protected in California. This has allowed the animal
something of a come-back, mainly in the western states where natural
habitat is more extensive. According to Howard B. Quigley, President of
Hornocker Wildlife Research Institute, the state of California now harbors
an estimated 5,000 cougars.*

The cougar ranges from central Canada to Patagonia, and survives equally
well at sea level, in swampy terrain, jungles, deserts, forests, and high alpine
regions. Depending on location, it is also called the mountain lion, puma, and
panther.

I have seen only one in the wilds. Jenny and I were hiking the PCT in
Washington when suddenly there came a deep throated, spine chilling growl,
unlike anything we had heard. We backed off and saw the animal flash
through the nearby brush. Then we heard a soft "meow." It seems that mother
cougar was only protecting her kitten. And rightly so, for judging by the
sounds we had approached to within a dozen feet of the little tike. Needless to
say, we didn't investigate.

Many cougar-related stories that we hear or read about in the media may
have basis, but might not have been reported accurately or interpreted correctly. I wonder whether the two runners killed in the mid 1990's, one in
California and one in Colorado, might have been unknowingly threatening a
kitten.

Still, cougar-related stories are subject to over-dramatization. For example I know of one hiker who frequents the PCT and puts Jim Bridger to shame with his tall tales. Local residents have told me that bears have ripped this fellow's sleeping bag off him at night, that cougars have stalked him for days, and so forth. I mention this only because you may hear some of these fanciful stories yourself.

But back to reality. The cougar is swift, sharp toothed, and powerfully built. It is an extremely efficient hunter, sensing its prey at a distance and stalking it with almost otherworldly stealth. But is the cougar dangerous to hikers? I don't think so. If it wanted to eat hikers it would have eaten most of us long ago. The fact remains that most humans have a genetic fear of being preyed upon by large animals. For our primordial ancestors this was a good type of fear. It helped alert them to danger and greatly increased their chances of survival. Even today, large predators still roam the wilderness. But statistically, the cougar has endangered people in only two basic scenarios: One, a young, inexperienced cat wanders into the suburbs to see whether it might snatch a lone child. And two, a mother cougar acts defensively to protect her kitten from someone racing along and paying no heed. I have not heard of a cougar pouncing on someone hiking or camping.

But let's think of this in cougar terms for a moment: when modern man devastated its niche, he eradicated most of the animal's natural food sources and introduced livestock instead. The cougar has had no choice but to prey on livestock. I liken it to putting a child on a diet, then setting barrels of candy in his bedroom. The temptation would be to gobble as much as possible, and to take possession of the rest before it got away. This is how cougar sometimes behave around sheep. And as Edward Abbey pointed out, "Any animal that eats sheep can't be all bad."

In the extremely unlikely event that you are approached by a cougar, back away slowly. You might be near its kitten. Running away could trigger its "chase" instincts. If the animal persists, defend yourself if necessary by throwing rocks or sticks. In every incident that I've read about, this tactic has frightened the animal away.

Bear

When a man wants to murder a tiger he calls it sport;
when a tiger wants to murder him he calls it ferocity.

– George Bernard Shaw

Native peoples of North America hunted the bear for its meat as food, its fat as lamp oil, and its skin as clothing, rugs, etc. And they often used its teeth and claws as jewelry. Other Indians considered the bear to be a reincarnated relative, or sacred in other ways, and left it strictly alone. As settlers moved west, the bear, cougar, wolf and wolverine all began losing habitat to land cleared for agriculture. The strictly carnivorous predators are losing out, but the bear is omnivorous: its molars are flat-topped, allowing it to eat plants as well, and this has helped it adapt to the changing ecology.

The grizzly bear: California state animal, last seen in that state in 1924. Completely eradicated from its former habitats across the western and southwestern states – ostensibly for sport but in reality for fear. To my knowledge no PCT hiker has ever spotted one anywhere along the trail.

The black bear: less aggressive and far more predictable, and therefore not as greatly feared, it continues to flourish all across the more remote regions of the US. Still, with keen senses and an opportunistic behavior it tends to gravitate to clusters of civilization seeking food, where it inevitably loses in its confrontations with modern man.

As for PCT environs, even as late as 1990 the black bear was rarely found south of Walker Pass. But being the mobile and inquisitive sort, it has since been migrating south. Today's PCT hiker is likely to encounter "Blackie" almost anywhere along the full length of the trail.

The two types of black bear

The black bear is not always black. It can also be cream, blond, cinnamon, reddish, or brown. Despite the coloration, all black bears are powerfully muscled, armed with claws and incisors, and almost always hungry, yet they do not view humans as food. Yes, there have been remote incidences of black bear attacks on humans, but in light of the thousands of black bear-human encounters every *day*, those incidents are so remote that for all intents and purposes they hardly exist.

Based on my experience with black bears, which goes back to 1961 when I worked in Yellowstone National Park, and which includes 11 years coexisting with them in Yosemite National Park, I divide the black bear species into two distinct types: the "wild" bear and the "park" bear. As far as PCT hiking is concerned these two are as different as Peter Pan and Elmer Fudd.

Wild Blackie

The "wild" variety of black bear is found mainly outside the National Parks, where every hunting season it becomes prey to big-game hunters and their hounds. These remind it that humans can be dangerous.

While hiking the mega-trails Jenny and I have encountered literally hundreds of "wild" black bears. Almost without exception they have fled into the woods. Cubs and yearlings are different. Often they will stop and stare curiously for a few moments before scurrying up a tree or running away into the forest. But left alone, wild black bears pose not the slightest danger to you or your supplies. Yes, they are big and powerful and fully capable of ripping hikers to shreds. But no, they virtually never do. And as for the "factoid" that hikers should never get between a sow and her cub: I consider it just another myth. My only advice with wild black bears is to leave them alone. In every likelihood they will reciprocate.

Park Blackie

Inside National Parks, where hunting is generally not allowed, the black bear is an entirely different animal. Whether it wanders across the park boundary as an adult, or whether it is born inside the park, it tends to gravitate to the nearest black hole of humanity. Once there, it becomes "habituated" to people and begins raiding campsites and vehicles for food, or objects resembling or possibly containing food. And being remarkably intelligent, it devises all sorts of clever tactics to get it.

In these struggles with humans it loses more of its innate fear and becomes more of a menace – sometimes even a hazard to the imprudent. And when finally its havoc wreaking grows intolerable, the rangers break out their dart guns and bear traps.

Once caught, "Bruin" is drugged and ear-tagged or body painted, and removed to some far away forest. But it does not forget its associations of humans with food. Using its remarkable homing skills it will often return to the scene of the crimes, however far away – only to be caught again and tagged on the other ear. Or it might simply descend to the nearest outpost and resume its pillaging there, only to be shot, as likely as not, on sight. How do we know this is a relocated bear? The ear tags.[1]

Outside National Parks, bears are hunted to the ends of the earth. Inside them, our protectorates of the natural world relocate them to the outside.

Dangerous to hikers?

Rarely, a park bear will injure a tourist stupidly teasing it with food. Even though the bear may act tame, it will still exhibit certain requirements for personal space. Normally it will only growl or act defensively if someone ventures too close. But instincts can surface, for example when a touron[2] instructs his or her children to pet the bear or its cuddly-looking cubs for a family photograph.

The park bear, like all bears, is almost always hungry. Yet once again it has no appetite for the flesh of campers. It wants only their food; no, it *demands* their food. And considering that about only one in fifty campers will defend their supplies, it usually meets with success.

Protecting your food

Unable to solve the bear problems, the "authorities" mandate that we hikers solve them. First, they instruct us to camp only in designated campsites. Effectively, they are corralling us into known, and therefore easily regulated sites. But imagine the irony: this corralling is a convenience to rangers and to bears.

I don't mean to depreciate backcountry rangers. Only after we have walked a mile in their moccasins will we begin to appreciate the problems these hardy souls face. In popular areas such as along the John Muir Trail they are inundated with unconscionable and "lazy" campers, who every night of the season leave their food and gear scattered all over their camps. Hence the bear problem.

But because the rangers can't fine the bear when it steals our food, they fine *us* when the bear steals our food. Currently, the fine is up to $500 for not bear-bagging our supplies. Official literature depicts various methods of suspending food from tree branches, so many feet above the ground, and so many feet out from the tree trunk. This is conservation? – killing a tree branch by sawing into its bark with a thin line hoisting heavy bags?

---

[1] I once talked with a landowner outside one of the National Parks, who called the officials to report a tagged bear prowling his property. The advice: "Shoot, shovel, and shut up."

[2] A term of affection used by park residents, combining the words "tourist" and "moron."

Nevertheless, I reckon that many bears of the National Park backcountry owe their livelihood to gullible hikers trusting in this system. Nocturnal bruin is incredibly resourceful at retrieving comestibles, and the nights are long. I've seen the results of scores of bags plucked from remarkable heights. Even lost one myself many years ago, hung so high that the bear would have needed a step ladder to reach it. But reach it, it did; and the massive branch supporting my bag narrowly missed smashing my tent. Alas, while new bear-bagging techniques come up into vogue as fast as they go down, the food bags, and the branches supporting them, mainly just go down.

Realizing this, the rangers supplied many backcountry campsites with metal storage boxes and overhead wires from which to suspend food. Lately they have been withdrawing them, outwardly to return the wilderness to its utopian wildernesshood, so to speak, and inwardly maybe to discourage backcountry visitors. Again, such irony! But under this system everyone loses. The campers lose their food; the rangers lose their fondness for campers; and the bears often lose their lives. I recommend a method where the thru-hiker, the bear, and even the ranger, unknowingly, usually win. I call it "stealth camping," detailed back on page 186. Of course, if each of the thousands of backcountry visitors practiced this method then the bears and rangers would catch on, and things would quickly return to everyday chaos. The method works mainly because it is out of the ordinary. It is not infallible, but since the *Handbook's* introduction many distance-hikers have used it with success.

The Park Service is now recommending the use of personal bear-proof food canisters, and I imagine that one day they will actually require their use. Currently, these are too heavy for most long distance hikers, particularly considering the quantity of food we sometimes need to carry. And while they may keep our food from being taken, they will not prevent bears from prowling through our camps. Once bears learn to associate hikers with the food they carry, they will usually try to obtain that food no matter how many times they meet with failure. If they spot an opportunity, they will tend to pursue it.

I realized the futility of bear-proofing my supplies long ago. Instead, I attempt to outwit the ravenous bear. Let's look at the typical scenario:

The Park bear associates backpackers with food, and it recognizes a pattern with most of them. The overwhelming majority of backpackers:

- camp in designated sites, every one of which lies on the bear's nightly marauding route (no coincidence there).

- They advertise their presence with campfires, the smoke of which sends an olfactory signal clearer than any siren.

- They cook food, the aroma being a thousand times more alluring than smoke.

- They hang their food in sight as though advertising it.

- And they are terrified by the beast's intrusion and flee, leaving Bruin to feast on the spoils of victory.

For the bear roving in search of plunder, I can't imagine a scenario more conducive to success. As a long distance hiker, though, I need to turn the tables. Otherwise, the results, as thousands of backpackers have learned, are not likely to fall in my favor.

To avoid park bears I need to stay away from the places they frequent, at the times when they frequent them. During the summer, and in the backcountry, the park bear will be found almost exclusively within range of the designated campsites. These, in turn, are predictably located near lakes and streams. Moreover, in the wilds, campsite marauding in the presence of humans is almost invariably a nighttime activity.

I avoid bears by not camping in their zones of activity, populated by hordes of unenlightened campers acting as bait, and by not attracting them to my stealth camps.

Therefore:

☑ I refrain from sleeping within several miles of the nearest designated site, and/or a creek or lake.

☑ I do not advertise my impromptu camp with a campfire.

☑ I avoid cooking and eating within several miles of where I sleep.

In PCT environs I sleep with my food at my head, and with my flashlight near at hand. Many wild creatures are nocturnal, and a shuffling or scratching around outside could be a deer, porcupine, mouse or vole. Or a bear. But so far I have not heard or seen a bear at any of my stealth campsites. If and when I do, I will simply rise, break camp, and move on.

❊

None of the methods in this book come with any guarantees, particularly those in this chapter. If you emulate my methods and Blackie grabs your food anyway, the tables are irrevocably turned. In the interests of personal safety do not attempt to steal it back.

Rain

May the warp be the white light of morning,
May the weft be the red light of evening,
May the fringes be the falling rain,
May the border be the standing rainbow.
Thus weave for us a garment of brightness.

— *Song of the Sky Loom (Tewa Indians)*

When rain falls heavily, weekend hikers usually pack up their belongings and retreat to their cars. Once home, they rid themselves of their wet clothing by chucking it into the washing machine and clothes drier, and the wet tent and dank sleeping bag by airing them in a warm room. How fiercely we have come to rely on our civilized amenities, and how forlornly we have abandoned the skills needed to thrive in the natural world.

I doubt whether our primal ancestors suffered every time it rained. Unlike us today, they wore clothing that worked. Of course, they had adequate shelter too, or could construct it when needed, I suppose. Still, their clothing was tantamount to survival. We distance hikers emulate their lifestyles in many ways, and we, too, need clothing and equipment suitable for use in inclement weather. If we have it, and know how to use it properly, then we need not suffer the effects of a cold, pouring rain.

The umbrella

In the past twelve thousand miles of hiking Jenny and I have spent a lot of time in the rain. Cold rain, warm rain, rain that comes straight down and rain driven sideways in a gale; rain that lasts a few minutes and rain that lasts for days and soaks everything. And through it all, our umbrellas have been our first line of protection. I discussed this back on page 69. However, if the wind is frigid and blowing gale force, we would put away the umbrellas in favor of waterproof-breathable parkas. I have experienced an umbrella blowing apart, not while on journey but in a severe, late-autumn storm. So I know that the potential for a suddenly destroyed umbrella will always exist, and that if and when it happens, the hiker had better be carrying back-up storm clothing. So let's discuss which clothing is appropriate and how best to use it.

The storm parka

Today's market is aglut with rainwear. Judging by the price tags and hang tags on most parkas and rain pants, the marketeers seem to be preying on the fears of outdoor enthusiasts unaccustomed to living with rain. But they do not seem to be addressing their needs very well, mainly due to the extreme lack of ventilation of these garments.

So my first caution is to avoid the hyper-expensive rainwear. Those who buy it might be investing in their images by surrounding themselves with visible evidence of money spent, but they are probably not keeping themselves any dryer than with less expensive, but equally functional apparel. Most of the rain protection comes from the fabric, not the dazzling colors, the pit zips, the plethora of cargo pockets and their zippers and storm flaps, the mesh liners, Velcro tabs, loops and bookmarks plastered everywhere about. Designer seams crisscrossing the fabric are potential leaks. They make the garment more colorful and appealing in the stores and glossy advertisements, but in the field they are little more than extraneous plumbing. And in particular, the rain protection does not come from the brazen logos.

Distance hiking can be extremely hard on any storm parka. Where the pack straps bear against it they can abrade the waterproof-breathable membrane within. Thus, if used in lieu of an umbrella the parka's lifetime for the thru-hiker will be about one season. After that it can start leaking. For this reason I recommend a less expensive parka, detailed below.

Desirable features in a parka

The hiker's storm parka should not be insulated. Otherwise, even in cold weather the insulation is likely to become sweat soaked. This increases the garment's weight, decreases its serviceability at the rest stops and at camp, and makes it much slower to dry. The parka and the insulating shirt or sweater underneath it should be two separate units.

I recommend that when selecting a parka you choose one made of waterproof-breathable material, or of some other vapor permeable system. Make sure it has a full-length, front-opening zipper. And even while wearing your insulating garments under it, make sure that it doesn't bind across the back and shoulders. This will allow you ample room for swinging your arms wildly, for example while pitching your $600 tent in the pouring rain. The sleeves should extend well beyond your wrists, covering your mittened hands. The parka itself should extend below the crotch, protecting your lower body. And its hood should not be too large. Otherwise, as you jounce along the trail, and as your pack drags the back of your parka slowly up your back, the hood can slip forward and down over your eyes.

Two types of waterproof-breathable fabric

The thru-hiker's ideal parka would be made of a waterproof-breathable fabric. Generally, this comes in two or three ply. The two-ply (two-layer) comprises the W/B membrane bonded to a layer of nylon fabric. The mills leave it to the manufacturers to protect the vulnerable membrane's exposed side. This is accomplished by sewing a liner into the garment. In the store this liner gives the parka a nice feel. And granted, on the trail when perspiration condenses on the membrane's inner surface, the liner acts as a buffer, making the garment more comfortable. But that buffer actually reduces the membrane's ability to transfer vapor by reducing the temperature gradient across it.

Three-ply waterproof-breathable fabrics are made by sandwiching the vulnerable membrane between two protecting layers of nylon. They do not sell as well in the shops because they do not look and feel as luxurious as their two-ply counterparts made with liners. Nonetheless, three-ply is my choice for a rain parka, particularly as the design *can* be more basic, which *can* translate to being less expensive.

Seal *every* seam

Every seam of the parka should be sealed. On a parka made of two-layer material with a separate liner, look for faint impressions of the sealing tape. And try to suck air through the seams. On three-layer garments the seam tape is visible. Where the seams are not factory taped you must seam-seal them yourself. Unsealed wrist cuffs, for example, can soak a pair of mittens very quickly.

Heat is a byproduct of work

A car's motor burns fuel to generate power (and heat). It is cooled by its fan and radiator. If the engine becomes hot, does that mean it is working too hard? No, it indicates that it is working, period, and probably as designed. However, if the thermostat should malfunction, blocking the flow of coolant, then the radiator would soon boil over.

Likewise, human muscles burn fuel to generate power (and heat). Sweat exuding from glands acts as the muscle's and the body's main coolant. Does the presence of sweat indicate that the hiker is working too hard? Again, not at all. But the last thing we want to do is block the body's natural cooling.

The poached Wienerwurst

Imagine you are hiking up a long hill while carrying a loaded pack. A cold rain is falling but you came prepared with the latest technology. You are wearing a $90 wicking shirt beneath a $460 waterproof-breathable parka. The farther you hike, the more heat your muscles produce and the more sweat your body exudes in an attempt to rid itself of all that excess heat. You respond by unzipping the parka's front opening, to little effect. Then the pit zips. Ditto. The sweat wicks into your shirt. The humidity inside your parka soars to 100% and the parka's inner surface becomes coated in condensation. And there you are, struggling along in the cold rain feeling like a $3.25 poached Wienerwurst.

The solution is to remove the parka and wicking shirt, *before* breaking into a sweat, to don a lightweight polyester shirt and shell jacket (of thin, *breathable* nylon) if the day is quite cold, and to hike beneath your umbrella.

At the rest stops, remove your sweaty polyester shirt and slip back into your wicking shirt and W/B parka. Indeed, these high-tech "active wear" garments work well when worn at rest. (!)

Wearing the parka backward

If wind-driven rain prompts you to wear your parka while hiking, you will hike with greater efficiency by wearing it backward. This helps ventilate the back of your neck and your back muscles which are already over-insulated by the backpack. Should the day warm you could remove the backward-worn parka without having to stop and unharness the backpack. Simply slide it off your arms. For stowage, fold and drape it over the lower portion of a shoulder-strap, beneath your arm. This easy-on, easy-off feature is particularly useful when hiking in cold wind, where the trail weaves in and out of the protection of hills or stands of trees.

To secure the backward-worn parka in place while hiking in stronger wind, remove the windward arm (the side toward the wind) from the parka's sleeve and from the backpack's shoulder strap. The other shoulder strap should hold the backpack in place if you lean over a bit. Insert the free arm back into the parka sleeve, then back through the pack strap. The pack strap is now on top of the parka sleeve, pinning it in place. Repeat with the other arm.

In winds coming from the side, you can remove the leeward arm (side away from the wind) from the parka sleeve and fold the garment inward, diagonally across your chest, tucking the sleeve in as well. The sleeve that remains on your other arm, and it's half of the parka, would protect your windward side.

Rain pants

In frigid Arctic conditions a pair of waterproof-breathable pants might be most welcome. Particularly for someone with a higher inert factor. In a worse-case scenario the more nimble could descend to less hostile climes and crawl into the tent or under the low slung tarp, and hit the sack. The fact is, though, for the high-mileage hiker W/B pants restrict ventilation and insulate the legs too much. The legs are mostly hard-working muscles, pumping out large quantities of heat and needing to be kept cool. W/B pants also tend to bind at the knees with every step, especially when damp or wet inside from perspiration, as they usually are after having hiked in them awhile. The pure friction of this retards progress and increases fatigue. Yet another discouraging factor is that they will probably be wet, inside and out, when you arrive at camp, and they can be very slow to dry. The parka shares this problem, but it opens wide for airing, except for the sleeves.

On the trail I prefer wearing shorts of polyester or Lycra.™ Lightly clad and working hard, my legs do not mind the wet. And when I arrive at camp I wring out my fast-drying shorts and hang them to dry beneath the tent's awning. Scurrying into the tent I put on dry clothing, and slide comfortably beneath my sleeping quilt.

If I am wearing shorts and hiking in the rain, and if the day begins to chill, I pull on my shell pants (of lightweight breathable nylon). These offer quite a lot of warmth and protection from wind and scraping bushes, without sacrificing much breathability. They bind at the knees very little because they are more supple and lighter in weight. (Pants that do bind can be articulated by safety-pinning a tuck just above each knee.) And when given the chance they are very fast to dry. Only in the most persistent downpour will they still be wet when I reach camp. And even then I can wring them out and bring them into the tent or under the tarp with me, and either hang them on the inside clothesline, or place them somewhere down by my legs. By morning they will be reasonably dry, and ready to go another 30.

If the day is colder still, I may wear a pair of full length, wicking-fabric pants – Thermax™ or the equivalent – under the shell pants. If I arrive at camp with both wet, then I will have to rely on the sleeping bag alone for warmth. This is ok, for should the storm persist into the next day I can don these damp garments (with a slight grimace), and once I have gained some momentum on the trail they will have warmed, and will again perform as favorably as before.

Mittens

In heavy rain you must hold your parka sleeves in the down position. If you raise your arms, for example to hook your thumbs into the pack straps or thumb loops, your parka sleeves act like funnels. Which is another reason I prefer the umbrella. In the always-down position, though, longer parka sleeves will cover your mittens nicely. This means that the mittens can be made of simple fleece. When they become wet you can remove them and wring them out. If you find yourself without mittens, you could try wearing extra socks on your hands. I have never found the need for W/B mittens along the PCT.

Footwear appropriate for wet conditions

Dry feet are a misconception when it comes to hiking in extended periods of rain, even in the most expensive boots. I recommend lightweight, breathable shoes or low-cut boots, and socks made of nylon, or in colder weather of wool-synthetic blend. See the "Footwear" chapter starting on page 90.

The rain hat

Here again, the umbrella in conjunction with a fleece cap will usually suffice, even in the heaviest rain. Those not using an umbrella would use the parka's hood, but this restricts ventilation in the shoulder area and the back of the neck where it is needed. A better option might be to wear a fleece hat having a W/B covering. This leaves the shoulders and neck more free to ventilate. If the hat has a brim to shelter the eyeglasses, so much the better.

Pack cover

Despite the skyrocketing price of backpacks these days, few are waterproof. In years past I wasted a lot of time trying to rectify this problem with my store-bought packs, waterproofing their seams – without success. Then I bought a commercial pack cover. Despite its cost it was baggy and tended to flog in strong wind. It was heavy. And rain still soaked the pack between it and my back, and pooled in the sagging pack cover bottom. Tired of dumping so many liters of water out of my pack cover, I started making my own. I custom fit them and went through several design improvements. And Jenny and I hiked with them for thousands of miles. Still, they were far from ideal.

Finally we found something that would keep the contents of our packs dry: simple plastic trash bags, lining the insides of our packs and twisted closed at their tops.

The tent awning

Most tents are not designed to be used with their vestibules or doorways open in rainy weather. With the door open, rain falls or drips into the tent's living quarters. If your tent is like this, then you are not adequately equipped to camp in extended periods of rain. That being the case, I recommend you sew an awning over the tent's doorway. See page 60.

Rainy weather hiking strategies

Wet weather hiking is a skill. And like most skills it is easier said than done. But in a nutshell the concepts are these:

- Keep your equipment and clothing to a minimum. The more items you have, the more time and effort you will spend trying to keep them all dry. And as the rain persists and these efforts fail, the more time you will spend trying to dry them. For the "well equipped backpacker," life in the rain can be a real hassle.

- Dress lightly and hike briskly. Ridding your body of restrictive clothing frees you to move ahead with far less effort and improved heat dissipation.

- Snack often, both for energy and metabolic warmth.

- Rest frequently but briefly. Hikers with many thousands of trail miles behind them might require fewer rest stops throughout the day. Thus, they tend to handle cold, wet weather better because they are not repeatedly subjecting themselves to the penetrating chill at the rest stops. But for the first or second-time thru-hiker, frequent rest stops – perhaps hourly – are beneficial in extending the day's overall travel. Still, these rest stops must be kept very brief during rainy weather. When hiking minimally dressed during cold, rainy weather we are operating metabolically. Consequently, at each of our rest stops we must consider ourselves in a red-alert situation in terms of hypothermia. Bundle up at the rest stops and keep those rest stops brief. Otherwise make camp.

- At day's end, pitch the tent, remove and wring out your wet clothing, hang it to dry on a clothesline strung inside your tent or beneath your tent's awning or tarp, and crawl straightway into your sleeping bag.

While distance hiking in rainy weather you might be tempted to stop and make camp early in the day. Try to nurture the momentum to move ahead regardless of the weather's mood – within reason of course. As with any "obstacle" we benefit tremendously by learning to project our consciousness through it. And remember that the umbrella can greatly improve your enjoyment of the day's travel by allowing you to essentially ignore the rain.

Lightning

Lightning sometimes kills people and animals, yes; but that is one of its few negative deeds. Starting forest fires would seem to be another, and this is generally true with today's multi-clear-cut "tree farms." Actually, fires are a necessary and beneficial aspect of old-growth forest ecology. And it plays an even greater role in the ecology of the Earth as a whole. As a bolt rips though the sky it breaks loose nitrogen. Twenty million lightning storms annually deposit some 100 million tons of nitrogen on soil and plants, as brought to the earth by rainfall. Nitrogen is sustenance for the world's flora. Have you ever stood at the base of a colossal tree and wondered where all that mass came from? Surely not from the earth, otherwise the tree would have made a giant indentation in the ground. No, the mass came mainly from the nitrogen and carbon dioxide in the air, created in lightning storms and brought to the earth by rain.

When Thor is hurling his mighty charges in our direction, he doesn't really take aim. His bolts can strike just about anywhere as a matter of chance. Still, we can take a few precautions that can greatly reduce our chances of being hit.

Avoidance

Along the PCT, lightning is most active on the higher mountains during afternoon thunderstorms. These thunderstorms are fairly predictable. Let's look at the cycle:

Initially, the early morning sky will be cloud free, but little puffy cumulus clouds will develop and grow throughout the morning. In the first few days of the cycle these clouds will remain benign, although they grow more extensive each day. Then one day they will "over-develop" and fill the sky. The next day they will do the same, and may become very black. It is these black clouds that spawn lightning. Succeeding mornings may start out clear, then the clouds will over-develop into various thunderstorms. After a few days of this, a front will pass through and fill even the morning sky with clouds. Rain may or may not fall but lightning will have ceased. Then after the front has passed, the weather cycle will begin anew, initially with clear skies throughout the day.

Observing these cycles allows us to predict the afternoon's weather with fair accuracy. That way, if our route ahead climbs to an exposed position we know whether or not we may safely proceed. If the previous afternoon brought thunderstorms, and if this afternoon's hiking would place us in a high, exposed place, then we know we should wait. We might haul off the trail, pitch our tent or tarp, cook a meal, and enjoy a nice nap, hopefully uninterrupted by the clapping of thunder striking the ridges above. Then after the storm has passed we could break camp and resume our journey. And of course along the way we might meet descending white-faced hikers who regale us with tales of horror.

If we find ourselves on an exposed ridge above treeline, with black clouds approaching, we would commence a descent immediately. Meanwhile, we could watch the flashes and count the seconds until hearing their thunder. To estimate the bolt's distance in miles, we divide the number of seconds by five.

If we find we cannot descend, perhaps because of cliffs on both sides, and if we are caught in a lightening storm, then we would remember that lightning tends to seek the highest grounded object in its vicinity. We make ourselves as low as possible by descending as far as we can, removing our packs, then assuming the lightning defensive position. This consists of crouching low on both feet (taking advantage of the shoe or boot sole's dielectric insulation), of keeping the knees together to lessen the spark gap between them, and of keeping the mouth open to reduce the pressure differential in the ear canals. Members of the group should spread out. That way, should one person be struck, the others would not be injured from the "splash," and would be available to administer CPR (cardiopulmonary resuscitation) to the strike victim. Also, metal objects including pack stays, umbrellas and ice axes should be set well aside.

Below timberline we would take refuge in the trees, but we would not sit beneath a tree for its protection from the rain. The rule is: be among the trees but not too near any one of them.

First aid

Being struck by lightning has been described as sustaining a total-body blow by a white-hot sledgehammer. The results are usually unconsciousness, a shut down of the heart beat and breathing, rupture of the eardrums, and possible burns. The strike victim will appear dead. In most instances, however, the heart is in a quivering state known as ventricular fibrillation. Usually it can be restarted with CPR, even though this may take an hour or sometimes much longer.

Umbrella Hazard

Obviously, carrying a deployed umbrella when the air is electrically charged is asking for trouble. If you are holding the umbrella in your hand, avoid touching the metal shaft. I credit the plastic handles for saving our lives once:

While hiking through New Mexico during our CDT trek, Jenny and I were splattered by a nearby strike. One minute we were hiking along under our umbrellas in a pouring rain – with no evidence of lightning anywhere – and the next minute an explosion knocked us momentarily senseless. We found ourselves chasing after our umbrellas, with no recollection of having dropped them.

Creek Fording

In many years of backpacking, climbing, long distance hiking, and kayaking adventures I've gained a reasonable amount of experience in fording creeks and rivers. The result is an enormous respect for the power of moving water.

As fledgling professionals in charge of various wilderness programs, we Outward Bound instructors experimented with every technique we could think of, related to using ropes as security for crossing creeks and rivers.

Initially, we scheduled arriving bus loads of students to disembark at the bank of some daunting river. After unloading, we instructed the students to line up, lock elbows, and not let go. Then we marched them across, mid-torso deep. This technique worked well, until one time a student did let go, and was swept down river at great peril. So the next time we rigged a safety line, angling obliquely across the river and out of sight downstream. The next student who let go of the gang was swept by the current into our rope, only to become trapped like a fly in a spider's web. The director dove in headlong, swam to the student's rescue, and pried him bodily off the "safety" rope.

Trial and error

In the ensuing years we experimented further. We tried wading a river while holding onto a rope, fed from a belayer – only to find that the rope drag drastically compromised the wader's balance and concentration. We installed "sky-lines" over creeks, tree-to-tree, and experimented with various tensions and heights of rigging them. At first we secured the students to a sky-line using long lanyards and carabiners. This proved dangerous because the stretching sky-line offered little balance, yet its tension tended to drag the wader face first into the river. Then we tried using the sky-line for hands-on balance; but with much the same results.

We set Tyrolean traverses: pairs of taut ropes across which students hauled themselves while suspended by harnesses and carabiners. But the weight of even one person hanging on the block-and-tackle-stretched ropes elongated them beyond their elastic limits, and ruined them for future use. And we constructed complicated rope latticeworks as make-shift Burma bridges. Both these techniques required that someone first swim across the river while towing a pilot line, and this was genuinely dangerous.

These "trial and error" experiments may sound clumsy, but they only illustrate how firmly we believed the myth that ropes could be used to safeguard river crossings.

A roped drowning

A friend of mine and his climbing partner had completed a technically difficult, multi-day ascent of the Leaning Tower, in Yosemite. After climbing down the Tower's back side they decided to descend to the valley via a shortcut that led across Bridalveil Creek. The precipitous falls lay immediately downstream, so as though climbing rock, my friend waded in with his climbing rope attached to his harness and leading back to his partner seated on the riverbank in the standard belay position. The creek bed was polished bedrock, made slippery with algae; and within seconds the wader became a submarine. The belay rope, meant as a safety device, now acted as a drowning device. The torrent's force, countered by the strain on the rope, submerged the victim to the riverbed. Yet his belayer could not pay slack because of the nearby waterfall. The belayer later told me that the force on the rope was unimaginable. After struggling to secure the rope to his anchors, he rigged a haul system that climbers use to hoist bags of water, food and bivouac equipment. After a protracted struggle he winched the body out of the water.

If I seem to be painting a grim picture, so much the better. In Yosemite alone, a dozen or more hikers drown each season. Remember that the water is usually deeper (due to refraction of light), colder, and more swift than it might appear from the bank. And no matter how swift the current, and no matter how cold and clear the water, algae will be growing on the riverbed, whether or not you can see it. So before starting across any creek, via a log, a series of rocks, or a wade, stop and consider the peril. And never step into water, however placid, where whitewater lurks downstream.

Creek crossings along the PCT

Creek crossings are an unavoidable part of a PCT thru-hike. Most are reasonably benign and present little danger. And theoretically all the unwadeable torrents are bridged, although floods and avalanches have a way of displacing bridges. Also, because some of the creeks which are easily forded in summertime can be roaring gushers in spring, early season PCT thru-hikers can expect to encounter a few creeks that are quite dangerous. These are not to be experimented with. If the crossing looks in the least questionable, hike upstream until you find a log on which to cross, or turn back and take another route – even if it means a several day detour.

The natural bridge

Many creeks along the way are bridged naturally by rocks or fallen timbers. Negotiating these often requires a good sense of balance. None of us are born with this skill, just as we are not born with the skill to ride a bicycle. Back on page 34 I explained how to improve one's sense of balance. This is important material which could spare you a few dunkings into shallow water.

Where the water is deep and swift you would not walk across a log. The preferable method is to sit down and straddle it. Your feet dangling on both sides would contribute greatly to balance, and you could even squeeze the log between your legs for added security. In this position you would skooch across a few inches at a time, shoving your backpack ahead. One caution: before straddling any log make sure it can't roll.

The fording staff

When approaching a creek where wading will be necessary and presumably safe, half a mile back you might begin looking for a stout stick as an aid to balance. Should campers cease from burning fording staffs we would probably find many on both sides of nearly every creek. But because firewood is such a scarce commodity at the creek-side campsites, fording staffs are considered fair game. So whenever you cross a creek with one, carry it well beyond the campsites and deposit it alongside the trail for use by those coming the other way.

Unlatch the backpack's waist strap

Before taking the first step across any creek, large or small, unlatch the buckle of your backpack's hip belt. Novices might be reluctant to do this, thinking that a poorly balanced backpack could topple them into the water. And they might worry about losing their packs in the process. Granted, with the pack cinched tightly around the waist they would save their packs, but they might lose their lives instead. One cannot swim very well, if at all, strapped to a heavy backpack. Your shoulders alone are fully capable of keeping the pack on your back. And should you slip and fall into the water you should be able to shrug the shoulder straps off in one quick motion.

In fact, make a habit of unlatching your hip belt when tackling *any* situation where a heavy object strapped to your body could increase the danger. This applies when balancing across fallen logs, stepping from rock to rock, and traversing precipitous terrain and steep snowbanks.

The ford

While thru-hiking the PCT you may come to the occasional creek that is deep and flowing fast enough to cause concern, but not so much so that it cannot be safely forded. As a general rule, if the water is moving swiftly and knee deep or deeper, forget it. Scout the bank for a natural bridge. Jenny and I have hiked as much as 5 miles along creeks looking for safe crossings. And if you find what appears to be a safe place to cross, but where whitewater lurks directly downstream, don't risk it. One slip and you could be swept into it. And if the creek bed is solid rock, find somewhere else. That rock is probably coated in translucent algae, and it can be deathly slippery because one you fall into the fast water it can prevent you from crawling out.

Look for a wide but shallow area, as opposed to a narrow one where the water is deep. Some exposed rocks offer security part way across, but others create turbulence which forms deep holes surrounding them. Make sure your way is clear of submerged logs and branches, and check that the opposite bank is climbable. Lastly, check your confidence level, and be sure it is tempered with caution.

Once you have decided that all looks well, wade into the creek slowly while carrying your stout balancing stick, braced upstream. Holding it downstream would place much more strain on it. If it snaps, you could lose your balance. Test the waters. Is the riverbed dangerously slippery? Is the current more swift than you imagined? If so, return to the bank and look for a crossing somewhere else. Is the water deeper than it appeared from shore? Don't try it. Otherwise, proceed ahead, step by cautious step. Don't place your weight onto your next leg until you have explored the bottom by feel and found secure footing. Rivet your eyes on the far shore, to prevent the water's motion from upsetting your equilibrium. But don't make the far shore your goal at the expense of your judgment. Gaze ahead, but anchor your mind on your present situation. Feel the current pressing strongly against your legs. Feel it trying to wrench each foot as you lift it free to take the next step. Keep a cool head and maintain control. If you feel the slightest insecure, turn around and carefully, step by calculated step, work your way back. Returning will be easier because you will have practiced the moves and you will know the ground.

Otherwise, before you reach the half-way point, assess your strength. If you are tiring, consider turning back. Fatigue can greatly undermine composure. But don't let the numbing coldness alone dissuade you.

Having nearly reached the far shore, you might find that the water ahead becomes deeper and more swift than expected. This is often the case at the outside bend of a river, where the water's centrifugal force drives it into the far bank. Do not let the nearness of shore tempt you into bolting for it. If prudence suggests turning back, do it. I have done the same a number of times.

Of all the safety precautions for creek crossings, the most important is to remain on your feet. Do not assume that you can swim a torrent. If the water is too swift and deep to wade, and the bottom is too slippery, then you must not assume that in a last ditch effort you will be able to swim across. Strong turbulence can make swimming impossible.

Foot protection

For demanding creek crossings, always wear shoes. First, though, remove your socks to lessen the drag, then tighten your shoe laces to increase security. From the far bank you would hike on a ways, drying your shoes somewhat before putting your socks back on.

During our CDT trek Jenny and I hiked for a month in extremely wet weather though northern Montana, often wading dozens of creeks every day. We rarely removed our shoes or socks, and without ill effect.

In situations where the wade will be minor you might remove your dry shoes and socks and tie them to your pack, then don a pair or two of dirty or wet socks. These would provide more cushioning and protection, as well as moderately good traction. And they would insulate your feet somewhat from the crushing cold. Once at the creek's far side you would remove the socks, wring them out and hang them on your pack to dry. Then you would slip back into your dry socks and shoes, and continue on your way.

Jumping small creeks

The PCT features hundreds of creeklets of a size that tempt the hiker to jump over them. Don't. The rocks or logs on the other side could be coated in algae and extremely slippery. And in early morning, the diffused light might not reveal the glimmer of verglas – condensed and frozen dew. Either way you could land crooked and pull a muscle. When it comes to logs and rocks there are jumpers and there are experienced hikers, but there are no experienced jumpers. If you cannot find a place to step across, then wade.

Build your fording experience day at a time, and always with prudence. The more creeks you wade, the better you will be able to assess their dangers. The creeks along the PCT which are the most dangerous tend to vary from year to year, depending on the snowmelt run-off, and where any naturally downed log bridges might lie. Rarely do these natural log bridges remain in place from year to year. However, the later you arrive at these fords, the smaller they will be, and the less their dangers. This is one of the main reasons that I discourage early-season PCT trekking.

Hot!

I walked in a desert.
And I cried:
"Ah, God, take me from this place!"
A voice said: "It is no desert."
I cried: "Well, but—
The sand, the heat, the vacant horizon."
A voice said: "It is no desert."

— Stephen Crane

The PCT is not all majestic forest and craggy mountains. The trail crosses many desert-like regions. These are not true deserts like the Sahara or even Death Valley, but lowlands of creosote scrub, grassland and chaparral offering mostly easy trekking, a fascinating array of plant and animal life, and exemplary camping under the stars.

Arabs survive and flourish in their torrid environments wearing heavy clothing to shield them from the powerful ultraviolet radiation and to insulate them from the intense heat. Obviously, while cloaked in this insulation they must not over-exert. Otherwise, the heat of exertion would convert their garments into kilns.

We distance hikers, too, need to protect ourselves from the sun, but we cannot wear heavy, Arab-type clothing while exercising strenuously. So instead, we regulate our temperature primarily by shading ourselves with umbrellas covered with reflective mylar, by wearing minimal, loose-fitting and lightweight clothing, and by drinking lots of water. The umbrella protects us from the sun's radiation, and the minimal clothing and generous fluid intake allow the perspiration to cool us, as designed.

Where are the warmer regions?

The terrain between the Mexican border and the flanks of Mt. Laguna can be quite warm, even in early and late season. The stretch between Chariot Canyon and Barrel Springs might be the hike's most torrid, although it is well known for its stormy weather, and some hikers have reported traversing it in parkas. Other hot areas are the Agua Dulce and Tehachapi environs, the Hat Creek Rim, and the Castella area. Of course, variations occur each summer, and you may find hot weather in other sections in addition to, or instead of these.

233

Night hiking

Jenny and I enjoy hiking far into the evenings, sometimes very far into them. Yet we consider walking through the desert at night impractical. The reduced pace and chances of stepping into pot holes are minor inconveniences compared with the chances of treading on a rattlesnake. And talk about frayed nerves! The subdued light makes every stick look like it might be a snake, and contrary to expectations a full moon only worsens the situation by casting suspicious shadows over every creosote bush. A flashlight would help, but enough batteries to last all night, every night would be impractical to buy, carry, and dispose of in an ecological manner.

The mylar covered umbrella

Traditionally, desert trekkers start hiking when the light of dawn is sufficient to reveal the presence of any rattlesnakes. They hike until the day grows intolerably hot, and rather than struggle beneath the afternoon sun they stop and rest in the shade, reading or napping until late afternoon. Then they set off again, and hike until the fading light of dusk precludes watching for snakes. Jenny and I tried this method and found that mid-day shade in the desert is a figment of someone's fecund imagination. So we decided to make our own shade, and it was then that I originated the idea of the mylar covered umbrella.

The mylar I am referring to is a silver polyester film, a Space® Blanket or the equivalent, which looks rather like aluminum foil. Cut to the approximate shape of the umbrella and taped to its perimeter,[1] it blocks nearly 100% of the sun's ultraviolet radiation and about 80% of its heat.

The hiker's main source of heat in desert-like environments is solar radiation bombarding the clothing and skin. While hiking beneath a mylar covered umbrella, wearing minimal, loose and airy clothing, and while carrying plenty of water and drinking copiously, Jenny and I find that we can hike throughout the day.

Sunburn

The effects of ultraviolet rays are cumulative, and the dangers of skin cancer are real. Again, my primary line of defense from the desert sun is the mylar covered umbrella. Beneath this I walk in almost total shade during the hottest times of the day. The protection it gives is so good that I cannot imagine hiking in the desert without one.

---

[1] In addition to tape, use small rubber bands to secure the mylar to the tip of each of the umbrella's tines.

My second line of defense is light weight clothing, covering the skin but fitting very loosely for better ventilation. Light weight clothing is not a primary defense because most of the sun's ultraviolet rays penetrate it. According to dermatologist and long distance hiker Tom McGillis, the SPF[2] rating for most lightweight fabrics is only 8 to 10. And when this clothing is wet its SPF drops almost to zero. Compare that with the mylar umbrella's SPF of nearly 100.

My third line of defense against sunburn is sunscreen with a high SPF. However, note that PABA and benzophenone, the two active ingredients used in most sunscreens, can produce allergic reactions, one of which is photodermatitis.

Photodermatitis

Photoallergenic and phototoxic contact dermatitis are commonly experienced by hikers over-exposed to the sun. These skin problems manifest themselves as exaggerated sunburns, following the application or ingestion of certain chemicals that lessens the skin's resistance to ultraviolet radiation. The chemical might be in a food or drink such as fruit juice, or in soap, shampoo, hand lotion, insect repellent, or ironically even in the sunblock cream.

Photodermatitis manifests itself as small blisters that sometimes itch like poison oak. If left exposed to the sun it can rapidly worsen. Rinse the affected parts repeatedly and gently in cold water, using no soap, then apply a hydrocortisone cream or dab the affected areas liberally with antiseptic, then cover them with cloth adhesive strips. Be extremely careful when removing the strips; otherwise they might peel away the blistered skin.

Most importantly, cover the affected area to minimize its exposure to sunshine, and uncover it at night for ventilation. It is most common on the back of the fingers and hands, when hiking at higher altitudes, and especially on glaring snowfields. Wear protective mitts made from an old pair of socks with their toes cut off for better ventilation.

How much water to carry?

In late April on our first thru-hike Jenny and I experienced the hottest temperatures of our career. Initially we tried carrying little water and traveling swiftly from one water source to the next. After one particularly torturous jaunt we reached a water source and chugged five quarts of water each. In the ensuing days we tried other strategies, but finally decided that the weight of

---

[2] Sun Protection Factor: The percentage of ultraviolet radiation blocked by the sunscreen or garment.

water is inconsequential compared with its value in sustaining life. And it was then that we resumed hiking in reasonable comfort and health, despite the loads and temperatures. By the time we reached Walker Pass the heat had eased to 110° and we were each consuming three gallons of water a day.

On our most recent journey we hiked the trail south of Walker Pass in late August. To accommodate the 100° temperatures we hiked beneath mylar covered umbrellas while wearing minimal clothing. We kept careful track of our water consumption, and found that it averaged about two gallons per person per day, which included water used for cooking corn pasta.

As a northbound hiker, rarely will you have to carry more than a day's supply of water. Although carrying two gallons is a hefty addition to your packweight, as the day progresses that load will lighten considerably. And I might note here that the desert is not a good place for the long distance hiker to consume diuretics, such as coffee, tea, and alcohol. These fluids extract water from the body rather than add to it.

Cold!

Even in July and August, strong, icy winds can lash the alpine crests, bringing rain and sometimes snow. Hikers unaccustomed to these conditions often focus on the discomforts and attendant dangers - such as hypothermia. In this chapter we examine the more essential techniques of cold weather camping and travel, designed to reduce the discomfort and danger and to inspire more self confidence with the journey as a whole.

The basics of long distance trekking should be apparent by now: moving along at a constant, steady pace, eating high quality meals, snacking often, and drinking plenty of water. In cold weather these principles become even more important. In addition, we must remain particularly aware of whether we are overheating or losing heat. This requires, first, constant monitoring; and second, remedying any deficits in their early stages. Overheating? Yes, the overdressed hiker is an overheated one, and as sweat soaks the clothing it reduces its ability to insulate. All is apparently well until this person stops for a long rest, and begins to chill.

Heeding all of these factors will go a long ways in adding to your safety and enjoyment of cold weather hiking. Ignoring any one of them can indeed lead to hypothermia.

Eating well

As you hike along the trail your muscles "burn" fuel and oxygen. If the hiking is fairly strenuous and prolonged, then the heat of this "combustion" will likely keep you plenty warm. Food plays another key role, and Jenny and I have found that a steaming pot of corn pasta has a tremendous warming effect. But I wouldn't recommend stopping alongside the trail in very cold weather to cook. You could become deeply chilled while sitting there. The answer is to eat well at camp, from the warm confines of your sleeping bag, and then to eat snacks every hour or so while on the trail, keeping the rest periods brief and the water intake regular and ample. And while I don't recommend sugar and fat-laden foods as energy, I have found that when eaten in very small quantities at frequent intervals they can provide a certain amount of metabolic warmth. I recommend planning ahead for those chilly days by carrying a few snacks in your pockets, and a supply of them in the top of your pack.

Drinking plenty of water

While hiking in cold and blustery conditions we must drink water often. We lose a fair amount in our breath, and from our insensible perspiration. And if not careful we can lose a lot from sweating. The resulting dehydration thickens the blood and reduces its volume. This hampers circulation, which in turn affects our ability to warm our extremities.

Wearing clothing dynamically

Mother's instructions for bundling warmly on those cold days do not apply while distance hiking. Granted, you would start out from the rest stops wearing an extra layer or two. But as soon as your body regains operating temperature you would stop and remove them, specifically to minimize sweating. Learning to attune to your body temperature is a skill. Concentrate on whether your body feels a little sweaty or a little chilled, and correct immediately. Or better yet, anticipate and make the appropriate adjustments slightly ahead of time.

If the temperature drops and the terrain levels, and you find yourself feeling a little chilled, put your hat back on. Heat rises, and a hat can catch a great deal of heat emanating from your body via your head. If colder still, put on your sweater or parka. If you find yourself feeling deeply chilled despite being well bundled, play it safe: stop and make camp.

Hiking clothing

Heat is a natural byproduct of work, and the hard working hiker must dissipate the excess. So the hiking clothing should be thin and lightweight, minimizing sweat and allowing the greatest ventilation.

Resting clothing

Conversely, the resting clothing would comprise thicker garments providing insulation and protection from the wind chill. At each rest stop, preferably at a place sheltered from the wind, you would remove your sweat-dampened, lighter-weight hiking clothing and hang them to air. Then you would quickly don your heavier clothing, carried handy in your pack. After the rest period you would change back into your hiking garb and put most of the warmer apparel away. In only a short ways you will be back to operating temperature, and can remove whatever insulating garments you still have on.

However, in an emergency you would wear all your warm garments while hiking, regardless of how wet they become. And in such a situation you would hike *down* out of the more exposed regions, seeking a sheltered place to camp.

Hypothermia

The term hypothermia describes a decrease in normal body temperature (hypo - meaning low, and therm - meaning heat). I recommend Dr. James A. Wilkerson's *Medicine for Mountaineering* (see Bibliography) which contains one of the best descriptions on the subject I've read. Generally, hypothermia progresses in stages from mild: with shivering, chilliness, and loss of dexterity in the fingers, to severe: unconsciousness and death. The malady can be particularly dangerous because it affects the victim's ability to detect it, and increasingly so as it progresses though the stages.

These dangers are minimal for the person exercising vigorously, especially when traveling uphill and generating ample metabolic heat. But while resting in damp clothing one becomes immediately susceptible. Body heat is lost, and this, combined with a lack of energy from not eating enough good food, and the typically severe dehydration, can lead to a case of hypothermia.

One must act definitively in such circumstances. If the condition is fairly mild you would try to descend and make camp in a sheltered area. Otherwise, don't hesitate to pitch your tent right there on the trail. After doing so, remove your wet clothing and climb into your sleeping bag with a few energy snacks. If you are using a tarp instead, locate a place protected from the wind, and which has good drainage. Pitch your tarp extremely low lying, with its two edges flush to the ground and in a direction perpendicular to the wind.

Cold weather camps

In cold weather, avoid camping in areas where the trees are stunted or entirely absent. These could indicate katabatic pockets. If they are too cold for trees to flourish then they would be too cold for you to camp. For more about avoiding katabatic air, refer to page 189. That entire chapter contains many more tips on choosing the warmest and most secure campsites.

Snowpack

Every land has its own special rhythm.
Unless the traveler takes the time to learn the rhythm
he or she will remain an outsider there always.

— *Juliette De Baircli Levy*

Alpine snowpack is one of Nature's most beautiful compositions, lending spectacle and splendor to the mountains and high forests. The snowpacked landscape is pristine, void of sound but never quiet, tranquil but never still. To tread slowly and methodically across some vast glacial-like expanse can be a humbling but mind escalating experience. So much so that at times we might feel almost as though trespassing Mother Earth's inner sanctum. Often, though, we find dainty tracks of small animals and birds, or the heartening furrows of large animals. These remind us that life does indeed thrive in the alpine winter wonderland.

And when at last the snowpack steepens, we eagerly draw our ice axes and climb into a playground of unparalleled grandeur. Alpine air beneath our heels has a way of intensifying reality; and no scene on earth is more sublime, more rewarding than the sudden view over some hard-won spine of the frozen High Sierra.

The PCT is a trail of adventure. And the *Handbook* is meant to insure that those adventures are all safe and rewarding. The hazards along the way are not many, at least for those who exercise skill and sound judgment. But they can be quite real for the person who chooses to ignore them. Mountain snowpack has the potential to be hazardous, but with a knowledge of when and where it is genuinely dangerous, and the skills for safe travel, the snowpack can add immeasurably to the summer's adventure.

Misconception: southern California is all desert

In the past, thru-hikers would set off from the Mexican border in early spring believing that the trail would lead them mainly through deserts in southern California. And thinking in terms of a 6 or 7 month trek they were trying to avoid the late-spring heat of the deserts, and to beat the early-winter snowfall in the North Cascades. What they didn't realize was that the PCT confronts a succession of mountains which begins near the Mexican border and continues all the way into Canada. Granted, in southern California these mountains are interspersed with relatively arid and often fairly hot lowlands of chaparral and creosote. But we must also take into account the high mountains, where spring usually looks and feels more like winter. And typically, those who tried to traverse these snowy regions too early in the season toiled needlessly, only to become disenchanted and return home. Others admitted temporary defeat by walking roads circumventing the mountains, or finding themselves waylaid somewhere en route, waiting for the snowpack to melt and perhaps wishing they had waited, instead, at home.

Much of this early-season snow along the PCT in southern California is gently inclined and not particularly dangerous. Granted, it can obscure the route and make it harder to follow – and of course the consequences of getting lost could be serious, as could those of becoming hypothermic. And when soft, the gently inclined snow can increase the labors of wallowing through it enormously, while retarding mileage to the same degree. However, some of the snow is not so gently inclined, particularly in the High Sierra. Avalanches have buried a few early-season hikers, and steep, icy slopes have sent many careening into rocks or trees far below. But let's return to the mountains of southern California, and take a closer look at the typical spring snow conditions there.

Mt. Laguna

The first of these is Mt. Laguna, standing 5,900 feet high and about 43 trail miles from the Mexican Border. For most hikers this is only two or three days into the journey. Those starting according to one of the *Handbook's* itineraries are likely to find this mountain entirely snow free. But those starting early can encounter up to 30 trail miles of deep and pervasive snow. And early spring storms are well known for depositing more.

The Desert Divide

Beyond Mt. Laguna the trail leads through warmer, drier climes for a hundred miles until it rises again to the Desert Divide. Beyond is a region of surpassing beauty; and for the unsuspecting hiker ahead of the *Handbook's* itineraries it can also be a region of considerable peril. Here, much of the trail was blasted out of precipitous rock, and when snowbound it can call for the skills of an accomplished and well equipped mountaineer.

Mt. San Jacinto and beyond

Beyond the Desert Divide the PCT traverses the lofty flanks of Mt. San Jacinto, which in early season can harbor snowpack so deep and pervasive that it can obscure the route almost completely for 14 miles from Saddle Junction, along Fuller Ridge to the northern terminus of Black Mountain Ridge. Beyond that, en route to the High Sierra the trail traverses the San Bernardino range, staying lower and away from most of its snowpack; and the San Gabriel Mountains, climbing high and leading straight through the snow there.

Normal and abnormal snow deposition

After a winter of normal snow deposition, hikers who start according to one of the *Handbook's* itineraries should encounter relatively little snow. "Relatively," because still they are likely to find at least a few steep and icy patches covering the trail, possibly on Mt. San Jacinto but mainly in the High Sierra. Accordingly, each hiker will need to carry an ice axe through these areas and know how to self-arrest with it. I described the techniques back on page 35.

It *is* possible to chose a year of normal snowpack for your PCT thru-hike. As the winter unfolds you could read the Sierra snowpack reports in the newspapers and on the Internet, keeping in mind that they can be somewhat slanted toward encouraging tourism in the ski areas. Nevertheless, if the snow is accumulating deeper than normal, simply postpone your journey and watch the reports the following winter. Of course, this scheme is not too practical. Most hikers choose the year of their journeys regardless of what conditions may be in store. If the winter's deposition exceeds 200% of normal, however, as it did in 1995 for example, I recommend two options: One, that you post-pone your trip a year. Or two, that you start not until late May, that you pre-pare to hike many miles of snowpack in southern and central California, and that beyond the High Sierra you press ahead with a will in order to finish be-fore the early-winter snowstorms hit the North Cascades.

If the winter snowfall was normal or below, and if you plan to start ac-cording to one of the book's itineraries, then you should have very few snow-pack worries. The following discussions deal with heavier than average snowpack – caused either by a heavy deposition or by starting too early.

Should you find yourself in this category, a word of warning:

Avalanche!

When the High Sierra is deeply snowbound, avalanches can make travel quite dangerous. To increase your margins of safety, learn to recognize the condi-tions of greatest peril and avoid the danger zones. The problem is, the PCT leads straight through a number of them.

Let's look at a few of the principles: The steeper a slope is, the more gravity pulls on the snow covering it, and the more that snow is liable to ava-lanche. Also, a winter's snowpack is like a multi-layer cake, with each layer consisting of the snow deposited by successive storms. And because each storm is different, so is the snow it deposits. The greatest avalanche danger occurs, then, when a heavier layer rests upon a lighter and less cohesive one.

So, if you find yourself hiking the PCT through the Sierra in its snow-packed condition, you would avoid traveling beneath steep snow slopes. And even then you would refrain from making a lot of noise. Sometimes just a sharp sound will trigger an avalanche. Where the trail climbs a steep slope, you might start climbing it off to one side, one person at a time. Part way up, dig a slot a couple of feet deep, very carefully with the ice axe. Examine the layers. If you find that all layers are compact, then the slope is probably safe to climb. However, if you find an icy layer, or a layer which lacks cohesion – "corn snow" it is called because the individual flakes have metamorphosed without bonding together – then however thin that layer might be, do not proceed. Your weight could be the proverbial straw that breaks the camel's back, setting the entire slope in motion.

Otherwise, as you climb the slope, keep your backpack's hip belt unlatched. The unfortunate hiker caught in an avalanche should shrug off the backpack and swim frantically for the surface. When avalanche alluvium comes to a stop it tends to set up like concrete. A friend of mine was once caught in a small avalanche that buried him only partially, yet he could not struggle free. Fortunately he was not alone, but by the time his buddies dug him out they had to administer artificial respiration. If you are planning to hike through the Sierra in early season, (usually prior to mid May but much later in a year of heavy snowpack) then you and your party would do well to study a few books on avalanche safety, and to carry transponders and probes.

My advice regarding snowpack is this: First, if you have very little experience in winter mountaineering, and if you are not too keen on the whole idea, you should avoid the snowpack. Second, if you have little experience, but are genuinely intrigued, you might want to learn the theories and techniques ahead of time and experiment with them carefully. And third, if you have the confidence that comes from years of experience, enjoy the snowpack!

How much snow, and where?

The amount of snowpack northbound hikers encounter at any given place along the PCT in southern and central California depends on the elevation and latitude, the time of year, the previous winter's deposition, and the spring-time's melt rate. Hikers have no control over the winter's deposition, the spring's melt rate, or the trail's elevations. But they can choose the time of year they hike the trail. And the good news is that this variable has perhaps the greatest influence of all. In terms of safety and enjoyment, timing is all important.

Categories of snowpack coverage

I have divided the PCT Universe into four categories of snowpack coverage: Little, Light, Medium, and Heavy. The definitions of the categories are given in the table below. You can estimate which category you will be hiking in by researching the depth of snow in the High Sierra. This information is published regularly in the San Francisco Chronicle and Los Angeles Times newspapers. And I imagine that by the time you read this it will be available on the Internet. At any rate, with a rough idea of snow deposition in the Sierra you then begin your journey according to an itinerary. When you reach two key locations, or indicators, in the San Jacinto Mountains, you will know what to expect throughout the remainder of your summer's journey.

Estimating the category ahead of time

Assuming you will be hiking in accordance with one of the *Handbook's* itineraries, we can take an educated guess as to what snowpack category you will likely be hiking in, based on the percentage snowpack figures for the High Sierra, as mentioned above.

Winter's Snow Deposition in the High Sierra	Will You Be Following a *Handbook* Itinerary?	Snowpack Category
74% of Normal and Below	Yes	"Little Snowpack"
75% to 99% of Normal	Yes	"Light Snowpack"
100% to 139% of Normal	Yes	"Medium Snowpack"
140% of Normal and Above	Yes	"Heavy Snowpack"

Those who start ahead of the *Handbook's* itineraries automatically place themselves in a higher snowpack category. Generally, for each two weeks earlier, they would place themselves in the next higher category. This figure is based on the average rate of melting in the springtime.

A visible clue

As you reach the Pines to Palms Highway you may decide to hike northwest one mile to the Backcountry Inn restaurant for water and a meal. While walking along the highway, if the weather is clear you should catch a glimpse of Mt. San Jacinto, standing away to the north. If you see even a little snow up there, then you are probably hiking in a "Medium Snowpack" or "Heavy Snowpack" category.

As you continue following the trail, now along the Desert Divide, if the sky is clear then you should occasionally see Mt. San Jacinto, still in the distance. If the mountain appears very white, then you are even more sure to be in a "Medium Snowpack" or "Heavy Snowpack" category.

The two indicators that specify your category exactly

Indicator 1 ➠	The trail in the general vicinity of Antsell Rock, just beyond the Desert Divide (WP Guide book map B8).
Indicator 2 ➠	The trail traversing west along the north slopes of Red Tahquitz Peak, 8 miles beyond Indicator 1 (map B9).

Taking into account these two factors - Snowpack Category and Indicator - what follows is a description of the snow conditions you are likely to encounter all the way through the Sierra and beyond, and how best to deal with them.

Determining the category from the indicators

❶	If you find both indicators snow free, you are in Category **"Little snowpack"**.
❷	If you find indicator 1 snow free, and indicator 2 with patchy snow, then you are in Category **"Light snowpack"**.
❸	If you find indicator 1 with patchy snow, and indicator 2 snowbound, then you are in Category **"Medium snowpack"**.
❹	If you find both indicators snowbound, you are in Category **"Heavy snowpack"**.

Once you have determined what category you are traveling in, refer to the appropriate table below. And once again, please note that regardless of the snowpack category you find yourself hiking in, you should always carry an ice axe and know how to use it.

Snowpack descriptions for each category

❶ Category "Little Snowpack"

You will probably find the trail snow free throughout southern California. In the High Sierra you are likely to encounter snow only on the higher passes, and mainly on their north-facing slopes. Beyond Donohue Pass the trail is likely to be clear all the way to Canada. Early-winter storms could strike northern Washington prior to your arrival. But if you have traveled expeditiously from Tuolumne Meadows, then you should arrive well ahead of them.

Because this category involves very little snowpack, you might be tempted to start earlier. Normally, this would not be to your advantage. The earlier you start, the more snow you will encounter. This snow will increase the difficulties enormously, and slow your progress.

❷ Category "Light Snowpack"

You are likely to find Mt. Laguna snow free, as well as the Desert Divide. You will encounter patches along the north slope of Red Tahquitz Peak, but most can be circumvented. The trail is then likely to be snow free to the Fuller Ridge, where again you might encounter lingering patches, some of which might be more expansive. This will be your last snow until reaching the High Sierra.

Your first snow in the High Sierra will probably be near Cottonwood Pass, at 11,160 feet. And what conditions you find there will indicate what you will encounter at this approximate elevation all the way to Donohue Pass. You will probably find the south-facing, sun-facing slopes harboring much less snow than the north-facing ones.

Beyond Donohue Pass you should encounter only patchy snow all the way to Leavitt Peak. Beyond there you will descend for the last time past 10,000 feet, and should confront no more snow the remainder of the way to Canada – with two possible exceptions: The trail above the Packwood Glacier in the Goat Rocks Wilderness might harbor snow, and this can be frozen hard early in the mornings. If so, wait a few hours for it to soften. And Fire Creek Pass on the slopes of Glacier Peak usually has snow on its northern slope. Carry an ice axe for this one just in case.

❸ Category "Medium Snowpack"

Mt. Laguna might harbor some snow, but no more than a few miles of it. And barring any recent storms, this snow should not be more than a foot deep.

While hiking along the Desert Divide you may see what appears to be a dusting of snow on distant Mt. San Jacinto. In reality you are looking at up to 30 trail miles of snow. If you are not proficient with the ice axe self-arrest, and with map and compass navigation, you might consider leaving the PCT at one of the spur trails (bomb-offs) leading down and west, and proceeding to Idyllwild. From there you could follow the Black Mountain Road, and rejoin the PCT at the northwest end of Fuller Ridge.

Otherwise, continuing along the Desert Divide you may encounter patches of snow along its far northern reaches. And if you arrive there early in the morning you will probably find these patches ice-skating-rink hard and slippery. You may also find that they are quite exposed, meaning that a slip on any one of them could prove fatal. Proceed ahead only with great caution. Otherwise, turn around and hike back along the PCT to one of the Desert Divide bomb-offs, and descend to Idyllwild; then hike back up to rejoin the PCT either at Saddle Junction or via the Black Mountain Road.

Back on the PCT along the Desert Divide, where the trail swings west around Red Tahquitz Peak you may encounter pervasive, hard-packed snow on its northerly, shaded slope. If this snow is too dangerous to negotiate, turn around and hike back along the PCT to one of the bomb-offs leading down and west, and head for Idyllwild.

Instead of turning back, you could use your ice axe to safeguard your descent, diagonally down and west into the drainage north of Red Tahquitz Peak. Once at the bottom, follow that drainage uphill to the southwest and into Tahquitz Valley, where you are likely to find water in the south branch of Tahquitz Creek, and patches of snow free ground for camping. Continue west to rejoin the PCT.

From the PCT at Saddle Junction your choices are essentially two: You could descend to Idyllwild along the Slide Trail, then hike the Black Mountain Road to rejoin the PCT on the northeast slope of Black Mountain. From Idyllwild, this road walk is approximately 15 miles. Or you could continue following the PCT across the somewhat daunting Fuller Ridge.

Assuming the latter, after climbing 1,000 feet above Saddle Junction on Mt. San Jacinto, if the trail is snowbound you might experience some difficulty finding where the PCT forks left from the Mt. San Jacinto summit trail. If so, traverse west to the drop-off and look across to the distant and probably snow free slope to the northwest. There you should see the PCT snaking across the mountainside.

Beyond Deer Springs Campground the PCT will likely disappear beneath the snow and remain so for many miles. This is the route-finding crux of the San Jacinto traverse, if not the entire PCT. The Forest Service has adamantly refused to blaze the trail; and granted, hikers coming along a few weeks behind you will find the trail mostly snow free.

The length of the Fuller Ridge is exposed to the elements and affords very little bare-ground camping during early season. It is best traversed in a single day, if possible. Along the way keep generally to the crest, but traverse around the rises, keeping to the eastern slopes a hundred feet or so from the crest. In some places the trail dips briefly down the sunnier western side. At any rate, the PCT in this area is rather nondescript. Don't look for the usual thoroughfare-type trail here. Also, don't bomb off the Fuller Ridge to the east. The slope below is extremely long and dangerously precipitous in many places. And don't shortcut down the slope toward the Black Mountain road until you actually *see* it. Once at the road, descend it to the northeast, then take the spur road to the northwest to rejoin the trail, which at that point should be snow free. Along this spur road you should find water flowing here and there. Stock up, as it might be your last for a ways.

Your next snowpack will be in the San Bernardino Mountains, but here it is normally nothing as daunting as on Mt. San Jacinto. About the only region you may encounter it in quantity is between the Mission Creek Trail Camp and the Coon Creek Jumpoff. Carry an ice axe for safety.

Beyond the Jumpoff the next snow will be the occasional patches above and north of Big Bear Lake, and then on the upper reaches of the Blue Ridge above Wrightwood. The snow here can actually be to your advantage, as you can melt it for drinking water. Hikers later in the season will not have this luxury, although they should find water in some of the campgrounds farther along.

Mt. Baden Powell can be another daunting height of land, and a rather hazardous one in the mornings when its steep snowpack is frozen. One option would be to walk along the Angeles Crest Highway, normally closed to traffic that time of year, from Vincent Gap to Islip Saddle. Otherwise, follow the PCT up the flanks of Mt. Baden Powell and leave the trail at whatever elevation it becomes pervasively snowbound. Climb straight uphill, tree to tree and holding your ice axe at the ready. This snow is often sun-cupped this time of year, making for good footing. Gaining the high shoulder you may find bare ground leading to the summit. Ignore the PCT, which cuts off just below the summit and leads perilously in early season across northern exposures. Instead, from the summit follow the ridgeline generally west, then southwest, down into every notch and back up over every peak. Descend Mt. Hawkins and out of the snow, and resume following the trail. From Islip Saddle and the highway, the trail leads up the south-facing slopes, which should be mostly snow free.

Beyond, the PCT should be generally snow free all the way to the High Sierra.

Beyond Kennedy Meadows you may encounter patchy snow in the higher, shaded regions. But it won't be until reaching the vicinity of Cottonwood Pass that it will become pervasive.

The depth, extent of coverage, and density of the snowpack in the vicinity of Cottonwood Pass, and for the next few miles beyond, are entirely indicative of the prevailing High Sierra snowpack. What you encounter here is generally what you can expect to encounter at equivalent elevations during the next few weeks to Tuolumne.

So, if you find that you are sinking into the crotch here with every step, think twice about proceeding. You are sinking in because the Sierra snowpack has not yet consolidated. And as such you will probably have a lot of struggling ahead of you. A much better plan would be to leave the trail, hike down to the Horseshoe Meadows trailhead, and hitchhike down to the town of Lone Pine for an extended layover, perhaps a week or two while waiting for the snowpack to consolidate and much of it to melt.

Personally, I would resist the temptation to flip-flop ahead, or to bypass the High Sierra altogether by hiking the Owens Valley. I have heard that the hike through the Owens Valley can be interesting, if hot. Because of the numerous side roads, one can purportedly avoid the busy highway. And as a bonus, one could visit a few hot springs along the way. However, the magnificence of the High Sierra is such an integral part of the PCT experience that the hiker who avoids it is missing a great deal.

The Nine Passes Of The High Sierra

Assuming that the snowpack at Cottonwood Pass has consolidated and will generally bear your weight, and assuming that you are aware of the avalanche danger and that you are prepared to navigate largely by map and compass in the higher regions, you might feel inclined to proceed. I will give directions for surmounting the major passes along the way:

1) COTTONWOOD PASS qualifies as one of the PCT's high passes in every regard but one: the PCT does not climb up, over, and down it. Instead, the trail remains at 11,000+ feet for several miles in its proximity to the north. Once again, the snow conditions at this pass are indicative of those throughout the alpine regions all the way to Tuolumne Meadows. If you are post-holing and bogging down here, then prudence might suggest

bombing off to Lone Pine, and waiting for the snowpack to coalesce.

2) FORESTER PASS is the PCT's highest, and in very early season it can be a genuine mountaineering challenge, requiring all the right gear and experience. It's south side is a cliff, and the upper reaches of the trail were blasted from its sheer granite. Usually, the winter's snow plasters these blasted out switchbacks, making the "hiking" both difficult and dangerous. The more daring among the early season hikers are likely to find themselves kicking steps across steep faces of snow, and gazing straight down several hundred feet to the ground. Seventy feet below the pass, the trail traverses a steep couloir which can be frozen and corniced before mid June, calling for extensive step-chopping with an ice axe. Note that the route does not climb the couloir, but traverses it and climbs the buttress to the left (direction given while facing in).

As I understand it, winter mountaineers normally avoid the blasted-out switchbacks by taking a line which climbs to the high saddle 1/8 mile east of Forester Pass, mid-way between Forester Pass and Junction Peak. This avoids the blasted-out switchbacks. I have no experience with this route, but should someone require an option, it might be a feasible one.

Once at the pass, we see that the slope beyond is much less steep. If deep snow pervades, one can descend the fall line, angling slightly to the left (direction given while facing out). Although the terrain below will initially remain hidden, this slope leads to the frozen tarns below. A word of caution: avoid walking on the frozen tarns, as the ice could be thin. Plunging through would almost certainly be fatal. Back at Forester Pass, if the snow is not pervasive, then one would follow the trail in order to circumvent the exposed and steep scree below the pass.

3) GLEN PASS provides an intimidating, but fairly straightforward romp up its south side. Barring any avalanche hazard, early season trekkers would wend steeply up the slope a few hundred feet left (facing in) of the actual pass. Near the top they would traverse right to the exposed ridge crest.

The opposite side presents us with a classic North Cascades type of snowfield: steep, unbroken, and expansive. If the Sierra snowpack has consolidated, and if you arrive here early in the morning, then you might find the snow plastering this northerly slope rock-hard. If so, do not proceed until it has softened, usually by mid-morning. Otherwise, plunge-step down and to the right (facing out), with caution.

4) PINCHOT PASS is technically uncomplicated, although it might require some step chopping while climbing its southeast side. The descent is a

walk-down.

5) MATHER PASS is relatively short, but in early season it can be extremely daunting. Like Forester Pass, Mather is a perfect example of the trail builders leading early season hikers straight into danger. When buried, its southeast face is a steep and massive snow field of questionable stability. If tackling it in early season, rather than follow the buried trail, take a line to the left (facing the pass) of the lake. Stay to the left of the face in order to avoid the steep slabs hanging beneath the notch. When you reach an elevation slightly below the pass, diagonal over to it and climb its cornice.

If prudence dictates that you not tackle Mather, you could bomb-out of the Sierra via Taboose Pass. Again I have no experience with this route, but park rangers tell me that it is viable in early season. This drops you steeply down to a trailhead at the end of Taboose Creek Road, which leads out to Highway 395.

The descent of Mather is straightforward if one does not try to follow the trail, but rather picks a way carefully among the ledges and slopes.

6) MUIR PASS is a walk-up, and a walk-back-down the other side. In early season this area can provide rewarding winter-like travel amid spectacular scenery.

7) SELDEN PASS is more than a thousand feet lower than Muir Pass. If you've reached this point, then you have climbed the most arduous passes. Selden Pass generally lacks technical difficulties.

8) SILVER PASS: ditto the above.

9) DONOHUE PASS in early season will probably stand as your last reminder of the grandeur that is the High Sierra, and of the arduous passages leading through it. Unlike its kin to the south, Donohue is reasonably accessible, so you are likely to find the way graced with myriad boot tracks. As for the approach, the PCT "High Trail" would be far easier than the JMT or the River Trail, because of its greater exposure to the snow-melting sun. Beyond Thousand Island Lake, if the trail is buried then you will do well to refer often to your compass and map. The way ahead is usually fraught with the constantly diverging tracks of other hikers, and these tracks are often unreliable as guidance.

The descent is straightforward, but some who have tried to short cut down the northeast-facing slope lying between 10,800 feet to 10,400 feet have injured themselves quite seriously. Traverse above this dangerous slope to the west, cross the outlet creek or snow-buried drainage, and follow the trail's line as it descends diagonally into the meadows.

North of the High Sierra

Beyond Tuolumne you will probably encounter far less snowpack. Still, it will exist in the higher regions and make route-finding difficult at times. The southwest declivity of Benson Pass could be extensively snowpacked, and I might point out that the trail beyond Smedberg Lake traverses the slope to the southwest quite a ways, even climbing a bit, before making its descent toward Benson Lake. Early season hikers commonly fail to traverse far enough before descending, and find themselves clambering down all sorts of steep and awkward sections. Another potential problem area is the northwest slope beyond Seavey Pass. Note that the trail heads northeast from the pass, through some interesting rock outcroppings. Hikers have reported crossing Kerrick Creek where the PCT first approaches it. This might reduce the creek crossing difficulties and avoid the snow-plastered northwest facing slopes, which the PCT traverses for about 4 miles.

As mentioned earlier, although snow is not usually a problem for the early season hiker in this part of the Sierra, the snowmelt runoff can be. The "Creek Fording" chapter, page 228, gives the details.

One last section in the High Sierra is worth mentioning: the stretch of trail between Leavitt Peak and Sonora Pass. Here, the early season snowpack can be extensive. And where the trail turns abruptly to the southeast and traverses the bowl above Sonora Pass there is one dangerous section that crosses above a cliff. Follow this section of buried trail only with ice axe in hand and the skill to self-arrest with it. Otherwise, after climbing above Kennedy Canyon, descend to Leavitt Lake and follow its road down to the highway, then hike up the highway to Sonora Pass to rejoin the PCT.

Beyond Sonora Pass and Wolf Creek Lake the PCT descends below 10,000 for the last time. You can avoid most of the snow along the East Fork Carson River drainage by crossing the creek and hiking along its northeast, and sunnier bank.

Beyond, the snow will be intermittent and sometimes expansive much of the way to Sierra City and perhaps beyond. Map and compass skills will be essential for safe and expedient travel. In particular, the ski slope on Granite Chief mountain can be treacherously icy in the early mornings.

Descending Gibralter Mountain, north of Sierra City, you may need your ice axe in the morning. Beyond, the trail will probably be snow free, depending on the season. However, I might mention the short but often dangerous snowfield above Cliff Lake in the Marble Mountain Wilderness, along an old section of PCT. The new route bypasses it.

Again depending on the season, your next snow will probably be in central Oregon, intermittently at first then more pronounced in the Three Sisters Wilderness, and beyond to the flanks of Mt. Hood. In Washington you may find snow on the trail above the Packwood Glacier in the Goat Rocks Wilderness, and on the far slopes of Fire Creek Pass in the Glacier Peak Wilderness. Carry an ice axe for both, just in case.

❹ Category "Heavy Snowpack"

Hikers in this category are likely to wallow through some 30 miles of snow on Mt. Laguna, a trend which will continue throughout. In the higher regions they will not be hiking but winter mountaineering, an activity beyond the scope of this book.

Snow conditions

Snow can be fluffy soft, as deposited by a recent, cold snowfall, or it can be consolidated and frozen as hard as ice. The casual observer may not differentiate the two by sight alone. To illustrate this: every spring, people drive from their sultry cities into the mountains seeking relief from the heat. Some run from their cars and leap out onto a snowbank, which extends far down the mountainside. Well enough if that snowbank is fluffy soft. But sometimes it is hard and slippery, and just about every year people go sliding to their deaths into the trees and rocks far below.

While thru-hiking the PCT you must always test steeper snow before stepping out onto it. Probe it with your ice axe. If the snow is soft, proceed ahead while holding your axe in the self-arrest position, in case you should slip. If rock-hard, as often is the case in the early morning, you might have to circumvent the snow, or you might decide to forge ahead, chopping steps across the less yielding places. A few words about chopping steps: chop them large. Also, don't try chopping them down a long, steep slope. If you lose balance and have to self-arrest, you may not be able to stand back up without the benefit of chopped steps at your feet.

The coalescing snowpack

Winter snowfall is usually soft and fluffy, depending on the ambient temperatures. In the spring, the warmth of the daytime sun begins metamorphosing the snow crystals, and the nighttime cold freezes them. This morphing-freezing cycle begins to coalesce the snowpack from the surface down. In the mornings when the more consolidated surface is frozen, the hikers' boots may break through the surface crust with each step, and plunge deeply into the soft snow beneath. This is called "postholing," and it can be very strenuous. (It can also be dangerous if moving downhill too quickly, and a foot suddenly postholes deeply into the crust and jams between underlying rocks or logs.) As the weeks pass and as the snowpack coalesces further, it will support the hiker's weight better, until eventually it will barely indent.

So the condition of snow that you encounter is not a matter of chance. It is a matter of timing. Much too early in the season and you will flounder in it to the crotch. Only a little too early and you will posthole through it laboriously. Just right and you will walk on its surface. Moreover, the snow's depth is of little concern. Walking on consolidated snow that is one foot deep is the same as walking on snow that is 20 feet deep. What does matter is the snow's condition; and as I've said, that is a matter of timing.

Special equipment for snow travel

Snowshoes

Snowshoes can be quite effective for negotiating soft and gently sloped snow. And granted, the PCT is gently graded throughout the vast majority of its length. However, it often traverses steep slopes, and when these are covered in snow, the "trail" will become steeply sloped in the lateral direction. But back to my basic premise: Snow that is soft enough to require the use of snow shoes has not yet consolidated. It indicates merely that you are there too early in the season.

Even so, you can find yourself slogging in mush or postholing later in the afternoons when the sun has been softening the crud all day. At night, if the sky is clear (allowing radiant cooling) the crud will probably re-freeze from the surface down. In the early mornings, then, this frozen crust might again support your weight, and this is the appropriate time to boogie. Let the snow-shoers sleep in, while you make tracks – miles of barely indented ones.

Skis

If you are considering skiing through the Sierra in early season, then your mountain-skiing proficiencies would be of sufficient caliber. In the late spring when the snow has coalesced, I leave my skis behind in order to save weight. Granted, many times while hiking the PCT I've longed for a pair of skis to swish down several miles of pristine snowpack. But even several miles would not justify carrying them the remaining several hundred.

Ski poles

Swashbuckling up the trail with a ski pole in each hand is supposed to give "a total body workout." No doubt long-distance hikers could use a little more exercise of the upper body; but to me, ski poles are just more superfluous equipment. Granted, they can serve as third and forth legs, helping the adventurous arthropod maintain balance on rocky terrain. But most hikers carrying reasonably lightweight packs don't require that kind of support. A ski pole would be a good rattlesnake poker, were it long enough, or a good third leg for fording creeks, were it strong enough. But then, so would a stout stick found lying about.

I have seen advertisements which attempt to impart magic qualities to hiking poles. The inference is that they almost spring the hiker along the trail. Baloney. Along these lines, some mountaineering equipment salespeople (trying to sell gear, but not necessarily the right kind of gear) and some uninformed hikers have been known to recommend the use of crampons and ski poles in combination, instead of *maybe* crampons and certainly an ice axe. Should the hiker fall and accelerate wildly down a steep slope, the efforts of self-arresting could snap a ski pole like a match stick. Unless you are extreme skiing and genuinely require ski poles, stick with an ice axe.

Crampons

Imagine a neophyte pilot, launching a hang glider from a lofty seaside cliff and flying far over the ocean. Now imagine a novice mountaineer, strapping on a pair of crampons and venturing across a steep and frozen void of snow. Both activities would be fairly easy. And both would have grave consequences if the person goes down.

Crampons can fail in many ways, mostly through misuse; and it is the novice who is most prone to misusing them. In order for crampons to function, obviously the wearer must remain upright. A person wearing crampons can experience a moment of vertigo from looking far down into the valley, and lose balance. He can stumble on an unseen dip or rise, or catch a crampon prong on the other crampon, on its strap, or on a pant leg or gaiter. A crampon strap can work loose, or a tooth or other metal component can fracture. Moreover, if the snow is wet it can stick to the bottom of the crampons and accumulate with every step until the hiker is walking, not on perforating spikes but on slippery snowballs.

If and when you fall onto hard, steep snow, whether wearing crampons or not, the laws of physics suggest that you would immediately accelerate downward. Plummeting down a slope is not a favorable time to deliberate the proper techniques. Well practiced, lightning-fast reflexes will be your only hope of avoiding the rocks below. So you initiate a speedy self-arrest, using your ... crampons? Nope. Touch those spikes to the snow and they will cart-wheel you wildly out of control. With your gloved hands? No, they will do nothing to slow you. With a stick, walking staff, or ski pole? Sorry, those feeble implements could snap like toothpicks. Ok, prudently you were carrying an ice axe in the self-arrest position. You jam in the pick, and shards of frozen snow rooster-tail down the frozen declivity a short ways... and you drag to a secure halt. Crampons greatly facilitate climbing out onto steep, hard-packed slopes where a fall would be dangerous. But should a fall occur, they are less than useless at helping arrest the slide, because they prevent the wearer from using the feet to assist in the self-arrest.

If you need crampons to climb a frozen slope, then in most cases you are there too early in the day. The morning's warmth will probably soften the snow and allow you to kick perfectly adequate steps. If not, then you could chop the steps with your ice axe.

Climbing rope

A short length of rope can provide greater safety for two hikers traveling the snowbound Sierra together, but only if one hiker is experienced with its use and the other not. If both are inexperienced, a rope can double the danger; for if one person slips, the rope could wrench the other off balance. If both are experienced then they will not need a rope for extra security, not only because they know how to handle themselves on steep, compact slopes, but because they will be more apt to look for a safer way.

I recommend a 20 foot length of 7-millimeter Spectra rope. This material is very strong and lightweight. However it is so slippery that ordinary knots can work loose, particularly the bowline. Instead, use an overhand on a bight, secured with a couple of half-hitches. Leave plenty of free end, and check the knots regularly.

Protective clothing

The month of May is normally stormy in the High Sierra, but the first day of June usually brings sunny skies. After that date the sun can reflect powerfully from the snowfields and create a severe sunburn hazard. As such, the early season snow-tromper will need to cover virtually every square inch of the skin. Wear a long-sleeve shirt, lightweight mittens, and a wide-brimmed hat. Cover the face with a bandanna and apply a high SPF sunscreen to the ears and nose. Apply the cream inside the nose a little ways and try to keep your mouth closed. The sun reflects from every direction, and can sunburn these sensitive areas painfully. As you hike across the snowfields in the glaring sun, the temperature can be quite hot. Lightweight clothing is essential. I normally wear my polyester short-sleeve shirt, to which I safety-pin a pair of sleeves, cut off from an old shirt. Once off the snow I remove the sleeves. These sleeves also work great in the desert.

Descending a snow slope

Having labored up one side of a snowbound pass, you might feel you deserve to slide down the other side. This can be hazardous, and remember that you are probably a long way from help. The slope below may feature rocks or soft spots which might not be apparent from where you stand. The soft spots are by far the more dangerous. Boot skiing is a good technique, as long as one doesn't build up much speed. Otherwise, should the feet suddenly plunge through the crust, a leg could become trapped in a hole between rocks, and the body's forward momentum could break that leg. The same is true for glissading. And only the foolish would slide down such a slope while seated on a ground sheet, a technique which adds speed and subtracts control.

But back to the PCT: The snow conditions on both sides of a major pass can be as different as day and night. Reaching the crest and gazing down the far slope, remember that it could be frozen. And don't be fooled by deeply set boot tracks. They might have been made in the late afternoon when the snow was mushy. So, exercising the utmost caution, proceed gingerly down. If the snow is hard, if it resists the kicking of adequate steps, then return to the crest and enjoy a long rest. Otherwise, proceed cautiously while assessing the avalanche hazard.

The safest descent is with the "plunge step." As you take each step, lock the knee and let your body weight pile-drive your heel down into the snow. And again, watch for soft spots in the snow where your foot might break through to the underlying rocks.

Brain lock

By far the most dangerous aspect of snow climbing and descending is a phenomena I call "brain lock." Remember the cartoons of the coyote forever chasing the road runner? The road runner zooms off a cliff and into space – after all, it is a bird – and the coyote unthinkingly pursues. Suddenly realizing that something is dreadfully amiss, the coyote stops. Suspended in mid air, it ponders the enormity of the situation for a few moments before giving the audience that look of utter resignation, then plunges.

This is not so far from reality. Despite the actual circumstances, a hiker on a steep slope does not drop until the brain suddenly tells him that he must. As an example, I was leading a group of students across a snowfield in which our boots were imprinting only slightly. At that point in my career I had become so accustomed to walking on steep snow that I could easily secure myself, when needed, by stomping the edges of my boots aggressively into the snow. The slope gradually steepened but we were doing fine until one fellow piped up: "Hey, this is steep!" Suddenly five of them went down like bowling pins and slid a dozen feet into the rocks, fortunately not hard enough to sustain any injuries. The others held fast, and together we traversed off the slope.

This is an example of brain lock. I've witnessed it many times, and have noticed that once the brain locks out, the effect is virtually irreversible. The situation must resolve *itself*, for better or worse. Brain lock is caused by fear and panic. It's a natural mechanism designed to relieve us of having to deal with a frightful situation. Yet the consequences of not dealing with it can be fatal.

As another example, I was cruising solo near the Continental Divide in the Colorado Rockies, planning to meet with students farther along. I came to a snow slope and found it in excellent condition, so I began boot-skiing down it. Farther down, the slope steepened and I happened upon a most unexpected scene. Someone was lying on the slope, clinched in the self-arrest position. Three others were seated in the talus, 50 feet safely off to one side but afraid to risk their lives to help the person in trouble, even though all of them had ice axes and wore stout mountaineering boots. The person on the snow was brain locked. I sped to her assistance, and was able to escort her safely off the slope.

A life might have been saved that day, for the woman might have ultimately lost strength and tobogganed at break-neck speed into the boulders far below. But the point is, her brain lock was caused by a fear of the *possibility* of plunging down the slope, not by the *probability* of doing so. Once I had her safely in my grasp, the possibility of her sliding away vanished. The situation resolved itself for the better, her brain unlocked, and together we easily walked across the slope to join her friends. In actual fact, she didn't need me to reverse her brain lock. Had she kept her timbers tight together at the outset she could have traversed off the slope by herself just as easily.

How do you anticipate brain lock, and how do you prevent it? Early one morning during our second PCT hike, Jenny and I were descending Fire Creek Pass, not too far from the Canadian border. A hundred miles earlier I had consigned my trail ragged shoes to a trash can, and in order to avoid hitchhiking to civilization to buy a new pair I had appropriated Jenny's spare shoes. They were three sizes too small for me, but I had slit them all manner of ways, enlarging them just enough. Part way down from the pass we came to a steep, frozen slope that dropped far away to a batch of cliffs. This slope was inconvenient to circumvent, as often they are; so, exuding confidence despite our lack of safety gear, I led across and Jenny followed. The farther we traversed, the harder was the snow's surface. And my shoes were so tight that the uppers bulged far over both sides of the soles, rendering the soles useless for edging.

To hack each minuscule step, I slashed repeatedly with my blunt shoes, and in retrospect I probably could have done better wearing roller skates. A few dozen feet from the far side I deemed that the ever steepening slope was getting too dangerous to proceed. Feeling a brain lock hovering menacingly overhead, I clinched my resolve and very matter-of-factly told Jenny that we were, ho hum, turning around. Unaware of how insecure my footing was, she easily walked back across our footholds.

I prevented brain lock in myself by keeping a cool head. And I prevented it in Jenny by projecting my coolness. We circumvented the slope by climbing around it, and I went away with an increased distrust of those shoes.

Niels Bohr, the famous Danish physicist, once said: "An expert is a man who has made all the mistakes which can be made in a very narrow field." I've highlighted a number of the more predominant mistakes of my hiking career so that you can learn from them as I did. Carry an ice axe and wear proper footwear. And avoid stepping out onto steep, frozen slopes which hang dangerously on the heights. But should you find yourself in dire straits, realize that the danger lies primarily in your own mind. Use foresight to keep yourself out of trouble, and a level head to get yourself out of trouble when you do get into it.

Plying the transition zones

On a spring day in the snowclad mountains, the ambient temperature depends on the altitude and time of day. As we begin a descent from a high pass early in the morning, the snow is likely to be frozen, as in the above example. The deeper into the valley we descend and the more the morning unfolds, the softer the snow beneath our feet. Our boots will begin sinking in. Yet typically all will be well as long as the snow remains deeper than about three feet. Less than that and it is likely to be "rotten" in most places.

Snowpack melts in three ways. On the surface it sublimates, meaning that it simply evaporates directly from the solid state. Sometimes on a crisp morning you will see the snowfields steaming. This is the vapor of sublimation condensing into visible form. Snowpack also melts on the surface, from the sun and the sun-warmed air. Puddles do not form because the underlying snow absorbs the water. And thirdly, snowpack melts from the heat of the earth, rocks, trees and vegetation. It is this latter effect which most concerns the hiker. Snow deeper than about three feet absorbs the moisture of melting and remains structurally intact, able to bear the hiker's weight. Less than this, generally, and it becomes saturated. Saturated snow is a much better conductor of heat, and this accelerates its melting.

I refer to this rotten, fast-melting snow as transition snow, because it is soon to vanish, and also because for the hiker it is the transition between relatively solid snow and bare ground. Transition snow occurs mainly near a snowfield's lower boundaries. It can fool unsuspecting hikers climbing up from the valleys and reaching snow for the first time. Trudging through this up to their knees, they might imagine that all the snow ahead is equally slushy. This false assumption can dissuade them from continuing, and it tends to reinforce their suspicions that all snow is best avoided. This is why we don't see many of these people in the higher regions.

Depending on the depth of snowpack, the transition zones can be from one to several hundred feet wide. And usually they provide many clues as to the best routes through them. Not all of the snow is rotten. Far from it. And once you learn to read these clues you will travel across snowpack far more quickly and with far less effort. And you may be amazed at the tracks of those who struggled ahead of you, at how they stepped consistently in the soft spots.

How to read the snow

Note that the following clues apply only to the coalescing snowpack of late June and early July. It does NOT apply to winter and early spring conditions when the transition zones are minimal.

- Look for willows or other branches barely protruding from the surface, or scan ahead for a darkened hint of buried branches. The heat of these plants has probably desiccated the substrate and weakened it considerably. Give these areas a wide berth. They are booby traps.

  As you hike near the snowfield's transition zone, yet as you are still managing to keep your boots on the surface, or sinking in only a little, observe the boot tracks of those who proceeded you. Notice how they course more or less directly ahead, and therefore how they plunge repeatedly into barely protruding patches of brush. You, on the other hand, deviate around both the brush and the multitude of hiker's post holes.

- In meadows and gradually sloped and more open areas, the transition zones can be hundreds of yards broad. In them, pick a line that keeps the farthest from rocks and trees. And try to pass uphill of these objects. Why? Because they absorb the sun's heat and carry it beneath the snow's surface, slowly melting the surrounding snow. The resulting moisture flows imperceptibly downhill, not near the ground as one might expect, but actually as a horizontal effusion throughout. This effusion begins saturating and weakening the snowpack as it goes. To step onto this weakened snow is to posthole suddenly into it. Recognize it in two ways: One, by what objects are uphill of it. And two, by the subtle sagging, or depression, in the snow's surface, running downhill from the object causing it.

- In any type of snow, avoid the margins around protruding, or noticeably underlying, rocks. Rocks transmit the earth's heat, even when deeply buried, and melt the surrounding snow. The resulting void, often covered, is known as a moat. Generally, the larger the rock the more capacious its moat. If you have not inadvertently fallen waist deep into hidden moats at least ten times, then you have not yet qualified for the Cosmos-is-avenging-me merit badge. Those who have seen gaping moats as large as dump trucks might not care to qualify for the badge.

- Most importantly, when you are descending a snowfield and are about to reach its lower margin, watch for very subtle lines indicating the boundaries of the transition zone. The rotten snow is often a little more crystalline in appearance, and sometimes slightly more yellow. Time and again during our trek of '91, I noticed a crystalline margin and stepped only a few inches to one side of it (and to one side of someone's post hole) and avoided sinking in.

Keep in mind, however, that no matter how assiduously you adhere to these recommendations you may still wallow a fair amount. Faced with acres of unavoidable, rotten and thigh-deep snow, it's time to change your priorities. Switch off the speedometer. Banish the urge for forward progress. Mitigate your pace and concentrate solely on your heart rate. Think of a soft snowfield as a steep hill. If you feel that you are clawing ahead at a mere snail's pace, then you have not yet conquered your impatience nor relinquished your crusade for speed. Using brute force will deplete you very quickly. Instead, proceed thoughtfully and in control, striving for the proper balance of pace and mental serenity. Once achieved, you will cruise through that snow with much less effort.

Following a snowbound trail

When snowbound in early season, the PCT can be difficult to follow, mainly because it is not blazed at regular intervals. Perhaps technology will one day remedy this. A GPS receiver coupled with a microchip containing the trail's coordinates, could pinpoint the hiker's location and specify, generally, where to look for the trail – depending on whether the GPS unit is differentially co-ordinated, hence its accuracy. This technology exists today, but the system is unlikely to become viable until the receivers are made sensitive enough to register satellite signals consistently through forest canopy. And although this technology could simplify route-finding through snowpack, it would do nothing to simplify the physical labors of trudging, nor to alleviate the dangers of avalanche and snowmelt run-off. And of course, not all hikers are going to carry it.

So I think we might benefit by learning a few trail sleuthing techniques.

The most important concept here is in knowing your whereabouts with reasonable accuracy. So before entering a region of snowpack, study your map. Examine the topographical features denoting the layout of the land, so that you will know what features to look for, ahead. Note your location on the map, and look at your wristwatch and note the time. And most importantly, study the map's line of the trail, looking for switchbacks. It is the switchbacks that cause the most route-finding problems. At them the trail suddenly changes direction, often without any indication above the snow's surface.

The trail does not lead directly through a tree. Therefore, where you see a tree, you know the trail is not there. And conversely, where you see no tree, the trail *might* be there. And continuing with this logic: where you see a line of no trees in an area of otherwise regularly spaced trees, the trail is *probably* there. The trail builders probably felled that line of trees. These treeless corridors are your best clues in areas of densely growing smaller trees. They are common, except where the trees are growing large and farther apart, encouraging the trail builders to simply route the trail around each tree, leaving no evident corridor.

Even in areas lacking corridors the trail builders may have left clues. When Jenny and I hiked the trail southbound we traveled a deeply snowbound trail much of the way through Washington. I reckon we navigated about 60% of the way by snipped tree branch stubs. You don't see them much while hiking a bare trail because you don't need to see them. In winter-like conditions, you *need* to see them, because they are often the only part of the trail there is to see. When hiking through the forest with no hint of a trail, if you find a snipped branch stub which has a clean edge that appears to have been cut with a saw, you have almost certainly found the trail.

A log that has one end cleanly sawed off is sometimes an indication of the trail and sometimes not. When the trail builders saw an offending log they discard the part blocking the trail. They might give it a shove and send it rolling down the slope, but usually they will carry it a ways into the forest, out of sight of the trail, nice and tidy like. And there you may find it, protruding above an ocean of snow.

In addition to snipped branch stubs, Jenny and I navigated about 20% of the way through Washington by shovel cuts. Look for them on steeper terrain, in the vicinity of large trees. Each large tree normally has a snow free mote around it, caused by the melting action of the tree. Very often where the trail nears a tree on steeper ground the trail crew's shovel cut will lie close enough to the tree to be visible in the tree's mote. The shovel cut will not look like fresh-cut dirt. But it will look like dirt. Exposed dirt is rare in timber country, especially near trees. If you find even a little, the chances are, it was shovel-cut.

Following a snowbound trail is much easier while hiking in a northerly direction. Looking ahead, you are looking at the south-facing slopes. These are exposed to the sun's warmth and are far less snowbound than their north-facing counterparts. By constantly looking ahead, you can often locate a small piece of the trail on a patch of snow free ground. As you climb over a rise and start down the other side, the trail may again disappear beneath the snow. But by looking far ahead you may see at least a piece of it climbing the next slope.

We navigated about 10% by studying the terrain far ahead for a faint line leading across unbroken snow slopes. Straight lines leading across slopes are unnatural. Each time we saw one, we memorized where it started and where it went. Even though fairly apparent from a distance, these lines can be virtually impossible to discern at close range. So rather than search for the trail at your feet, search for it well ahead of you.

Where the land is covered in tall but patchy snowdrifts, don't walk around them. You might save energy, but you also might become disoriented as to the trail's directional trend. Follow the trail up and over every snow-bank. If they are five or ten feet tall then so much the better because they will allow you to see that much farther ahead.

Finally, when trying to follow a snowbound trail through the forest, resist the temptation to strike out cross-country unless you know exactly where you are going. Remember that you have only so much trail-searching time in one day. Spend it near the trail rather than far from it.

Bypassing snowbound sections altogether

Hikers who start their journeys too early in the season often find themselves bypassing the mountainous snowbound sections and walking the lowlands around them. Or they will flip-flop ahead, with the intent of coming back and finishing the job later. (As though they are undertaking some sort of work project.)

The simple fact is, too much snow in the mountains does not indicate that Nature's timing is off, but that the hikers' timing is off. And skipping ahead does not solve the problem, which is: the hikers are there too early in the season. Skipping ahead will only make them earlier still. The PCT has its own rhythm, and I've found that I do best when hiking in accordance with it. And this seems to work equally well going in either direction.

I've designed the itineraries in this book around the trail's natural rhythm. Regardless of how many miles you hike each day, the itinerary of your choice will keep you reasonably in tune with the natural flow of the trail. With one exception. During a year of abnormally heavy snow deposition, you would delay all the itinerary dates by at least a few weeks.

But back to the too-early hikers. Those who skip the higher sections by walking lower ones are missing a great deal of what the PCT has to offer. Such is the price of impatience. And in many ways the road walking can be as dangerous as any snowbound mountain pass. My advice is this: At the first indication of too much snow, take a vacation. Hitch out to a town and grab a bus to somewhere interesting, and kick back for a few weeks. The trail isn't going anywhere, and as long as you keep yourself in shape by going on long walks, your focus is not likely to dissipate. Returning, you should find the trail much more snow free, allowing you to resume your journey safely and enjoyably.

Those who decide to skip ahead must then decide where to rejoin the PCT, and this can be an enigma. Granted, they will find long, hot stretches of trail, but each will ultimately lead to more snowpack. Seeking solutions they often telephone various ranger headquarters asking about the current snow conditions in their districts. The usual reply is that the trail is snowpacked, extremely dangerous, and basically closed. What they are saying is exactly what I am saying. Don't start your hike too early.

Part 3
Planning Details

Itineraries, Resupplies, Permits

Hiking Standards

> The ultimate goal of transport technology
> is the annihilation of space,
> the compression of all Being into one pure point.
>
> *— Edward Abbey*

Freedom, autonomy and independence are the hallmarks of long-distance trekking, and the choices of route, style, and itinerary are entirely up to the individual. For many, though, a PCT thru-hike is a once in a lifetime experience, and most will want to make the best of their investment in time, money and effort. However you define your summer's trail goals, I recommend that you define them before starting out, and that you also decide on your degree of adherence to them. This can go a long ways in helping you stay on track in the face of the inevitable temptations and enigmas. And in so doing, it will also help insure the greatest satisfaction, as you look back on your journey, years from now.

Currently, the PCT is about 2,650 miles long, and we can add another 80 miles of hiking out and back from the resupply stations. At the same time, the straight-line distance from the Mexican border, south of Campo, to the Canadian Border, at Monument 78, is about 995 miles. Hiking the trail's length is therefore like hiking the straight-line distance, turning around and hiking all the way back, and turning around a second time and hiking almost three-quarters of it again. The trail obviously takes a roundabout course. And not only that, it climbs and descends prodigiously for much of its distance. Yet the idea is not to cut the country as directly as possible. Leave that to the airliners. The PCT takes the scenic route, contouring among the hills and mountains, and entire mountain ranges themselves. And the fact is, valid reasoning underlies most of the trail's meandering even where not apparent. For example it might be circumventing private property. But sometimes the trail's routing simply defies logic, and that seems to be its own form of logic, fair enough.

In choosing to hike from border to border rather than ride an airliner, you are making a decision about your method of travel and basing that decision on its potential for greater meaning and reward. Abandoning modern methods of transport in favor of your own two legs, you are exchanging ease and rate of travel for adventure and personal discovery. And as for the rewards: at journey's end you will have, not an in-flight magazine full of irrelevant advertisements, but a summer of memories, photographs, experiences, and a trail journal bulging with the many wonderful details of your own adventures as they unfolded each and every glorious day.

Decisions of style

But here in the planning stages you must make a few more decisions pertaining to the style of your Walk of Wonder. Will you indeed hike all the way, or will you hitchhike some of it? (We hope not.) Will you stick to the trail where safe and practicable, or will you take alternative routes that short-cut some of the main track? Will you start at one end and thru-hike all the way to the other? Or will you flip-flop the route, using a vehicle to avoid sections which may seem undesirable at the time? Will you hike the trail all in one summer, or just a part of it, large or small?

Before we examine these possibilities, let's consider my phrase "where safe and practicable." The hiker intent on doggedly following every inch of the trail may not be approaching the task with an open mind. Personal safety in regards to the trail's conditions might recommend a certain amount of flexibility. Recollect my hypothetical "avalanche of adversity" ripping stalwart timbers by their roots while leaving willow and young aspen to spring back upright when the avalanche has passed.

Following the route to an exposed mountain crest in the face of a powerful lightning storm, for example, might be akin to playing Russian roulette. And we could all be drowned who unthinkingly try to ford every early season creek where the Congressionally designated trail crosses them. At times, some parts of the trail are subject to avalanche. Dangers aside, the hiker is likely to find places where the trail is impossible to lay foot on. A large tree may have fallen over it, requiring circumventing. In the high mountains, snowpack can bury the trail deeply, mandating a bit of cross country travel. And what's more, virtually all sections of PCT are subject to rerouting, minor or major. The section you hike this year might not be official route next year.

Trail adherence

Even in terms of wanting to stick to the route I recommend a certain amount of flexibility. For example, during Jenny's and my most recent PCT thru-hike our goal was to hike 99% of the trail. Such a concept is still very nebulous, I know. But it did provide us with a sense of purpose, and reminded us all along the way exactly what we expected of ourselves. And that 1% freedom in our choice of routing was enough to keep us from feeling like bona-fide trail slaves bulldozing ahead on principle. I don't think we used the entire 27 miles, but still we felt that they were ours to use if needed.

In playing the percentage game we might wonder where we should draw the line. "Thru-hikers" skipping the High Sierra, for example: when they return home can they realistically claim to have hiked the PCT? What about those who skip the Fuller Ridge, or those who leave the trail momentarily to avoid a fallen tree? Of a truth, the only rules are those which we make for ourselves. So when someone says they are hiking the trail, then that is good enough for me. I am not trying to make their decisions for them, nor provide their rewards. I leave it up to the individual to base his or her decisions on personal circumstances and objectives.

In the same vein, there are no judges governing the ethics of PCT hiking. So when I hear someone criticizing someone else's style, I let it pass. Yes, it is easy to be judgmental. But I believe that Shakespeare summarized these principles well when he wrote: "This above all: to thine own self be true." True to your own style of hiking and your claims about same, and true to your acceptance of all others.

So let's take a look at the various options, and consider them in more detail:

Possible scenarios

As mentioned, some thru-hikers want to walk the entire tri-state distance, intent on following as much PCT as proves safe and practicable. They might go to considerable lengths to remain on the trail. And true enough, in many places they will be performing the regimen for its own sake. But I suspect that more often they will be seeing a great deal of interesting country that the short-cutters will miss.

Other thru-hikers want to walk the entire distance, but they care not whether they walk the PCT, various alternative trails, cross country, or roads. They arrange their resupplies and scheduling to coincide with a hike of the PCT, and they hope to hike a great deal of the main trail. But by design they are not willing to shackle themselves to the tyranny of the trail. For them the summer's journey is more extemporaneous. They allow themselves the independence to hike where they feel like hiking. And perhaps they enjoy the challenges of finding and planning more expedient ways. And incidentally, cross-country travel can be challenging, and can impart a higher sense of pioneering. But for the unwary it can also lead to trouble. I don't recommend it where one is not absolutely certain of one's location in relation to that of the trail.

Some thru-hikers might want to strike a compromise somewhere between absolute tyranny and absolute freedom. They might want to walk the entire distance with intentions of following most of the trail; but also they might not be opposed to taking various short-cuts. For instance, after leaving the trail to visit a resupply station, rather than backtrack they might hike ahead and re-join the trail farther along.

Kicking a boulder

Hitchhiking out and back might be necessary at times, to buy a new pair of shoes or to get medical attention. I like the way George Meegan described his style in his book *The Longest Walk*, (see Bibliography) which details his seven year, continuous trek from the tip of South America to the top of North America:

"If I left the route because I needed to seek water, or wanted to visit an ancient temple, or simply wished to post a letter, I would conscientiously mark my farthest point of advance, note my exact distance, run my errand, eventually return to the 'mark,' and start clocking my distance again. Setting my mark might involve circling a conspicuous tree two or three times, scoring the dirt in the shape of an arrow, or kicking a boulder. This was crucial; if I didn't take these precautions, the entire line of my steps would be irreparably broken and the journey compromised – and my peace of mind destroyed forever."

Hitchhiking for forward gain

I know many so-called thru-hikers who hitchhiked ahead, and I have nothing against this practice. But I have noticed, time and again, how it can discourage hikers to such an extent that they ultimately quit the game and return home. Perhaps riding ahead degrades a person's resolve to continue, by breaking the journey's continuity. Or conversely, perhaps a degraded resolve merely leads to hitchhiking around various sections. Either way, hitchhiking is used as a means of dealing with an undesirable section of trail. Again, there is nothing wrong with this, as long as we recognize that it tends to reinforce a reliance on vehicles as a means of solving the problems at hand.

"Alternate" routes

The authors of the Wilderness Press PCT guide books formulated their profusion of alternative routes mainly for the benefit of section hikers. I have hiked a number of these, and yes, most were interesting. And I have also hiked a very high percentage of the official route. In no instance have I found the main route inferior to any alternative route.

The thru-hike

The word "through" denotes going in one side and coming out the other; as in: going through a tunnel; or: I read the article through. The word "thru" is the informal use, which I find more in keeping with the informal activity of hiking. By definition, "thru-hikers" start at one end of the trail and proceed to the other in one continuous journey. As though on an odyssey, they may make side trips out for supplies. They might take rest days and maybe even a week or two "vacation" while waiting for safer conditions such as the snowpack to melt or the snowmelt torrents to subside. Still, they attempt to preserve the expedition's general continuity.

In my mind, the thru-hike has a certain dignity about it, and a sense of import in the same manner as a migration. Many mammals, birds, fish, and even insects migrate. And so did some tribes of early humans. So to me the thru-hike is a migration that carries its hikers with the flow of Nature.

Flip-flop, slack pack

As the term implies, a flip-flop entails breaking the hike at some point, catching a ride to a distant location, then hiking back to close the gap. A common flip-flop is to hike from the Mexican border to Walker Pass, skip ahead to Castella, continue on to Canada, then return to Castella and hike back to Walker Pass. The variations on the theme are practically unlimited. I would not do it because I would have the nagging feeling that I was attempting to hack Nature down to my level with the use of transport technology. More important to me would be the break in the journey's flow. But once again there are no rules. Each hiker is free to pursue the dream however he or she chooses.

Some hikers use vehicles for support, imagining that they are distance hiking. Often they will even resort to "slack-packing," a system whereby a vehicle meets them always at the next trailhead, transporting not only their supplies but most items from their packs as well. This is supposed to reduce the difficulties, but I suspect that it actually increases them by complicating the logistics enormously. Jenny and I have hiked in the company of slack-packers for many hours at a time, all of us carrying equivalent loads. This illustrates merely that more efficient methods can achieve the same results, and then some: we were not ensnared by the automobile at day's end.

Of course, sometimes a medical condition might necessitate vehicle support. In those cases, these hikers would be commended for their efforts, despite the compromises they have to make.

Section hiking

Section hikers cover the trail bits at a time. Sometimes they will start at one end and work their way toward the other, year by year. In so doing they are simulating a thru-hike by stages. These people are thru-hikers at heart, even though they may lack the time or resources to make the jaunt all in one go.

I have corresponded with many people who tell me that it has always been their dream to hike the PCT, were it not for various misgivings about setting out on a multi-month thru-hike. Lack of time and experience are the usual concerns. I believe the best approach in some of these cases would be to hike a shorter section first. If a thru-hike is the ultimate goal, then why not try a 400 or 500 mile section first? Such an adventure would demonstrate whether long distance hiking is as personally gratifying as it might seem.

The PCT offers several possibilities. One popular option is to hike it southbound from Castella, in northern California, to Mt. Whitney – a trek of about 750 trail miles. Another is to hike the PCT through Oregon, starting perhaps in Seiad Valley, in northern California, and ending 500 trail miles later at the Columbia River. And yet another excellent segment is the 510 mile stretch of PCT through Washington. Normally, the months of July and August would be most suitable for each of these.

⁕

During the course of your summer's trek you are bound to meet hikers from every walk of life, from a broad range of age, from various locations on the Pyramid of Style, and with very different hiking standards. Sometimes it is this variety in kindred spirits that remains in the memory long after the hike is finished. Viva les différences!

Permits

Documents granting authorization to travel in our Public Lands

This land is your land, this land is my land,
From California to the New York island,
From the redwood forest to the Gulf Stream waters,
This land was made for you and me.

— *Woody Guthrie*

In theory, I shun excessive regulations, including permits of any kind. But I also realize that not every backcountry visitor practices no-trace hiking and camping methods. Obviously, the activities of the more unconscionable must be regulated in some way. Today's backcountry permit system attempts to do this, and although it might be a good start on the long path toward wilderness preservation, I see it as fatally flawed. Why? Because it regulates every person's freedom to enjoy America's "public" lands. It limits traffic somewhat, but it does not limit the abuse of the unprincipled. If the agencies doling out the permits were genuinely concerned about reducing environmental impact they would ban pack and saddle stock straightway. I feel that this single measure would reduce the forces damaging most wilderness areas to a mere fraction of what they are today.

To a large extent, humans are not what impact the wilderness environment, but the implements they bring with them. The day-hiker wearing running shoes and carrying no overnight gear causes very little harm. Ideally, people wanting to camp overnight might be required to attend a class on low-impact practices, and to present evidence of such when applying for a permit to carry camping gear. This system would not restrict the individual from going into the backcountry, but only what that person could carry and use. Heavy hiking boots, for example, wood cutting saws and axes, and in the more frequented areas, even tents and sleeping bags. And this system would of course forbid the use of pack and saddle stock, ORV's, dirt bikes, and so forth. Under this plan, anyone willing to leave these things behind would be most welcome.

I also feel that the trailhead parking areas should be eliminated, along with the roads leading to them. This would make the wilderness a little less accessible in some of the more overcrowded areas.

And finally, I would like to see a wider variety of trails, dispersing the hiking and camping community over a broader area. If these new trails were built to hiker-only standards they would be much less costly to build and maintain than if built to stock standards, thus decreasing the impact drastically in those areas. And because they would not be open to domestic stock, they would not be eliciting the greater impact associated with them.

In my opinion the permit system in existence today is but another product of equestrian monarchy. The National Forest Service and National Park Service are not in complete control of their respective domains. Rather, they are told what to do by Congress, which, in turn is lobbied heavily, in this case by stockmen, packers, guides, outfitters, and equestrian-interest organizations. So about all that we hikers can do is apply for our permits to enjoy America, shrug our shoulders, and get on with our treks.

Those planning to flip-flop the PCT, or to hike only a section of it during the height of summer, might need a variety of permits. They would contact the appropriate ranger districts for details.

Those planning to thru-hike the PCT will need:

- In California, a "joint use permit," from the USFS, good for the whole of the state. Available from Cleveland National Forest, 10845 Rancho Bernardo Rd., San Diego, CA 92182; Phone (619) 673-6180.

- In Oregon, a permit for traversing a trio of wilderness areas in that state. Northbounders may obtain this permit on reaching the Shelter Cove Resort, listed on page 308.

- In Washington, self-issue permits are currently available where the trail enters each wilderness area.

Remember that this information is subject to change.

Permit for entry into Canada

Like all politically sovereign nations, our friendly neighbor to the north expects its foreign visitors to abide by its immigration and customs regulations. Hikers are allowed to enter the country via the PCT as long as they carry the appropriate permit. This permit is free, and obtaining it is hardly an inconvenience compared with being turned back at Monument 78 by a tall, chain-link fence. Don't laugh. Non-compliance could turn this into a reality.

During the preparatory stages, all northbound, non-Canadian PCT hikers planning to cross into Canada should request the form for entering Canada on the Pacific Crest Trail. It is available from the Canadian Immigration Centre, Huntington, B.C., Canada V0X 1M0.

Those planning to thru-hike the trail northbound according to one of the *Handbook's* itineraries would request the form during their planning stages. They would then fill it out and place it in their resupply parcel going to whatever resupply station they plan to reach two months prior to their estimated arrival in Canada. From that station they would then mail the form to Canadian Immigration, using General Delivery, Snoqualmie Pass, WA 98068 as their return address. They would also request that the clerk write: "Please Hold For PCT Hiker" on the outside of the envelope. From Snoqualmie Pass they would then carry their permit into Canada.

Choosing An Itinerary

No matter where I am,
I can't help thinking
I'm just a day away
from where I want to be.

— Jackson Browne

Of all the decisions to be made in regards to thru-hiking the PCT, the timing is perhaps the most important. Important because it must agree, generally, with the timing of Nature. If it doesn't, hardship and possible dangers will almost inevitably result. I've experienced this myself, and have seen it happen with many other hikers. The sum total of my knowledge on the matter is embodied in the itineraries, presented in the following chapter. Yet these itineraries still leave plenty of latitude, which I discuss in this chapter.

Prior to the advent of *The Pacific Crest Trail Hiker's Handbook*, thru-hikers, what few of them there were, normally spent six months hiking the PCT. Why this long? They ate low-nutritive food, carried heavy packs, and wore heavy boots. And their role models were the authors of the books they had read, and who had spent six months hiking the trail.

During our most recent PCT hike, Jenny and I met about 35 northbound thru-hikers, going the opposite way we were. Most were using the *Handbook's* concepts: carrying fairly light packs, wearing running shoes or lighter-weight boots, and eating corn pasta regularly. Of these, nearly all said they were on the book's five month itinerary. And indeed, we met the majority of them within a few days. Why had they chosen the five month itinerary? My guess is that the human mind prefers round numbers, and for these hikers six had seemed too long and four too short.

Let's compare their five month itinerary with Jenny's and my southbound hike:

Journey's duration	Five Months	3 Months & 4 Days
Layover days	1 per week	4½ total
On-trail days	130	92
Distance covered, including side trips to resupply stations.	2,740[1]	2,700
Average daily mileage	21.1	29.3
Assumed average hiking speed	2¾ mph	2¾ mph
Hours hiking each day	7.7	10.6
Hours sleeping each day	8	7
Hours left for loafing each day	**8.3**	**6.4**

Examining this table we see that the differences between a five month plan and a three month one are not all that great. Both allow for plenty of off-trail time.

Jenny and I are not super-hikers, nor do we possess uncanny endurance. Quite the contrary. We have simply learned, over the course of many thousands of hiking miles, how to travel less inefficiently. Because we carry lighter loads we do not become as tired, and this allows us to enjoy more time on the trail each day. This is important because we do, indeed, enjoy the hiking.

In terms of hiking inefficiently, I've analyzed the mistakes of scores of thru-hikers, and a great many of my own, and have completely re-written this *Handbook*. The book you are now reading is not the same one that the five month sloggers read. The techniques here are much more refined and I hope more universally applicable. Then again, maybe you *want* to spend 8.3 hours loafing every day. The choice is yours, and it makes no difference in the cosmic sense, as long as you start at the proper time and finish before the snow flies. Let's delve into the specifics:

The itineraries, described

I have arranged the itineraries according to duration – four to five months in quarter-month intervals. I have also included two southbound itineraries. As the trail becomes better marked through the far-northern Cascade mountains,

---

[1] 2,660 trail miles plus 80 miles to and from the resupply stations.

southbound thru-hiking is bound to become popular, despite its being a little more challenging, or perhaps because of it.

The best feature of these itineraries is that, as much as possible, they place the hikers in the right places at the right times. This insures the optimum (as opposed to the perfect) weather, and minimum snowpack and snowmelt-runoff all along the way. Secondly, the itineraries take into account the varying difficulties of terrain throughout the full distance of the trail. For each duration category, the computer then used this information to suggest the appropriate resupply stations, based on the number of hiking days between them, and on their off-trail distances. It then calculated the average daily mileages between those resupplies – for comparative purposes only. And it detailed the number of days' food and supplies you would need to include in each parcel going to each of those resupply stations.

Again, as wilderness travelers we abide by Mother Nature's rules. Our computer planned schedules mean nothing to her. Still, I feel these itineraries can be of tremendous help in avoiding the standard pitfalls.

The planning information embodied in the itineraries represents something of a breakthrough. No longer do hikers need to pore over unfamiliar place names while planning their food drops. No longer do they need to calculate mileages between possible resupply points, or guess how much food and supplies to put in each resupply parcel. The itineraries spell it all out in black and white. If you want to hike the trail in four and a half months, for example, select the corresponding itinerary, load the detailed number of resupply parcels, each with the specified number of days food, arrange to have them mailed to the stations, and hit the trail, confident that your planning was expertly done. And how will you know you are most likely to reach Canada in four and a half months? The itineraries suggest your departure dates from each station.

The northbound thru-hike

As a thru-hiker-in-planning, your first concern is whether to hike the trail northbound or southbound. Thru-hikers have almost universally hiked from south to north. The benefits of this approach are:

- A longer season and therefore a better chance of completing the trip in one season.

- A much less demanding initial few weeks.

- The Wilderness Press guide books detail the PCT from south to north, and southbound hikers have reported that these guides are difficult to translate for travel in the opposite direction.

A northbound trek involves only one section that has the *potential* to slow the thru-hiker considerably: the snowbound High Sierra. Normally, though, by following a *Handbook* itinerary you could expect most of that snowpack to have melted. The southbound trek is almost guaranteed to feature two slow sections: the snowbound North Cascades, and the hot and dry stretches of southern California where hauling very heavy loads of water is usually necessary that late in the year.

The southbound thru-hike

Southbound thru-hikers face a much more abrupt start. If they begin in mid June on a year of average snowpack, then only a few days into their treks they are likely to encounter deep and pervasive snowpack. The trail is unlikely to be wholly snowbound. Where it descends to lower climes it should be snow free. Still, the southbound thru-hiker can expect to wallow in snow for much of the initial two or three weeks.

Unlike in the Sierra (where the terrain is quite open above tree line, and the understory is not particularly dense below tree line), cross country travel is not as practical in the snowbound far-north Cascades. Its terrain is steep and its underbrush is often impenetrable. Here, the hiker must stick with the trail. When you lose it, as Jenny and I did hundreds of times, you must return to where you last had it, and begin searching ahead until you find it again. This may take only a few moments, or much of the day. A lesser problem is that of fog or ground blizzards bringing progress to a standstill. Sometimes about all you can do is abandon your search and follow your tracks back down the mountain and bivouac for the night, and try again the next morning.

The High Sierra is much higher than the North Cascades, so its winter can come earlier and with more severity. Southbound thru-hikers must traverse the High Sierra prior to late September, but sometimes early September can be pushing it. After winter strikes, the hiking season is essentially suspended until the snow consolidates the following spring.

And finally, hiking the deserts of southern California in late season requires carrying large quantities of water between domestic sources. Most of the natural water sources will have dried by then. This means that your pack will be quite a lot heavier, and that you will be continually pushing hard to reach the next source before your water runs out. The days can be very hot that time of year, and the consequences of running out of water on some of those remote stretches would be rather unpleasant. Of those who have tried to thru-hike the trail southbound, most have reverted to walking roads the final 500 miles.

The southbound trek does have its benefits. Hikers do not have to deal with the springtime-flooded creeks of the Sierra. These will have dwindled to rock-hopping levels by that time. Nor will they encounter nearly as many ticks in southern California. By late season these pests are inactive. Still, I believe southbound PCT thru-hiking is a more ambitious undertaking, and I recommend it for the very hardy and more experienced.

Assertive planning

After deciding in which direction to hike the trail, your next task would be to decide how long you want to spend hiking it. I have already detailed the considerations in previous chapters. But keep in mind that your body will most likely toughen to the rigors of hiking during those weeks and months, particularly if you are following the concepts in this book. As your journey unfolds, then, you are likely to find yourself hiking many more miles each day than you might imagine. So be careful when choosing a longer itinerary, against the tendency to later find yourself psychologically restrained by it.

Selecting an itinerary

To determine which itinerary is likely to serve you best, let's start by looking at the summary:

ITINERARY SUMMARY

	Duration in Months	Start Date	Finish Date	Number of Re-supplies	Hours Per Day Hiking	Extra Miles Hiking To Resupply Stations	Number of Hitch-Hikes
North	4	May 11	Sep 10	26	9.4	58	1
	4¼	May 9	Sep 15	28	8.8	76	2
	4½	May 7	Sep 21	28	8.4	79	3
	4¾	May 4	Sep 26	30	7.9	79	3
	5	May 2	Oct 1	32	7.5	79	5
South	4	Jun 15	Oct 14	26	9.4	57	2
	4½	Jun 15	Oct 29	28	8.4	76	2

The computer assumes that all hikers average the same speed: 2¾ mph. Those who travel more miles each day, do so merely by hiking more hours each day.

As we see, the five-month hikers average 7.5 trail hours a day, 6 days a week. Were they to hike an additional 1.9 hours a day they would find themselves on the 4 month itinerary, shortening their journeys by an entire month! And assuming they sleep 8 hours a night, still they would have a full 6.6 hours each day for leisure. And this is in addition to their weekly layover day.

Once again, starting your hike ahead of the *Handbook* itineraries will not help you complete your journey before season's end. Instead, it will only subject you to considerably more snowpack, and snowpack which would be less consolidated and capable of supporting your weight. The way to increase your chances of success is to start on time, and to spend a bit more time hiking each day.

The table above gives the side-trip distances out for supplies to those stations which are normally hiked to. And it gives the number of hitchhikes required. By necessity the longer-duration itineraries use more resupply stations, and consequently more side-trips out to them.

Layover days

The most economizing distance-hiking tactic is to tramp with a purpose between resupply stations, and then to rest, or layover, near the stations. **Built into the itineraries is one layover day for each six days of hiking.** This explains why the number of days' supplies and the station departure dates don't match. For every six on-trail days, the calendar advances seven, as it accommodates the weekly layover. Which days you select as layovers, and where, are your choices.

The "day's food" detailed in these itineraries represents the amount of food needed to hike from one station to the next. It does not include the layover or stopover food. For those layovers where a store is lacking, you would supply yourself with extra food. But where a store and/or café is available, you might purchase that food there. The list of resupply stations starting on page 296 tells you where the stores and restaurants are.

In terms of a *Handbook* itinerary, the moment you leave the PCT to visit a resupply station, your are effectively beginning a "layover." If you plan on backtracking to the trail, rather than short-cutting ahead, then while hiking out to the station and back, you are not making trail mileage. So technically, if you spend a half day walking or hitchhiking out, and an equal time returning to the trail, you have just expended a layover day. Hikers on the shorter itineraries bypass stations distant from the trail, and therefore they avoid the associated off-trail exercise, which in some cases can be considerable. The lesser duration itineraries also reduce the amount of hitchhiking.

Psychologically, layover time can be extremely volatile. On the trail the clock seems to run at its normal rate, but at the resupply stations it races. Hours and even days can evaporate. But you may find that extended layover time has little effect at restoring vigor. Soon after setting out again you may feel as tired as before, even though you might have rested for several days. For the well-conditioned, fed and hydrated distance hiker, the best plan is to rest well in the evenings and at night, and to minimize layover time.

Avoiding early-winter storms

Northbounders adhering to the shorter duration itineraries are more likely to reach Canada before its early-winter storms. Those in the 5 month category, and who are planning to adhere to the PCT where safe and practicable, take note: In order to hike the entire tri-state distance in one season you must not dally. Generally, your count-down clock begins ticking from Kennedy Meadows. From there you need to redouble your hiking efforts. The way is long and the early-winter snowstorms of the North Cascades loom over the far horizon. The 5 month itinerary reaches Canada October 1. In the "average" year, storms begin hammering northern Washington in mid October. But in some years they arrive much earlier. Even so, they usually last only two or three days each, after which time the sun may reappear for several days until the onset of the next storm. And typically, the first few snowfalls remain powdery and fairly easy to traipse through. The water sources begin freezing in late season, though, requiring hikers to carry more stove fuel. Indeed, the late-season days are brisk and short, but they usually offer hiking and camping no less rewarding for those who persist.

Those who find themselves falling vastly behind schedule might be tempted to flip-flop to the Canadian Border and hike south. They might keep in mind that the early snowstorms normally extend most of the way through Washington to Mt. Adams.

The 5½ month Plan

I have not included a 5½ month itinerary because it is too likely to drag hikers into the early-winter storms of the North Cascades. The unsuspecting might imagine that they could simply start their treks two weeks earlier than the 5 month itinerary. But as I have described, the greater snowpack they would almost certainly encounter would hamper their progress significantly. Starting early is no short-cut to success. In fact, there are no shortcuts to success. By far the best method is to train well prior to the hike, to eat well, carry a lighter pack, and wear lighter footwear during the hike. This should allow even the most inexperienced hikers to follow one of the *Handbook's* itineraries.

The Kennedy Meadows hinge point

The itinerary of your choice specifies your start date. Of necessity, lower daily mileage hikers would begin earlier than higher ones. This means that while hiking northbound through southern California, most of those ahead of you will be traveling fewer miles per day than you, and most of those behind are likely to be traveling more. This is good news, for it greatly increases your chances of meeting other distance hikers somewhere along the way. In fact, that somewhere is Kennedy Meadows. All itineraries are designed to converge there. So plan on spending a few days at the Kennedy Meadows PCT thru-hiker's annual conclave. As yet this is an unofficial event, but considering its potential I hope that something grand will someday become of it.

All northbound itineraries specify setting off from Kennedy Meadows on June 15. This mass exodus would have a number of advantages. Banding loosely together in the High Sierra, hikers would benefit from each other's route finding and footsteps in the snow. This in itself would increase almost everyone's chances of success. And should someone encounter difficulties, others could render assistance.

As I mentioned in the chapter on snowpack, when you reach Cottonwood Pass, then based on the snow's depth and consistency there, you will know what to expect of the snowpack throughout the higher regions of the Sierra. If you find yourself wallowing or postholing laboriously at Cottonwood Pass, then rather than fighting the snow, your best tactic would be to descend to Horseshoe Meadows and hitchhike down to Lone Pine for a long layover.

Station departure dates

The itineraries in the following chapter specify the resupply stations appropriate for each schedule, and the approximate dates of departure from those stations. I am setting something of a precedence by not using between-resupply-station trail mileages. Mileage figures are a spin-off of our highway and transportation systems. Hikers have little use for them, especially as they do not reflect the many variables which can make those miles easier or tougher: the steepness of terrain, the weather, and other elements that can retard or favor progress. Nor do hikers carry odometers with which to measure long-term mileages. My itineraries more realistically use the overall time frame: the number of day's travel between each resupply station. If you arrive at a resupply station a day or so behind schedule, either pick up your pace on the next stretch, or throw in a little extra food. It's that simple.

The dates listed in the itineraries are station departure dates. They are not intended to be adhered to strictly. Use them as guidelines, but travel in accordance with your abilities and motivation. On journey, should you find yourself falling behind schedule, then your chosen itinerary will suggest the need to increase your daily and weekly mileages. And instead, if you find yourself pulling ahead, then you can be assured that you are traveling in good form.

Itineraries

4 Month Northbound Itinerary
Copyright (c) 1996 by Ray Jardine

Departure Date	Days Food	MPD	Departure Date	Days Food	MPD
Mexican Border			**Old Station (0.1)**		
May 11	**2.1**	21	Jul 17	**1.6**	30
Mt Laguna (0.6)			**Burney Falls Camp Store (0.1)**		
May 13	**3.4**	21	Jul 19	**3.1**	28
Warner Springs (1.3)			**Castella (2.5)**		
May 17	**3.4**	21	Jul 22	**5.5**	28
Idyllwild (4.5)			**Seiad Valley (0.0)**		
May 21	**4.2**	23	Jul 29	**3.1**	29
Big Bear City (3.0)			**Hyatt Lake (0.7)**		
May 26	**3.6**	25	Aug 1	**2.8**	31
Wrightwood (4.4)			**Crater Lake Lodge (0.2)**		
May 30	**3.6**	25	Aug 4	**2.5**	31
Agua Dulce (0.0)			**Cascade Summit (1.4)**		
Jun 3	**4.0**	25	Aug 7	**5.2**	27
Tehachapi (10h) or Mojave (10h)			**Olallie Lake G. S. (0.2)**		
Jun 8	**5.5**	26	Aug 13	**1.9**	28
Kennedy Meadows (0.7)			**Timberline Lodge (0.1)**		
Jun 15	**8.4**	21	Aug 16	**1.8**	28
Vermilion Valley Resort (6.0)			**Cascade Locks (0.4)**		
Jun 24	**3.2**	21	Aug 18	**5.6**	27
Tuolumne Meadows (0.3)			**White Pass (0.7)**		
Jun 28	**6.0**	25	Aug 24	**3.5**	29
Echo Lake Resort (0.0)			**Snoqualmie Pass (0.3)**		
Jul 5	**3.6**	28	Aug 28	**7.3**	24
Sierra City (1.5)			**Stehekin (10 bus)**		
Jul 9	**3.3**	28	Sep 6	**3.3**	25
Belden Town (0.0)			**Canadian Border**		
Jul 13	**3.1**	28	Sep 10		

The figures in parentheses are off-trail miles to the resupply stations. The "h" indicates hitch-hiking miles.

4¼ Month Northbound Itinerary

Copyright (c) 1996 by Ray Jardine

Departure Date	Days Food	MPD	Departure Date	Days Food	MPD
Mexican Border			**Old Station (0.1)**		
May 9	2.2	20	Jul 19	1.6	28
Mt Laguna (0.6)			**Burney Falls Camp Store (0.1)**		
May 11	3.6	20	Jul 21	3.3	26
Warner Springs (1.3)			**Castella (2.5)**		
May 16	3.6	20	Jul 25	5.8	26
Idyllwild (4.5)			**Seiad Valley (0.0)**		
May 20	4.5	21	Jul 31	3.2	27
Big Bear City (3.0)			**Hyatt Lake (0.7)**		
May 25	3.8	23	Aug 4	2.9	29
Wrightwood (4.4)			**Crater Lake Lodge (0.2)**		
May 29	3.8	23	Aug 8	2.7	29
Agua Dulce (0.0)			**Cascade Summit (1.4)**		
Jun 3	4.2	24	Aug 11	5.5	26
Tehachapi (10h) or Mojave (10h)			**Olallie Lake G. S. (0.2)**		
Jun 8	5.8	24	Aug 17	2.0	26
Kennedy Meadows (0.7)			**Timberline Lodge (0.1)**		
Jun 15	4.5	20	Aug 20	1.9	26
Independence (9.0 + 15h)			**Cascade Locks (0.4)**		
Jun 20	4.5	20	Aug 22	5.9	25
Vermilion Valley Resort (6.0)			**White Pass (0.7)**		
Jun 25	3.4	20	Aug 29	3.7	27
Tuolumne Meadows (0.3)			**Snoqualmie Pass (0.3)**		
Jun 29	6.5	23	Sep 2	3.5	21
Echo Lake Resort (0.0)			**Skykomish (17h)**		
Jul 6	3.9	26	Sep 6	4.4	22
Sierra City (1.5)			**Stehekin (10 bus)**		
Jul 11	3.5	26	Sep 11	3.5	24
Belden Town (0.0)			**Canadian Border**		
Jul 15	3.3	26	Sep 15		

4½ Month Northbound Itinerary

Copyright (c) 1996 by Ray Jardine

Departure Date	Days Food	MPD	Departure Date	Days Food	MPD
Mexican Border			**Burney Falls Camp Store (0.1)**		
May 7	2.3	18	Jul 23	3.5	25
Mt Laguna (0.6)			**Castella (2.5)**		
May 9	3.8	18	Jul 27	3.9	25
Warner Springs (1.3)			**Etna (10h)**		
May 14	3.8	18	Jul 31	2.3	25
Idyllwild (4.5)			**Seiad Valley (0.0)**		
May 18	4.7	20	Aug 3	3.4	26
Big Bear City (3.0)			**Hyatt Lake (0.7)**		
May 24	4.0	22	Aug 7	3.1	27
Wrightwood (4.4)			**Crater Lake Lodge (0.2)**		
May 28	4.0	22	Aug 11	2.9	27
Agua Dulce (0.0)			**Cascade Summit (1.4)**		
Jun 2	4.4	23	Aug 14	5.8	24
Tehachapi (10h) or Mojave (10h)			**Olallie Lake G. S. (0.2)**		
Jun 7	6.1	23	Aug 21	2.2	25
Kennedy Meadows (0.7)			**Timberline Lodge (0.1)**		
Jun 15	4.7	18	Aug 23	2.0	25
Independence (9.0 + 15h)			**Cascade Locks (0.4)**		
Jun 20	4.7	18	Aug 26	6.3	24
Vermilion Valley Resort (6.0)			**White Pass (0.7)**		
Jun 25	3.6	18	Sep 2	3.9	26
Tuolumne Meadows (0.3)			**Snoqualmie Pass (0.3)**		
Jun 30	6.9	22	Sep 7	3.7	20
Echo Lake Resort (0.0)			**Skykomish (17h)**		
Jul 8	4.1	25	Sep 11	4.6	21
Sierra City (1.5)			**Stehekin (10 bus)**		
Jul 12	3.7	25	Sep 16	3.7	22
Belden Town (0.0)			**Canadian Border**		
Jul 17	3.5	25	Sep 21		
Old Station (0.1)					
Jul 21	1.7	26			

4¾ Month Northbound Itinerary

Copyright (c) 1996 by Ray Jardine

Departure Date	Days Food	MPD	Departure Date	Days Food	MPD
Mexican Border			**Burney Falls Camp Store (0.1)**		
May 4	2.5	18	Jul 25	3.7	23
Mt Laguna (0.6)			**Castella (2.5)**		
May 7	4.0	18	Jul 29	4.1	24
Warner Springs (1.3)			**Etna (10h)**		
May 12	4.0	18	Aug 3	2.4	24
Idyllwild (4.5)			**Seiad Valley (0.0)**		
May 16	5.0	19	Aug 6	3.6	24
Big Bear City (3.0)			**Hyatt Lake (0.7)**		
May 22	4.2	21	Aug 10	3.3	26
Wrightwood (4.4)			**Crater Lake Lodge (0.2)**		
May 27	4.2	21	Aug 14	3.0	26
Agua Dulce (0.0)			**Cascade Summit (1.4)**		
Jun 1	4.7	21	Aug 17	2.0	23
Tehachapi (10h) or Mojave (10h)			**Elk Lake Resort (1.3)**		
Jun 7	6.8	21	Aug 20	4.1	23
Kennedy Meadows (0.7)			**Olallie Lake G. S. (0.2)**		
Jun 15	5.0	18	Aug 24	2.3	24
Independence (9.0 + 15h)			**Timberline Lodge (0.1)**		
Jun 20	5.0	18	Aug 27	2.1	23
Vermilion Valley Resort (6.0)			**Cascade Locks (0.4)**		
Jun 26	3.8	18	Aug 30	6.6	22
Tuolumne Meadows (0.3)			**White Pass (0.7)**		
Jul 1	7.2	21	Sep 6	4.1	24
Echo Lake Resort (0.0)			**Snoqualmie Pass (0.3)**		
Jul 9	4.3	24	Sep 11	3.9	19
Sierra City (1.5)			**Skykomish (17h)**		
Jul 14	3.9	24	Sep 16	4.9	20
Belden Town (0.0)			**Stehekin (10 bus)**		
Jul 18	3.7	24	Sep 21	3.9	21
Old Station (0.1)			**Canadian Border**		
Jul 23	1.8	25	Sep 26		

5 Month Northbound Itinerary

Copyright (c) 1996 by Ray Jardine

Departure Date	Days Food	MPD	Departure Date	Days Food	MPD
Mexican Border			**Old Station (0.1)**		
May 2	**2.6**	17	Jul 25	**1.9**	24
Mt Laguna (0.6)			**Burney Falls Camp Store (0.1)**		
May 5	**4.2**	17	Jul 27	**3.8**	22
Warner Springs (1.3)			**Castella (2.5)**		
May 10	**4.2**	17	Jul 31	**4.3**	22
Idyllwild (4.5)			**Etna (10h)**		
May 15	**5.3**	18	Aug 5	**2.5**	22
Big Bear City (3.0)			**Seiad Valley (0.0)**		
May 21	**4.5**	20	Aug 8	**3.8**	23
Wrightwood (4.4)			**Hyatt Lake (0.7)**		
May 26	**4.5**	20	Aug 13	**3.5**	25
Agua Dulce (0.0)			**Crater Lake Lodge (0.2)**		
Jun 1	**4.9**	20	Aug 17	**3.2**	25
Tehachapi (10h) or Mojave (10h)			**Cascade Summit (1.4)**		
Jun 6	**4.5**	21	Aug 21	**2.1**	22
Onyx (17h)			**Elk Lake Resort (1.3)**		
Jun 12	**2.5**	20	Aug 23	**4.3**	22
Kennedy Meadows (0.7)			**Olallie Lake G. S. (0.2)**		
Jun 15	**5.2**	17	Aug 28	**2.4**	22
Independence (9.0 + 15h)			**Timberline Lodge (0.1)**		
Jun 21	**5.2**	17	Aug 31	**2.2**	22
Vermilion Valley Resort (6.0)			**Cascade Locks (0.4)**		
Jun 27	**4.0**	17	Sep 2	**7.0**	21
Tuolumne Meadows (0.3)			**White Pass (0.7)**		
Jul 1	**3.8**	20	Sep 11	**4.3**	23
Bridgeport (33h)			**Snoqualmie Pass (0.3)**		
Jul 6	**3.6**	22	Sep 16	**4.1**	18
Echo Lake Resort (0.0)			**Skykomish (17h)**		
Jul 10	**4.6**	22	Sep 20	**5.1**	19
Sierra City (1.5)			**Stehekin (10 bus)**		
Jul 15	**4.1**	22	Sep 26	**4.1**	20
Belden Town (0.0)			**Canadian Border**		
Jul 20	**3.9**	22	Oct 1		

4 Month Southbound Itinerary

Copyright (c) 1996 by Ray Jardine

Departure Date	Days Food	MPD	Departure Date	Days Food	MPD
Canadian Border			**Belden Town (0.0)**		
Jun 15	4.2	20	Aug 16	3.1	30
Stehekin (10 bus)			**Sierra City (1.5)**		
Jun 19	5.0	20	Aug 20	3.5	30
Skykomish (17h)			**Echo Lake Resort (0.0)**		
Jun 25	3.8	20	Aug 24	5.4	28
Snoqualmie Pass (0.3)			**Tuolumne Meadows (0.3)**		
Jun 30	4.5	22	Aug 30	2.3	28
White Pass (0.7)			**Vermilion Valley Resort (6.0)**		
Jul 5	6.8	22	Sep 2	6.6	26
Cascade Locks (0.4)			**Kennedy Meadows (0.7)**		
Jul 13	1.7	28	Sep 9	5.4	26
Timberline Lodge (0.1)			**Tehachapi (10h) or Mojave (10h)**		
Jul 15	5.0	30	Sep 16	4.6	22
Elk Lake Resort (1.3)			**Agua Dulce (0.0)**		
Jul 21	4.2	30	Sep 21	4.1	22
Crater Lake Lodge (0.2)			**Wrightwood (4.4)**		
Jul 26	2.9	30	Sep 26	4.1	22
Hyatt Lake (0.7)			**Big Bear City (3.0)**		
Jul 29	3.0	30	Oct 1	4.0	24
Seiad Valley (0.0)			**Idyllwild (4.5)**		
Aug 1	5.2	30	Oct 5	3.2	22
Castella (2.5)			**Warner Springs (1.3)**		
Aug 7	2.9	30	Oct 9	2.9	24
Burney Falls Camp Store (0.1)			**Mt Laguna (0.6)**		
Aug 11	1.6	30	Oct 12	1.5	28
Old Station (0.1)			**Mexican Border**		
Aug 13	3.0	30	Oct 14		

4½ Month Southbound Itinerary

Copyright (c) 1996 by Ray Jardine

Departure Date	Days Food	MPD
Canadian Border		
Jun 15	**4.7**	18
Stehekin (10 bus)		
Jun 20	**5.6**	18
Skykomish (17h)		
Jun 26	**4.3**	18
Snoqualmie Pass (0.3)		
Jul 1	**5.1**	19
White Pass (0.7)		
Jul 7	**7.6**	19
Cascade Locks (0.4)		
Jul 16	**1.9**	25
Timberline Lodge (0.1)		
Jul 19	**2.1**	26
Olallie Lake G. S. (0.2)		
Jul 21	**3.6**	26
Elk Lake Resort (1.3)		
Jul 25	**4.7**	26
Crater Lake Lodge (0.2)		
Jul 31	**3.2**	26
Hyatt Lake (0.7)		
Aug 3	**3.3**	26
Seiad Valley (0.0)		
Aug 7	**5.9**	26
Castella (2.5)		
Aug 14	**3.2**	26
Burney Falls Camp Store (0.1)		
Aug 18	**1.8**	26
Old Station (0.1)		
Aug 20	**3.3**	26

Departure Date	Days Food	MPD
Belden Town (0.0)		
Aug 24	**3.5**	26
Sierra City (1.5)		
Aug 28	**3.9**	26
Echo Lake Resort (0.0)		
Sep 2	**6.0**	25
Tuolumne Meadows (0.3)		
Sep 9	**2.6**	25
Vermilion Valley Resort (6.0)		
Sep 12	**3.7**	23
Independence (9.0 + 15h)		
Sep 16	**3.7**	23
Kennedy Meadows (0.7)		
Sep 20	**6.1**	23
Tehachapi (10h) or Mojave (10h)		
Sep 27	**5.1**	19
Agua Dulce (0.0)		
Oct 3	**4.6**	19
Wrightwood (4.4)		
Oct 9	**4.6**	19
Big Bear City (3.0)		
Oct 14	**4.5**	21
Idyllwild (4.5)		
Oct 19	**3.6**	19
Warner Springs (1.3)		
Oct 24	**3.3**	21
Mt Laguna (0.6)		
Oct 27	**1.7**	25
Mexican Border		
Oct 29		

Resupply Parcels

The Pacific Crest Trail is routed well away from towns in order to maintain its wilderness character. For its hikers, this means that grocery stores and backpacking equipment outlets are generally unavailable. Not to worry. In order to resupply with food and gear we can mail parcels containing the needed items to ourselves, in care of the resorts and small post offices along the way.

This does mean that we must plan carefully ahead of time. The needs for sustenance must be met. Equipment fails or wears out. Clothing becomes needed or not, according to the season and geographic location. New shoes will be necessary every so often, as the "old" ones begin breaking down. This chapter details these considerations.

Hikers following the *Handbook's* 4¾ month itinerary, for example, will be resupplying at 30 stations. This means that while preparing for the journey they will need the same number of shipping boxes in which to load their supplies. These cardboard boxes are for sale commercially, but you should be able to salvage equally suitable ones from recycling bins at various stores in your area. Or ask the store manager for discarded boxes. Bookstores often have particularly strong and durable ones.

Keep in mind that resupply parcels are subject to rough handling en route to their destinations. Paying extra for "Special Handling" is unlikely to help. Select sturdy boxes *only*; and once home, tape any suspect edges, double-tape the bottoms across the center joint and along both sides, and remove or cover any address labels.

Arrange the boxes in a line, and onto each one tape a temporary label specifying its destination. According to your chosen itinerary, fill each box with its specified number of days' supplies. These supplies will normally include food for hiking and for eating there at the resupply station, film and processing mailers, the appropriate section of the guide book (cut from the glued binding and re-bound with adhesive tape) any additional maps, flashlight batteries, first aid items, and any replacement or additional articles of clothing and footwear. If the parcel weighs more than 50 pounds, for example if it contains supplies for two or more hikers, repackage it into two or more smaller boxes.

And incidentally, if your resupply box will contain supplies for your partners as well, include their names on the mailing address. One of you might reach the supply station ahead of the others. Or one person might be elected to detour to the station to collect the parcel. Postal regulations forbid handing over a box to someone who's name is not on the address label.

Mailing the parcels

Most distance hikers enlist the services of a relative or close friend, who "volunteers" to mail the resupply parcels. This is a lackluster job, driving interminably to the post office or UPS station, lugging ponderous boxes inside and standing in line with them. But the arrangement has decided advantages for you. For example, you could leave the boxes open so that your helper could add things prior to sending it. For example they might add home-baked goodies, fresh potatoes, and any items of clothing or equipment that you might have requested by telephone.

Other than potatoes, beware of adding fresh produce. As it rots it gives off terribly foul odors which can not only spoil much of the box's contents, but which can also strain our relations with the resupply station managers. Yes, it does happen. Along these lines, avoid packing soap next to food. Its essence will leak through the plastic bags and permeate those of its neighbors. Soap flavored corn chips have little to recommend them.

Sample shipping label

From: (Hiker's Return Address)
NAME(S) OF HIKER(S) C/O General Delivery Post Office, Resort, or Store ADDRESS, STATE, ZIP
PLEASE HOLD FOR PCT HIKER ESTIMATED PICK-UP DATE _____

Be sure to write your expected arrival date on your shipping label. This helps the station masters organize the parcels. And in the unlikely event of a possibly missing hiker, it could provide useful information. And don't forget to include a return address on all packages.

Jenny and I send our resupply parcels "First Class" so that they will arrive with the greatest expediency, and so that we can request that they be forwarded or returned without incurring extra cost. The same with our Drift Box (see description, below) which we send ahead. We send our unneeded items home more economically via Third Class.

Make a schedule showing which parcel is to be mailed to where, and when. Three or four weeks ahead of your planned arrival date should be about right, depending on what part of the country you will be sending the boxes from. Leave this list with your home base person or people, and keep a copy for yourself. And once on the journey, telephone them occasionally to relate the news of your progress, and more importantly to encourage them and to let them know you appreciate their help.

In addition to your box mailing schedule be sure to carry your driver's license or other form of picture identification. Postal Service policy requires that you show this when collecting your parcel.

The return parcel

At those resupply stations with post offices, you might decide to send unneeded items back home. Plan ahead and include a shipping label and a small roll of boxing tape in each resupply parcel. Simply roll some tape around a cylindrical object – such as the cardboard insert from a roll of paper towel or toilet paper. Once at the station, recycle your resupply box by cutting it down to size. Fill it with the items to be returned, tape it closed, tape the new shipping label in place, and mail the parcel home.

The drift box

You might consider also using a drift box: a small parcel sent ahead rather than home. This could contain items maybe needed later but not presently, for example a spare pair of shoes and fresh insoles, a spare water filter cartridge, an extra camera battery, a miniature whetstone, a utility knife with disposable blades, a tube of seam-sealing compound and its small bottle of accelerator, a spare spoon, an extra sweater, and a roll of boxing tape. Send the drift box First Class, two weeks ahead. And be sure to write your forwarding instructions beneath the mailing address in case the parcel is delayed. Or send it Priority Mail a week ahead if you will be needing something then. Priority Mail also works well for having things sent from home base to your present location or your next resupply station.

If you use drift boxes, keep a record listing the contents of each, the date you mailed it, and where you mailed it to. This will reduce the chances of your losing track of these parcels.

Quitting the hike early

During the course of the summer, should you change your mind about continuing your trek, be sure to arrange for your parcels to be returned. Visit your local post office and ask for a set of Change of Address forms. Including one with each request of return can save you money.

For those lacking a home base

Hikers visiting from other countries, and hikers without a home base of operations, can use either of these two methods to resupply themselves:

1) Take your resupply parcels en masse to a professional mail forwarding service. I have done this twice. The first one was a disaster – I had to return to it, collect my parcels, and mail them all to a friend who agreed to handle them. The second service, in a different state and year, was a resounding success. So if you decide to use a mail forwarding service, plan for contingencies.

2) The second method is more complicated, but gives you far better control. The *general* game plan is as follows, and the variations are practically unlimited: Every six weeks, hitchhike out to a town and buy food for the next six weeks. After loading your pack with a two week supply, send another two week supply two weeks ahead. And send an additional two week supply four weeks ahead.

To shorten the two week interval, load two or three larger drift boxes with more than ample supplies, and leap-frog them ahead of you.

Remember also that tourist-type foods are available at many of the resupply stations along the way. The next chapter describes where these stores are located.

Resupply Stations

I journeyed fur, I journeyed fas';
I glad I foun' de place at las'!

— *Joel Chandler Harris*
Nights with Uncle Remus

*I use the term "Resupply Station" to describe a place to which hikers can
mail their supplies. This is not to infer a large building of brick and stone in
the sense of a train station, but merely a resort, small store, or post office.
However nondescript, this is a traditional place where the friendly postal
worker or proprietor is well accustomed to handling supply boxes for hikers. The stations featured in this chapter are linked with the computer-
generated itineraries beginning on page 283. In fact, the computer recommended which stations to use with which itineraries.*

I have organized the stations into three general types:

- **Post Office**, offering the usual receiving and sending services. In many
  cases along the PCT they are housed in their own buildings, typical of
  any small town. They do not accept parcels sent by the United Parcel
  Service (UPS). Most are closed on weekends, though some have limited
  hours on Saturdays. And they are closed during national holidays. In the
  trekking season these are: Memorial Day (the last Monday of May), Independence Day (July 4), Labor Day (the first Monday of September),
  and Columbus Day (October 12).

- **Resort or store featuring a small post office inside its building**. These
  offer hikers the best of both worlds. They accept parcels sent both via the
  US Postal Service and the UPS. They will normally hand over your box
  anytime they are open, usually seven days a week throughout the summer
  season. And they can handle outgoing parcels, although usually only
  during official postal hours.

- **Resort or store with no post office**. These are commercial enterprises
  that receive and hold parcels only, sometimes for a fee. On the plus side,
  they will normally hand over your parcel anytime they are open, usually
  seven days a week. And this is a big plus. On the minus side they cannot
  normally handle outgoing packages. Most of these establishments prefer
  that you send your boxes to them via UPS. This company delivers the
  packages to their door, while the Postal Service delivers them only to

their P.O. box, usually miles away in the nearest town. To save the management the trouble of retrieving your box from town, and to better insure that your supplies will be awaiting your arrival, use UPS. And for the cheapest rates, indicate that you are sending it to a commercial address rather than a residential one. I have indicated these stations as "Resort-no P.O." or "Store-no P.O."

Handling charges

For the people running the resorts and stores, handling scores of hikers' resupply parcels is a big job. Naturally, some of them charge handling fees. Those that don't are acting out of pure generosity. Make sure you express your appreciation.

Minimum-impact resupplying

A delicate subject, but hikers headed into town usually don't realize how strong their body odor can be, or how it can offend the folks in town. But the fact is, the hiker who offends a post master or a resort manager is, in effect, working to discourage the continuation of these valuable services. Reading this at home, you might imagine this could not apply to you. But be advised that after you have been on the trail awhile the dreaded BO can prevail, and that you will hardly detect its presence. In rare instances, bathing ahead of time is not possible. But in most cases it certainly is possible, usually with the dundo[1] method, using a little soap. Make an effort to rinse out a shirt, also. And once in town, a trip to the laundromat and showers should take first priority.

As you pass through the resorts and small resort-type towns, remember that you may be the only distance hiker that some of the tourists ever meet. If they seem interested, stop and chat awhile. And don't be put off by their often standard questions. In their eyes you are one of the trail's representatives, so anything you say to promote hiking would be of benefit.

But don't go overboard by declaring a hiatus in public view and spreading gear haphazardly about. This creates a scene that some locals find distressing. Laundromats are particularly vulnerable to distance-hiker anarchism. In all the above, try to be considerate, and practice minimum impact resupplying.

---

[1] Described on page 180.

Station data

The hours listed for each station, below, are those of the post offices. Any stores in the area will usually be open 7 days a week, morning to evening. All the data here is subject to change. In particular, the out-of-the-way stores might be well stocked or not, depending on when the staff last traveled to town for supplies. The station hours are subject to revision, as are any package handling fees. If in doubt, call or send an inquiry with an SASE to the stations you plan on using, before mailing your parcels.

FROM THE MEXICAN BORDER:

Post Office CAMPO, CA 92006 619-478-5466		
SUN	MON - FRI	SAT
	7:30 a - 11:30 a 12:30 p - 4:30 p	7:30 a - Noon

CAMPO (.5 mile off route) From the well-stocked store head south along Forest Gate Road, turn left at the first street, and walk 2 blocks east to the post office. About the only other amenity in town is a laundromat.

Post Office MT. LAGUNA, CA 91948 619-473-8341		
SUN	MON - FRI	SAT
	8:00 a - Noon 1:00 p - 5:00 p	8:00 - Noon

MT. LAGUNA (0.6 mile off route) Leave the trail at the northern boundary of Burnt Rancheria Campground. Proceed west through the campground, then veer north-northwest and ascend a dirt road (quietly) past a few cabins. Descend their access road to the paved highway. Turn right, cross the highway and reach the Laguna Mountain Lodge, the Mt. Laguna Store, and the post office. Ask the clerk whether the café down the street (to the south) is open.

Post Office WARNER SPRINGS, CA 92086 619-782-3166		
SUN	MON - FRI	SAT
	8:00 a - 4:00 p	8:00 a -1:30 p

"Due to space limitations, we can hold parcels for a maximum of 30 days."

WARNER SPRINGS (1.3 miles off route) On reaching Highway 79, collect a bit of water at the fire station if needed, then continue following the PCT. Leave the trail at the next Highway 79 crossing, after determining whether Agua Caliente Creek is flowing. Hike east along the highway to the post office, currently in a converted mobile home. If you found Agua Caliente Creek dry, fill your bottles at the gas station. The area lacks public amenities and camping facilities.

Post Office IDYLLWILD, CA 92349 909-659-2349		
SUN	MON - FRI	SAT
	9:00 a - 5:00 p	7:00 a - 8:30 a Parcel pick-up only. (Knock on front door)

IDYLLWILD (a 4.5 mile, 2,300 foot descent from Saddle Junction) Features a post office, a mountain shop with sporadic hours, plenty of camping, showers, laundromat, restaurants and supermarkets.

Post Office BIG BEAR CITY, CA 92314 909-585-2322		
SUN	MON - FRI	SAT
	9:00 a - 4:30 p	1:00 p - 2:00 p

BIG BEAR CITY (3.0 miles off route) Leave the trail at Van Dusen Canyon Road. Proceed down-canyon, south, along the dirt road, turn left onto Highway 38, hike ½ mile northeast, then turn right onto Greenway and walk south ½ mile to Country Club Blvd. Turn right and walk west 1 block to the post office. Within one block are a laundromat, medium size market, and restaurants. The vicinity lacks camping facilities.

Post Office WRIGHTWOOD, CA 92397 619-249-3112		
SUN	MON - FRI	SAT
	8:45 a - 5:00 p	9:00 a - 11:00 a Parcel pick-up only.

WRIGHTWOOD (4.4 miles off route) Reached via a 2,500' descent of the Acorn Canyon Trail. The town has a post office, well stocked stores, and the usual amenities.

Notes: There are two principal faltering points along the PCT where hikers are most likely to drop out. One is in the vicinity of Mt. Laguna and the other is along the trail just beyond Wrightwood. Mt. Laguna is the trail's first challenge. It is nothing prodigious, mind you, but it does bring hikers to a better awareness of the scale of the endeavor. Many find that they are not prepared to deal with this much reality. Of those who continue, many quit not far beyond Wrightwood. I doubt whether it has anything to do with the trail within a hundred miles on either side of this town. It is no more difficult than anywhere else. Rather, it seems to be related to the town itself. Why, I'm not sure; Jenny and I normally bypass it because it is too far from the trail. But the fact remains that hikers who visit this black hole tend to lose their resolve to continue.

Statistically, if you make it to Agua Dulce, having followed the trail the whole way, then you have every chance of making it all the way to Canada.

Post Office AGUA DULCE, CA 91350 805-268-0559		
SUN	MON - FRI	SAT
	9:00 a - 5:30 p	9:00 a - 4:00 p

The post office is in the Hallmark store.

AGUA DULCE (on route) (ah-*gwa DOOL-say*) This burgeoning community features a large grocery store, a well-stocked mini-grocery and a few restaurants; but it lacks camping.

Post Office TEHACHAPI, CA 93561 805-822-3276		
SUN	MON - FRI	SAT
	8:30 a - 5:30 p	10:00 a - 2:00 p

Tehachapi (*Tuh-HA-cha-pee*) Reached via a 9½ mile hitchhike northwest along the Tehachapi Willow Springs Road. Tehachapi is a pleasant town featuring the usual amenities. The post office is at 105 East E Street, off Grain Street.

Notes: Highway 58, seven miles beyond the Tehachapi Willow Springs Road, is a high-speed, limited-access freeway on which hitchhiking is not allowed. However, you could walk 2 miles along the highway, turn left onto Tehachapi Boulevard, and hike or hitchhike west 7 miles to town.

Post Office MOJAVE, CA 93501 805-824-4561		
SUN	MON - FRI	SAT
	8:30 a - 5:30 p	10:00 a - 5:00 p

MOJAVE (*mo-HAH-vee*) (10 miles off route) An option to Tehachapi. From the Tehachapi Willow Springs Road, turn right and walk southeast 0.3 mile to the Oak Creek Road, which leads to Mojave. Oak Creek Road is much less traveled than the Tehachapi Willow Springs Road leading to the town of Tehachapi. Mojave is a highway town, featuring a post office and the usual amenities. Inquire at the trailer park, two blocks east of the McDonalds restaurant, for showers, laundry, and spartan camping.

Post Office ONYX, CA 93255 619-378-2121		
SUN	MON - FRI	SAT
	9:30 a - 1:00 p 2:00 p - 4:00 p	7:30 a - 10:30 a Parcel pick-up only.

ONYX (*ON-ex*) Reached via a 17 mile hitchhike from Walker Pass west along Highway 178. Onyx has groceries and a post office.

KENNEDY MEADOWS GENERAL STORE P.O. BOX 3A-5 INYOKERN, CA 93527
7 Days
9:00 a - 5:00 p
Store-no P.O. "These hours are effective from April 25 to October 31. After May 20th, the store is normally open until 8 pm on Saturday."

KENNEDY MEADOWS (0.7 mile off route) At the Sherman Pass Road, leave the trail near the bridge, turn right, and hike southeast along the road to the friendly general store. A busy campground lies a few miles north along the PCT.

Post Office 101 S. EDWARDS ST. INDEPENDENCE, CA 93526 619-878-2210		
SUN	MON - FRI	SAT
	8:30 a - 5:00 p	See below

"Although not open for regular business on Saturdays, this office is 'PCT Hiker Friendly' and will deliver packages through our 'will-call window' from 7 am until Noon if the hiker knocks for service."

INDEPENDENCE (off route) Reached by hiking over Kearsarge Pass on the trail of the same name, 9 miles to Onion Valley, then by hitchhiking 15 miles down the mountain (sometimes easy, sometimes not). Located on busy Highway 395, Independence has a post office, cafés, motels, mini-markets, and a grocery & mercantile.

VERMILION VALLEY RESORT P.O. BOX 258 HUNTINGTON LAKE ROAD LAKESHORE, CA 93634 209-855-6558 (office) 209-259-4000 (resort)	
SUN - FRI	SAT
7:00 a - 7:00 p	7:00 a - 8:00 p

Resort/Store-no P.O.

VERMILION VALLEY RESORT (1½ miles of walking and a 4½ mile boat ride - twice daily) The resort features a café and small store, showers, laundry, phone, and fuel by the ounce. Camping is nearby. Write to the management for information regarding fees for ferry and parcel handling services. Send your parcels a week earlier than you would otherwise, as UPS delivers only to Rancheria Garage, 23 miles away, and the resort management collects the parcels only once a week.

Notes: Hikers have asked me about resupplying at the Muir Trail Ranch. Very expensive, and the management packs in its supplies and parcels using horses and mules. The person who uses these animals, however indirectly, is contributing to the associated trail damage and pollution.

REDS MEADOW RESORT P.O. BOX 395 MAMMOTH LAKES, CA 93546 619-934-2345 1-800-292-7758
7 Days
7:00 a - 7:00 p
Resort/Store-no P.O. "Please call or write for our Package Pick-Up Authorization. We charge $20 per package pick-up, plus a storage fee."

RED'S MEADOW RESORT (0.3 mile off route) Leave the PCT at the abandoned stage coach road. In season, the store is usually well stocked with picnic items, and a café is adjacent. However, the resort does not normally open until early or mid June, and sometimes much later if the snowpack has been heavy. A campground is nearby, as are the naturally heated showers, which are free. One can ride the shuttle to the ski resort, then hitchhike or walk the remaining 5 miles downhill to the town of Mammoth Lakes, which has a post office (Zip 93546) and the usual amenities. Northbound hikers pressed for time might simply buy a few picnic supplies at the Red's Meadow store, if open, and "tough it" to Tuolumne Meadows.

Post Office TUOLUMNE MEADOWS STATION YOSEMITE NATIONAL PARK, CA 95389 209-372-1329		
SUN	MON - FRI	SAT
	9:00 a - 5:00 p	9:00 a - Noon
Opens approximately June 15, depending on the snowpack. Until then, parcels are held in Yosemite Valley, accessible via hitchhiking.		

TUOLUMNE MEADOWS P.O. (0.3 miles off route) (*TWAH-luh-me*) Leave the PCT at Highway 120 in Tuolumne Meadows. To reach the tent-cabins, restaurant and showers turn right, cross the bridge, and follow a road-side trail 1 mile. Otherwise, from the trail turn left and hike southwest along Highway 120 to the well-stocked store, grill, and post office. The Mountain Shop, presently located in the gas station a short distance west, sells back-packing gear.

Post Office ECHO CHALET, INC. 9900 ECHO LAKES RD. ECHO LAKE, CA 95721 916-659-7207		
SUN	MON - FRI	SAT
	11:00 a - 2:00 p	11:00 a - 2:00 p
Store-P.O.		

ECHO LAKE RESORT (On route) A small, usually well-stocked store open 7 days. Camping in the vicinity of Echo Lake is prohibited.

Notes: The "hiker friendly" Tahoe Sunset Lodge, located in the community of South Lake Tahoe, about 8 miles from Echo Lake along Highway 50, offers a free shuttle for its guests coming from the trail, and a free ride back. You can call them from Echo Lake at 1-800-755-8246. The management will hold resupply parcels for guests, sent via UPS "commercial" to: Hiker's Name c/o Tahoe Sunset Lodge, 1171 Emerald Bay Rd., South Lake Tahoe, CA 96150. To economize, up to 4 hikers can share a room. Guests are also welcome to use the hot tub and picnic/BBQ area. Within half a mile of the lodge are the following amenities: laundromat, post office (Main Post Office, South Lake Tahoe, CA 96150), restaurants, large sporting goods store, supermarket, natural foods store, and a movie theater.

Post Office SODA SPRINGS, CA 95728 916-426-3082		
SUN	MON - FRI	SAT
	8:30 a - 4:30 p	

SODA SPRINGS (3 miles west along Old Highway 40) Features a small grocery store, a restaurant, and a laundromat.

	Post Office SIERRA CITY, CA 96125 916-862-1152	
SUN	MON - FRI	SAT
	8:30 a - 4:30 p	

"Due to a lack of space, we prefer that parcels arrive no earlier than 15 days ahead of their owners."

SIERRA CITY (1½ miles southwest along Highway 49) The town has a post office, a normally well-stocked store, a restaurant, and a laundromat; but it lacks camping facilities other than the Wild Plum Campground, near the PCT.

	Post Office BELDEN TOWN, CA 95915 916-283-2906	
SUN	MON - FRI	SAT
	8:30 a - 5:00 p	8:30 a - Noon

"We recommend a Saturday arrival so you can share our potluck supper!"

BELDEN TOWN (on route) The small store is normally well stocked with picnic items. Showers and laundromat facilities are adjacent. A campground is nearby.

	Post Office OLD STATION, CA 96071 916-335-7191	
SUN	MON - FRI	SAT
	8:30 a - 4:30 p	1:30 p - 2:15 p Parcel pick-up only. (Knock on side door)

OLD STATION (0.1 mile off route) Pass through a metal gate and follow the dirt road to the resort. Or continue along the PCT, and after seeing the buildings from the trail, continue to the gravel road, turn left and in 100 feet cross a yellow cattle guard. Turn left again on another dirt road and follow it to the Hat Creek Motel & Resort. There you will also find the post office, Old Station Pizza, and Hat Creek Store, which carries mainly picnic items. There are 3 restaurants along the highway 1½ miles northeast of the Old Station Post Office: Uncle Runts Place, Old Station Café and Pub, and Rainbow Restaurant. Also, there is the Rim Rock Ranch Store and Resort, and a mini mart at the gas station next to the Rainbow Restaurant.

BURNEY FALLS CAMP STORE McARTHUR-BURNEY FALLS STATE PARK 24900 HIGHWAY 89 BURNEY, CA 96013 916-335-4214
7 Days
8:00 a - 8:00 p
Store-no P.O. "We are open mid-May through early October, everyday including holidays."

CAMP STORE in McARTHUR-BURNEY FALLS STATE PARK (0.1 mile off route) Within earshot of Burney Falls, leave the trail and turn right, cross the bridge over Burney Creek, and proceed to the store, stocked with tourist food and camping supplies. Coin-op showers and camping are nearby.

Post Office CASTELLA, CA 96017 916-235-4413		
SUN	MON - FRI	SAT
	8:30 a - 5:00 p	8:30 a - 10:30 a

CASTELLA (2.5 miles below the PCT at its intersection with the Bobs Hat Trail.) The campground has a site for PCT hikers, and shower facilities. Descend the paved road leading out of the park to the post office, and Ammirati's Market which is normally well stocked, and its adjacent bar which serves hot meals. Cross under the Interstate to reach the laundromat.

	Post Office ETNA, CA 96027 916-467-3981	
SUN	MON - FRI	SAT
	8:30 a - 5:00 p	

ETNA (a 10 mile hitchhike northeast from the PCT) Has a post office, a medium size grocery, motels, and restaurants. It lacks public showers, but allows free camping in the city park.

	Post Office SEIAD VALLEY, CA 96086 916-496-3211	
SUN	MON - FRI	SAT
	8:30 a - 5:00 p	Noon - 2:00 p

SEIAD VALLEY (on route) (*SIGH-yad*) In the building housing the post office is a usually well stocked store and a café. Take the chef up on his PCT Pancake Challenge, if you dare. Camping, coin-op showers and laundry facilities in the adjacent RV park.

Notes: According to Jeffrey Schaffer the Mid River RV Park will handle your resupply parcels, and is open 7 days a week. Before mailing your parcels there, check with the management by writing to them at P.O. Box 707, Seiad Valley.

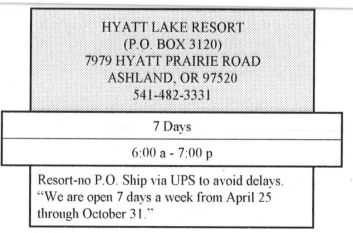

HYATT LAKE RESORT (P.O. BOX 3120) 7979 HYATT PRAIRIE ROAD ASHLAND, OR 97520 541-482-3331
7 Days
6:00 a - 7:00 p

Resort-no P.O. Ship via UPS to avoid delays.
"We are open 7 days a week from April 25 through October 31."

HYATT LAKE RESORT (0.7 mile off route) At Hyatt Lake Road, ignore the sign to Hyatt Lake Resort, as the road is far longer than the short cut. Instead, follow the signs to the recreation area and then to the overnight camping. Near the lakeshore turn left onto a trail and proceed to the dam. Crossing the dam you will see the resort. It features a laundromat and showers, a campground, a restaurant, and a snack bar. At publication time the restaurant was open Wednesday through Sunday, 8 am to 8 pm. The snack shop, where hiker resupply parcels are kept, was open 7 days, 6 am to 7 pm.

CRATER LAKE LODGE 400 RIM VILLAGE DRIVE CRATER LAKE, OR 97604 541-594-2511
Open 24 hours, 7 days a week.
Resort-no P.O. Packages sent via the Postal Service will be held down at the post office.

CRATER LAKE LODGE (0.2 mile off route, handles parcels sent *only* by UPS) Located in the Rim Village atop the caldera. Parcels are held at the Lodge's front desk, open 24 hours, 7 days a week. Nearby is a cafeteria, open 6 am to 10 pm, and a take-out pizza and frozen yogurt shop.

If you prefer to send your resupply parcel via the US Postal Service, address it to yourself in care of General Delivery, Crater Lake National Park, OR 97604. You'll have to collect it at the post office, located at Park Headquarters at the base of the caldera, and open weekdays 10 am to 4 pm, and Saturdays 10 am to 2 pm. The Mazama Campground has showers, laundry, a camper-oriented store that usually carries stove fuel, and cabins.

Post Office CASCADE SUMMIT, OR 97425 541-433-2548		
Sun	Mon - Fri	Sat
	8:00 a - 2:00 p	8:00 a - Noon
Resort/Store-P.O. "Hikers can receive their parcels anytime the store is open, but can only mail things out during postal hours."		

CASCADE SUMMIT (1.4 miles off route) 1.6 miles southwest of Highway 58 near Willamette Pass, leave the trail at the 4WD road signed "Pengra Pass," and which appears to be an unofficial trailhead. Turn sharply right, descend the road to the railroad tracks, cross them and descend to the paved road. Turn right and walk along the road 1.1 miles to the Shelter Cove Resort. The moderately-stocked store (open 7 days, 5 am - 6 pm and usually later on weekdays and Saturdays) houses a deli and small post office. This friendly establishment lacks laundry facilities, but offers coin-op showers and a deep sink to wash clothes by hand and two free campsites for PCT hikers.

ELK LAKE RESORT
CENTURY DRIVE
(P.O. BOX 789)
BEND, OR 97701
541-317-2994
7 Days
8:00 a - 8:00 p
Resort/Store-no P.O. "We are open Memorial Day through late September. Please send your parcels via UPS."

ELK LAKE RESORT (1.3 miles off route) The resort has a moderately stocked store and a grill. A Forest Service campground is nearby. Ask ahead of time about handling fees.

OLALLIE LAKE GUARD STATION
C/O CLACKAMAS RANGER DISTRICT
61431 EAST HIGHWAY 224
ESTACADA, OR 97023
7 Days
See below
Ranger Station - No P.O. "Other duties require the guards to be away from the station for up to eight hours. Evenings are usually the best time to pick up packages. Allow plenty of time for mail delivery and please secure food packages against mice."

OLALLIE LAKE GUARD STATION (0.2 mile off route) The Olallie Lake Store, just east of the Guard Station, is usually reasonably stocked with expensive picnic goods. Camping abounds in the not-too-immediate proximity. No restaurant, showers, telephone or laundromat. The Guard Station is normally open mid-June to mid-September, but has irregular hours during the day. For this reason thru-hikers might plan on buying a few supplies here only, rather than sending a resupply parcel.

TIMBERLINE SKI AREA WY'EAST STORE TIMBERLINE LODGE, OR 97028 541-231-7979	
SAT - SUN	MON - FRI
7:00 a - 6:00 p	8:00 a - 5:30 p
Resort-no P.O.	

TIMBERLINE LODGE (0.1 mile off route) Walk across the paved drive from the massive lodge and enter the WY'East Annex. The store, which sells no food but which handles resupply parcels for a fee, is on the lower floor of the annex. The cafeteria is on the upper level. This busy area lacks camping.

Post Office CASCADE LOCKS, OR 97014 541-374-8410		
SUN	MON - FRI	SAT
	8:30 a - 1:00 p 2:00 p - 5:00 p	

CASCADE LOCKS (0.4 mile off route) Nearly to the Bridge of the Gods, turn right and walk along Wa Na Pa Street to the post office. The town features the typical amenities, including a well stocked grocery and a laundromat. The marina has showers, and free camping on the adjacent lawns. Don't miss the Char Burger Restaurant, 50 yards east of the Bridge of the Gods on Wa Na Pa Street.

I certainly don't recommend this, but if you plan on short-cutting to Carson via Stevenson, (both full service towns), rather than using Cascade Locks as a resupply station you might use the post office at Carson, WA 98610. Be advised that this short-cut involves hiking along minimum shoulder roads which in some places can be quite dangerous.

KRACKER BARREL 48851 US HWY. 12 NACHES, WA 98537 509-672-3105	
MON - THU	FRI - SUN
8:00 a - 6:00 p	8:00 a - 8:00 p
Store-no P.O.	

WHITE PASS (0.7 mile off route) At Highway 12 near White Pass, turn left and walk uphill along the highway to the small and moderately stocked Kracker Barrel Grocery and laundromat. Camping is nearby. The Summit House Restaurant is next door (closed on Tuesdays) as is lodging at the Village Inn.

Post Office SNOQUALMIE PASS, WA 98068 206-434-6141		
SUN	MON - FRI	SAT
	7:00 a - 3:00 p	7:00 a - Noon
Store-P.O. "We make exceptions for PCT hikers, allowing them to pick up their parcels anytime between 7:00 am and 11:00 pm, 7 days a week."		

SNOQUALMIE PASS (0.3 mile off route) Near Interstate 90 at Snoqualmie Pass, leave the trail by turning right and walk the frontage road to the village. A short ways past the motel/restaurant complex is the well-stocked Time Wise Grocery and Deli, which houses the post office. A Forest Service campground lies one mile northwest of the village.

Notes: The Wardholm-West Bed and Breakfast, located half-a-mile east of the Time Wise Grocery, is a friendly stopover for the PCT hiker stumbling from the disheartening big stump bio-regions to the south. It offers reasonable rates, particularly for those willing to share a room, up to four in a room. Shower and laundry is also available for those not wanting to stay the night. Contact the Wardholm-West B&B, P.O. Box 143, Snoqualmie Pass, WA

98068, 206-434-6540. If you telephone from the village, the proprietors might be able to pick you up. Otherwise, follow the frontage road east, continue past the freeway on-ramp, staying on Yellowstone Road. House #861, the only 3 story chalet on the road.

Post Office SKYKOMISH, WA 98288 360-677-2241		
SUN	MON - FRI	SAT
	9:00 a - Noon 1:00 p - 5:00 p	8:00 a - 10:00 a Parcel pick-up only.

SKYKOMISH (*sky-KO-mish*) (a 17 mile hitchhike along well traveled Highway 2, west from Stevens Pass) The town has a post office, lodging, restaurants and well stocked mini-markets. It lacks laundry facilities.

Post Office STEHEKIN, WA 98852 (no phone)		
SUN	MON - FRI	SAT
	8:00 a - 4:30 p	10:45 a - 12:45 p
"We are open 2 hours on Saturdays. Which two depends on the ferry's arrival time."		

STEHEKIN (*steh-HEE-kin*) (a 10 mile shuttle-bus ride) On your way to and from town the bus might stop at the Stehekin Pastry Company, in itself well worth the side trip. In Stehekin the store is usually not well stocked, and the camping can be austere and often overcrowded. Shower, laundromat, and telephone (credit card or collect calls only) are located at the public restroom building. Meals and lodging are available at the nearby North Cascades Lodge, and the distant Stehekin Valley Ranch (a.k.a. Courtney's) which offers transportation to and from town. For more information on the shuttle bus and its summer schedule, contact North Cascades National Park, 2105 Highway 20, Sedro Wolley, WA 98284, 206-856-5700.

MANNING PARK LODGE: See page 143.

Trail registers

At these resupply stations you will find PCT registers. Most of these were placed by the late Warren Rogers under the auspices of his now-defunct "PCT Club." As I see it, the purpose of the registers is to augment communication among hikers, to document trail conditions first-hand, and to archive some of the trail's history as it unfolds each hiking season. Additionally, hikers might describe wildlife sightings, give bits of wisdom inspired by trail life, or draw cartoons or compose poems and limericks that reflect some aspect of their journeys.

One purpose the registers do *not* serve is to accredit your journey. Logging in to a register is no evidence of having hiked the section of trail leading to it. And not logging in would not indicate you didn't hike the section. So there is no rule that says you have to sign every register. Nor do you have to leave your address, unless you want to be contacted.

Another point: the PCTA tends to use the registers to showcase its promotional material. Most of us hikers feel that this PCTA register pollution is in the same category as their horse apples on the trails. As an emissary of the trail you are encouraged to maintain the registers in a minimum-impact condition, by (discreetly) relieving them of this type of pollution.

Part 4
Trail-Related Ideals

The Trail's History

And the History of its Guide Books

To succeed in the higher sense, the PCT hiker must undergo two stages of personal growth. First, a metamorphosis from city dweller to distance hiker, as we learn to shed the dictates and hoary misconceptions of civilization, and begin to adapt to life more on Nature's terms. And second, the return to civilization and the application of this new-found wisdom and self-confidence in educating and encouraging other people to hike, conserve, and maintain the trails, ensuring future hikers the same potential for their own personal growth. In this we can learn much from the trail's history. How did it come into existence? What forces shaped its destiny? And what changes might be beneficial? These are questions we need to ask when considering the trail as a whole, rather than merely as a long pathway through the highlands.

Construction on the initial segments of what is now the Pacific Crest Trail began in the 1920s. Originally these segments were not meant to be connected, yet the idea was apparently being discussed in certain circles, as inspired by a similar concept with the Appalachian Trail, then under construction also. But it wasn't until the early 1930s that Clinton C. Clarke actually started turning the dream of a border-to-border trail into reality.

Clinton C. Clarke – father of the PCT

Clarke was a retired oil man with tremendous imagination and bureaucratic know-how. He "discovered" hiking and backpacking not until later in life, and by then considered himself unable to participate physically. But realizing what he had missed, and knowing how threatened were the remnants of western America's wildlands, he dedicated the rest of his life to establishing and promoting the Pacific Crest Trail, and to preserving the lands it passes through.

Always the organizer, Clarke set four general goals for himself (the quotes are from his book, discussed momentarily):

- To build a "continuous wilderness trail across the United States from Canada to Mexico, passing through the states of Washington, Oregon, and California. ... along the summit divides of the mountain ranges of these states, traversing the best scenic areas and maintaining an absolute wilderness character."

- To preserve the wilderness regions flanking this "Pacific Crest Trailway."

- To encourage young people to enjoy backpacking and "knapsacking" adventures by establishing "programs of exploratory expeditions for adventure and romance that will create leadership, self-reliance and sound physical development."

- And to "lead people back to a simpler and more natural life and arouse a love for nature and the outdoors."

Clarke wanted to encourage young people to enjoy the glorious and rigorous outdoor life that he had missed. He contacted the Boy Scouts and YMCA, which is how he met Warren L. Rogers, a 23 year old YMCA volunteer. Rogers caught Clarke's enthusiasm, and for the next 25 years the two corroborated, often working together in Clarke's southern California home.

After the two had laid out the initial sections on the maps, Rogers hiked some of them, and in 1932 when the two had formulated a satisfactory route Clarke drafted and sent proposals to the Forest Service and the National Park Service. "At the end of three years, [in 1935] a complete, detailed report and maps showing the entire route was sent to Washington. The report was then examined by field men of the National Forest and National Park Services on the Trail, corrected, and approved. From this report, the route was adopted as the official Pacific Crest Trail System."

The first hike of the PCT – 1935-1937

Also in 1932, "The Explorers Project of knapsacking exploratory expeditions over divisions of the P.C.T. was offered to the Boy Scouts... [and] adopted by the National Office as an advanced camping program for Senior Scouts. The same program was adopted by the National Y.M.C.A. The summer of 1935 the trail from Mexico to Tuolumne Meadows was covered by 15 relay teams. They averaged 15 miles a day for 805 miles. The summer of 1936, 14 teams knapsacked from the Tuolumne Meadows to Odell Lake in Oregon, 790 miles in 69 days. In 1937 the "Y" hiked on to Canada."

As Ann and Myron Sutton wrote:[1] "Sponsored by some thirty Y.M.C.A^s along the West Coast, these hikers carried from Mexico to Canada a logbook in which were recorded the comments by people encountered. Thus was completed the first exploration of the route."

---

[1] In their book *Pacific Crest Trail; Escape to the Wilderness*. See Bibliography.

This was a milestone. The PCT had been hiked, end to end, thanks to the skill, foresight, and determination of Clinton Clarke and Warren Rogers, and to the efforts of the YMCA and the Explorer Scout teams.

The first PCT guide book emphasizes preservation

In 1935 Clarke published the trail's first guide book, entitled *The Pacific Crest Trail, Canada to Mexico*. Work continued through the next decade, and Clarke published an improved guide in 1945 entitled *The Pacific Crest Trailway*. In many ways this humble little book set the standard by which all future PCT guide books would be judged. In its simplicity and unbridled enthusiasm, *The Pacific Crest Trailway* rings with the joys of hiking the PCT. But far more important is its appeal for environmental preservation, which pervades the book cover to cover.

"Explored by only the few adventurers, [the wilderness] is unknown and unappreciated by the many. And it can be destroyed without the people understanding what has happened. With the great increase in motor cars and road building, ...only a few primitive regions are left. It is absolutely vital that a great mountain, waterfall, canyon or forest be kept in its natural state.

"In few regions of the world – certainly nowhere else in the United States – are found such a varied and priceless collection of the sculptured masterpieces of Nature as adorn, strung like pearls, the mountain ranges of Washington, Oregon, and California. The Pacific Crest Trailway is the cord that binds this necklace; each gem encased in a permanent wilderness, protected from all mechanization and commercialization.[2] Our wildernesses are about gone. The primitive regions are being destroyed. The high mountain divide where runs the Pacific Crest Trail System is the LAST FRONTIER."

In a monumental effort which was to have consequences on par with those of John Muir, Clarke established conservation programs that quite literally saved most of the PCT corridor from development (or at least forestalled it). And in his words: "To almost complete this project in ten years against general disapproval by the citizens, especially of California, was a major achievement."

The book concludes with a sizable chapter on natural history, reflecting the author's appreciation of Nature. "In our hurry-scurry world of machines, noise and distractions, the mind becomes confused and our sense of values is lost. Throw down your sleeping-bag beneath a pine high on a mountain side, and get acquainted with that vast world of God's creatures that are more and

---

[2] Pack and saddle outfitters are commercial enterprises, and the laws have failed to protect the wilderness from them.

more being banished. Peace and contentment come, and events that yesterday seemed so vital shrink to their true worth."

In addition to inspiring people to hike the PCT, and greatly encouraging its preservation, Clarke's book discouraged the use of pack and saddle stock. This is yet another of his illustrious legacies, because it legally sets this important proviso. "In order to maintain the trail region in a wilderness condition and preserve the meadows and flower gardens from deterioration by pack and saddle animals, backpacking is recommended over the Pacific Crest Trailway." Clinton C. Clarke, founder of the Pacific Crest Trail, meant it to be a hiker-only trail.

The work of Warren Rogers

Today, we hear the argument that horses were involved with the trail's history from the beginning. This is not true. When Clarke passed away in 1957 at the age of 84, Warren Rogers continued the work. Rogers was a staunch advocate in the use of horses and mules along the PCT, and he seems to have set the precedence.

At any rate, and in the words of Roger's son, Donald: "My father knew what his purpose in life was – to keep the Pacific Crest Trail alive." And over the next 35 years Warren Rogers worked hard doing just that. In addition to answering innumerable inquiries and compiling articles, he tried repeatedly to develop trail-related products to finance his activities. One was a set of "waterproof maps of the trail, published in 1972, which could be tucked inside a hiker's glove." This *Pacific Crest Trail Pocket Guide,* referred to as "strip maps" comprised five volumes which covered Washington, Oregon, and Northern, Central and Southern California. In 1975, authors Ann and Myron Sutton called these maps "One of the most complete series available." Rogers died at the age of 83, one year prior to the trail's official completion in 1993.

In 1968, Congress passed the National Trail Systems Act, which granted the PCT the status of National Scenic Trail. The relevant USFS and BLM agencies became responsible for trail routing and construction, a process that altogether spanned over 60 years. The result is a continuous trail over two and a half thousand miles – a fitting tribute to the foresight and determination of Clinton C. Clarke and Warren L. Rogers.

The trail gains popularity

In June of 1971, National Geographic featured a cover story on the Pacific Crest Trail. Then in October of the same year Chronicle Books published Eric Ryback's "true story" *The High Adventures of Eric Ryback.* These two publications precipitated a trail-rush in which hundreds of hikers traveled the route, all or in part, during the early 1970s.

Perhaps inspired by the market this trail rush created, Thomas Winnett, of Wilderness Press, hired a few writer-hikers to scout the trail in piecemeal fashion and to compile their material into guide book form. Winnett published Volume 1, his delineation of the trail through California, in 1973. And a year later he published Volume 2, covering the trail through Oregon and Washington.

Since then these guide books have undergone five revisions. They now contain all the maps that thru-hikers are likely to need, as long as those hikers stay more or less on the trail. And they contain a wealth of guide book type of information. Not everyone agrees with every opinion or piece of advice the guide book authors give, but still they have written the definitive work on the PCT route.

According to the authors, they intended these guide books mainly for day and weekend hikers, which comprise the bulk of their market. Thru-hikers are likely to find snow covering vast stretches of trail which the authors saw in mid-summer conditions. Frozen lakes, for example, are described as "warm for swimming." In these circumstances, map and compass skills are very important.

My only real complaint with the guides is their austerity in terms of trail conservation. They reflect the sentiments of the mid '70s when the authors were scouting the PCT, and when horses were not yet present on trail in sufficient numbers to cause the problems they are causing today. The guide books openly condone the use of pack and saddle stock on the PCT, and in this I feel they are encouraging even more trail damage and pollution.

Hiking the PCT without the guide books is entirely possible, and Jenny and I have met a number of people doing just that. In fact, during our most recent PCT thru-hike we did not use them. But of course we had hiked the trail twice before and knew what to expect. Our main concern was to save weight, but also we wanted the least complicated hike with the greatest freedom. We carried broad maps of the areas, and these easily showed where to expect water ahead. We were not playing the numbers game, and had no interest in trail mileages. To stay on schedule we hiked according to my computer-generated itinerary, and this worked nicely.

If and when the PCT becomes properly marked, we may see the advent of a new type of streamlined guide booklet designed specifically for thru-hikers. Until then, those preparing to hike the PCT for the first time might cut the Wilderness Press guide books into sections – the sections pertaining to your resupply stations, not to the books' highway-oriented sections – and place each one into your corresponding resupply box.

Those planning on taking alternative routes and short-cuts might find the Forest Service maps quite useful. For a master list of maps of the districts in California, contact USDA Forest Service, 630 Sansome St., San Francisco CA 94111; (415) 705-2784. For Oregon and Washington contact Nature of the Northwest, USDA Forest Service, 800 NE Oregon St. Rm. 177, Portland, OR 97232; (503) 872-2750. An excellent source of commercial maps is the Map Link, 25 E. Mason St., Santa Barbara CA 93101; (800) 627-7768.

Trail Improvements

Manifesto: Separation of Wilderness and Civilization

> Hurt not the earth,
> neither the sea,
> nor the trees.
>
> *— Revelations 7:3*

If Disney entertained us with amusements, then Muir, Abbey and Thoreau enlightened us to the beauty and power of the natural realm. I regret the prospects of the PCT becoming more diluted with civilized amenities.

Shelters

During our southbound PCT hike, Jenny and I reached a place known as Government Meadow, or Camp Urich. There, we read an official sign informing visitors that the old cabin had been torn down "...to provide a more primitive Wilderness Experience as mandated by the 1964 Wilderness Act." That sounded pretty good to us, until five minutes farther along when we came to the newly built Mike Urich Cabin.

The PCT has very few such shelters, yet. I feel that such civilized conveniences rob us of the lessons and rewards of the natural world. A shelter is an eyesore in the natural realm, robbing it occupants of fresh air, solitude, the sounds of the night and the multitude of other sensations waiting to be discovered. Granted, on the Appalachian Trail rain is more frequent, and its shelters and huts are an integral part of that trail's rich culture and history. But I feel it would be wrong to try to make the PCT into another AT. The PCT has a more wild flavor, which I and many others consider one of its finer aspects.

Water spigots

Artificial water sources along the trail fall into the same category. They are man-made articles of convenience. Rather, I feel we benefit the most by accepting the natural water sources where, and sometimes if, they are to be found. Where they are 20 miles apart and more we can carry extra water. And sometimes we may have to go thirsty for a while. This, too, is part of the experience. Even in times of drought we can pack extra water, go the distance, and collect water at the next outpost of civilization as Jenny and I did in southern California during our southbound hike.

Vandalism

Vandals have a bad name. And rightly so; most of us abhor the idea of people tearing down things without authority or good reason. But what authority does Nature have when she tears things down? In some ways, then, vandals might be thought of as agents of Mother Nature working (thanklessly) to hasten the process of removing man-made, trailside objects of convenience. For further amusement along these lines I recommend Edward Abbey's *The Monkeywrench Gang*, and Dave Foreman's *Ecodefense*.

"Improvements" by dynamite

Speaking of vandalism, consider loggers clear-cutting entire forests. And imagine the PCT trail crews dynamiting the trail into existence. Rocks, tree stumps, and sometimes entire cliffs were obliterated, leaving many miles of otherwise pristine rocky sections permanently scarred. Aesthetics aside, sometimes the results of the explosions are as dangerous as the explosions themselves. And they can be just as inconvenient as the original obstacles. In the higher elevations a trail blasted from steep rock will fill in with equally steep snow. And if that snow is frozen solid it can make a very short runway. Dynamited trails such as these usually have extremely friable edges as well. Stepping on these edges could also precipitate disaster.

Trail maintenance

The fact that the PCT is federally funded and operated, so to speak, is a mixed blessing. We get an easy grade and nice tread most of the way. But hiking this type of trail tends to be a "hands off" experience. If hikers encounter something amiss, however minor, they hike on, deferring the work to the trail crews. Ditto with blow downs, overgrown brush, bridges out, eroded trail, and so on. The more demanding might voice their complaints with the Forest Service. The meek or apathetic usually just hike on. I think this mindset has a negative effect on both the hikers and the trail. These people are bringing their expectations with them, rather that bringing a willingness to assume at least some responsibility. Rather than complain about the problems, we might benefit by rolling up our sleeves and doing something about them.

Volunteer trail work

Volunteer trail work parties can be fun and rewarding. They can be a time for repaying the trail for what it has given, for getting together with like-minded friends, and for enjoying the fresh air and exercise. In light of the ineffable experiences gleaned during the summer's trek, I recommend laboring a few days, maintaining the trail. For after all, we who have traveled it know better than anyone where the maintenance needs lie.

While working on the trail, we must resist the temptation to try to civilize it. An all too common mistake is to hack the trail into a condition resembling a horse-chewed rut. This rut, some people imagine, is what a trail should look like. The fact is, using tools to chop through the earth's indurate layer exposes the loosely held undersoil to the ravages of erosion. As a rule, try to hurt the earth as little as possible.

As Ruben Rajala wrote in *The American Hiker*: "The focus should be on maintaining basic passage, rather than creating a manicured trail corridor. A more natural look is desired. Smaller blow-downs that can be easily stepped over might be left. Because we are striving for a natural environment, re-source protection is the key. The overall goal should be to keep the wilderness experience as natural as possible through trail work that is simple and that blends in."

Trail signs

In the 1930's the Forest Service placed diamond shaped emblems in Oregon and Washington, reading: "Pacific Crest Trail System." In the 1970's the agencies placed PCT logo emblems along the trail's full length. Plinkers found both types ideal targets. In the mid 1990's the Forest Service removed most of these markers in an effort to restore the wilderness to its former pris-tinehood. Never mind their road building, clear-cutting, and livestock ranging policies. In place of these historic emblems they installed branded wooden emblems at many of the trail junctions only. "Tree warts" is a term that came to me via one of the trail crew members installing them.

I believe the PCT would benefit from AT-style blazes: paint marks, 6-inches high by 2-inches wide, on the trees or posts at frequent intervals. Very frequent intervals, and facing in both directions. Like other man-made arti-cles, blazes can shatter the illusion that we are pioneering. So yes, they are unnatural, but so is the trail itself. And I consider proper blazes an important part of any trail, particularly of a National Scenic trail. Their purpose is to specify the trail at each junction, and far more importantly, to reassure hikers between junctions that the trail they are following is the intended one. These between-junction markers are vital in early season, when hikers find them-selves wallowing around searching for the trail. Appropriate markers would inform them which trail they have found. And in fact, proper tree blazes would keep early season snow sloggers from having to search for the trail.

These painted blazes could be applied to trees which have rough bark by shaving the bark, but not into the cambium. Where the bark is too rough for that, filler could be used. Either way, this type of blaze would have a number of additional advantages. It is very cost effective and easily applied. It is not subject to theft and not an attractive target to plinkers. When the paint fades it can be reapplied. Should the trail be realigned, the paint can be removed, or darkened and allowed to efface naturally over time.

Presently, the overseeing agencies are opposed to such markings along the PCT, ostensibly because of a Congressional mandate to maintain the wilderness in its natural state. (Never mind the huge amount of construction on the trail itself.) But I suspect this will change. Such trail markings would increase hiker safety and decrease government search and rescue costs. And they would increase public awareness, which in turn would elicit more enthusiasm for fiscal support and for public trail maintenance activities.

Preservation

Once you have journeyed through the magnificent regions flanking the PCT, you will have gained a first-hand awareness of the need for ardent preservation. This corridor through the timeless but vulnerable succession of ecosystems, how shall we attempt to leave it for those who will follow in our footsteps? Aldo Leopold wrote, "We abuse land because we regard it as a *commodity* belonging to us. When we see land as a *community* to which we belong, we might begin to use it with love and respect." Alas, the PCT hiker sees innumerable examples of how our culture has been treating the land as a commodity, taking from it and giving nothing in return. And I hope that more of us will begin to realize the dire need to reverse this trend. The PCT and the nation's other long trails are not commodities belonging to the hiker, but communities to which all hikers belong. The wild places the trails pass through are not waste lands, nor do they represent miles to be gained. Instead, they are marvelous ecologies to be reveled in, to be loved and respected. Their survival depends on our caring and fighting for them, just as our survival depends on them.

The PCT offers a reasonably convenient means of spending a block of time with Nature. And if hiking and living in its wilds teaches us anything, I like to think that it teaches us greater self-reliance. It teaches us that we can survive very nicely without a hot shower every day. That we can live outdoors and sleep in our tents. That we can walk all the way across the country, perhaps without resorting to the use of vehicles. And it allows us to spend time in the great Quiet, free of the distractions of society. Dragging bits of civilization closer would dilute the wilderness experience and make hikers more dependent on that civilization. And that, I believe, would be a mistake.

As Edward Abbey was fond of saying, "God bless America. Let's save some of it."

Plowing and Polluting

Welcome to The Pacific Crest National Scenic Stock-yards

> "At least as far as the Pacific Crest Trail is concerned,
> I am prepared to invoke the wisdom of Thomas Jefferson:
> *'Walking is the best possible exercise. Habituate yourself to walk very far.*
> *The Europeans value themselves on having subdued the horse*
> *to the uses of man; but I doubt whether we have not lost more*
> *than we have gained by the use of this animal."*
>
> *The Pacific Crest Trail by William R. Gray*
> *Special Publication, 1975 by National Geographic.*

First time PCT hikers may not see a great deal of trail damage caused by horses, mules, and llamas – even though they are walking in the ruts caused by these animals for many hundreds of miles. Self-evident though this damage is, they tend to accept it as normal, and view the domestic animals causing it as their own kith and kin of the trails.

I know this was Jenny's and my impression during our first PCT hike. But the second time we hiked the trail, four years later, we witnessed a dramatic increase in the damage. And after seeing how that damage was spreading like a cancer from one end of the trail to the other, we realized the simple but painful truth that domestic animals no longer belong on the PCT.

When we hiked the PCT the third time, three years later, we saw, not just another dramatic increase in the damage, but an astronomical one. The stretches of trail pulverized by horses and mules were no longer short. And the associated ruts were far deeper. We examined and documented this all along the way, and ultimately concluded that:

The damage by pack and saddle stock is doubling every three years.

DOUBLING !!

While hiking through the High Sierra during that third journey we met four professional trail crews of about 15 members each. Each crew had been working to restore the trail since early spring, and planned to continue well into the fall. I asked one supervisor what percentage of the damage had been caused by horses and mules. "If it wasn't for them," he replied, "we wouldn't have anything to do!" What were they doing? Paving the trail with rocks. This is a form of road building, and I wonder where it will take us...

Even deeper into politics, no doubt. Cobblestone paved trails are just another result of equestrians rallying for their rights to (ab)use the PCT. They have the numbers. They have the money. And they have the lobbying power. And they have been using these to their advantage for decades, and will no doubt continue doing so. And the simple fact is: until hikers resist, the equestrians are fighting a one-sided battle; and they are winning by default.

Let's learn a little about these animals.

Horse facts

Each horse or mule weighs between 1,000 and 1,200 pounds, and carries a load of 150 to 250 pounds. Compound this into a string of a dozen animals and we have the equivalent crushing, lacerating weight of a Sherman tank, including the steel tread. With one major difference: The Sherman tank doesn't poop on the trails. Pack animals do, and each one disperses between 15 and 25 pounds of manure a day, anywhere it likes, including on the trail, in the campsites, and even in the creeks and lakes. And yes, packers can legally stand their animals in the water, even though these animals often urinate and defecate in that water. As for the manure on the trail, if not pulverized into the earth by the passing of hooves and boots, it can endure for years; and so can the pathogens teeming within it. Washed away in the run-off of rain and melting snow, these fecal and urinary coliforms head for the creeks and lakes.

Horses and mules were not built for mountain travel; rugged terrain would break up their hooves. So they require steel shoes. The calks, or protuberances on these shoes are even more damaging, especially at the camps and rest stops where these animals often paw and dig. Where tied to trees or between trees with picket lines, they compact the ground, effectively sterilizing it against regeneration.

Induration

In its natural state, the earth's surface has been hardened by the elements. This is a process known as "induration," and it acts to protect the underlying soil from erosion. Steel horseshoes work like farmer's plows, chopping through the indurated surface layer, breaking it apart, and turning it under. This is because these animals don't walk flat-footed, but pivot and gouge with each step. Once they expose the soft, underlying soil, erosion begins taking its toll. The "experts" tell us that the trail ruts are caused by wash-outs linked to poor trail construction. But water coursing downhill cuts a V-shaped trough. If water was the main eroding factor, the trails would all be V-shaped. But more importantly, they would not be channeled in areas where the terrain is level.

U-shaped ruts are caused mainly by horse and mule hooves. Hikers avoid walking on the steep edges of the ruts to prevent twisting their ankles. Horses and mules don't. Each time they step on the edge of the trail-rut they cut another vertical slice from its edge. This is why the "horse ruts" are steep sided. The more cohesive the soil, the steeper the sides.

When we think of the saying "hit the dusty trail," we might remember that horses initiate the process by cutting through the indurate layer. Deprived of its protective overlayment, the dry and dusty material is exposed. And when both horses and hikers raise this dust, the wind blows it away. This is how the trail is eroded on level ground. It is the erosion of wind not water. Trail maintenance crew members work to repair this damage, filling in the ruts with dirt and rocks. Conservationists work to remove the horses and mules which are causing it. Some soils along the PCT are loose to begin with, and lack much of an indurate layer. These are particularly susceptible to stock erosion.

Pro-equestrian myths

If pack animals are so damaging to the ecology, why are they permitted in the backcountry? Apathy among "conservationists," as promulgated by a widespread belief in myths. John F. Kennedy put it well when he said: "The great enemy of the truth is very often not the lie – deliberate, contrived and dishonest – but the myth – persistent, persuasive and unrealistic." Nowhere is this more apparent than in wilderness issues.

Whenever someone raises the issue of whether or not pack animals belong on the trail, we hear the same old arguments. Almost invariably these come from the pro-equestrians. And by the term "pro-equestrian" I mean anyone, horse rider or hiker, who favors the equestrian presence. I have no animosity with any of these people. Nor do I dislike horses, mules and llamas. What I am discussing here is the plowing and polluting, and the plethora of misinformation and myth that clouds the entire issue.

The standard arguments in favor of trail riding have been perfected over the years, and are so effective that they persuade hikers to become pro-equestrian hikers. But it goes beyond that, into the realm of blindness and intolerance. Join the PCTA and speak out against horse use and you will see what I mean. Here in the real world there are two sides to every story. So let's look at some of the standard pro-equestrian arguments and contrast them with pro-conservation responses.

Myth: Pack and saddle stock have the right to use the trails.

Pro-conservation: Horses, mules and llamas are like motorbikes and ORVs. They are vehicles; objects of conveyance used to transport people and loads. Vehicles have no rights in the wilderness.

Myth: Horse, mule and llama manure is nothing but fertilizer.

Pro-conservation: Backcountry trails, campsites and water sources do not need to be fertilized. Manure often contains the grain seeds of invasive plants that can take root in alpine meadows. Cow birds are attracted to these seeds, and tend to follow livestock into the backcountry. There, they invade the nests of the indigenous songbirds, not occasionally, but exclusively.

Myth: The horse rider dressed in traditional western garb – the cowboy hat, cowboy boots, and the bandoleer of 30-30 cartridges draped over the chest – is a *REAL* cowboy.

Pro-conservation: The "real" cowboy is a Hollywood invention. John Wayne was an actor, and all the romance associated with his fanciful western escapades was dreamed-up by script writers. In the name of recreation, to-day's Hollywood cowboys are plowing and polluting western America's wild lands, meadows, lakes, and streams.

Myth: Saying anything against pack and saddle stock is taboo.

Pro-conservation: The horse is sacred to the "real" cowboy in the same way that the cow is venerated by the Hindu, but in reality it is just another domestic animal. Horses, mules and llamas degrade the outdoor experience by their abusive treatment of the environment, and hikers have absolutely no reason to refrain from discussing the issue.

Myth: Equestrians have done much to preserve the PCT.

Pro-conservation: Equestrians have done much to establish trails and trail-side amenities for themselves. And they have lobbied to preserve their rights to "use" the PCT. But they have done very little to further the cause of trail preservation. What they have done is to exclude those other vehicles which terrify their animals. Bicycles and hang gliders for example. They have lobbied for the construction of trail-side packer amenities such as well appointed horse camps and water troughs – none of which are of use to hikers due to the stench and pollution. They have lobbied to insure the packer's rights to exploit the wilderness for hire. And most important in this case, they have promoted their own interpretation of wilderness; one which overlooks the negative impact their animals have on the land.

Myth: Equestrians are becoming more conscientious about low-impact backcountry practices. By adopting light weight backpacking gear, they will reduce the number of pack animals they require, and thus their impact.

Pro-conservation: Promoting and practicing are two different things. Even so, lightening a 150 pound load on a 1,000 pound mule by 50 pounds still leaves the impact of 1,100 pounds chiseling the trail with every step. And even if some "conscientious" packer reduces his dunnage enough to decrease the number of animals needed to carry it, say from 6 to 5, the remaining 5 would still impact the back country enormously. If the equestrians are going to carry lighter-weight backpacking gear, perhaps they will also carry it as designed: on their backs, as they hike along the trails.

Myth: The wilderness managers of the Sierra are concerned about the growing impact of pack and saddle stock.

Fact: FINAL POLICY, *Submitted to the Federal Register for publication on October 23, 1991, drafted by the Central Sierra Interagency Wilderness Managers*: "*Maximum number of pack and saddle stock: 25 head per party.* [27,000 pounds of crushing, trail chiseling weight depositing 500 pounds of manure per day, per party.] *Exceptions may be granted, with an application submitted 30 days in advance.*"

Myth: Pack and saddle stock on the National Scenic Trails is a fact of life. They were written into the 1964 Wilderness Act, and removing them would require rewriting the Act.

Pro-conservation: The Wilderness Act was muscled in by lobbyists supported by outfitters, guides, and packers. The entire Appalachian Trail is congressionally designated wilderness, yet horses are banned from the vast majority of it's length. If AT hikers can exclude these animals from their National Scenic Trail, then PCT hikers can do exactly the same with theirs.

Witness the segment of PCT leading to the caldera rim in Crater Lake National Park. The Park's Superintendent, David K. Morris, and the Chief of Resource Preservation and Research, William M. Brock proposed in May of 1994 that this segment be designated for foot traffic only. When this proposal was approved, a bold, new precedent was set.

Comments and my responses

Pro-equestrian: Without the influence of stockmen and packers, the PCT may not have come into existence.

Response: The main difficulties of bringing the trail into existence involved the horrific expense of building it to stock standards. Without their influence I imagine that the trail would have been completed a decade earlier.

Pro-Equestrian: Now is not the time to pick fights. In these days of budget cutbacks, the de-fanging of environmental regulations, and ever-increasing pressure on our remaining wild areas, we must build environmental coalitions, not tear them apart.

Response: Equestrian groups are not environmental coalitions.

Pro-equestrian: The PCT was originally meant to be shared by hikers and equestrians.

Response: Clinton C. Clarke, the originator of the PCT, was wholly opposed to the use of horses on the PCT. He intended the trail to be used by hikers only, and documented this repeatedly in his writing.

Pro-equestrian: The Sierra Club tested the relative impacts of a horse's hooves and a hiker's boots. The results were recorded as equal.

Response: A 200 pound hiker in two rubber-soled boots having the same impact as a 1,200 pound horse on four steel shoes? Give us a break! While the Sierra Club has promoted conservation in many areas, in a few others it has turned a blind eye. Case in point: since the club's beginning it has promoted the use of pack and saddle stock on the trails. Why? Tradition, equestrian interests among some of its principals perhaps, and the same old politics.

Pro-equestrian: Studies have shown that horses and mules do not cause giardia.

Response: From Chris Oswald, biologist and research physiologist: "The current [1995] consensus among biologists is that livestock contribute to the spread of giardia. I think it would be best for the PCT (and many other trails) to prohibit the use of pack animals in the backcountry."

Pro-equestrian: Most erosion is not caused by horses, but by the loose nature of the decomposed granite or volcanic pumice over which the trail passes.

Response: The looser the soil and the more subject to erosion, the more impact horses have on it, and the greater the need to keep them off it.

Pro-equestrian: To minimize trail erosion, we need to build well-engineered trails.

Pro-conservation: Paved in cobblestones, for example? Why not use asphalt instead? Banning livestock and discouraging the use of heavy hiking boots would obviate the need to pave our National Scenic Trails.

Pro-equestrian: In the Sierra, hikers outnumber horses by 100 to 1.

Response: Horse and mule teams ply the high country in strings of 15 to 25 animals every day of the summer. The ratio of 100 to 1 seems highly exaggerated. Even so, comparing hikers to horses is absurd. The horse is massively heavier, it chisels the trail with steel shoes, and it poops where it pleases.

Pro-equestrian: For every horse camp, there are 10 hiker camps.

Response: Those 10 hiker camps don't come with corrals reeking of manure and trampled inside and out, picnic tables, metal fire pits, stock loading ramps, hitching posts, and sometimes even stacked cordwood.

Pro-equestrian: Equestrians are friendly people who love the wilderness.

Response: Many act with friendliness, but many act with startling aggression. However, the issue is not how amicable or surly they are, or how much hikers like or dislike them or their horses. The issue is how much damage these animals are causing.

Comment: Much of the conflict between the two groups results from a kind of cultural clash.

Response: No, the conflict results from the damage and pollution.

Pro-equestrian: If we want to ban horses, then to avoid being hypocrites we will have to ban hikers also.

Response: Assuming that hikers and horses belong together, either on the trails or banned from them, is an error in logic. If any two activities belong together it would be the two vehicles: horses and motorbikes. Both are capable of great impact, and in fact motorbikes were once legal on the trails until outlawed for the damage they were causing.

Pro-equestrian: The PCT "community" consists of hikers, equestrians, members of the trail-related organizations, trail maintainers, affiliated agents of the Forest Service, Park Service, and BLM, sponsors both individual and corporate, and guide book authors.

Response: How cozy. But as I stated at the beginning of this chapter, the amount of damage that pack and saddle stock are causing the PCT is doubling every three years. So, as impressive as this "community" sounds, it is not effectively preserving the trail of its namesake. And until it reverses this trend I am not one of its members.

Pro-equestrian: Instead of threatening to ban pack animals from the PCT, we need to be educating their owners to the ways of low-impact travel. Rather than the steel shoes, horses and mules need to start wearing low impact footwear.

Pro-conservation: In the same way that a Sherman tank could not possibly travel in the high country with low impact, neither could a horse. Low impact footwear on an eleven hundred pound animal is an oxymoron.

Pro-equestrian: Archeologists tell us that man and horses existed in prehistory.

Response: There is no evidence to suggest that domestic horses existed on the North American continent prior to the early 1500's, when the Spaniards introduced them from Europe. This introduction occurred 2,000 years after "prehistory."

Pro-equestrian: Research history and it is the men who defied tradition that have plunged the world into its gravest disasters: Hitler, Mussolini, Stalin come to mind.

Response: So does Patrick Henry, father of the American Revolution. We celebrate his vision every Fourth of July.

Pro-equestrian: Pack animals have the legal right-of-way.

Response: Like almost every aspect of the trail, the horsemen lobbied for this "law." Why? Perhaps they feel superior to pedestrians and want them out of their way. Hikers favoring an untrammeled earth are wearying of this Marlboro Machismo.

Hiker safety

When we hikers encounter pack animals on the trail, for our own safety we should stand well clear. The average mule or horse is innately afraid of hikers, especially those carrying large backpacks. Thus, we should never try to pet the animals, lest they over-react by biting or stomping. And beware: these animals are well known for kicking bystanders. When a horse strikes out, the thrust is usually blindly to the side. But a mule can take deadly aim; its blow is likely to connect, and the resulting injuries can be maiming.

If a horse should suddenly bolt, and if you are down slope of it, it could fall on you, or buck its rider or panniers onto you, or kick rocks onto you. Or the horse could kick out and knock you down the slope. So remember that the highest position is by far the safer. When giving way to equestrians, always leave the trail by climbing the slope.

Author and hiker Charlie Hoeppner states it well: "I fear horses. They are very unpredictable no matter what all the horse lovers say. I know many horsy people, and every one of them has been injured (broken arms, ankles, etc.) from a horse getting away while riding it, or from being thrown by it. Of course, they all claim it was their own fault. But the simple fact is, these animals are very dangerous."

Other hikers speak out

Namie Bacile, II (AT 89, PCT 92, CDT 94 and 95; Current President, The American Long Distance Hikers Association, Western States Chapter): "As for horses on the trail, I've seen enough. Slogging through the Bob Marshall Wilderness during my CDT hike this year was the worst backpacking experience of my life. The trail was churned to slop, causing me to slip and slide with every step. I felt lucky to still be walking after twisting my knee in a fall. I've never seen so much tax money being spent re-routing trail because of horse damage, only to have the new trail churned to soup as soon as it opened. Horses don't like walking in mud a foot deep either, as they too seek the dry edges, which soon turns an 18-inch trail into an 8-foot wide disaster. Now get this: posted regulations state that in order to reduce impact parties shall be limited to 15 people and 35 stock. How does this make sense? It boils down to money, greed and politics. Outfitters seeking income, subsidized by taxpayers, at the expense of the wilderness.

"It's not just the outfitters either. Hiking behind Ben York, President of the Pacific Crest Trail Association, on the PCT in '92 I saw damaged switchbacks, manure along the trail and in the creeks, pawed up campsites and urine spots the size of my tent, to go along with piles of manure and the horseflies and stink that go with it. Perhaps all of this is quite natural to the equestrian, but it isn't my idea of wilderness. Unfortunately the damage goes even further. Stream crossings that you could otherwise hop across get eroded into fords. Water bars are often destroyed or rendered useless. Steep grades become dangerous slides of dust and rock when dry, and wash out into ruts, sometimes several feet deep after the rains. I've seen a single trail turn into as many as eleven as stock spreads out across meadow sections. I've also seen horses ridden knee deep into ponds and lakes to drink, often leaving as much fluid as they consume.

"I believe there are places for horse riding and the National Scenic Trail is not one of them. The work and money equestrians put into the trail can't make up for the damage they do, which in many cases is permanent. It's not the horse's fault - they are just too heavy. Just as roads, highways and bridges have weight limits, so should the trails."

Garrett Holmes (four years as Backcountry Ranger in the Three Sisters Wilderness): "We are now at a critical time for the future of our nation's wonderful trail systems. Our current, slashing congress has deleted the majority of trail maintenance funds with the simple swath of a pen. Trails are disappearing at an alarming rate! Trails that were the work of the Civilian Conservation Corps, miners, and even native Americans are returning to nature.

"The results of today's vogue to be "outdoorsy" are more pressure, more people, more horses, and oops, less trail maintenance money. In the Three Sisters it is not uncommon to encounter 400 people a weekend on just one stretch of the PCT. Yet in my view 90% of the immediate damage could be stopped simply by discontinuing horse use. Plain and simple, a creature weighing a thousand pounds with metal shoes does a lot of damage. Alpine meadows whose growing season might only be 2½ months can be scarred for decades by one group of thoughtless horse users.

"In my experience, equestrians are rarely present at trail maintenance sessions. During the summer of 1990, the Foley Ridge trail was nearly destroyed due to horses going around blowdowns. Eventually our trail crew was forced to pull off other projects to fix that trail. Meanwhile the Forest Service re-built its parking area, installing horse loading ramps, hitching posts, and making it much more horse accessible.

"For the preservation of certain habitats and ecosystems, I believe measures should be taken. Due to its crestline, exposed, and fragile nature, I do not feel the PCT is an appropriate route for horse use. There are thousands of miles of low-land, more durable trails for these steel shod creatures to tramp. Leave the PCT to those who feel its surging length through the soles of their feet, not to those who are distanced by mounting some beast of burden. The PCT has been given an enormous amount of respect by being named a National Scenic Trail. Now it is time to show that respect by securing its preservation for future generations. The key step is to make the PCT hiker only!"

Frank Spirek and **Diane Ensminger** (PCT 92): "We began our PCT thru-hike about 8 hours behind PCTA President Ben York, his wife, and 5 pack animals. By the second night we caught up to them. It surprised us that we could out-pace the horses. As we reached the high country, his pack train was forced to look for alternate routes to avoid the higher elevation snow packs. We leap-frogged with them all the way to Kennedy Meadows, during which time the Mrs. fell from her horse and broke her arm, and had to drop out. From Kennedy Meadows York and his animals were obliged to skip around the High Sierra. As the months and miles stretched onward, we again found ourselves catching up to them. We may hold the record for continuous miles walked through fresh animal waste! In all seriousness, the presence of pack animals greatly detracted from the overall trail experience.

"Throughout our trip, it never ceased to amaze us at how heavily laden the animal packers would travel. In northern Washington, we met up with pack trains of 18-animals each, carrying circus style tents and large metal wood-stoves. No trace camping it ain't!!

"Animal packers seem to be clinging to the romantic days of the "Cowboy West" – an era concerned with taming the wilds instead of preserving them. We've met lots of animal packers, and despite their almost universally poor back-country practices we can't imagine that they really enjoy damaging the very source of their pleasure. Maybe from high in the saddle they can't see the damage caused by those many steel-shod hooves."

Charlie Hoeppner: "My gut feeling is that horses, mules, and llamas have no place on trails such as the PCT. It has to do with fragility, and the need for a dignity about our uses of the ever shrinking wilderness. I've talked to people who were packed into the back country on horses and served gin and tonics before a dinner of filet mignon, totally insensitive to anything between their air conditioned car at the trailhead and the book they were reading with sherry at the lakeside camp. In one such group, only 2 persons had even walked around the immediate lake in their 4 day stay. I thought of how I had trudged boot deep in dust, rock and rubble into the basin, full of anger because what was causing it was not appropriate to the wilderness.

"I've often wondered when hearing about the studies of meadows and campsites being damaged by pack animals, why one never hears of all the damage and impact of the delicate vegetation alongside the trail: tall, barren stocks where one knows well a horse ate them. The telling tale is that horses tend to yank at vegetation and then drop it in the trail. A deer just nibbles and eats that which it picks.

"To me, the whole purpose of hiking a trail is to observe the natural world, both distant and close at hand. Unfortunately, close at hand all we can see is the impact of pack animals. I strongly favor a hikers-only PCT."

Karl Diederich, (PCT '91, M.S., Mechanical Engineering) "If with a declaration and a wave of my hand I could change any one thing about the PCT, banning pack and saddle stock would be it. I used to estimate that one pack animal did as much damage as 10 to 20 people, depending on the trail conditions. In watching large hiker and stock groups pass by during this summer, I specifically looked at the trail damage they did in passing. I am forced to revise my estimate upward to one stock beast causing as much damage as one hundred backpackers. But trail damage is only their first offense. Their urine causes the trail to reek long after the manure is pounded into dust.

"Being designed for horse travel, the trail detours away from scenic areas that would be too heavily damaged with stock access. Trailside trees were cut out, and this exacerbates the brush problem. Foot bridges were build much heavier and obviously placed exclusively with stock in mind. In many places the trail detours away from areas where it could not have been constructed to stock standards, but where a perfectly acceptable foot trail could have been built. This translates to greater costs in building the trail to stock specifications, and also in repairing the stock damage."

The days of innocence and apathy

The golden era of the PCT and its resplendent 2,700 mile wilderness corridor is now in its twilight. The trail is in enormous need, and hikers will have to rally if they are to save it as a Mecca for future generations. Not with trail maintenance outings, for although these are highly beneficial in clearing brush, they do not address the much deeper problems of conservation. Hacking brush is destruction, not conservation. And so is digging, prying, sawing, and dynamiting. Filling long stretches of equestrian rut is not conservation either, but cover-up work. And cover-ups don't endure because they address the results rather than the causes.

Horses and mules are not the only forces threatening the PCT. Motorbikes, logging operations, cattle and sheep grazing are all hanging ominously over the trail's future. And so is the Forest Service road building task force. But as it stands today, all of these pale in comparison to the systematic plowing and polluting by horses and mules.

In the history of major hiking groups in the western states, I can't think of a single one that survived very long without accepting the all-pervading equestrian influence. Those which resisted were summarily divided and conquered.

The PCT needs its thousands of voiceless hikers to form coalitions on its behalf. These grass roots organizations would strengthen and unite the hikers, and provide them a means of repaying the trail for the many experiences it has provided. These groups must forget any petty differences, and work together for a common cause. And if they are to solve the problems, they must solve them in Washington DC. The equestrians have been doing this for decades, while the hikers stand idly by, watching the trail ruts grow deeper.

Advanced Techniques

Jettison as many of your belongings as you dare.
Nothing serves better than a long climb
in identifying the essentials of life.

– Adam Nicholson

As Jenny and I were hiking through Oregon during our most recent PCT thru-hike, we found ourselves hurrying along one afternoon, trying to reach the store – and our resupply box – at the Timberline Lodge before it closed for the day. The late evening and early morning hours are among our favorite for hiking, and we knew that if we didn't hurry we would have to forfeit them and make an early camp somewhere near the lodge. So at my suggestion Jenny handed me her backpack, pocketed some cash and her ID, tied her shell jacket around her waist, and took off at a run. We figured it would take her about an hour to reach the lodge.

This left me carrying two backpacks. To most backpackers this would have been a considerable extra burden, but since I normally carried my 8½ pound pack on one shoulder only, I simply slung Jenny's pack onto my other shoulder and continued ahead. The additional load slowed me, but still I was able to hike at a reasonable clip. And I deemed this rather novel configuration my 17 pound "backpackpack."

Farther along I overtook a pair of backpackers lumbering beneath typically huge loads. Their trail-weary appearance suggested they had been hiking for several days, so I slowed my pace and struck up a conversation. The fellow and his wife said they were hiking the section of PCT from the Columbia Gorge to central Oregon, and that they had left the Gorge five days ago. I mentioned that Jenny and I were thru-hiking the PCT, and that we had left the Gorge yesterday. After a few minutes I noticed that they were laboring to keep up, so I bid them good-bye, saying I hoped to meet them again at the lodge.

Jenny and I were sorting our resupply items inside the lodge when our friends arrived. Right away they began asking a lot of questions. It turned out that they had read the first edition of our *PCT Hiker's Handbook*, which described some of our earlier lightweight methods, but they admitted that they simply "didn't believe any of it."

A matter of style

The reaction of these two was typical of the hundreds of backpackers we met that summer. On paper my methods may seem "radical" and idealistic. But when these people saw how easily we were almost doubling and sometimes even tripling their daily mileages they tended to become less skeptical.

I don't mean to suggest that Jenny and I were trying to set speed records. We were not. Our higher daily mileages were merely a spin-off of our more efficient style. Our main purpose was to enjoy the hike, and indeed, our light-weight approach granted us that ten thousand times over.

How true that the essence of hiking is enjoyment. Most backpackers enjoy their hikes, else why would they bother with them? But I doubt whether they are enjoying them as much as they could. The heavy clothing, boots, backpacks and other gear make for tough traveling. And they also reduce the daily mileages dramatically. I realize that most backpackers are not interested in high daily mileages. Most often they can be seen enduring a five-mile slog to their favorite lake, with the idea that once there they can finally relax and start enjoying their weekend. The hiking itself, they merely put up with. But this book is mainly about the hiking itself, and how to enjoy it to its fullest.

Individual freedom

Much later in that same journey we met a woman hiking the PCT through California. After we had talked a while she admitted that she had taken a lot of flack from the "Jardinites." These, she explained, were the zealots following the techniques in the *Handbook* to the letter, so caught up in their newly adopted methods that they now felt that everyone else was doing it all wrong. The woman said that some of these hikers had ridiculed her heavy backpack and slow pace. "I love my backpack," she said, "and I don't see anything wrong with it." I told her that I saw nothing wrong with it either. "It looks like a great pack, and if you're enjoying your hike, then that's what's important." She said she was surprised to discover that I was not as obsessed as some of my "followers." I told her that I am concerned mainly with my own methods, and that I wrote the book only to introduce and discuss some of them. If someone adopted some of them, I said, then that was great; but if not then that was perfectly ok, too.

Use with discrimination

What follows are some of the more advanced ideas that have worked for Jenny and myself. If you find any of them appealing, feel free to give them a try. But please do so with caution. Most of them are geared for the more skilled adventurer, and some can actually increase the dangers when used improperly. Experiment with only one new concept or item of gear at a time.

Do this during your training hikes, and always carry backup gear and have backup plans.

At the very least, I recommend that all hikers carry spare clothing that is both warm and protective. And if conditions deteriorate they should put that clothing on. As Chris Townsend reminds us, "wet and warm is better than wet and cold." Many backpackers have died from exposure with spare garments in their packs. I imagine they were simply reluctant to get those clothes wet.

Lightening our minds

Before we can seriously lighten the loads in our backpacks we need to lighten the loads in our minds. One way to help release ourselves of our iron clad misconceptions is to think about where our beliefs came from. Perhaps it was from the Boy Scouts. Were the scout leaders experts in ultra-long-distance hiking? Perhaps it was from books. Were the authors merely parroting other authors in regards to the Standard Backpacking Method? Maybe some of our ideas came from the trendy monthly magazines, written by professional writers often posing as daring adventurers. The point is, actions speak louder than words. One of the best ways to learn about adventuring, or anything else, is to study the methods of those whose actual accomplishments align with your goals.

Reducing packweight to a minimum requires bold imagination. So in addition to shedding misconceptions, we should never limit our imaginations. This applies to every aspect of our lives, not just to hiking. But here are a few examples from the hiking world: Imagine hiking the Appalachian Trail from Springer Mountain, 2,150 rugged miles to Katahdin, turning around and hiking all the way back to Springer, and turning around once again and hiking back to Katahdin. Without stopping. Two individuals have done this "triple AT yo-yo." Imagine thru-hiking the AT with a 50+ mile-per-day *average*. It has been done twice. Imagine thru-hiking the AT blind, as Bill Irwin did with his guide dog Orient in 1990[1]. Imagine hiking from the tip of South America to the top of Alaska in one continuous journey of 7 years, as George Meegan[2] did. And imagine walking 250 miles in 76 hours, as Dick Crawshaw did. (That's 3.3 mph non-stop for 3.16 straight days.)

People who accomplish notable undertakings are usually single minded. And there are vast differences between being single minded and narrow minded. Single minded people create goals for themselves, and they are will-

---

[1] *Blind Courage*, by Bill Irwin; WRS Publishing 1993. Autographed copies from Irwin Associates, Inc, 2013 Fox Run Road, Burlington, NC 27215. See also article in Guideposts magazine, March 1993.

[2] See Bibliography.

ing to explore at least some of the many avenues and possibilities that might help them achieve those goals. They are not afraid to experiment because they are not afraid of "failure" or criticism. And because their successes have won them self-confidence, they are open to personal growth. Single minded individuals cross oceans in small boats, break track and field records, and explore vast regions on foot. Narrow minded individuals are usually too busy criticizing to pursue goals of their own.

As Harry Browne noted in his book *How I Found Freedom in an Unfree World*[3], "Sometimes a thing turns out different from what you thought it was. A comparison of the first impression with later impressions can show that the earlier view was insufficient. So in terms of possible later discovery, all current knowledge is incomplete, or will be enlarged later." Be careful about barricading yourself inside a cage of certitude. Give yourself room to expand your horizons. Reducing your packweight to 10 pounds or less will require this type of thinking.

The Standard Backpacking Reasoning:
It is better to have a piece of gear and not need it,
than to need it and not have it.

Jardine Reasoning:
If I need it and don't have it, then I don't need it.

Minimalist mobility

One rainy afternoon on the Appalachian Trail Jenny and I stepped into a shelter for a short respite. There, we greeted a lone hiker lying in his sleeping bag, brewing tea, and listening to a weather forecast on his radio. "My trail name is Fairweather," he said, "I got it because I never hike in bad weather. Been here for two days."

After a pleasant chat we wished the fellow good luck, deployed our umbrellas, and stepped back outside into the "bad" weather. And while rambling along I thought about ourselves, years ago, when we too had been intimidated by prolonged wet weather, and had usually endured most of it inside our tent. The contrast made me appreciate our present lightweight system, in terms of how it had released us from those weather-related concerns.

---

[3] See Bibliography

Minimalist equipment and philosophy adds greatly to one's mobility, and conversely, mobility enables minimalist hiking. Backpackers who carry heavy loads of durable and weatherproof gear (bulky clothing, 4-season tents, heavy sleeping bags, inflatable mattress, etc.) will very likely need to rely on these items, because they will be far less able to descend quickly to a more protected environment. They will be, in effect, sitting ducks, subject to everything the sky can hurl at them.

Mobility depends on physical fitness, proper nutrition, and an ultralight weight system of clothing and equipment. It allows us to keep moving throughout the day regardless of the weather, because it makes us far more capable of finding a protected campsite when genuinely needed, and to descend to lower and more sheltered environments should a major storm eventuate. As such, this mobility allows us to flow more in harmony within our dynamic weather environment.

System of equipment and philosophy

Each item in my equipment inventory fits into an overall system like a piece in a jigsaw puzzle. Each works only in conjunction with all the others; and none of my ideas will work properly out of context. And the same would generally hold true for anyone serious about optimizing packweight. Only by looking at the bulk of gear as a system and the methods of its use as a philosophy can we even begin to approach the higher regions on the Pyramid of Hiking Style.

The two items which can turn backpackers into hikers are the 10½ ounce shoes and the 1 pound backpack. But note how these are connected in the system: I recommend hiking in running shoes or sandals. But before backpackers can safely retire their boots, they would need to reduce their packweights. To do that, they would first reduce the quantity, sizes, and weights of the items that fit into their backpacks, and then they would choose smaller and lighter backpacks. It all works together, like synergy in motion.

Back on page 25 we saw how most backpackers can be found low on the Pyramid of Hiking Style's flanks, carrying loads of heavy-duty and heavy-weight equipment, much of which is superfluous. Each time they shed weight from their packs, feet, bodies or minds they climb a little higher on the Pyramid. They will be able to hike a little farther each day if they like, and with greater enjoyment. Jenny and I exert ourselves no more than other hikers; we simply use more of our energy for forward progress and less for hauling loads and fussing about. From Manning Park to Kennedy Meadows we easily adhered to our three month itinerary, despite pervasive and deep snowpack in the North Cascades and a 3½ day stopover in central Oregon. Yet in the arid lowlands of southern California we had to haul large quantities of water for long distances, and the added packweight cost us four extra days. I mention this merely to illustrate the dramatic effects of increased packweight.

The backpack

Imagine pulling a six pound object from your backpack and sending it home. That would lighten your load considerably. You probably don't have anything in there that heavy. But how about the backpack itself? Most large packs on the market weigh around seven pounds (on the scales, rather than on the published spec sheets). Yet they add nothing to the journey; they are merely containers for the necessary equipment, clothing and food. To me it makes no sense that the container should be the heaviest item in the entire inventory.

The pack I used on our most recent PCT hike weighs 13.5 oz. Jenny's is slightly less. Each one took us about 12 hours to make, and cost $10.40 in materials. Throw-away models? Hardly. Their condition has not deteriorated in more than 3,000 miles of use. What strains a pack is all the mass crammed into it. With a lighter load the pack doesn't need to be nearly as robust.

The accompanying illustration shows how we make our packs. Before starting any project we make a set of patterns, using sheets of paper taped together. These patterns catalog the shape and size of the pieces, and are invaluable when making improvements the next year. To begin, you could take measurements from a commercial pack of the size you are interested in, and transfer those measurements onto your paper patterns. Otherwise, you could start with a commercial pattern. One possibility is the "Alpine Rucksack" from The Rain Shed (541) 753-8900. At 2,200 cubic inches it is about the right size for a thru-hiker serious about cutting down on the bulk of gear. And it comes with instructions.

Another advantage of making your own pack is that you can customize it to your needs. You can omit most of the straps and fancy do-dads. You can add a netting water bottle pocket on one side, a netting fuel bottle pocket on the other, and a netting tent-fly or tarp pocket on the back. Elasticized at their tops to prevent loss of contents. If your load will most often be below 25 pounds you could even dispense with the internal stays and the hip belt. Jenny and I discovered this on our AT thru-hike. A couple of days into that journey we realized that the hip belts and internal aluminum stays of our home-made packs were of no benefit, so at the next town we dispensed with them.

We reinforce all stress points with small patches of material. These spread the load over a wider area, and reduce the chances of a pull-out. The area of greatest stress is where the shoulder straps attach to the upper part of the bag, so the reinforcement patches there are quite large.

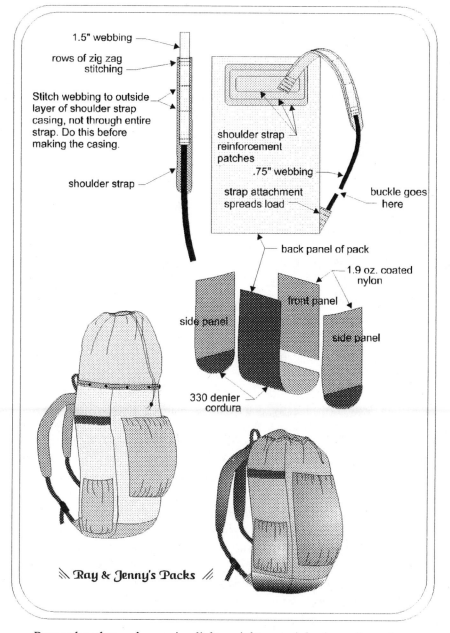

1.5" webbing

rows of zig zag stitching

Stitch webbing to outside layer of shoulder strap casing, not through entire strap. Do this before making the casing.

shoulder strap

shoulder strap reinforcement patches

.75" webbing

strap attachment spreads load

buckle goes here

back panel of pack

1.9 oz. coated nylon

front panel

side panel

side panel

330 denier cordura

Ray & Jenny's Packs

Remember that we're sewing light weight materials. An ordinary home sewing machine works just fine, and it doesn't need any features beyond a straight stitch, a zigzag, and a reversing lever. Just be absolutely certain to start with a new needle of the highest quality, such as the ones made by Schmetz.

Heavy thread and light weight materials don't mix. Use medium weight, long fiber polyester thread. Triple stitch all your seams to achieve the needed strength, and be sure to back-stitch each row half-an-inch to prevent raveling. Use parallel rows of tight and wide zigzag stitches to attach webbing, such as the shoulder straps and clothing hanger straps.

Before you start any project, sew together a few scraps of the same material you will be using, and examine the stitches. Adjust the tension on both the top and bobbin threads as necessary. For more information refer to your sewing machine manual, a book on the subject, or someone knowledgeable about sewing.

Where can you buy the materials? Try your local fabric shops first. And while there, look for the book *Sewing Activewear*, in the Singer Sewing Reference Library series. It is an excellent source of ideas and instruction. Otherwise, check with some of the mail order fabric outlets, and be sure to compare their prices, as they sometimes vary considerably. In addition to the Rain Shed you could contact Outdoor Wilderness Fabrics (800) 693-7467, Quest Outfitters (800) 359-6931, and Seattle Fabrics (206) 632-6022. All these firms sell fabric, supplies, and a variety of patterns.

For the backpacks, we use 330 denier coated Cordura™ for the bottom and the panel that rests against the hiker's back, and 1.9 ounce coated nylon for most of the remainder. Our packs are little more than large, durable, custom-made stuff sacks with shoulder straps attached to them. We even close them with draw cords. Ideally, one would use Airex™ high density foam for the shoulder straps, as it resists flattening over time. Beva II™ foam works about as well. We use Cordura for the shoulder straps casings, and attach them to the packs with 1½-inch flat nylon webbing at the top and ¾-inch flat nylon webbing at the bottom.

The Tarp

During my summers as a professional wilderness instructor, we did not use tents. Instead, we slept beneath tarps. Initially these were nothing but sheets of clear polyethylene, although later I made my own of coated nylon. To secure the sheets of plastic we tied lengths of cord to the corners with sheet-bend knots, which are extremely strong. I never saw one tear out.

Tarp corner

Sheet bend

To ground peg

These tarps had many advantages and very few disadvantages. They cost far less than tents. They had no zippers or poles to break and render them immediately unserviceable. They weighed less than half of what a tent weighs, yet they provided twice the living space. But most importantly they permitted the best possible ventilation. We, our clothing and our equipment stayed much drier. This made them eminently suitable for living in for weeks at a time, especially during inclement weather. And in those high Colorado Rockies there was plenty of that. The two disadvantages of a tarp are its lack of mosquito netting and apparent lack of protection in strong winds. I'll discuss these first:

Using a tarp in mosquito season

Jenny and I used a tarp during our most recent PCT trek. On those days when the bugs were swarming with a vengeance we hiked in bug-proof clothing. The shell jackets and pants we made of 1.9 ounce *breathable* nylon, so they are light in weight and very fast drying. At the rest stops we removed our shoes and donned booties and mittens of the same material. The shell jackets have hoods which protected our necks and heads, except for our faces of course. On the trail we wore mosquito headnets; otherwise we wore our shell jackets with their hoods, and a little repellent on our faces. Aside from the headnets, these garments work equally well at night. Sleeping beneath an open tarp and an open quilt, our main problem was not the mosquitoes but the ants. They are not aggressive but can be annoying, crawling around on one's skin during the night. Our mosquito clothing solved the problem.

In addition to our bug-proof clothing we also used a large piece of mosquito netting sewn to the top edge of our sleeping quilt. This netting we pulled over our faces at night to help keep the mosquitoes away. On nights too warm for the quilt we slept only in the mosquito proof clothing, after dabbing a bit of repellent on our faces. It was then a simple matter to drag the quilt over us in the wee hours, when needed.

Using a tarp in strong wind

One of the tarp's finest features is its adaptability. The more the rain slants down, the lower the tarp can be pitched. One summer our Outward Bound group spent two weeks on the Continental Divide in Colorado's San Juan range. There, powerful winds called for a little ingenuity in pitching our seemingly frail plastic tarps. We laid out our ground sheets, set our packs between them, covered the lot with a tarp, then placed smooth rocks all around the tarp's perimeter. This created the ultimate in aerodynamic structures. To enter, we used the standard spelunking techniques of squirming and crawling. And no matter how tightly we had rocked the tarp's perimeter, the gale-force winds provided ample ventilation.

These were experiments and I do not recommend camping on exposed ridges, especially when lightening threatens. Climb high and camp low. On the PCT when the wind is slanting with rain Jenny and I usually pitch our tarp with its ridgeline broadside to the blow. We set it low, and place its windward edge on the ground. If the wind is angling unavoidably into one end, we set the tarp even lower and deploy our umbrellas at the windward end. The more vicious the weather, the lower we set the tarp. This provides a streamlined, low lying shelter, customized to the situation – something unattainable with tents. And speaking of which, should a tent pole break during strong conditions, the tent becomes far less serviceable. If a tarp support fails you, it is because you failed to choose one stout enough. And even then you would normally be able to find another one fairly readily.

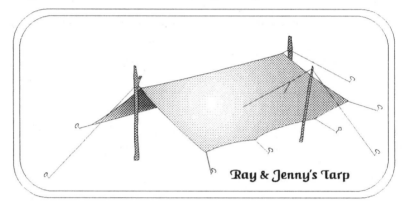

Ray & Jenny's Tarp

Standard Pitching

The illustration shows the tarp pitched in its usual configuration: the A-frame mode. The ridgeline in this case is stretched between two sticks, but it could be between two trees, or one of each. We usually use two sticks because they allow us to choose the ground for best drainage, irrespective of where any trees happen to be growing. And because trees are known for dropping massive branches during storms. Normally we start looking for these tarp support sticks well before reaching our stealth camp, and even more so in areas where trees are sparse. In places where trees are lacking we carry a couple of sticks. In the desert we have used dead century plant stalks as tarp poles, and as a last resort we have even used our umbrellas. The thing to avoid is laying the tarp directly on the sleeping bag, as it will soak it in condensation.

In its standard mode we pitch the tarp by guying its four corners out, pulling each guyline 45° out to the side (the direction that bisects the corner angle of the tarp). A strong wind can apply huge forces to a tarp, so its guylines must be attached only to objects which are very secure. We use tent stakes only in firm ground. Otherwise we use logs (placed endwise to prevent rolling), large flat-bottomed rocks, or bushes. Even small bushes can be well anchored, and guys attached to their bases can be very secure.

The tarp has its own rule: if you fail to pitch it securely, it will fail you in a storm. It's just that simple.

In addition to the four corner guys, we secure the tarp further against strong wind with its edge guys, two on each side. And, we use a pair of pull-out lines attached central to both halves of the tarp. These raise the ceiling and provide far more interior space. They also help stabilize the tarp in gusts, and help support it beneath snow accumulation.

A tarp lacks the bathtub-type floor with its raised lip, as is typical of most tents. This means that we tarp users can't camp in ponds. Or more to the point, that we shouldn't camp in low places that might become ponds during heavy rain.

Specifications

Making your own tarp is fairly easy. Jenny and I make ours by sewing two lengths of 1.9 ounce coated rip-stop nylon together along one edge. The seam running down the centerline is the tarp's ridgeline, and of course we seal it with compound. And after hemming the perimeter we fit the guy-attachment loops. These are very short loops of thin webbing, sewn to the tarp. The guylines are tied to these loops. Our tarp measures 8 feet 8 inches square, and weighs 1¾ pounds, including the guylines. A tarp for one person could be a few feet narrower, and would be even lighter. In addition, we use 8 aluminum tent pegs that weigh a total of 2½ ounces. When more stakes are needed we use rocks, logs, or bushes instead.

Differences in Ventilation

In prolonged rainy conditions a *properly* pitched tarp will keep you much drier than a tent. Because of its design and lack of ventilation a tent can gradually fail. Rain might fall or drip into its open doorway, or splash up from the gap around the fly. Severe weather can even drive rain straight *through* the fly, particularly when its coating has deteriorated somewhat from prolonged exposure to sunshine. Moreover, the occupants emit quite a lot of moisture from their breathing and insensible perspiration. All this moisture pumping into the interior has nowhere to go. As the humidity reaches the dew point the vapor begins condensing on the tent fly's inner walls. If the tent is steep-walled, like an A-frame or pyramid, the condensation is more likely to run harmlessly off to one side. In a free-standing dome type tent, though, the overhead ceiling is gradually sloped, forcing condensation to drip from the fly onto the tent fabric, which will eventually begin to drip also, this time onto the occupants and their sleeping bags and clothing. Lack of ventilation is not as significant for the weekend backpacker who can cart the wet gear home and be rid of it. But it can cause real trouble for the long distance hiker who must live with the gear, and depend on it every day and night as though his or her life depends on it. Which it generally does.

Condensation will form on the underside of a tarp, just as it does on the underside of the plant leaves all about. But it will rarely form heavy enough to drip. And unlike the air trapped inside a tent, the air beneath the tarp is far less humid, meaning that all that moisture does not pervade the clothing and sleeping bag.

Camping in the rain

Pitching a tent in the rain can be frustrating. First, you have to lay out your ground sheet, and while it is acting inadvertently as a rain catcher you quickly pitch the tent on it. And while the tent is soaking water like a sponge, both from above and below, you madly fit the fly. Welcome to a soaking wet home.

Now that you're in, you cannot cook a meal. For safety's sake you must venture outside in the pouring rain, and perhaps pitch a separate cooking fly. And there you sit, hunkering over your stove for what little warmth it provides, soaking wet and becoming more miserably chilled all the time. This is not too troublesome for a few days in succession, but it can grow intolerable in continually wet weather. I doubt whether even our primal ancestors lived as miserably.

You can pitch a tarp in the rain without all the worry and rush of keeping things dry. Just be sure to do it right the first time, keeping it low if there is much wind, orienting its ridgeline perpendicular to the wind, and attaching all its guy lines to well secured objects. After pitching the tarp you crawl beneath it and bring in your pack, setting it to one side. Preening the ground of sticks and pine cones, you lay out your ground sheet, dry side up. Next, you remove your damp clothing, wring it out if necessary, and hang it from a clothesline strung lengthwise along the underside of the tarp's ridgeline. Quickly, you then put on dry clothing and crawl into your sleeping bag. Welcome to a warm, dry home.

If rain has been falling all day, you may not have stopped to cook a hot meal, and now would be a good time to do so, as long as you are not in National Park bear country. Being able to cook while seated or lying under your tarp is another of its many advantages, as long as you leave both ends open for good ventilation. Simply reach beyond your ground sheet, ignite the stove, and cook a hearty corn pasta dinner. Make sure, though, to keep your flammable clothing, sleeping bag and equipment well away from the flames. And be sure to locate your stove in such a place that should it tip over, it will not spill hot liquids onto you or your ground sheet.

Heavy rain rebounds into the tarp's interior just as it does into the gap around a tent fly. But because the tarp is so much larger than the tent, this rebounding doesn't even come close to you. And unlike inside a tent where this rebounding moisture becomes trapped, beneath a tarp it soaks into the ground or evaporates. The same happens with the rain running off the tarp's perimeter. Any ground water will flow away from you if you have selected a site which is naturally well drained, for example one on a slight rise. If the rain is pouring and you are camping on a slope, then you might have to trench a V in the ground uphill of you, to channel the groundwater away from your living quarters. This would be extremely uncommon, though. I have done it only twice.

Striking camp in the rain

On those mornings pouring with rain, breaking camp will be far easier if you are using a tarp instead of a tent. You simply load your pack while underneath the tarp, deploy your umbrella, step outside, and set your pack beneath a sheltering tree. Then you break down the tarp, give it a few vigorous shakes, and stuff it into an external netting pocket of your backpack. Or you roll the tarp tightly and insert it into its waterproof stow bag. Persistent rain will prevent you from airing your tarp during the day. This means only that the tarp will be a little heavier. The wetness will not affect its performance the following evening.

The open shelter

One of the features we like best about the tarp is how it doesn't shut us out from the environment the way an enclosing tent does. It allows us to stay more in tune with what's happening outside, to watch the sunset if we are retiring early, and to listen to the birds, insects, and any animals roving about. So it provides the best of both worlds: shelter with a sense of openness.

Develop the skills

Of course, using a tarp safely is a skill. It will withstand stormy weather only if properly pitched. If you decide to try using a tarp, take it on a few overnight training hikes first, and carry your tent as a back-up. Start with mild weather and work up to stormy.

My clothing system

During our most recent PCT hike, Jenny and I started out carrying back-up waterproof-breathable parkas, which we had made ourselves. This was a southbound journey, beginning with a few weeks of wallowing through the snowbound North Cascades. We met with some fierce storms, yet every time we retired our umbrellas in favor of our parkas we soon grew chilled. Trudging through endless miles of snow is hard work, and the parkas caused our sweat to remain near our skin. The entrapped moisture sapped the heat out of us. We also tried sleeping in the parkas for added warmth, only to meet with the same results. We sent the parkas home from the first resupply station.

But again for safety's sake I recommend that all hikers carry W/B parkas and a few extra garments for emergency use. We were living closer to the edge – by choice – relying more on our skills and mobility.

While hiking we normally wore fast-drying shirts of polyester, and shorts of polyester or Lycra.™ If the day was cold and breezy we also wore our shells (lightweight breathable nylon jackets and pants). On days when the temperature plummeted we added wicking shirts. And in rain we used the umbrellas. One might imagine we were cold in such thin clothing. Rarely. While hiking vigorously our bodies generated quite a lot of heat. And we knew that if needed, we could make camp and crawl beneath the quilt.

Covering higher daily mileages, we needed maximum energy, provided mainly by corn pasta, and maximum ventilation, provided by the lightweight breathable clothing, and in inclement weather by the umbrellas. And when I mentioned that we got cold only rarely, it was while hiking snow free trail across level or downhill terrain, where we could not work hard enough to generate the needed warmth. We felt in no danger because these conditions are quite suitable for making camp, if needed.

The sleeping bag

For many years I used the standard mummy-style sleeping bag. Typically, a few hours after falling asleep I would awake with the urge to claw out of it. I solved the problem by placing a water bottle in the foot of my sleeping bag each night. As my body, particularly my feet, radiated excess heat, (or so it seemed) the water absorbed it. In the morning I would awake comfortably, with a bottle of non-frozen water.

The open sleeping bag

I didn't realize it then, but I was trying to adjust to too much insulation. I discovered this one night when I opened the bag and used it as a blanket. This worked so well that it quickly became my standard procedure, and by the time Jenny came into my life I had not slept in a zipped closed sleeping bag for 10 years, despite the fact that I had used sleeping bags most of that time. So it was only natural for us to share a single sleeping bag, used as a blanket. This system has once again proven so successful that we use it to this day. It saves us half the weight of two sleeping bags, half the bulk, and half the cost.

Most store-bought sleeping bags are not designed to be used open like a blanket. The upper and lower parts are not symmetric, and in many cases they contain unequal thickness of insulation. Suitable models do exist but you might have to search for them.

One problem with just about any kind of sleeping bag is its loss of loft, or thickness, during a long summer's journey. Because of this we had to buy a new bag each year. Eventually tiring of the expense, we started making our own.

Making your own sleeping bag

If you and your mate are thinking of trying our quilt system, or if you will be hiking alone and prefer a mummy-style bag, you, too, can save a lot of money by making your own. Manufacturers tend to complicate their designs in order to attract customers, but we distance hikers need only a simple bag or blanket. Making these at home is easy and straightforward, particularly with today's synthetic insulation materials which do not require myriad baffles as do the down bags. And these materials are available via the mail-order outlets.

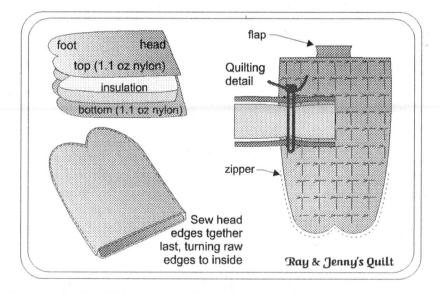

foot   head
top (1.1 oz nylon)
insulation
bottom (1.1 oz nylon)

flap

Quilting detail

zipper

Sew head edges tgether last, turning raw edges to inside

Ray & Jenny's Quilt

Our sleeping "quilt" lays over us like a blanket, but has a foot pocket formed by a short zipper. The foot pocket positions the bag over our feet. We make these quilts fairly light so they are easier to stow and carry, and faster to dry. If the night is cold we sleep in our clothes as well. With the two of us sleeping together beneath the quilt, a gap occurs between our necks, permitting an undesirable draft. To stop this draft we sew an insulated flap to the quilt. It hangs down between our necks and closes the gap.

Five steps, and you have a sleeping bag or quilt as capable as anything on the market:

❶ Cut out two pieces of 1.1 ounce breathable nylon to the desired shape of your bag, as it would be laid flat on the floor. Sew the two pieces together around their edges, but leave the top open like a pillow case. I recommend white nylon for the top layer, to minimize radiation heat loss, and black for the bottom, which when exposed to the sun will dry very quickly. The black-side-up is also less conspicuous when sleeping under the stars.

❷ Lay this "pillow case" on a sheet of insulation, then cut the insulation to the same size and shape. Any synthetic insulation will do, as long as it holds together and does not require the use of baffles to keep it in place. But try to choose a type which compresses well yet which has good loft retention.

❸ Insert the insulation into the nylon pillow case, and sew the case closed along its top edge. You may need to pin the insulation in place to keep it from shifting as you sew this final seam.

❹ Grid the bag off in 12-inch squares, and quilt it with synthetic yarn to hold the insulation in place. Be careful not to compress the loft at each quilt.

❺ The zipper is optional. Sew on a full length zipper if you like. Or as Jenny and I do, sew only a 26-inch robe (lightweight) zipper at the bottom. Either way, the bag must open fully for faster drying.

Stoveless cooking

Because most of the information in this book is original, I've gone to great lengths to recommend how to use it properly. Obviously, I have no control over how this information is misused. Stoveless cooking falls squarely into this category. I know there are thoughtless individuals out there capable of misusing the technique and causing ill feelings both with other hikers and the authorities, and possibly even starting forest fires. But at the same time I'm not going to censor this information on their behalf.

Please note that I am not suggesting that hikers have *carte blanche* to cook over camp fires. Open fires are illegal in many areas, for example throughout the whole of southern California and in most of the National Parks along the way. And they are decidedly unsafe at every stealth camp where pine needles and duff have accumulated deeply – whether the woods are dry or wet.

However, in certain circumstances open fire cooking could be life saving, and in actual fact, when done correctly it can be quite safe. I recommend that all distance hikers use gas-burning stoves. These leave no trace, they are legal virtually everywhere, and they can be used safely at most stealth campsites. But depending on the circumstances, hikers might resort to the cook-fire technique if the stove breaks down or runs out of fuel in a place where more cannot be obtained.

At the outset, I'd like to make the distinction between the campfire and the cook-fire. The campfire is more or less thrown together. The cook-fire is an art form, much smaller and meticulously done. It is crafted to cook the meal quickly and then to consume itself. The campfire leaves a deep scar, and usually a large pile of coals surrounded by blackened rocks. The cook-fire is completely erasable.

The cook-fire

In a nutshell the cooking technique is this: Fashion a tripod about 3 feet tall using three sticks tied together near their tops. Place this structure over the cook-fire and suspend your cooking pot from it.

The specifics:

Start looking for the tripod sticks about an hour before mealtime. When found, carry them to where you want to cook. I know of only two places where cook-fires are sometimes safe. In an existing fire pit at an established campsite, and on the trail. I say "sometimes" because neither would be safe on a windy day. And I've seen impromptu campsites with campfire-ring rocks placed squarely on deep duff. How these senseless campers avoided igniting the forest I can't imagine. The trail is also covered deeply in duff and pine needles in many places. But in other places a cursory scraping with the shoe will expose the underlying dirt very easily. My suggestion of building a cook-fire on the trail might seem outrageous, but when built, tended and extinguished correctly it will be undetectable by anyone, and will have close to zero impact. If done incorrectly it can create a big mess, like any campfire, leaving an eyesore for other hikers. I don't appreciate seeing where someone had stopped to build a fire on the trail, and I'm sure other hikers feel the same way. But as I said, I have no control over how these techniques are misused. If you build a cook-fire on the trail, try to find a less populated area, and wait until evening when the other hikers have stopped to make camp. If you see someone with a cook-fire on the trail during normal hiking hours, then you are seeing someone mis-using the technique very blatantly.

Prior to fashioning the cook-fire, choose an area where the trail is wide enough to prevent any shooting sparks from reaching the needles and duff of the forest floor. And don't imagine that because the duff is soaking wet that it is fireproof. Even though a cook-fire is quite small and compact, it is very hot and it's radiant heat can dry its surroundings quickly. And don't forget to con-sider the direction of any breeze.

Carefully scrape away flammable materials such as pine needles, pine cones, twigs, and so forth. The fire must be built on dirt or sand. Nothing else will do. What we need is a circle of dirt at least two feet in diameter; ideally three. The cook-fire will go in the center. Don't scatter the materials when scraping them away. Save them in little piles off to the side. You will scatter them back over the area when finished.

Collect sticks which are about the diameter of a pencil. Anything larger will not burn completely, and will prevent you from restoring the site to its original condition. And for the same reason, try not to collect sticks which are damp to the core. Break the dry sticks into 4- to 6-inch lengths and pile these "fire sticks" neatly and conveniently to one side. Amass all your fire sticks ahead of time because once you start cooking you will have little time to col-lect more.

Fabricate the cooking tripod by lashing the tripod sticks together with a short length of cord. Pour the correct amount of water into your cooking pot and fit its lid, to keep the water clean.

Start the fire with twigs, then begin adding your fire sticks. As the cook-fire comes to life, place the tripod over it and press the tripod sticks gently into the ground to prevent them from shifting. Then suspend the cookpot from the tripod. Adjust the length of the suspension cord so that the pot hangs about an inch off the kindling. You want the pot *in* the fire, not so close that it suffo-cates the fire and not so high above the fire that it is cooled by the air. Ideally, you want the cook-fire to cover the entire bottom of the pot, but no more. Keep the fire small so that it doesn't ignite the tripod sticks or melt the sus-pension cord.

Fire sticks burn quickly, meaning that you will have to continually add more. Resist the temptation to use larger wood. It will leave ugly coals which are just about impossible to eradicate, and which could spark a fire later. Continue adding fresh fire sticks, as well as the ends of those that did not burn completely. Done correctly, this little cook-fire will boil water as fast as any stove.

If a draft is sweeping the heat away from the cookpot, seat yourself to windward and block it. If this proves unsuccessful you might have to place a few rocks to windward of the cook-fire. However, don't place them against the fire or it will blacken them with soot. If they become accidentally blackened, leave them in dirt, black side down. Theoretically the earth will transform the carbon faster than the atmosphere will.

When the water comes to a boil start adding the corn pasta, if that is what you are cooking. Stirring with the spoon would place your hand too close to the fire, so stir with a longer stick. Once the meal is ready, lift the tripod carefully away, and lean it over to bring the pot to rest on the ground. Then untie the suspension cord and set the tripod aside.

The small bed of coals could then be used for baking a dessert. Jenny and I use the term "scones" to refer to any kind of cake-like, baked dessert. Probably the easiest scones to bake on cook-fire coals are the store-bought "just add water" muffin mixes. Even the mixes that require egg and oil will bake nicely without the extra ingredients. Mix the batter inside the packaging or resealable plastic bag, adding water a few dollops at a time while stirring with a small stick. The key is to use as little water as possible. The drier the batter the faster it will bake and the less the finished scones will stick to the "baker."

For a "baker," use a sheet of aluminum foil about 12 inches square. Scoop the batter onto the middle of the foil, then fold the foil over it as though wrapping a loaf of bread. Seal the ends to contain the steam. If handled carefully, one sheet of foil will survive several bakings. Place the foil-packaged batter on a *small* bed of coals, then scoop more coals over the top. If the coals are too hot they will burn the scones. Cool them by spreading them out. Turn the packet over occasionally for better heat distribution. Continue adding a few glowing coals to the top of the packet as the old ones cool. Properly baked, the scones will be nicely browned on the outside, and cooked all the way through.

When finished cooking, rebuild the cook-fire just a little and place all the unburned ends of the fuel sticks into the tiny fire. You can now also burn any paper scraps you may have accumulated. Don't burn plastic, though, because it will produce toxic fumes, and will not burn completely. Tend the little fire carefully, encouraging the small flame to consume the last of its embers. When only ashes remain, use a stout stick to stir in water, dirt, or both. This extinguishes any remaining traces of fire, and cools the ashes and the ground. Next, it's time to do the Monster Mash.

Properly done, the Monster Mash will erase any indication of the cook-fire. Step on the cooled ashes with the ball of your shoe, and twist. This grinds the ashes to powder. Kick in a bit of dirt and continue stepping and twisting, one foot after the other, as though dancing some sort of ceremony. Call it the cook-fire-monster-mash-leave-no-trace-ceremony. A few *minutes* of this will work the last traces of carbon into the earth.

If possible, camp in the vicinity after the meal, then return to the site early the next morning and erase its presence. This will better guarantee that every last ember has extinguished. If you must move on right away, feel the ground and make sure that your cook-fire site is only warm. If it is too hot to leave your hand on for long, then your fire was too large and you will have to cool the ground by pouring water on it, if available. If not, you will have to wait. Whatever you do, don't restore the original materials (duff, pine needles, sticks, etc.) over hot ground. The possibility is slight, but an unseen ember under the hot ground could ignite the materials long after you've gone.

If you made your cook-fire properly, the ground should be only warm, and you may safely restore the site by spreading the original materials back into place. If thoughtfully done, they will erase any hint of your cook-fire's presence. And this is exactly the desired effect.

Lastly, disassemble the tripod and place the tripod sticks where they cannot possibly start a fire. They should not be charred, unless your fire was too large. And by now they should no longer be hot to the touch. Never disperse hot or charred tripod sticks into the forest. Leave them on a snowbank, dunk them momentarily in a creek or pond, or carry them a distance until they have cooled.

The power of focus

Focus is the driving force behind any endeavor. It promotes determination and strength, but paradoxically it is extremely fragile. We must nurture and guard our sense of focus as though our journeys depend on it. Because they do.

A study of successful adventurers past and present will reveal that the paramount ingredient for success is focus. The more focused we are, the more in tune with the natural environment and the nature of the journey, and therefore the more capable we are. The less focused, the less our chances of success.

Like happiness, our focus must be engendered from within and nurtured. The best time to start is in the planning stages. Focus yourself on your objectives and practice screening out the inevitable distractions. Nor will focus automatically follow you along the trail. Distractions will again attack your resolve. Distractions in the form of wayside amenities, for example. For the long distance hiker, civilized-type amenities come in two forms, one necessary and beneficial, the other unnecessary and potentially detrimental.

Unnecessary amenities might include a motel room for three nights, or a stay in someone's home while being fed and entertained. These people may feel they are doing hikers a service, when in fact they are dispensing weakness in wholesale quantities, as evidenced by the hiker drop our rate just beyond that location.

Necessary amenities include a laundromat, store, restaurant, post office, and litter bin. Like a sortie, we go into town, do what has to be done, and come back out - in full possession of our focus. In foul weather, indeed, we might indulge in a night's motel room – long enough to dry our gear and spirits. Then we set off refreshed, with renewed purpose.

The artistry of hiking

Maintaining perspective on your summer's journey, moment to moment, will not always be easy. Like the artist who dabs just the right colors of paint in just the right places, the distance hiker paints a canvas with a million steps. Up close you may see only the rough brush strokes: the dust, fatigue, heat, mosquitoes and rain. But unlike the artist, you cannot stand back to appraise your work. So you must depend on your vision, rather than your sight. And when at last you stroll to the border, like the artist you will indeed stand back and admire the labor of love, and suddenly your hard-wrought masterpiece will snap into focus. So do not expect to see much of the work while it is in the making. Maintain focus, and make each step a brush stroke of love.

At the same time, it is important to live in the moment. During the hike, the far border may seem impossibly distant, almost unreachable. But in a few short months your hike will be history, and you will be left with memories – of the people and places, the interesting events, the stupendous vistas, the flora and fauna, and the new ideas and feelings you entertained along the way. Living in the moment insures the greatest memories and the greatest enjoyment. And make no mistake, on a big thru-hike there are joys to be had every minute of every day.

✳

In this chapter, and indeed throughout the book, I have shared many of my hiking techniques and philosophies. Some are what people like to call "radical." To me they are merely ideas that have worked for myself and others. Try some of them at home if you like, on your training hikes, or on shorter trips. And once tried, don't be reluctant to adapt them to your longer hikes. But of course you would always plan for contingencies. Always carry a back-up set of warm, wind-protective clothing. Use your imagination and stay flexible to the possibilities.

Ray & Jenny's Equipment, PCT '94

Ray's packweight 8.44 lb

Jenny's packweight 7.12 lb

(Not including food, water, and clothing worn)

	Weight	Cost of materials	Hours to Make
Ray's Gear			
Pack	13.5 oz	$10.40	12.0
Umbrella	9.0 oz	$12.99	1.0
Mylar umbrella covering, with rubber bands and tape for attaching mylar to umbrella	0.8 oz		
Sleeping quilt: PrimaLoft® synthetic fill, includes mosquito netting. 79" long, 58" chest, 44" foot	49.0 oz	$34.00	9.0
Sleeping bag stowbag, 2 ply W/B	2.5 oz	$6.00	3.0
Stove, fuel, windscreen, in coated nylon stowbag	24.8 oz		
Water bottle (empty soda bottle)	1.6 oz		
Ray's Clothing			
Hat: fleece	1.2 oz	$0.50	0.3
Shell jacket: breathable nylon	6.0 oz	$8.00	6.0
Mittens: fleece, home made	1.0 oz	$1.00	1.0
Shell pants: breathable nylon	3.0 oz	$4.00	3.0
Socks: 2 pair thin nylon	1.2 oz		
Shower booties, coated nylon	0.8 oz	$0.50	1.0
Face towel: cotton, 12" square	1.8 oz		
Clothing stowbag (plastic garbage sack)	1.3 oz		
Ditty Bag #1, nylon mesh	0.2 oz	$0.50	0.5
Windex for cleaning eyeglasses and camera lens	0.8 oz		
Half a cotton bandanna for cleaning eyeglasses and camera lens	0.1 oz		
Compass	0.8 oz		

Spoon: Lexan	0.2 oz		
Prescription dark glasses	1.2 oz		
Eyeglasses bag: fleece with velcro	0.2 oz	$0.25	0.5
Flashlight with single AAA battery and spare bulb	1.0 oz		
Pocket knife	0.8 oz		
Toothbrush	0.1 oz		
Dental floss	0.1 oz		
H_2O_2 (antiseptic) in small plastic bottle	0.5 oz		
Cord	0.5 oz		
Ditty Bag #2	0.6 oz	$0.50	0.5
Medical kit: Betadine, Metronidazol, Diasorb, Amoxicillin, Campho-Phenique Antibiotic, zinc oxide, Mycelex (for athlete's foot), 1 T. salt in tiny resealable plastic bag	4.0 oz		
Sewing kit: heavy thread, 3 safety pins, 3 needles	0.1 oz		
Emergency fire starter kit in resealable plastic bag: small lighter, stick matches, birthday candles	0.9 oz		
Spare flashlight battery, size AAA	0.5 oz		
Valuables: traveler's checks, cash, credit card, driver's licenses, in resealable plastic bag	1.0 oz		
Toilet kit: toilet paper & Dr. Bronner's soap in plastic vial	2.0 oz		
Journal pad, maps & pen	2.0 oz		
Ray's Total Pack Weight	**8.44 lb**		

Jenny's Gear			
Pack	11.5 oz	$10.40	12.0
Umbrella	6.0 oz		1.0
Mylar umbrella covering, with rubber bands and tape for attaching mylar to umbrella	0.8 oz		
Tarp: 1.9 oz coated ripstop nylon, 8'8" square	28.0 oz	$15.00	5.0
Tent pegs: 8 aluminum, 7" long	2.5 oz		
Tent peg stowbag: nylon	0.1 oz	$0.25	0.5
Ground sheet: 81.5" long. 48" wide at head, 34" at foot	6.5 oz	$13.99	0.1

Foam pads: two 3/8 inch thick closed cell polyethylene. 19.5" wide at head; 17.5" at hips; 36.5" long	9.5 oz	$6.99	0.1
Camera with 1 roll film	6.0 oz		
Camera stowbag: coated nylon	0.5 oz	$1.50	0.5
Camera kit: 1 roll of film, spare battery, and bulb brush	1.4 oz		
Water bottle (empty soda bottle)	1.6 oz		
Water scoop: breakfast cereal cup, plastic	0.1 oz		
Water trough: cookie package, aluminum foil	0.2 oz		
Jenny's Clothing			
Hat: fleece	1.0 oz	$0.25	0.2
Shirt: Thermax, long sleeve	3.0 oz	$9.75	3.0
Shell jacket: breathable nylon	6.0 oz	$7.50	4.5
Mittens: fleece	1.5 oz	$0.75	0.3
Shell pants: breathable nylon	4.0 oz	$7.61	4.0
Socks: 3 pair, thin nylon	1.8 oz		
Shower booties: coated nylon	0.8 oz	$0.50	1.0
Half of a cotton bandanna as towel	0.3 oz		
Clothing stowbag (plastic garbage sack)	1.3 oz		
Jenny's Ditty Bag, nylon	0.2 oz	$1.00	0.8
Flashlight with single AAA battery & spare bulb	1.0 oz		
Lighter	0.5 oz		
Comb	0.3 oz		
Toothbrush	0.3 oz		
Spoon: Lexan	0.2 oz		
Can opener: P-51	0.2 oz		
Repellent in pump spray bottle	1.8 oz		
Sunscreen	0.8 oz		
Note pad & pencil	0.3 oz		
Prescription dark glasses	1.2 oz		
Glasses case: fleece with velcro	0.2 oz	$0.25	0.1
Lip balm	0.5 oz		
Aspirin & vitamins together in small resealable bag	0.3 oz		
Foot Care in resealable bag: 13 adhesive strips, ½ sheet Moleskin, full pack of 2nd Skin & dressing, white adhesive tape, clear first aid tape, 3 Q-Tips, 3 pieces Molefoam	3.5 oz		

Cookpot with lid: aluminum, 2 quart capacity	7.8 oz		
Cookpot stowbag: coated nylon	0.5 oz	$1.00	0.8
Jenny's Total Pack Weight	**7.12 lb**		

Ray's clothing worn			
Sun hat with wire rim	2.0 oz		
Shirt: Polyester	4.0 oz		
Watch	1.5 oz		
Shorts: Lycra	4.3 oz	$2.00	2.0
Socks: 2 pair, thin nylon	1.2 oz		
Shoes	22.0 oz		

Jenny's clothing worn			
Sun hat	2.0 oz		
Shirt: Polyester	2.0 oz	$6.50	3.5
Underwear	0.5 oz		
Shorts: Nylon and Spandex	3.0 oz		
Socks: Nylon	0.6 oz		
Shoes	21.0 oz		

Ray's Additional Gear			
Head net: no-see-um netting (used in central OR only)	1.2 oz	$1.00	0.5
Hat: fleece & 2-ply W/B covering (used in northern WA only)	2.5 oz	$1.75	2.5
Jacket: 2-ply W/B (used first few days only)	6.0 oz	$7.00	4.0
Sweater: lightweight fleece (carried through northern WA, rarely needed)	14.3 oz	$13.00	4.5
Wicking shirt: Thermax, long sleeve (used in WA only)	8.0 oz	$7.50	4.0
Shell mittens: breathable nylon (used in central OR only, for mosquitoes)	0.2 oz	$1.00	0.5
Wicking pants: Thermax (used in northern WA only)	7.5 oz	$7.00	3.0
Snow boots: Avia N'yati (used in WA only)	26.5 oz		
Socks: 2 pair, polyester & wool blend (used in WA only)	2.2 oz		

Shell booties: breathable nylon (used in central OR only, for mosquitoes)	0.2 oz	$1.00	0.5
No-Fog cloth in resealable plastic bag (used in northern WA only)	0.2 oz		
Water bag: 2.5 gal (used in southern CA only)	3.5 oz		
Ice axe, modified (used in northern WA only)	12.8 oz		3.0

Jenny's Additional Gear			
Hat: fleece (used in WA only)	3.0 oz	$3.50	1.5
Sweater: lightweight fleece (used in northern WA only)	14.0 oz	$13.00	4.5
Jacket: 2-ply W/B (used first few days only)	8.3 oz	$21.50	5.5
Shell mittens: breathable nylon (used in central OR for bugs and southern CA for sun)	0.2 oz	$1.00	0.5
Wicking pants: Thermax (used in WA only)	7.0 oz	$7.00	3.0
Snow boots: Avia N'yati (used in WA only)	25.0 oz		
Socks: 2 pair, polyester & wool blend (used in WA only)	4.0 oz		
Socks: 1 pair, Ragg wool (used in northern WA only)	3.8 oz		
Shell booties: breathable nylon (used in central OR for mosquitoes only)	0.2 oz	$1.00	0.5
Water bag: 2.5 gal (used in southern CA only)	3.5 oz		
Ice axe, modified (used in northern WA only)	12.5 oz		3.0

Re-entry

The Descent Back to Civilization

Here I am, safely returned over those peaks
from a journey far more beautiful and strange
than anything I had hoped for or imagined.
How is it that this safe return brings such regret?

— *Peter Matthiessen*

If your long journey left you feeling a little alienated from society, welcome to the club. Such is the plight of the adventurer. But take heart! The same inner strength you won on the trail will serve you well in the cities. One of the greatest benefits of long distance hiking is how it builds self-confidence and a sense of independence. No longer will you need the acclaim of others to justify your existence. Nor will you have to rely on someone else to create your opportunities or shape your destiny.

Post-hike readjustment difficulties can be profound. In the hike's aftermath, the adventure, the challenges, the freedom, and the joys of living with Nature are suddenly no more. In their place come the responsibilities of jobs and families, and the hassles of intermixing with a society frenetically in quest of comfort, security, and social status.

How does a person who has just walked 2,700 miles in 4 or 5 months re-adjust back to the "real" world? My answer is this: Superficially.

We long distance hikers have seen and experienced the realities of Nature, and we now realize how myopic much of society is to those realities. Once we have opened our eyes to Nature, are we to close them? Are we to forget all the hard-won lessons learned through toil and privation and inexpressible joy? Are we to forget the freedom and child-like curiosities of wandering across the land, only to sit for endless hours before a TV, worshipping the gods of entertainment, commercialism, and absorbing (biased) news reports like the millions of "normal" people?

I feel that when we return to the cities we need to keep hold of those parts of ourselves which we fiercely discovered in the wilderness. But yes, compromises are necessary. Our journeys blessed us with greater independence, but they did not wean us from society altogether. We need society for food, shelter, and companionship, such as it is. So let's discuss a few ways of blending back in, superficially.

Splashdown

One of the key elements here is in planning ahead. During the final few weeks of your trek, think about what you might want to do when you return home. Project yourself ahead in time, and visualize yourself busy with a number of interesting projects. Give yourself something to look forward to so that you don't simply stumble off the end of the world at trail's end.

Long distance hiking teaches self-worth, and brings new-found confidence in dealing with challenges. We develop these skills on the trails, and we can use them equally well in the cities. So when returning home, remind yourself that you are now a much more capable person. Use this new energy to meet whatever challenges come your way.

Many distance hikers trying to adjust back to city life create even more difficulties for themselves by failing to eat quality foods, in moderation, and by failing to exercise regularly. The mind must be properly nourished in order to cope effectively, and the body properly exercised. I say eating "in moderation" because when returning from a long hike our metabolisms continue to resemble that of steam locomotives for a few months. As such, most of us are susceptible to gaining weight. Fat is the body's means of storing energy. So in effect, our minds are preparing our bodies for the next expedition.

Another problem when returning home is that hikers begin spending nearly all of their time indoors. Try to work and relax outside for a few hours every day.

The non-completed journey

For those who cut their journeys short, coming home can be even more difficult. My recommended approach is to accept our mistakes and learn from them. Each one can be a valuable opportunity for enlightenment and personal growth. Understand the lessons, and we are likely to do much better the next time. For after all, if our "failures" teach us anything, it is that we may not have achieved the proficiencies needed for success.

Before I climbed the Diamond[1] the first time, I "failed" on six attempts. But each failure taught me more of what I needed to know in order to succeed. My goal was to climb the face of that magnificent wall, and I was determined to succeed. And on the seventh try I did succeed. And once I had achieved the

---

[1] The East Face of Long's Peak in Colorado, a notoriously difficult rock climb, especially in the early days of ironmongery (heavy pitons).

skills I went on to scale the precipice six more times, each by a different route and with a different partner.

To the person who is genuinely determined, then, there is no such thing as failure. Nature allows no short-cuts. We can proceed ahead in our adventures only one step at a time, and only with the knowledge and skills which that step requires.

So remember that the trail will probably be there, if and when you choose to return. And like I have done many times, you might adopt the saying *"Reculer pour mieux sauter."* It means "Draw back in order to make a better jump."

Nightmares in utopia

Many of us returning from our long journeys feel alienated from society. This feeling can be profound and long-lasting, and it stems mainly from our new awareness. Suddenly we see how alienated most city people are from their natural surroundings. For those of you who sense that there was something more to your journey than just a long walk in the woods, here are a few of my thoughts:

The Earth's biosphere, a self-sustaining system for millions of years, is now dying. Granted, various organizations are struggling to save at least some of it, and I support several of them with donations, letters, and so forth. But quite frankly I suspect they are not going to enjoy a great deal of success. Mankind's greed and power are just too overwhelming.

However, as destructive to the ecology as "civilized" mankind is, he will always be caged in his own cities and automobiles. Those hardy adventurers who can survive and thrive outside these cages will remain invulnerable to civilization's decimating power. As with the terrible forces of an avalanche, those who try to stand up against it are subject to being knocked flat and hurled into a pile of debris. Those who know how to bend and flex to Nature's ways are far more likely to survive.

The long journey afoot teaches us how to move over the land. It teaches us how to live in the wilderness on Nature's terms. It teaches us that Nature's obstacles are not insuperable, but merely opportunities for further learning and growth. And it teaches us how to attune ourselves to Nature's messages, on which we must depend for our safety. I believe these skills could again become necessary for survival in the not-too-distant future.

In this book I have emphasized independence from commercialism: sewing your own clothing and making your own sleeping bag and backpack. Still, there are many more lessons to be learned: How to build a fire without matches. How to build shelter, track and forage; how to tan skins and thatch plants for clothing and bedding. These are not just fun crafts designed to entertain Boy Scouts. They are subsistence skills used by humankind for millennia. Our society is only a few hundred years old, yet already it has forgotten these skills of survival. Instead, it is leaning heavily on the fence posts of commerce. But those posts are rotting at their bases, and when they fall over, civilization as we know it will undoubtedly go with them.

The people who survive will not be the "survivalists" holed up in their retreats stockpiled with food and weapons. Retreats can be plundered. Food supplies will run out, and hunger will drive the "survivalists" back to the maelstrom of the cites where, indeed, they will need their weapons. The people who survive will be the small, nomadic tribes, eking out their existence upon a stormy, dusty earth. These will be the distance hikers of the Brave New World.

Poking At The Embers

One of trekking's quintessential benefits is the escape it provides from the distractions of city life. On the trail we can become more attuned with the natural world, as opposed to the material one. And indeed, we find the backcountry a marvelous creation, comprising expansive forests (hear those chain saws buzzing?), lofty, snowpacked mountain ranges, and pristine, trickling brooks teeming with myriad aquatic organisms, giardia included. Who can deny that in her astounding variety, in her immense and infinitesimal, Nature is inscrutable?

With each object in Nature, the more we examine its inner complexities, the more they befuddle us. How does the brain of a chipmunk work, and how does it grow from an embryo? How does the structure of its inner-atoms relate to that of the outer universe? Could the billions of similar unknowables represent an organized plethora of cosmological accidents? Maybe, but to me the odds seem immeasurably against it.

The Creation

I perceive all objects in Nature as wrought by the Creator. More importantly, looking inward I feel much of that same evidence of an Infinite Spirit. I love Nature; else why would I spend so much time bumbling around in it? And therefore I love God, who obviously (it seems to me) created Nature. Consequently, I have faith.

The Infinity Of Nature

Nature has strengthened my faith far beyond what she alone is capable of gratifying. Yet because Nature is infinite, it seems to me that my soul is also infinite, as is the soul of everyone else.

When I learned of the Gospel some 30 years ago it changed my life entirely. In a nutshell the tidings are these: By piling rocks we cannot reach the stars, and by practicing religion we cannot reach God's eminence. God loves the mountains, trees, and even our stealth campsites; otherwise why would He have created them? And He loves us too. And it is this love that prompted Him, some two thousand years ago, to send Jesus to provide transit across the colossal gap between God and us. The wages of sin are death, not the physical death but the spiritual one. And Jesus died on the cross to pay the price of our sins. When we accept Him as Lord and Savior we accept his gift of spiritual life.

So-called educated people don't believe in God on the basis of insufficient evidence, even though the evidence is all around them. But I think a lot of people are disgusted by the religious movements with their various preachers and do-gooders who look down on non-believers and who attempt to empower themselves by twisting the message of the Bible. They disgust me too. But my faith is in the Creator, pure and simple, not in these religious fanatics.

In his book *Into A Desert Place; a 3000 mile walk around the coast of Baja California*, (see Bibliography) Graham Mackintosh writes:

"I listened to the ayatollahs of America pumping out their incredible interpretations of Christianity. Why do most Christians use their religion to look down on and condemn others? Where is the humility and compassion? What would Christ have to say about such arrogance and selfishness? How can men be so blind as to miss the whole point of Christianity; to use the doctrine that bears Christ's name to further their own prejudices, insecurities, and hatreds? Wasn't Christ's mission to teach us how to rise above the worst aspects of our potentially evil human nature; and to sow love, trust and mutual understanding?"

In terms of distance hiking, I think of Nature as our compass, pointing the way to our Creator. The Holy Bible as our guide book, filling us with resolve and providing directions at each of life's confounding junctures. And Jesus as providing us passage over the unwadable gap, and to eventually triumph in our celestial quests.

"For God so loved the world,
that he gave his only begotten Son,
that whosoever believeth in him should not perish,
but have everlasting life."
– John 3:16.

I like to think that Jesus was a hiker. One of his last acts on Earth was to sit with a few of his disciple friends before a fire. They roasted fresh-caught fish, ate bread, and perhaps sat long into the night talking heavenly subjects while poking at the embers.

Select Bibliography

Books are but stepping stones to show you where other minds have been.

– John Muir

Guide books and history

The Pacific Crest Trailway, Clinton C. Clarke. The Pacific Crest Trail System Conference: 1932, 1945. The genesis of PCT publications, and the one which I feel has had the greatest impact. The book is a blueprint of Clarke's conservation efforts aimed at preserving the PCT environs.

Pacific Crest Trails, Joseph T. Hazard. Superior Publishing Company: 1946. The author mentions the possibility of a Pacific Crest Trail System extending from Alaska to Cape Horn, but he uses the idea mainly to impart a sense of grandeur to his irrelevant although often entertaining stories of his own ramblings.

The Pacific Crest Trail; Escape to the Wilderness, Ann and Myron Sutton. J. B. Lippincott Company: 1975. Discusses the PCT, its environs, history and natural history. The authors "hiked some of the trail but by no means all of it."

Pacific Crest Trail Pocket Guide, Warren Rogers. Rogers: 1972, 1980. The "Strip Maps" in five volumes, covering Washington, Oregon, and northern, central and southern California.

The Pacific Crest Trail Volume 1: California, Jeffrey P. Schaffer, Thomas Winnett, Ben Schifrin and Ruby Jenkins. Wilderness Press: Fifth Edition 1995. This book, and the one which follows, are the guide books in common use today.

The Pacific Crest Trail, Volume 2: Oregon & Washington, Jeffrey P. Schaffer, with Andy Selters. Wilderness Press: Fifth Edition 1990.

Trail description and narratives

Mexico To Canada On The Pacific Crest Trail, Mike W. Edwards and David Hiser. National Geographic: June 1971.

The Pacific Crest Trail, William R. Gray. Special Publication, National Geographic: 1975.

A Pacific Crest Odyssey, Walking the Trail from Mexico to Canada, David Green. Wilderness Press: 1979. The classic PCT thru-hiking narrative.

First aid

Medicine For Mountaineering & Other Wilderness Activities, James A. Wilkerson, MD. The Mountaineers: Fourth Edition 1992. Jim and I were members of the same climbing expedition to the Peruvian Andes in the late '70s. His book was the most thorough on the subject then, and still is.

Wilderness Medicine 4ᵗʰ Edition – Beyond First Aid, William W. Forgey, MD. ICS Books, Inc.: 1994. Contains a wealth of practical information, and is a great refresher on a subject which we all need to review on occasion.

Ice axe technique

Mountaineering: Freedom of the Hills. The Mountaineers: Fifth Edition 1992.

Food

The Natural Farms Cookbook, from Deaf Smith Organic Farms, Inc., Frank Ford. Harvest Press

Dry It-You'll Like It!, Gen MacManiman. Box 546 Fall City, WA 98024. A book about dehydrating food, including recipes and plans for building your own food dehydrator.

The Well-Fed Backpacker, June Fleming. Vintage Books

Supermarket Backpacker, Harriett Barker. Contemporary Books

Backpacker's Recipe Book, Steve Antell. Pruett Publishing Company

Simple Foods for the Pack, Axcell, Cooke, and Kinmont. Sierra Club Guide

Wilderness Cuisine, Carol Latimer. Wilderness Press

Information

Sewing Activewear, Singer Sewing Reference Library. Cy DeCosse Inc.: 1986. Look for this excellent book at your local fabric outlets.

Lightweight Camping Equipment And How To Make It, Gerry Cunningham and Margaret Hansson. Charles Scribner's Sons: 1976.

Richard Hittleman's Yoga: 28 Day Exercise Plan, Richard L. Hittleman. Bantam Books: 1969.

Bear Attacks, Their Causes and Avoidance, Stephen Herrero. Lyons & Burford: 1985. Excellent material on bear psychology.

Rattlesnakes, Laurence M. Klauber. University of California Press: Abridged Edition 1982.

Conservation

Dave Foreman's Books Of The Big Outside, available free from Ned Ludd Books, P.O. Box 1399; Bernalillo, NM 87004. The average citizen is not particularly concerned with the issues of wilderness preservation. If horses, mules and llamas hammer the trails into urine stenched manureways, and if they decimate every water source along the way, then so what? If motorbikes plow the trails down to their axles, and if the clear-cutting loggers drop every tree in sight, who cares? Let the strip-miners scrape away the mess. Perhaps upon the rubble, future generations will construct a new Utopia of asphalt and cement. Meanwhile, most of us who spend a lot of time in the wilds do care. I heartily recommend *Dave Foreman's Books of the Big Outside*. This is an annotated catalog of titles on wilderness issues. Buy some of these books and read them. Or at least read the free catalog.

Wilderness, the quarterly publication of The Wilderness Society, 900 Seventeenth Street NW, Washington DC 20006-2596. If you subscribe to only one conservation newsletter, this might be a good choice.

I heartily recommend the High Sierra Hikers Association, P.O. Box 8920, South Lake Tahoe CA 96158. These folks are working tirelessly to preserve the wilderness against the forces legally profaning it.

Other distance hiking narratives

The Longest Walk, George Meegan. Paragon House: 1989. A seven year, continuous trek from the tip of South America to the top of North America.

The Long Walk, A Gamble For Life, Slavomir Rawicz. Harper & Brothers: 1956. Literature's preeminent distance-hiking narrative.

Into A Desert Place; a 3000 mile walk around the coast of Baja California, Graham Mackintosh. W. W. Norton: 1995. Signed, hardcover copies available from Graham Mackintosh, P.O. Box 1982, Lemon Grove, CA 91946.

The Walker's Journal, Robert Sweetgall. Describes his non-supported journey through all fifty states in 364 consecutive days. Most of his 11,208 miles were on roads, and as any pavement pounder can tell you, these can be far tougher on the feet than trails. Published by one of his sponsors. Out of print but a gem if you can find a copy.

Author and lecturer **Chris Townsend's** is an authority on long distance backpacking in remote areas, and a close friend of mine. To date he has written nine books. Among them are:

- *The Great Backpacking Adventure*, The Oxford Illustrated Press: 1987. Contains what I consider to be the best account of a CDT thru-hike.

- *Walking the Yukon*, Ragged Mountain Press: 1993. Chronicles Townsend's epic backpacking journey through the Yukon Territory.
- *High Summer: Backpacking the Canadian Rockies*, Oxford Illustrated Press (UK) and Cloudcap (USA): 1990. Details Townsend's pioneering trek along the Continental Divide, north from the American-Canadian border.
- *The Backpacker's Handbook*, Ragged Mountain Press: Second Edition 1996. Townsend's knowledge of commercial equipment is impressive, and he details it well in this book, which is available in local bookstores. Autographed copies of this and his other titles can be purchased directly from Chris at Auchnarrow, Braes of Castle Grant, Grantown-on-Spey, Moray PH26 3PL, Scotland.

General reading

How I Found Freedom In An Unfree World, Harry Browne. Avon Books: 1973. When I first read this book in the mid 70's, it affected my thinking profoundly. Since then I have re-read it every few years. It is not a hiking book, but it discusses the manifesto of free-thinking.

Flow, The Psychology of Optimal Experience, Mihaly Csikszentmilalyi. Harper and Row: 1990. How the author pronounces his name I haven't a clue. But I find his insights equally applicable to long-distance hiking.

I also recommend any and all books by Edward Abbey and Tom Brown, Jr.

Index

Ray Jardine holds a degree in Aeronautical and Astronautical Engineering from Northrop University, and worked in the aerospace industry as a specialist in space-flight-mechanics. He retired at an early age to pursue his outdoor interests.

A mountaineer, he climbed most of Colorado's fourteeners, many in winter; and he climbed extensively in the Tetons and in South America. His highest peak was Peru's Huascarán, at 22,205 feet.

A wilderness instructor, he worked for the Colorado Alpine Winter Mountaineering School for two seasons, and for Outward Bound for seven. In the process, he backpacked several thousand miles. He also holds an EMT certificate from St. Anthony's Hospital in Denver, Colorado.

A rock climber for 25 years, Ray established some of the era's toughest climbs, including the world's first 5.12 graded climb: The Crimson Cringe, and the first 5.13: The Phoenix. He climbed extensively in Great Britain and across western America. His ascents in Colorado include seven Diamond routes. In Yosemite Valley he pioneered 50 first ascents, and was the first to free climb a grade VI, on El Capitan. He invented the protection and anchoring device known as the "Friend," which revolutionized the sport. And he originated the style of climbing used today which enables much tougher routes to be conquered. According to Rock & Ice magazine, "The brilliance of his routes, the undeniable contributions of his designs, and his yet-unrealized visions of the future of the sport place Ray Jardine among the rarest of climbing revolutionaries."

In 1982, Ray and his wife Jenny put to sea aboard their ketch SUKA (acronym for "Seeking UnKnown Adventures"), and sailed around the world in 3½ years.

Ray is also an avid hang glider pilot. He has logged some 400 hours aloft, flown to 16,000 feet, cross country 50 miles, and has thermal gained 9,100 feet (nearly two miles straight up). He has also flown sailplanes and small powered craft, and he holds an Australian Restricted Private Pilot's License.

Sea kayaking has also been a favorite pursuit. Ray has paddled several thousand miles in areas including offshore California, the Sea of Cortez, French Polynesia and Australia. Embarking from Anacortes, Washington in 1988, he and Jenny paddled a two-person kayak 3,300 miles north to the Bering Sea. Later, he developed an efficient sailing rig for kayaks, and the pair used it to advantage on a 650 mile expedition along the inside length of Baja.

In 1987 he and Jenny thru-hiked from Mexico to Canada, generally along the PCT, in 4½ months. Once wasn't enough, so in 1991 they thru-hiked the PCT again, in 3 months 3 weeks. In 1992 they thru-hiked the 2,800 mile Continental Divide Trail, in 3 months 3½ weeks. In 1993, the 2,100 mile Appalachian Trail, in 2 months 28 days. And in 1994 they thru-hiked the PCT southbound, in 3 months and 4 days.

The summer of 1995 Ray and Jenny paddled along the coast of Arctic Alaska in a kayak of their own design and construction. The lure of the Arctic must be strong, as that's where they are headed again as this book goes to print.